LOVERS OF CINEMA

studies in film

General Editors

David Bordwell
Donald Crafton
Vance Kepley, Jr.
Kristin Thompson, Supervising Editor

*Shared Pleasures: A History of Movie Presentation
in the United States*
Douglas Gomery

*Lovers of Cinema: The First American Film
Avant-Garde, 1919–1945*
Edited by Jan-Christopher Horak

*The Wages of Sin: Censorship and the
Fallen Woman Film, 1928–1942*
Lea Jacobs

Settling the Score: Music and the Classical Hollywood Film
Kathryn Kalinak

Patterns of Time: Mizoguchi and the 1930s
Donald Kirihara

LOVERS OF CINEMA

The First American Film Avant-Garde 1919–1945

Edited by
Jan-Christopher Horak

THE UNIVERSITY OF WISCONSIN PRESS

The University of Wisconsin Press
2537 Daniels Street
Madison, Wisconsin 53718

3 Henrietta Street
London WC2E 8LU, England

Library of Congress Cataloging-in-Publication Data
Lovers of cinema : the first American film avant-garde, 1919–1945 /
edited by Jan-Christopher Horak.
416 pp.   cm. — (Wisconsin studies in film)
Filmography: p. 363
Includes bibliographical references and index.
ISBN 0-299-14680-4 (cloth)
ISBN 0-299-14684-7 (paper)

1. Experimental films—United States—History and criticism.
I. Horak, Jan-Christopher.   II. Series.
PN1995.9.E96L68   1995
791.43'0973'09044—dc20   95-7399

CONTENTS

Illustrations   vii

Acknowledgments   x

Contributors   xi

1   Introduction: History in the Gaps   3
JAN-CHRISTOPHER HORAK

2   The First American Film Avant-Garde, 1919–1945   14
JAN-CHRISTOPHER HORAK

3   The Limits of Experimentation in Hollywood   67
KRISTIN THOMPSON

4   Robert Florey and the Hollywood Avant-Garde   94
BRIAN TAVES

5   Americans in Paris: Man Ray and Dudley Murphy   118
WILLIAM MORITZ

6   Startling Angles: Amateur Film and the Early Avant-Garde   137
PATRICIA R. ZIMMERMAN

7   U.S. Modernism and the Emergence of "The Right Wing of Film Art": The Films of James Sibley Watson, Jr., and Melville Webber   156
LISA CARTWRIGHT

8   Theodore Huff: Historian and Filmmaker   180
CHUCK KLEINHANS

9   Ralph Steiner   205
    Scott MacDonald

10 Straight Shots and Crooked Plots: Social Documentary and
    the Avant-Garde in the 1930s   234
    Charles Wolfe

11 Paul Strand and Charles Sheeler's *Manhatta*   267
    Jan-Christopher Horak

12 The City Viewed: The Films of Leyda, Browning,
    and Weinberg   287
    William Uricchio

13 Mary Ellen Bute   315
    Lauren Rabinovitz

14 Machines That Give Birth to Images: Douglass Crockwell   335
    Tom Gunning

Filmmakers of the First American Avant-Garde   363
Bibliography   383
Index   397

ILLUSTRATIONS

2.1. The Cinema Crafters of Philadelphia (1929)   16
2.2. 5th Avenue Playhouse, New York (1928)   21
2.3. Advertisement of Filmarte Theatre for *Prisoner* (1934)   22
2.4. Program brochure for the Little Theatre, Rochester, New
      York, November 1929   23
2.5. Still from *The Tell-Tale Heart* (1928)   26
2.6. Frame enlargement from *The Enchanted City* (1922),   39
2.7. Frame enlargement from *Light Rhythms* (1930)   41
2.8. Frame enlargement from *Lullaby* (1925)   46
2.9. Frame enlargement from *It Never Happened/Tomatoes
      Another Day* (1930)   47
3.1. Frame enlargement from *The Yellow Girl* (1915)   72
3.2. Frame enlargement from *The Blue Bird* (1918)   73
3.3. Frame enlargement from *Camille* (1921)   76
3.4. Frame enlargement from *The Old Swimmin' Hole* (1921)   78
3.5. Frame enlargement from *Greed* (1925)   81
3.6. Frame enlargement from *Beggar on Horseback* (1925)   86
4.1. Production shot on the set of *The Love of Zero* (1928)   101
4.2. Still from *The Love of Zero* (1928)   103
4.3. Still from lost film, *Johann the Coffin Maker* (1929)   109
4.4. Still from *The Preview Murder Mystery* (1936)   111
4.5. Still from film, *Skyscraper Symphony* (1929)   112
5.1. Frame enlargement from *Emak Bakia* (1926)   121

5.2. Frame enlargement of animation sequence of the Grim Reaper from *Danse Macabre* (1922) — 124

5.3. Frame enlargement of title animation from *Danse Macabre* (1922) — 125

5.4. Still from *Ballet Mécanique* (1924) — 128

5.5. Frame enlargement from *St. Louis Blues* (1929) — 131

5.6. Production still from *Black and Tan* (1929) — 132

6.1. Cover from *Amateur Movie Makers* (September 1929) — 138

6.2. Still from *The Last Moment* (1929) — 145

6.3. Program brochure from the Little Theatre, Baltimore — 148

6.4. Still from *The Fall of the House of Usher* (1928) — 151

6.5. Still from *Rien Que Les Heures* (1925) — 152

7.1. Still from *The Fall of the House of Usher* (1928) — 161

7.2. Still from *The Fall of the House of Usher* (1928) — 164

7.3. Still from *Lot in Sodom* (1933) — 165

7.4. Frame enlargement from *It Never Happened/Tomatoes Another Day* (1930) — 169

7.5. Homemade optical printer, constructed from old lathe by James Sibley Watson, Jr., for *Lot in Sodom* (1933) — 173

7.6. Still from *Lot in Sodom* (1933) — 175

8.1. Frame enlargement from *Hearts of the West* (1931) — 186

8.2. Frame enlargement from *Mr. Motorboat's Last Stand* (1933) — 189

8.3. Frame enlargement from *Mr. Motorboat's Last Stand* (1933) — 191

8.4. Frame enlargement from *Mr. Motorboat's Last Stand* (1933) — 192

8.5. Frame enlargement from *The Uncomfortable Man* (1948) — 193

8.6. Frame enlargement from *The Uncomfortable Man* (1948) — 194

9.1. Frame enlargement from *H_2O* (1929) — 210

9.2. Frame enlargement from *H_2O* (1929) — 211

9.3. Frame enlargement from *Mechanical Principles* (1933) — 214

9.4. Frame enlargement from *Mechanical Principles* (1933) — 216

9.5. Frame enlargement from *Panther Woman of the Needle Trades, or The Lovely Life of Little Lisa* (1931) — 217

9.6. Frame enlargement from *Pie in the Sky* (1935) — 221

10.1. Cover from *Experimental Cinema* (1934) — 241

10.2. Production still from *The Plow That Broke the Plains* (1936) — 243

10.3.	Still from *The City* (1939)	251
10.4.	Still from *Native Land* (1942)	252
10.5.	Still from *The Spanish Earth* (1937)	254
10.6.	Frame enlargement from *Pie in the Sky* (1935)	256
11.1.	Frame enlargement from *Manhatta* (1921)	272
11.2.	Frame enlargement from *Manhatta* (1921)	273
11.3.	Frame enlargement from *Manhatta* (1921)	274
11.4.	Frame enlargement from *Manhatta* (1921)	280
11.5.	Frame enlargement from *Manhatta* (1921)	283
12.1.	Photo of Jay Leyda and Serge Koussevitzky, no date	288
12.2.	Frame enlargement from *A Bronx Morning* (1931)	294
12.3.	Frame enlargement from *A Bronx Morning* (1931)	296
12.4.	Photographic portrait, Herman Weinberg	304
12.5.	Still from *Autumn Fire* (1933)	306
12.6.	Still from *Autumn Fire* (1933)	307
13.1.	Frame enlargement from *Tarantella* (1940)	316
13.2.	Mary Ellen Bute at work	318
13.3.	Still from *Rhythm in Light* (1934)	322
13.4.	Frame enlargement from *Escape* (1937)	324
13.5.	Frame enlargement from *Abstronic* (1952)	327
14.1.	Artwork for the *Saturday Evening Post*	337
14.2.	Portrait of Douglass Crockwell at work, ca. 1947	339
14.3.	Edison Kinetoscope parlor, ca. 1900	341
14.4.	Installation photo from Crockwell mutoscope exhibition, Museum of Modern Art (1967)	345
14.5.	Frame enlargement from *Glens Falls Sequence* (1946)	348
14.6.	Frame enlargement from *Glens Falls Sequence* (1946)	350

ACKNOWLEDGMENTS

This project began life as a panel at the Society of Cinema Studies in Montreal in 1987, after some preliminary research for my article on Paul Strand's *Manhatta* demonstrated to me the huge gaps in our knowledge of avant-garde cinema. That panel with Lucy Fischer, Anne Friedberg, and Bill Uricchio helped to clarify the parameters of this undertaking. Now it has been in the works for so many years that it is almost impossible to acknowledge all of the persons who have had a hand in its completion. First and foremost, I would like to thank all the authors of the present volume for putting up with my endless harassment, queries, and requests for revisions.

In the original research for this book I was greatly assisted and supported by: Tino Balio (Madison), Paolo Bertetto at the Museo Nazionale del Cinema (Torino), Barbara Galasso at George Eastman House, Robert Haller and Jonas Mekas at Anthology Film Archives, Harry Hay (Los Angeles), Lewis Jacobs (New York) Edith Kramer at the Pacific Film Archive, Ron Magliozzi and Mary Lea Bandy at the Museum of Modern Art (New York), Eddie Richmond at UCLA Film & Television Archives, David Trend (San Francisco), Jeffrey Fuller (Philadelphia), Paolo Cherchi Usai (Rochester), and Anne Fleming of the National Film & Television Archives of the British Film Institute. For helpful comments, thanks to Charles Musser and Bruce Jenkins, as well as Kristin Thompson, Vance Kepley, and David Bordwell, and Donald Crafton. Thanks, too, to my editor, Allen N. Fitchen.

Finally, I would like to thank my former staff at George Eastman House, Kay MacRae, Ruth Kanner, Edward Stratman, and Bob Ogie, for all their support over the years. Thanks to my wife, Martha F. Schirn, for giving up so much of our "quality time," and to my daughter, Gianna Mei Li.

CONTRIBUTORS

Lisa Cartwright received her Ph.D. from Yale University. She is Associate Professor of English and Visual and Cultural Studies at the University of Rochester, Rochester, New York.

Tom Gunning, who received his Ph.D. from New York University, is Professor of Radio, Television and Film, at Northwestern University, Evanston, Illinois.

Jan-Christopher Horak (Ph.D. Westfählische Wilhelms-Universität, Münster, Germany) is currently Director of the Münchner Filmmuseum and Professor at the Hochschule für Fernsehen und Film in Munich.

Chuck Kleinhans received his Ph.D. from Indiana University. He is Professor of Radio, Television, and Film at Northwestern University, Evanston, Illinois, and co-editor of *Jump Cut.*

Scott MacDonald teaches Film and American Literature at Utica College. He received his Ph.D. from the University of Florida.

Wiliam Moritz has a Ph.D. from the University of Southern California. He teaches film at the California Institute for the Arts.

Lauren Rabinovitz is Associate Professor in American Studies and Communications Studies at the University of Iowa. She received her Ph.D. from the University of Texas in Austin.

Brian Taves has a Ph.D. from the University of Southern California. He is on the staff of the Motion Pictures and Broadcasting Division of the Library of Congress.

Kristin Thompson, Honorary Fellow in the Department of Communication Arts at the University of Wisconsin—Madison, received her Ph.D. from that university.

William Uricchio, who has a Ph.D. from New York University, is Professor and Head of the Department of Cinema Studies at the University of Utrecht in Holland.

Charles Wolfe is Associate Professor of Film Studies at the University of California, Santa Barbara. He received his Ph.D. from Columbia University.

Patricia R. Zimmermann has a Ph.D. from the University of Wisconsin—Madison. She is a Professor at the Roy H. Parks School of Communication, Ithaca College.

LOVERS OF CINEMA

1

Introduction

History in the Gaps

JAN-CHRISTOPHER HORAK

In the canonical texts of film history, the evolution of avant-garde film has been telelogically structured as a progression toward ever more sophisticated forms of film art. Divided essentially into succeeding periods, each avant-garde has been connected to its predecessor by aesthetic and personnel continuities, constructing over significant gaps in time and geography a discourse on the evolution of personal expression in the film medium. Whether labeled avant-garde film (1920s–1930s), experimental film (1940s–1950s), or underground–independent film (1960s–1970s)—the terminology depending on the era—its history has been defined in oppositional relation to the commercial and/or propagandistic cinemas of its time. Floating freely outside social and political contexts, the artists in each period have been reified as knights of film art, fighting heroically, individually, only loosely bound together in a movement at the level of distribution, exhibition, and reception. Their artistic weight as a movement *ipso facto* was the result of a confluence of social, technological, and aesthetic forces, which miraculously move from one age to the next. Thus, the film avant-garde—as constructed in traditional histories—moves from Europe in the 1920s to post–World War II America and then to the global village of the 1960s, creating a narrative of birth and rebirth.[1]

This history begins in the 1920s, when the most important art movements on the continent—Dadaism, Futurism, Surrealism, *Neue Sachlichkeit*, Constructivism—spawn a European avant-garde in Germany, France, Holland, Czechoslovakia, and the Soviet Union. Avant-garde film production in these countries is facilitated and supported by the development of an art cinema movement, cinema societies, and other noncommercial exhibition outlets, all of which battle the crushing

3

dominance of mainstream narrative cinema, itself only recently instituted as the commercial cinema's preferred mode of articulation. The commercial introduction of sound film after 1927, with its attendant monopolization of sound film patents, the worldwide Depression, and the rise of Stalinism and Fascism all contribute in varying technical, economic, and political degrees to the demise of this first avant-garde.

With the emigration of Hans Richter, Oskar Fischinger, Man Ray, Alexander Hammid, and others to the United States to escape Fascism, a second avant-garde arises after World War II on the East and West Coasts, supported by the New York–based Cinema 16 and the San Francisco "Art in Cinema" initiatives. The stars of the second avant-garde—Maya Deren, Gregory Markopoulos, Kenneth Anger, Sidney Peterson, Harry Smith, and the Whitney brothers—are revitalized in the 1960s by the Filmmakers' Cinémathèque, Canyon Cinema, and a new generation of filmmakers on both sides of the Atlantic. Among this younger group are Stan Brakhage, Peter Kubelka, Marcel Hanoun, Michael Snow, Jordan Belson, George and Mike Kuchar, and Ron Rice. Lionized by Jonas Mekas as a canon of high art film, the *Essential Cinema* is born.[2]

Since the mid-1970s, this generation of avant-garde filmmakers has been superseded by postmodern, feminist, gay and lesbian, punk, African-American, Asian, and other currents in the film avant-garde. Not yet completely institutionalized in the history books, the latest wave of film and video artists are—like their predecessors—not easily categorized, nor have they embraced a homogeneous agenda. If anything unites filmmakers as diverse as Yvonne Rainer, Su Friedrich, Trinh T. Minh-ha, Lewis Klar, Ayoka Chenzira, and A. G. Nigrin, it is their very difference, their individual search for identity in a multicultural society. Meanwhile, some critics have proclaimed the final demise of avant-garde film in America, killed off by MTV's endless appropriations.[3]

Significantly, this periodization of avant-garde film history has always been closely identified with specific filmmakers, audiences, and spaces for reception, even though the critical focus has been on artists.[4] In fact, the valorization of the independent filmmaker, with the romantic image of the artist that such an inscription entails, has always been central to traditional avant-garde film histories. As Peter Lehman has pointedly noted, the history of the avant-garde as imagined by P. Adams Sitney and the Anthology Film Archives offers "at best a great man theory of the avant-garde to sit alongside the great man theory of the unnamed darkness"—that is, commercial cinema.[5]

Yet avant-garde film movements can only be historically circumscribed if they—like the commercial film industry—are constituted in terms of production, distribution, exhibition, and reception. Their role in the history of cinema should be gauged not only according to their individual aesthetic achievements, but also in terms of the myriad contexts of their institutional frameworks and reception.[6] If an avant-garde movement is defined in terms of film reception, as well as production and distribution, can other histories and other avant-garde film movements in fact be identified? Are there filmmakers whose work has remained hidden in the gaps, the fissures, those spaces where its reception has been repressed?

Indeed, while traditional film histories have most often served polemical argument, and the aesthetic legitimation of filmmakers enshrined in an established canon, this view of avant-garde film history has eliminated the discontinuities and dead ends that necessarily mark a film form based on individual and essentially isolated modes of production. Most avant-garde filmmakers have worked and continue to work independently, relying on personal finances, private donors, and sometimes public funding to create cinematic forms with little or no value in the marketplace. The reception of such work has likewise been sporadic at best, exhibition venues rising and falling, oftentimes victims of larger economic forces, while publications dedicated to the film avant-garde, too, appear more fragile than those catering to commercial markets. As a result, many histories have been lost.

Early cinema, for example, despite its intense formal and technological experimentation, was eliminated *a priori* from the classic avant-garde canon because of the post–World War II avant-garde's opposition to commercial, narrative cinema.[7] Yet early cinema's multifarious discursive practices were indeed avant-garde, so that the concept of an avant-garde in opposition to the norm appears only after the institutionalization of classical narrative in the mid-teens.[8] The debt to early cinema was acknowledged by the French avant-garde as early as the 1920s, especially its surrealist wing, when Georges Méliès and other so-called primitives were resurrected through soirees dedicated to their work.[9] In a 1932 issue of *Close Up*, the editors published a manifesto that exclaimed: "Back to Primitives, because cinema is in danger of losing—virility in cinematic idiom."[10] Jay Leyda suggested to Frank Stauffacher in the late 1940s that he do a program of early cinema in his "Art in Cinema" series.[11] Yet only recently has the avant-garde's debt to Méliès, Emil Cohl, William S. Hart, Mack Sennett, and Buster Keaton been acknowledged.[12]

The accomplishment of the new historians of early cinema has been to define what was previously known as "primitive cinema" as a system of representation of an entirely different order than classical Hollywood narrative with its inscription of the spectator in its mode of representation. Whereas classical cinema features central perspective, composition in depth, continuity editing, spectatorial identification through cross-cutting closeups, realist acting styles, and closed narratives, early cinema is defined through centrifugal, decentered compositions, discontinuous editing, long shots that block spectatorial identification, stylized acting, and open narratives demanding pro-filmic knowledge.[13]

If we take this definition of early cinema and use it as a basis for our thinking on avant-garde cinema—that is, see it as not only an economic/personal resistance, but also as a formal opposition to classical Hollywood cinema—then the field of avant-garde practice is indeed greatly expanded to include all those discursive practices outside the institutional mode of representation, including avant-garde, documentary, and amateur. Yet American avant-garde filmmakers working before Maya Deren (i.e., before the 1940s) have continued to be either completely ignored or devalued in importance. Critics and historians have treated them as mere epigoni of their European predecessors, their styles and aesthetic strategies essentially derivative. David Curtis, for example, noted of American city films by Herman Weinberg, Leyda, and others: "Although they added little technically or aesthetically to the European originals, they served to popularize the idea that the raw materials of art are everywhere."[14]

A similar attitude led the Anthology Film Archives to list only one American film from the 1920s, James Sibley Watson's *Fall of the House of Usher* (1928), and only one film from the 1930s, Joseph Cornell's *Rose Hobart* (1936), when it established its "anthology of the essential works of the art of cinema."[15] Not surprisingly, P. Adams Sitney's *Visionary Film: The American Avant-garde 1943–1978* denied the existence of an earlier American avant-garde in its very title. Writing of the gap between the European avant-garde and Maya Deren's work in the 1940s, Sitney noted: "In fact, in the 1940s, before the emergence of the American avant-garde, the sole locus of radical innovation in the cinema had been within theoretical articles and books by men who had made their most ambitious films almost two decades earlier."[16] Sitney is referring to Hans Richter and others who presented European avant-garde films to American audiences at the New School, the Museum of Modern Art, and elsewhere, and also wrote about them in American publications.[17] Arthur

Knight makes the same connection between the avant-garde of the 1920s and the post–Maya Deren avant-garde, mentioning the transplanted Oskar Fischinger and the Whitney brothers in the same breath, without acknowledging the existence of a longstanding American avant-garde.[18]

A quick survey of the literature confirms similar attitudes among most critics in the field: Sheldon Renan's *An Introduction to the American Underground Film* gives a perfunctory nod to the early avant-garde,[19] as does David Curtis' *Experimental Cinema*,[20] but both fail to go beyond a regurgitation of names and films culled from Lewis Jacobs' seminal 1947 article, "Experimental Cinema in America (Part 1)."[21] Stephen Dwoskin relies on the same (uncredited) source,[22] which in retrospect has been shamefully ignored by everyone else writing about American avant-garde film. Ironically, Jacobs, one of the most important figures in the 1930s avant-garde and a producer of numerous films, downplayed in his later writings the achievements of his own generation. After identifying more than thirty filmmakers from the 1920s and 1930s, not including the initial wave of post–Maya Deren artists, Jacobs concluded: "Its individual members remained scattered, its productions sporadic, and for the most part viewed by the few."[23] His later article, "Morning for the Experimental Film," contributed even further to this revision of avant-garde history, noting of the 1958 International Experimental Film Competition in Brussels: "For the first time in its history, the movie operating outside the traditional theatrical forms was given the opportunity to be seen . . . as an independent work of art—devoid of politics, box office values."[24] American avant-garde film production before Maya Deren had fallen into the black hole of history.

The goal of this book is to retrieve the history of this American avant-garde cinema. It argues that film historians should consider adopting a new terminology to differentiate between the "first avant-garde" of the 1920s and 1930s, and the "second avant-garde" of the mid-1940s through the 1960s. A "third avant-garde" might possibly encompass the last twenty-five years. Such a differentiation would clarify their separate institutional formations and histories, without denying the many aesthetic continuities that are not overtly the subject of this book but do constitute a subtext.

The following essays are a first attempt to rediscover and evaluate the work of a host of filmmakers from the first American film avant-garde. With one exception, all the articles were especially commissioned by the editor for this volume and are being published for the first time. In many cases they are the first comprehensive articles to appear in any language on these avant-garde filmmakers. Most of the filmmakers under discussion here were excluded from the canon of the avant-garde for the reasons listed above, and because their work fitted neither chronologically nor aesthetically into the standard histories of the American film avant-garde. These essays on various filmmakers and phenomena within the first American avant-garde demonstrate a broad range of historiographic approaches. This heterogeneity was the result of the editor's decision to give individual authors as much freedom as possible to develop their own theoretical frameworks and stylistic predilections, while at the same time keeping in mind a general approach to this critical *terra incognita*. While certain insights and analyses overlap, each author has a different perspective—differences that will, I hope, encourage further research and writing in this neglected area of film history.

The volume begins with my own broad historical survey of the first American avant-garde. This chapter attempts to contextualize the later essays by providing a first look at the production, distribution, and exhibition of avant-garde films in the United States in the 1920s and 1930s. It theorizes an avant-garde movement in this period, which, while fragmented and diverse, still managed to find the means for making films, as well as getting them screened and discussed in contemporary publications. It also attempts a general taxonomy of avant-garde cinema, which is not meant to be theoretically rigid, but rather allows for a structured discussion of this first American film avant-garde.

Kristin Thompson's chapter theorizes that film experimentation was not completely foreign to the Hollywood studios, at least before the studio system had hardened into a corporate monopoly. In "The Limits of Experimentation in Hollywood," she argues that Hollywood occasionally supported experimentation, although such avant-gardisms were often quickly integrated into classical Hollywood narrative. She also makes it clear that exhibitors' negative views of such oddities and their box-office failure made such experimentation short-lived.

If Hollywood and the avant-garde shared any values, even temporarily, a good place to look for overlap might be the career of Robert Florey, an "outsider" who nevertheless worked within the system. Brian Taves' "Robert Florey and the Hollywood Avant-Garde" argues that the director's avant-garde and commercial films, especially those produced in the 1920s and early 1930s, must all be seen as demonstrating similar thematic and formal concerns. With access to the Florey estate, Taves has expanded his work on Florey, previously published in a monograph,[25] focusing more closely on the way Florey straddled the institutional practices of both Hollywood and the avant-garde.

In his essay on another sometime Hollywood director, Dudley Murphy, "Americans in Paris," William Moritz sheds new light on both Murphy and Man Ray. He discusses in some detail Murphy's *Danse Macabre* (1922), as well as Murphy's other early experiments in Hollywood. The scene then shifts to Paris in the 1920s, where such American expatriates as Man Ray, Francis Bruguière, and Murphy lived. He manages to untangle a bit of avant-garde film history, explaining the intersecting and not often happy relationships between Man Ray, Fernand Léger, Dudley Murphy, and the Comte Etienne de Beaumont, coming to the startling conclusion that Murphy and not Léger was the primary creator of *Ballet Mecanique* (1924).

Another important facet of the early American film avant-garde was its relationship to the amateur film movement. Since writing her dissertation on the topic,[26] Patricia Zimmermann has spent a good portion of her academic career studying amateur films and the amateur film movement in America. In "Startling Angles: Amateur Film and the Early Avant-Garde," Zimmermann asserts that the nascent amateur movement was in fact always torn between the two poles of Hollywood professionalism and avant-garde experimentation. In this dichotomy, amateur film magazines gave space to avant-gardists, but usually as part of a more general discourse on artistic film.

Two "amateurs," Dr. James Sibley Watson, Jr., and Melville Webber, are the subjects of Lisa Cartwright's penetrating essay, "U.S. Modernism and the Emergence of "The Right Wing of Film Art." Basing her research on original documents in the Watson estate, Cartwright presents a wholly different side of Watson, connecting for the first time his filmmaking with his interest in the literary magazine *The Dial*, and paying particular attention to the influence of e.e. cummings on Watson's and Webber's work.

Chuck Kleinhans takes a look at another amateur filmmaker, Theodore Huff. Remembered as a member of the first generation of film historians and archivists, and the author of a pioneering work on Charles Chaplin,[27] Huff's work as an avant-garde filmmaker had been completely wiped out until George Eastman House preserved his films. Apart from presenting an analysis of Huff and John Flory's *Mr. Motorboat's Last Stand* (1933), Kleinhans looks at Huff's papers and discovers a true cinephile who never found an institutional home for his various activities.

The photographer Ralph Steiner also began as an amateur. Scott MacDonald questions the conventional wisdom that Steiner's early film experiments were "simple studies." Indeed, he documents the highly complex visual design of H_2O (1929) and its joyous pleasure in the camera's ability to document nature's infinite variety. Dividing Steiner's career into three periods, including his political films of the 1930s, MacDonald finally draws parallels to Steiner's film experiments in the 1960s, which brought him into the realm of structuralist cinema.

Steiner later became heavily involved in the documentary movement and is a good representative of the subject of Chuck Wolfe's chapter, "Straight Shots and Crooked Plots: Social Documentary and the Avant-Garde in the 1930s." Taking a slightly different approach than he did in his history of 1930s American documentary,[28] Wolfe argues succinctly that the early avant-garde and 1930s documentary are linked by both aesthetic/theoretic concerns and personnel. Like the 1920s avant-gardists, later filmmakers working in documentary were concerned with aesthetic innovation and the expansion of film as an art form, even when ideological matter also entered into the mix.

My article on Paul Strand and Charles Sheeler's *Manhatta* (1921) is a slightly abridged version of a previously published essay, in which I began the project of defining an early American film avant-garde, now the focus of this book. In that 1987 version,[29] I tried to set the parameters for further research. The present version narrows the focus on *Manhatta*, attempting to contextualize the film in terms of its aesthetic and literary predecessors, and especially its often-cited but seldom understood connection to Walt Whitman. Furthermore, I argue that *Manhatta* is a primary example of my thesis that the American avant-garde's relationship to modernism was far from unequivocal.

Rethinking some of the points made in his dissertation on the European city film,[30] William Uricchio's chapter, "The City Viewed: The Films of Leyda, Browning, and Weinberg," theorizes that these city films straddle the differing though not necessarily conflicting representational strategies of avant-garde and documentary works, as understood in contemporary discourse. Second, Uricchio argues that American city films utilized formal strategies quite unlike those of their European predecessors, strategies that appear to be in part a function of the differences between New York's topography and those of European cities, and in part a function of the American avant-garde's own vernacular.

Another American experimental filmmaker whose work remains relatively unknown today is the animator Mary Ellen Bute. While continuing a line of inquiry she began in *Points of Resistance*,[31] Lauren Rabinovitz enters new territory in her chapter in this volume. In retrieving the work of this important avant-garde filmmaker, who also happened to be a woman, Rabinovitz finds in Bute's abstract films a particular tension between "elitist modernist aesthetics and their popular reception as pretty amusements," a tension that seems to have been not uncommon for other early American avant-garde films. Rabinovitz also discusses Bute's highly successful self-distribution schemes, which ironically made her a *bête noire* for post–World War II American avant-gardists.

The film historian Tom Gunning, who has produced groundbreaking work on early cinema and the avant-garde, looks at the career of another animator in "Machines That Give Birth to Images: Douglass Crockwell." In his piece Gunning argues that Crockwell's animated films and his appropriation of "archaic" technologies such as mutoscopes were the result of his fascination with machine-crafted art. Gunning also sees Crockwell's animation as redefining the form as a series of temporal permutations of images, rather than a seamless reproduction of motion through illusion.

A filmography of seventy early American avant-garde filmmakers and a bibliography close out the volume. As film studies enters its third decade, it is fitting that this volume on the first American film avant-garde comes to fruition, catalyzing new research in the field of avant-garde film as a whole. An institutional history that goes beyond the hagiographies of the past is certainly necessary if we are to understand this important phenomenon of American filmmaking.

NOTES

1. See, for example, P. Adams Sitney, *Visionary Film: The American Avant-Garde 1943–1978* (New York: Oxford University Press, 1979); David Curtis, *Experimental Cinema* (New York: Universe Books, 1971); Sheldon Renan, *An Introduction to the American Underground Film* (New York: E. P. Dutton, 1967).

2. See *The Essential Cinema: Essays on the Films in the Collections of Anthology Film Archives*, ed. P. Adams Sitney (New York: New York University Press, 1975), pp. xiii–xviii.

3. See, for example, J. Hoberman, "Avant to Live: Fear and Trembling at the Whitney Biennial," *Village Voice*, 16 June 1987, pp. 25–28.

4. Apart from Scott MacDonald's article on Cinema 16, the institutional history of the American film avant-garde has indeed yet to be written. Where are the histories of Filmmakers' Coop, Canyon Cinema, the "Art in Cinema" series? See Scott MacDonald, "Amos Vogel and Cinema 16," *Wide Angle* 9, no. 3 (1987): 38–51.

5. Peter Lehman, "For Whom Does the Light Shine? Thoughts on the Avant-Garde," *Wide Angle* 7, nos. 1–2 (1985): 70.

6. Jeffrey Ruoff has begun this project for the post–Maya Deren American avant-garde in his recently published, "Home Movies of the Avant-Garde: Jonas Mekas and the New York Art World," *Cinema Journal* 30, no. 3 (Spring 1991): 6–28.

7. An exception to this rule is Peter Weiss's essay in German on the history of avant-garde cinema, "Avantgarde Film," *Akzente* 10 (1963): 297–319.

8. The work of Noel Burch is particularly important in this context. See, for example, Noel Burch, "How We Got Into Motion Pictures: Notes Accompanying *Correction Please*, *Afterimage* 8–9 (Spring 1981): 22–38. See also the pioneering work of Tom Gunning, "An Unseen Enemy Swallows Space: The Space of Early Film and Its Relation to American Avant-Garde Film," in *Film Before Griffith*, ed. John L. Fell (Berkeley: University of California Press, 1983), pp. 355–366; and "The Cinema of Attractions: Early Cinema, Its Spectators, and the Avant-Garde," *Wide Angle* 8, nos. 3–4 (Fall 1986): 63–70. See also Charles Musser, *The Emergence of Cinema: The American Screen to 1907* (New York: Scribners, 1990).

9. See Roland Cosandey, "Georges Méliès as *l'inescamotable escamoteur*: A Study in Recognition," in *A Trip to the Movies: Georges Méliès, Filmmaker and Magician (1861–1938)*, ed. Paolo Cherchi Usai (Rochester/Pordenone: George Eastman House/Edizione Biblioteca dell'Immagine, 1991), pp. 57–111.

10. Oswell Blakeston and Kenneth MacPherson. "We Present—Manifesto!" *Close Up* 9, no. 2 (June 1932): 92–105.

11. Letter, Jay Leyda to Frank Stauffacher, 31 August 1946, "Art in Cinema" papers, Pacific Film Archives (PFA), Berkely, Calif.

12. See Jon Gartenberg: "Reframing Experimental Film," in *Black Maria Film Festival* (brochure, 1985), n.p.; Scott MacDonald, *Avant-Garde Film: Motion Studies* (Cambridge: Cambridge University Press, 1993), pp. 8–12.

13. For an excellent summary of the discussion surrounding early cinema, see Bart Testa, *Back and Forth: Early Cinema and the Avant-Garde* (Toronto: Art Gallery of Ontario, 1992).

14. Curtis, *Experimental Cinema*, p. 42.

15. Sitney, *Essential Cinema*, pp. xiii–xviii.

16. Sitney, *Visionary Film*, p. 29; See also *The Avant-Garde Film: A Reader of Theory and Criticism*, ed. P. Adams Sitney (New York: New York University Press, 1978).

17. See also Jonas Mekas, "The Experimental Film in America," *Film Culture* 1, no. 3 (May-June 1955): 17.

18. Arthur Knight, "Self-Expression," *Saturday Review of Literature* (27 May 1950).

19. Renan, *Introduction to the American Underground Film*, pp. 75–81.

20. Curtis, *Experimental Cinema*, pp. 38–42.

21. Lewis Jacobs, "Experimental Cinema in America (Part I)" *Hollywood Quarterly* 3, no. 2 (Winter 1947–1948): 111–124; reprinted in *Experiment in the Film*, ed. Roger Manvell (London: Grey Walls Press, 1949), pp. 113–152; also reprinted in Lewis Jacobs, *The Rise of the American Film*, 2d ed. (New York: Teachers College Press, 1968), pp. 543–582.

22. Stephen Dwoskin, *Film Is The International Free Cinema* (Woodstock, N.Y.: Overlook Press, 1975), pp. 34–38.

23. Jacobs, "Avant-Garde Production in America" (1949), p. 113.

24. Lewis Jacobs, "Morning for the Experimental Film," *Film Culture* 19 (1959): 8. As late as 1979, Jacobs noted at the FIAF Conference in Lausanne, Switzerland, which was dedicated to the avant-garde at the end of the silent period:"L'avant-garde a donc une vie très brève puisque les moyens financiers disponsibles n'existent pas, très rapidement, et que, par ailleurs, les gens progressistes qui veulent faire du cinéma à cette époque-là cherchent d'autres sujets, dictés par la conjoncture, plutôt que les thèmes traditionnels de l'avant-garde de la fin des années vingt." See "Intervention de Lewis Jacobs," in *Travelling* 56 (Fall 1979), second volume of special issue dedicated to the fiftieth anniversary of the Congress of La Sarraz and an FIAF Symposium.

25. Brian Taves, *Robert Florey: The French Expressionist* (Metuchen, N.J.: Scarecrow Press, 1987).

26. Patricia Rodden Zimmermann, *Reel Families: A Social History of the Discourse on Amateur Film, 1897–1962* (Ph.D. diss., University of Wisconsin–Madison, 1984).

27. Theodore Huff, *Charlie Chaplin: A Biography* (New York: Henry Schuman, 1951).

28. Charles Wolfe, "The Poetics and Politics of Nonfiction: Documentary Film," in *Grand Design: Hollywood as a Modern Business Enterprise, 1930–1939*, ed. Tino Balio (New York: Scribners, 1993), pp. 351–386.

29. Jan-Christopher Horak, "Modernist Perspectives and Romantic Desire: MANHATTA," *Afterimage* 15, no. 4 (November 1987): 9–15.

30. William Uricchio, *Ruttmann's "Berlin" and the City Film to 1930* (Ph.D. diss., New York University, 1982).

31. Lauren Rabinovitz, *Points of Resistance: Women, Power, and Politics in the New York Avant-Garde Cinema, 1943–71* (Urbana and Chicago: University of Illinois Press, 1991).

2

The First American Film Avant-Garde, 1919–1945

JAN-CHRISTOPHER HORAK

A HISTORY OF AMATEURS

Contrary to the standard histories of American avant-garde cinema, numerous American avant-garde artists produced films in the 1920s, 1930s, and early 1940s. They include: Sara Arledge, Roger Barlow, Josef Berne, Thomas Bouchard, Irving Browning, Francis Bruguière, Rudy Burckhardt, Paul Burnford, Mary Ellan Bute, Joseph Cornell, Stanley Cortez, Douglass Crockwell, Boris Deutsch, Emlen Etting, Paul Fejos, Robert Flaherty, Robert Florey, John Flory, Roman Freulich, Jo Gerson, Dwinell Grant, Harry Hay, Jerome Hill, Louis Hirshman, John Hoffman, Theodore Huff, Lewis Jacobs, Elia Kazan, Charles Klein, Francis Lee, Jay Leyda, M. G. MacPherson, Jean D. Michelson, Dudley Murphy, Ted Nemeth, Warren Newcombe, Lynn Riggs, LeRoy Robbins, Henwar Rodakiewicz, Joseph Schillinger, Mike Siebert, Stella Simon, Ralph Steiner, Seymour Stern, Paul Strand, Leslie Thatcher, William Vance, Charles Vidor, Slavko Vorkapich, James Sibley Watson, Melville Webber, Herman Weinberg, Orson Welles, and Christopher Young.[1] Supporting these filmmakers was a network of exhibition outlets, art theaters, and amateur film clubs, as well as film publications. Together these filmmakers and attendant phenomena constitute an avant-garde film movement of more than marginal significance. Indeed, the sheer volume of activity demands attention.

To understand the dynamics of the 1920s and 1930s avant-garde in comparison with its post–World War II American successors, the different self-perceptions and material conditions of the two generations must be recognized. Both defined themselves in opposition to commercial, classical narrative cinema, privileging the personal over the pecuniary. However, the 1950s avant-gardists proclaimed themselves to be indepen-

14

dent filmmakers, actively engaged in the production of "art," while the earlier generation viewed themselves as cineastes, as lovers of cinema, as "amateurs" willing to work in any arena furthering the cause of film art, even if it meant working for hire.

The aesthetic position of the second American film avant-garde, defined exclusively in terms of personal expression, led this generation to reject any collaboration with commercial or public interests, any utilitarian usage of the medium, be it commercial, instructional, or ideological. Ironically, their self-conscious declarations about their roles as film artists indicated a romanticized professionalization of the avant-garde project. Of his own generation Jonas Mekas noted: "To former generations film art was something still new and exotic, but for this generation it is part of our lives, like bread, music, trees, or steel bridges."[2] This professionalization of avant-garde filmmaking was, of course, possible only because the institutions providing material support for the avant-garde had expanded to include university film courses (offering filmmakers a place to earn money while making their films), government and foundation grants (allowing them to finance production), and nontheatrical film exhibition within the institutional framework of museums, archives, and media centers (offering filmmakers a place to show their work).

Earlier filmmakers, on the other hand, thought of themselves primarily as film amateurs rather than as professionals. The professional was an employee in Hollywood, producing for hire a profit benefiting the corporate hierarchy, while the amateur was concerned with the cause of film art. Given this self-image, the agenda of the first American film avant-garde could be much broader: to improve the quality of all films, whether personal or professional, to create structures for distribution and exhibition, and to further reception through publications. These cineastes moved freely between avant-garde film and other endeavors: documentary, industrials, experimental narrative, film criticism, film exhibition, painting, and photography. Many were primarily painters or photographers who only "dabbled" in film.

Lewis Jacobs, as a member of a Philadelphia amateur film club (fig. 2.1), noted of his group: "Our club is composed of painters, dancers, and illustrators. . . . It is our aim to emphasize a direction that will result in cinematic form."[3] As a paradigmatic example of the contemporary 1920s cineaste, one might fruitfully look at the career of Herman Weinberg: in the late 1920s and early 1930s, he worked as a manager for a "little theater" in Baltimore, wrote film criticism for various magazines, and

Figure 2.1.
The Cinema Crafters of Philadelphia (1929), left to right: Tibby Lear, Jo Gerson, Betty John, Louis Hirshman, Lewis Jacobs. Courtesy of Mrs. Louis Hirshman

made avant-garde shorts.[4] This range of activities in different cinematic endeavors was of course economically determined, since no single effort offered a livelihood.

For Weinberg, the avant-garde constituted itself everywhere beyond the realm of classical Hollywood narrative. The amateur film enthusiast, "the lover of cinema," was seen as the most ardent supporter of an avant-garde. As Col. Roy W. Winton, managing director of the Amateur Cinema League, noted: "We are concerned about where this Eighth Art is going and we are concerned about it aesthetically as well as socially and ethically."[5] In making avant-garde works, even the professional could become an amateur, as Weinberg explained in the case of Robert Florey: "It was only when he was working on his own, after studio hours, with borrowed equipment, scanty film, a volunteer cast and the most elemental of props, that, released from the tenets of the film factories, he was able to truly express himself in cinematic terms."[6]

Ironically, the desire to improve the status of the film medium on many different fronts was characteristic of both the 1920s European avant-garde—a fact that has been often suppressed by later historians[7]— and the first American avant-garde. Both European and American avant-gardists entered film as amateurs because economics dictated it. At the same time, amateurs-turned-professionals, like Walter Ruttmann, Hans Richter, and René Clair, among others, thought of their contract and personal work as of a piece. Whether "city films" by Joris Ivens or Wilfried Basse or scientific views of sea life by Jan Mol, these documentaries were considered to constitute avant-garde cinema. Thus, Europeans and Americans shared a broader, inclusionist rather than exclusionist view of independent cinema.

While the first avant-garde pioneered alternative forms that survived on the fringes of institutional power, it was only sporadically able to support itself economically. The avant-garde itself had not yet been embraced by institutions that could have created the material conditions for its continued survival. As a result of such factors, it is extremely difficult, for example, to separate avant-garde film production from the production of some documentary films in the 1930s. Roger Barlow, Paul Strand, Willard Van Dyke, LeRoy Robbins, Irving Lerner, Henwar Rodakiewicz, Ralph Steiner, and others not only earned their livelihood during the Great Depression through organizational, governmental, and private documentary film production, but actually perceived such activity as continuing their experimentation with cinematic form. A history of the early American avant-garde, then, cannot help but broaden its definition to include other noncommercial film forms (e.g., amateur and documentary films), as well as unrealized film projects, film criticism, and film reception.

In its earliest phases the American avant-garde movement cannot be separated from a history of amateur films. Indeed, the avant-garde and a growing amateur film movement were two alternative discourses on the fringes of the commercial mainstream that for at least a few years overlapped.[8] As C. Adolph Glassgold wrote programmatically in 1929: "The artistic future of the motion picture in America rests in the hands of the amateur."[9] Both avant-garde and amateur film initiatives received a boost after the Eastman Kodak Company's introduction in 1924 of 16mm film and the easy-to-use Cine-Kodak 16mm camera. The new technology was not only cheaper and safer than 35mm nitrate film; it was also in many ways more versatile, allowing for hand-held camera work and shooting on location and under ambient light conditions. The Cine-Kodak made Everyman and Everywoman a potential film artist, and while some avant-garde filmmakers preferred 35mm, others, like Theodore Huff, could not have made films without the low-cost 16mm alternative. Thus technology played an important role in the development of this first avant-garde, as it did in the experimental film movements after World War II.

The first avant-garde defined itself in opposition to the commercial industry not only aesthetically, but also economically, producing films at minimal expense. Instead of large crews and expensive sets, avant-garde filmmakers worked with modest expenditures of money and materials, their films subject to the personal budgets of an amateur. When Slavko Vorkapich and Robert Florey completed *The Life and Death of 9413 — A Hollywood Extra* (1928), the press continually mentioned that the film cost a mere $97.50;[10] Florey's *The Love of Zero* (1928) was produced for approximately $120.00, and Charles Vidor's *The Bridge* (1929) for approximately $250.00, plus sound work.[11] Roman Freulich produced *Broken Earth* (1936) for $750.00, after earning a net profit of $200.00 on his first short, *Prisoner* (1934).[12] Two independent features, Paul Fejos' *The Last Moment* (1928) and Josef von Sternberg's *The Salvation Hunters* (1925), were both released for under $15,000. Roger Barlow made a film for supposedly no more than four dollars.[13]

The cause of the avant-garde and amateurs was given a concrete organizational form with the founding of the Amateur Cinema League in

1926, led in its early years by the inventor Hiram Percy Maxim. By June 1927 there were an estimated thirty thousand amateur filmmakers in the United States alone.[14] In 1928 more than a hundred amateur cinema clubs existed in the United States and abroad, while the Amateur Cinema League had more than twenty-three hundred members, all of whom were producing amateur films.[15]

Amateur, avant-garde groups sprang up all over the country, some shooting in 35mm, some in 16mm, some only spinning grandiose dreams. In New York, Merle Johnson, an amateur cameraman, shot *Knee Deep in Love* (1926), an avant-garde narrative in which the faces of the protagonists/lovers are never visible.[16] In Burbank, California, the experimental production group "Artkino" was founded in 1925 by two amateurs, Jean D. Michelson and M. G. MacPherson, the name suggesting a homage to Soviet cinema. They apparently produced at least half a dozen films, including *War Under the Sea* (1929), *The Trap* (1930), *The Power of Suggestion* (1930), and *Oil—A Symphony in Motion* (1933), of which only the last-named title seems to survive in any form. According to Arthur Gale:

> This interesting amateur unit has made experiments of a wider range than any other similar group and has the most original list of titles to its credit. In all instances, experimentation has been concentrated on continuity structure, camera treatment and lighting effects rather than upon camera tricks.[17]

In New York, the founding of Eccentric Films was announced in 1929. "The first avant-garde production unit in America," they planned the production of an expressionist film with action "harking back to Freud's notebooks."[18] In upstate New York the "Cinema Club of Rochester" was formed in 1928 under the chairmanship of Dr. James Sibley Watson. In Philadelphia, Lewis Jacobs, Jo Gerson, and Louis Hirshman belonged to "The Cinema Crafters of Philadelphia" (see fig. 2.1), founded in early 1928 to realize "pioneer experiments in the new field of photoplay production."[19]

Professionalism was equated with commercialism, while amateurism connoted artistic integrity. This discourse also identifies personal expression with formal experimentation, a dualism repeated continually in contemporary aesthetic manifestoes and reviews, and echoed in the polemics of the second American avant-garde. The emphasis on formalism is apparent in Frederick Kiesler's comment: "In the film, as in every other art, everything depends on *how* its mediums (means) are utilized and not on *what* is employed."[20] Lewis Jacobs concurred: "Such stuff as story, acting and sets are merely contributing factors to the more important element, form. We are trying to make film something restless, fluent and dynamic."[21]

AVANT-GARDE EXHIBITION AND RECEPTION

Just as avant-garde film production created an alternative discourse on filmmaking, the "Little Cinema" movement provided both an exhibition outlet for avant-garde and European art films and an alternative to the commercial cinema chains dominated by the major Hollywood studios. The establishment of art cinemas was apparently first suggested in March 1922 by the magazine of the National Board of Review of Motion Pictures, *Exceptional Photoplays*,[22] which specifically tied the founding of a little cinema movement to the growth of avant-garde cinema:

> The showing of experimental pictures in a special theatre or series of theatres, and the building up of an audience, would naturally be followed by the actual making of experimental pictures. Directors and actors, stimulated by what they had seen in this theatre and encouraged by the reception of new work, would feel impelled to try their hand.[23]

Three years later the "Little Cinema" movement took off when the newly founded Screen Guild in New York showed a series of Sunday films at the Central Theater and at the George M. Cohan organized by Symon Gould. Other series were programed by Montgomery Evans at the Klaw Theatre (New York) in March 1926, and by Tamar Lane, who formed the Hollywood Film Guild in the same month.[24] Gould, meanwhile, began the first continuous art film program, also in March 1926, at the Cameo Theatre, sponsored by the International Film Arts Guild.[25] Seating 540 persons, the Cameo scheduled many European and American films that had been failures in their first run because they were not "popular" enough.

In a speech before the Society of Motion Picture Engineers, Gould noted that the film art movement "had dedicated itself to the task of reviving and keeping alive classic motion pictures, as well as those films that may be noteworthy for the best elements." He concluded: "There is no doubt that this is the age of celluloid. We are only standing on the threshold of unforeseen developments in this momentous field."[26]

Meanwhile, in October 1926 Joseph Fleisler, Michael Mindlin, and the Screen Guild, acting as the Film Associates, Inc., took over the 5th Avenue Playhouse at 66 Fifth Avenue, proclaiming it the "first succinctly art cinema house in America"[27] (fig. 2.2). The first film on the program of the new cinema was the re-released *Das Cabinet des Dr. Caligari* (1919), often credited with initiating a film art movement in the United States.[28] Within a few years "little cinemas" sprang up all over the country. The Art Cinema League, meanwhile, remodeled a barn and presented experimental shorts.[29]

In spring 1927 the Little Theatre of the Motion Picture Guild, under the management of John Mulligan, was opened in Washington, D.C., the first "little cinema" outside New York City. This was followed by the Little Theatre of the Movies in Cleveland in late 1927, and almost

Figure 2.2.
5th Avenue Playhouse, New York (1928), frame enlargement from *The March of the Movies* (1928)

immediately by the Playhouse in Chicago. A. W. Newman, director of the Cleveland cinema, specifically referred to the exhibition of short films that "represent important experimentation" as a part of its mandate.[30]

In Hollywood the Filmarte was founded in 1928 by Ms. Regge Doran (fig. 2.3);[31] other little theaters were located in Boston (Fine Arts Theatre), Rochester (Little Theatre), New York (Carnegie Playhouse), Newark (Little Theatre), Buffalo (Motion Picture Guild), Baltimore (Little Theatre),[32] Philadelphia (Motion Picture Guild), Brooklyn (St. George's Playhouse/Brooklyn Film Guild), and East Orange, N.J. (Oxford Theatre).[33] The Motion Picture Guild, under the direction of Robert F. Bogatin, operated the theaters in Philadelphia, Buffalo, Cleveland, and Rochester. Michael Mindlin had his own subway circuit with the 55th Street Playhouse in New York, the St. George in Brooklyn, and the Playhouse in Chicago.

Figure 2.3.
Advertisement of Filmarte Theatre (Los Angeles) for *Prisoner* (1934), directed by Roman Freulich

In February 1929 Symon Gould opened the Film Guild Cinema on Eighth Street. Designed by Frederick Kiesler, it was in the eyes of its architect the "first 100 per cent cinema in the world."[34] The New York Film Art Guild's inaugural screening in 1929, which was attended by numerous dignitaries, including Theodore Dreiser, presented two avant-garde films by Americans, *The Fall of the House of Usher* (1928, Watson/Webber) and *Hands* (1928, Stella Simon), along with a Soviet feature, *Two Days* (1927). The premiere led the National Board of Review to name *The Fall of the House of Usher* in its "a Calendar of Progress," noting that: "Amateur experimentation reaches a sudden peak in this abstract film."[35]

The Little Theatre in Rochester (fig. 2.4) opened on 17 October 1929, with seating for 299. The opening-night program featured the French/

Figure 2.4.
Program brochure for the Little Theatre, Rochester, New York, November 1929

Italian silent, *Cyrano de Bergerac* (1923), with a three-man orchestra in the balcony providing musical accompaniment. With its slogan "The House of Shadow Silence," the Little Theatre consciously set itself against large commercial theatres, by now all wired for sound. It was dedicated to showing "art films that appeal to the intelligent and the sophisticated."[36] In early 1931 the theater was turned over to Ben and Florence Belinson, who ran it for the next thirty-five years. Today the Little Theatre is the oldest functioning art cinema in the United States.

Not surprisingly, art cinema programs often paired American avant-garde films with European, especially German and Russian, features. Dreiser commented on this mixture in the Film Guild's inaugural program brochure, which referred to "the little cinema theatres, which should, and I hope will, act as havens for artistic American as well as European productions and such experimental efforts of 'amateurs' here as many have the real interests of the screen as art truly at heart."[37]

The Life and Death of 9413 — A Hollywood Extra played at the Philadelphia Motion Picture Guild with the German/Indian production, *Die Leuchte Asiens/Light of Asia* (1926), while Robert Florey's second film, *The Love of Zero*, was billed at the Los Angeles Filmarte Theater with Gösta Ekman's *Klöven* (1927).[38] *The Story of a Nobody* (1930, Gerson/Hirshman) was exhibited with Paul Fejos' arty Universal feature, *The Last Performance* (1929),[39] while Charles Vidor's *The Bridge* premiered at the Hollywood Filmarte Theatre with another European feature.[40] Roman Freulich's *Prisoner* was shown at the Little Theatre in Baltimore with *Sweden, Land of the Vikings* (1934).

Ironically, obituaries for the Little Cinema movement appeared as early as 1929, when the movement was far from spent. John Hutchins' article in *Theatre Arts Monthly* noted in September 1929:

> That their bright day is done and they are for the dark, within only four years of their inception, is the unhappy comment on an art movement that from the first was characterized not so much by art as by a truly astonishing lack of foresight, and later by merely bad business methods.[41]

The fact that Hutchins wrongly proclaims the demise of at least two cinemas, and overlooks the imminent opening of two others in Rochester and Baltimore in October 1929, suggests that another agenda is at work. In fact, the author finds many of the foreign films distasteful, "static and inferior" (a consistent criticism of European "art" films from allies of the

American film industry), argues that the Little Cinemas had "little or nothing to offer," and accuses Gould's Film Guild, for example, of showing too many Russian films. Indeed, it would not be inferior foreign films, but rather a worsening economic climate, that would eventually contribute to the demise of many Little Cinemas. But that would take several more years.

Art galleries were another potential site for avant-garde exhibitions. In many cases gallery organizers screened the films of the artists whose works in other media they represented. Marius de Zayas' New York gallery showed Strand and Sheeler's *Manhatta* (1921) in 1922, after exhibiting Sheeler's photography, drawings, and painting. Jay Leyda's *A Bronx Morning* (1931) was premiered at the Julien Levy Gallery in New York, as was Lynn Riggs's *A Day in Santa Fe* (1931), Henwar Rodakiewicz's *Portrait of a Young Man* (1932), and Joseph Cornell's *Rose Hobart* (1936). Presenting European films as well, Julien Levy in fact built up a substantial collection of avant-garde films, which he hoped "to display on request."[42] Rodakiewicz's and Leyda's films were also shown at Alfred Stieglitz's An American Place, occasional showcase for American avant-garde films.[43]

Another exhibition outlet from 1930 through mid-decade was the Workers Film and Photo League, which was allied with the Communist Party, USA. Apart from its film production and photography activities, the League also set up local 16mm film distribution systems and, in 1934, a national one.[44] Presenting to its membership Soviet feature films, newsreels concerning left-wing political actions, and evenings of avant-garde films, the League was instrumental in developing an audience for art films, especially at the Hollywood chapter, which had an ambitious exhibition program under the directorship of Bill Miller.[45] League member Tom Brandon founded Garrison Films in 1932 to distribute to League organizations.[46]

The largest audiences were undoubtedly the Amateur Cinema League's local clubs in countless American cities. The ACL had begun to organize a lending library as early as 1927, in order, Arthur Gale wrote, to "provide an adequate distribution of amateur photoplays, secure a dependable event for club programs and, as well, encourage new groups to undertake amateur productions."[47] Its distribution catalogue included *The Fall of the House of Usher, The Tell-Tale Heart* (1928, Charles Klein, fig. 2.5), H_2O (1929, Ralph Steiner), as well as *Portrait of a Young Man* (1931, Henwar Rodakiewicz), *Lot in Sodom* (1933, Watson/Webber), *Mr.*

Figure 2.5.
Still from *The Tell-Tale Heart* (1928), directed by Charles Klein, with Otto Matiesen.
Courtesy of George Eastman House

Motorboat's Last Stand (1933, Huff/John Flory), and *Another Day* (1934, Leslie P. Thatcher), all of which were screened extensively throughout the United States. *The Fall of the House of Usher,* one of the most popular, was screened hundreds of times in ACL clubs.[48] Although ACL's interests turned in the 1930s increasingly to travelogues and other forms of home movies, these avant-garde films were still available through the League in the early 1950s.

The ACL awarded yearly film prizes, adding the winners to its library. *Photoplay* and *Liberty* magazine also staged amateur film contests, which offered public exposure to independent filmmakers. For example, *Photoplay* awarded its first prize in 1929 to Ralph Steiner's *H₂O*, which in turn led to a review in the *National Board of Review Magazine.*[49] In 1937 an amateur film contest announced in *Liberty* magazine was the occasion for LeRoy Robbins, Roger Barlow, and Harry Hay to produce *Even As You and I* (1937).

Other kinds of distribution were haphazard, usually dependent on the filmmaker's renting the film to individual exhibition outlets. Symon Gould, the founder of the Cinema Guild, apparently set up some kind of distribution network, renting films to both the little cinemas and commercial theaters. However, any profits realized never made their way back to the filmmakers. Strand and Sheeler, for example, complained that their film *Manhatta* disappeared after Gould got the print for a screening at the Cameo Theatre in 1926. Robert Florey was even more specific about promises made to him:

> Early in 1928, Mr. Simon [Sic] Gould, then manager of the 5th Street Cinema Playhouse [Sic] in New York offered to give World Wide exploitation to my experimental shorts . . . and to that effect I gave him *all* the negatives and prints that I had. I regret to say that I have not heard from Mr. Gould since 1929, I have never received an account of the rentals or sales of my pictures.[50]

When Frank Stauffacher, programmer for the "Art in Cinema" series at the San Francisco Museum of Modern Art (1946–1951), asked Gould in 1950 about the existence of certain avant-garde prints, Gould answered (on Film Guild letterhead) that he would be glad to undertake a search, for a twenty-five-dollar fee.[51]

Several film magazines were dedicated to promoting art films: *Close Up*, published in Switzerland in English; *Film Art*, published in London; *Experimental Cinema*, edited by Seymour Stern and Lewis Jacobs; and the *National Board of Review Magazine*, successor to the board's *Exceptional Photoplays*. The first three journals functioned briefly as critical voices in the discourse around both European and American art film, while the last continued its battle for better films for many years.

Close Up, in particular through its American contributors, Harry A. Potamkin and Herman Weinberg, documented the achievements of the American avant-garde from 1928 to 1934. The journal was initially impressed with the ability of the American avant-garde to produce low-cost films of high artistic merit, as evidenced in Kenneth MacPherson's editorial on Robert Florey's *Life and Death of 9413—A Hollywood Extra*.[52] In later issues, *Close Up* regularly published stills from new American avant-garde films, as well as reviews and news of future (sometimes unrealized) projects.

Film Art, published in London from 1933 to 1937, continued where *Close Up* left off, with many of the same contributors—Weinberg, Rudolf

Arnheim, Oswell Blakeston. The journal, published more or less quarterly, printed not only reviews of American avant-garde films but also stills from films by Lewis Jacobs and Joe Berne and information about new productions.

Experimental Cinema, published between 1931 and 1934, concerned itself primarily with leftist filmmaking but also considered avant-garde efforts. In issue number 5, for example, the magazine published stills from Steiner's *Pie in the Sky* (1935), Jacobs' unfinished *As I Walk* (1934), and Joseph Schillinger and Mary Ellen Bute's equally unfinished *Synchronmy* (1934), as well as a series of notes on various avant-garde efforts, including the Group Theatre project, *Cafe Universal* (1934).[53]

The *National Board of Review Magazine* reviewed not only commercial Hollywood films, but also European art films, and occasionally American avant-garde films.[54] Shortly after the magazine's founding in 1926, the journal published a series of articles on the Little Cinema movement. Its coverage of avant-garde films was more sporadic, since it apparently limited itself to reviewing films that were being distributed commercially.

Amateur Movie Makers, the official organ of the Amateur Cinema League, on the other hand, originally focused on amateurs, among them avant-gardists, but shifted away from the latter in the mid-1930s. As the organization became aesthetically more conservative, its members increasingly preferred polished travelogues and Hollywood's professional discourse to formal experimentation. In its early phase, though, articles by Theodore Huff, Jay Leyda, Henwar Rodakiewicz, and Herman Weinberg encouraged amateurs to experiment with film form. The magazine also published reports on local amateur cinema club activities, including screenings of films from the ACL library.

Thus, while the first American avant-garde relied on an institutional framework that was less well developed than that of the postwar avant-garde, their efforts did not exist in a complete vacuum, as has been previously assumed. Avant-garde filmmakers, while working essentially in isolation, were able to screen their films through a number of outlets and saw them reviewed in a variety of magazines. A public discourse on the nature and viability of amateur and avant-garde film first appeared in that period.

To be sure, as the 1930s progressed and the Depression deepened, possibilities for film production, as well as distribution and exhibition, steadily declined. By the late 1930s the ACL had turned completely to travelogues, a number of the Little Cinemas had failed, and money and jobs were scarce. Filmmakers emerging after 1935, like Sara Arledge, Rudy Burckhardt, Joseph Cornell, and Francis Lee, produced their films essentially in a void, until they were discovered by the second American avant-garde. Roger Barlow, LeRoy Robbins, Paul Strand, Willard Van Dyke, Ralph Steiner, and others turned to government- or politically sponsored social documentary as a means of expanding the borders of cinematic language.

It was, of course, at this very moment, in 1935, that the Film Department of the Museum of Modern Art was founded. Under its first curator, Iris Barry, the department's outlook was essentially Eurocentric: it exhibited the classic art and avant-garde films of the 1920s and 1930s, as well as the great silents, giving a new generation a film historical education. MOMA preserved the Berlin-produced avant-garde film, *Hands* (1928) by Stella Simon, but it also allowed the original and only surviving print of Jo Gerson and Louis Hirshman's *Story of a Nobody* to decompose in its vaults.[55]

Relegated to the dustbin of history, the first American avant-garde was not thought worthy of preservation. Many of the films produced by that avant-garde have been lost; others still await preservation. This survey, like the chapters that follow, must necessarily remain fragmentary.

EARLY AVANT-GARDE FILM PRODUCTION

Although European art and avant-garde films aroused intense interest in America and resulted in a degree of emulation, this volume will seek to demonstrate that American avant-garde films were unique products of American culture. The very fact that they were born out of the *reception* of European avant-garde films *in America* inscribed their position: while often borrowing or quoting the formal techniques of the European avant-garde, they demonstrated a certain wild eclecticism, innovativeness, and at times naiveté that was only possible for American filmmakers working far from Paris and Berlin, the centers of Western high culture. Contemporary critics condemned this eclecticism, as when Kirk Bond wrote of *Lot in Sodom*: "But by any worthwhile standard it is a chaos of conflicting mediums. Nothing is thought out in terms of any one, but the directors, like a painter with his colors, dip by turn into each, following the turn of the story."[56] Rather than denigrating American eclecticism, it might be fruitful to look at the early American avant-garde with a postmodern sensibility, appreciating the hodgepodge of styles (Expressionism, Cubism, Art Nouveau) and philosophical currents that make up the first American avant-garde.

The first American avant-garde—like the second, and unlike the European avant-garde—seems to have had an extremely contradictory relationship to the modernist project. Its utilization of modernist form in connection with expressions of highly romantic, even antimodernist, sentiments is symptomatic of this ambivalence toward modernism. A particularly American romanticism, which manifests itself in a longing for (wo)man's reunification with nature, informs the early American avant-garde's visualization of the natural environment and the urban sprawl. This kind of romanticism was quite absent from most of its European predecessors, with the possible exception of the French film Impressionists around Louis Delluc.[57] In European modernist films nature is seen at best as an abstraction, as an ideal aesthetic construct, not as a primordial force from which human society has been forcibly separated. While the European avant-garde is proudly modernist in its celebration of urbanism and the machine age, American avant-garde films are much more ambivalent, viewing the separation from nature with a degree of dread. This romantic view not only separates the early American avant-garde from its European models, but also connects it directly to filmmakers of the second American avant-garde, such as Stan Brakhage, James Broughton, and Ed Emschwiller.

Even within the first American avant-garde, differences can be ascertained. Avant-garde filmmakers in the 1920s produced experiments with the hope of distributing them through commercial channels; avant-garde filmmakers after 1929 produced their work with the expansion of the amateur film movement in view. While the former were often film professionals, working on their own time outside the commercial film industry, the latter were usually true amateurs. This loose division is also marked by the professional use of 35mm film stock versus amateurs' general use of 16mm at the very end of the decade and into the 1930s. Thus, filmmakers of the first generation, like Warren Newcombe, Boris Deutsch, Robert Flaherty, Charles Klein, Robert Florey, and Dudley Murphy, produced their avant-garde films and simultaneously or subsequently worked in the film industry in a professional capacity.

In 1929 Hans Richter created the first topology of avant-garde film for his seminal exhibition, "Film und Foto," held in Stuttgart, Germany.[58] In that exhibition, Richter differentiated between absolute *cinema pur* documentary and narrative *art cinema*.[59] Twenty-five years later, Jonas Mekas developed his own topology in his article on the American avant-garde. It included film drama, film poem, cineplastics, and document film.[60] P. Adams Sitney's topology in *Visionary Film* divides the avant-garde into five types: trance, lyrical, mythopoetic, structural, and poetic.[61] Dana Polan has rightly criticized this typology as incomplete and lacking "the kind of metacommentary that could concretize its categories in history."[62] Polan himself has suggested a typology that would take into consideration the "stances the films take (consciously or not) toward social experience."[63] He goes on to define the social and the lyrical, the structural and the physiological in avant-garde cinema, but ultimately admits that no topology can contain the diversity of avant-garde practice.

As stated in the Introduction to this book, it might be useful to look at all avant-garde films as discursive practices in opposition to classical cinema. We might also fruitfully think of avant-garde cinema as "pedagogical interventions, as works that allow us to see cinema again, in places and at levels where we had ceased to see it."[64] Looking at the avant-garde in this way allows us to see these films as critiques of mainstream, classical narrative, and as cinematic discourses on a whole range of issues. The subheadings below reflect this range of issues and can be divided into sets of polarities, depending on their referents: urbanism/nature, painting/dance, fiction/parody, and poetry. Clearly the theoretical question of topology remains unanswered, but such a project would demand an extended theoretical discussion that is not possible here.

THE POETICS OF URBAN SPACE

Paul Strand and Charles Sheeler's *Manhatta* (1921) was not only the first avant-garde film produced in the United States, and a model for subsequent "city films" in Europe and America, but also a highly contradictory film in terms of its modernist text. As I argue in Chapter 11, previous readings of the film have failed to take into account *Manhatta's* romantic subtext, which is visible both in the inter-titles, taken from the poetry of Walt Whitman, and in the film's overall narrative construction.

Manhatta was released commercially as a "scenic," a quasi travelogue, shown in cinemas as a short before the feature presentation, as was

Robert Flaherty's so-called scenic, *Twenty-Four Dollar Island* (1927). Financed by Pictorial Clubs of America, and released by Pathé, Flaherty's homage to New York City, ostensibly completed for the three hundredth anniversary of the landing of the Dutch in 1626, was in many ways less rigorous in its formal construction than *Manhatta*.[65] Flaherty's film was eventually used as a moving-image backdrop for a stage show at New York's Roxy Theatre titled "The Sidewalks of New York."[66]

The film begins with etchings of the Dutch buying Manhattan from the island's Native American inhabitants in 1624, then proceeds with a series of drawings and maps of what the Dutch called "Neiuw Amsterdam." Flaherty next cuts to an aerial view of the city, taken three centuries later. The following images, mostly held in long shot, and often taken from skyscrapers high above the city, focus on construction: cranes and excavators digging, a dredger working the river, bulldozers, workers blowing out bedrock with dynamite. Intercut with these images are shots of traffic and bridges on the Hudson and East rivers, on the one hand, and skyscrapers, on the other. Through the use of telephoto lenses and his bird's eye view, Flaherty collapses spaces, creating canyons of concrete and iron and giving the city a feeling of incredible density and power.

Unlike *Manhatta*, then, which ultimately attempts a visual symbiosis of city and country, man and nature, Flaherty, the romantic chronicler of "primitive cultures" in *Nanook of the North* (1922) and *Moana* (1926), here presents urban civilization as completely overpowering and destructive of nature, as when a lone tree is seen against a backdrop of the concrete jungle. The people of New York play no part in the film. Instead, as Flaherty himself noted, it was "not a film of human beings, but of skyscrapers which they had erected, completely dwarfing humanity itself."[67] The natural environment, then, has been replaced by an artificially constructed, primordial environment. Only the film's final image, an extreme long shot of Central Park, brings the film back to the first shots of the Dutch invaders and Native Americans, reminding the audience of that great absence that informs the film—the separation from the natural environment.

Much more celebratory of the city and also more humanistic in its view of city dwellers is Jay Leyda's *A Bronx Morning*, a tribute to one of his favorite photographers, Eugene Atget. It is a lyrical look at his Bronx neighborhood in the early morning hours before traffic and pedestrians crowd the street.[68]

An important city portrait from the early 1930s was Irving Browning's *City of Contrasts* (1931). Released commercially by Sol Lesser with a superficial "comic" narration to improve its box-office potential, the film nevertheless merits recognition in terms of its cinematography and sophisticated montage.[69] Browning, a photographer by trade, visually juxtaposes images both formally, contrasting light, shade, and form through extreme camera angles, and semantically, contrasting various ethnic neighborhoods, skyscrapers, and city parks, the wealthy at River-side Drive and the shantytown at Hooverville on the Hudson.[70] Its editing is thus much more ambitious than its soundtrack, creating a "New Realist" montage of the city's contradictions. The contradictory social forces and conditions visualized in the film are accepted as endemic to urban life. The unserious narration, added against the artist's intentions, positions the subject as a tourist, appealing to a desire for the exotic without forcing him or her to confront or analyze the juxtaposition of rich and poor, African-American and European.

The critic, film historian, and cinema manager Herman Weinberg produced at least two avant-garde films on the subject of the city, although the first, *A City Symphony* (1930),[71] was apparently chopped up to provide footage for the second, *Autumn Fire* (1931).[72] According to Weinberg, the latter film was a *romance sentimentale,* made not for public exhibition, but as a means of courting a woman he then married.[73] The film subjectively portrays two lovers who suffer through their separation until they are united at the end. Utilizing a Russian montage style, Weinberg intercuts continually between the two, juxtaposing their environments, identifying the young woman symbolically with nature and the man with the city (New York). That woman is identified with images of nature implies a whole set of textual referents: walking along the beach, gazing out her window at a field of flowers, she is inscribed as "the waiting woman," consumed by the emotional desire of man, an object of the male gaze. This gendered dichotomy is bridged by the film's reunification scene in a railroad station, which posits a form of narrative closure, cross-cutting images of nature (flowing water) with the station.[74] Thus, the film mixes elements of the city film with a portrait of nature, expressing a romantic longing for man's lost connection with the wilderness.

In the 1930s Lewis Jacobs also turned to documenting the city. While shooting footage for the Film and Photo League and working in New York as a cutter for advertising films, Jacobs began a project, *As I Walk,* which remained unfinished. It was to be a two-reel documentary of a working-class section of New York, following the "general trend of independent films to show the disgusting social conditions which exist in large and small cities."[75] A fragment, called *Footnote to Fact* (1934), was finished. A portrait of a young woman, it expressed in images the thoughts and scenes flashing through her mind: documentary shots of street life in New York. Jacob's inter-cutting between shots of the woman and her subjective views of reality accelerates until the film comes to a climax.[76] The film's other three parts were to be called *Highway 66, Faces in the Street,* and *Night Between the Rivers.* According to Jacobs, the whole was to be post-synchronized, "using sound in a stream of consciousness technique, including snatches of jazz, natural sounds, modern poetry and inner monologues."[77] The articulation of subjectivity was to become a lifelong preoccupation for Jacobs, as demonstrated by his later film, *Case History* (1956).[78]

American avant-garde films about the city, then, always seem to be about man and nature in the city. Such ambivalence toward urban spaces is nowhere as evident as in Willard Van Dyke, Henwar Rodakiewicz, and Ralph Steiner's government-sponsored documentary, *The City* (1939), possibly the last of the real "city films." From the very beginning the film sets up a country/city dichotomy, juxtaposing the opening "New England" sequence to the following scenes of heavy industry.[79] The metropolis is seen here as overcrowded, noisy, polluted, and unhealthy; images of smokestacks, traffic jams, and substandard industrial housing predominate. Only in the latter half of the film is a new vision presented: a city without a cityscape, a city in harmony with the environment, a city replicating a small-town feeling, the urban jungle miraculously metamorphized into suburbs. The film advocates a form of city planning where living spaces and work spaces are strictly divided, offering residents of newly constructed, individual houses clean, green suburbs in which the nature they crave and are denied in an urban environment is ever-present. Thus, while *The City*'s montage reproduces the formal aesthetics of earlier city films, its ideological position is far from modernist.

Toward the end of the 1930s, Rudy Burckhardt, a Swiss-born photographer who would become an important avant-garde figure in the 1950s and 1960s, made his first films with a 16mm camera. Burckhardt's city films, however, are not marked by the same ambivalence toward urbanism. Many in fact are conscious reworkings of the amateur travelogue, but constructed with an eye for composition, and for the unexpected, the incongruous, the off-beat. In 1936 Burckhardt shot *145 West 21,* a little silent comedy about a domestic quarrel with some of his artist friends as actors. That was followed by *Seeing the World—Part One: A Visit to New York* (1937), a spoof on travelogues.

Burckhardt lived in New York City, and many of his early films were visual poems to that particular urban landscape. In *The Pursuit of Happiness* (1940), his second film about the city,[80] Burckhardt's camera focuses on crowds, showing their collective power through fast and slow motion, analyzing their individuality through closeup still photographs of faces. In between we see shops, advertisements, and buildings, but these seem to be mere obstacles for the ever-moving crowds of pedestrians, that flow of humanity which had been so invisible in the avant-garde's first city films. Possibly because Burckhardt was a European, there is much less sense of nature's absence in the city or feeling that subjectivity can only be expressed through a reunification with the environment. Instead, like the European avant-garde, Burckhardt seems comfortable in urban spaces far from nature.

Surprisingly, then, most American "city films" seem to lack the unequivocal celebration of modernism and urbanism found in European "city films." In *Rien que les Heures* (1925, Alberto Cavalcanti), *Berlin: The Symphony of a City* (1926, Walter Ruttmann), and *The Man with a Movie Camera* (1929, Dziga Vertov), to name a few of the best-known feature films in this subgenre, the urban environment is celebrated for its excitement, speed, and modernity, with few references to nature, beyond its role in leisure-time activities for Sunday picnickers. The early American avant-garde, on the other hand, laments its separation from the country, a mood nowhere more evident than in its lyrical documentaries of nature.

LYRICAL NATURE

If we theorize that many of the city films of the American avant-garde constructed a mixture of modernist formal elements and romantic desires, then the avant-garde's depiction of nature seems to be a more direct expression of American romantic sensibilities. Certainly, the documentation of the natural environment seems to be almost completely absent from the European avant-garde, with its modernist fascination with speed, transportation, and the urban environment. The only exceptions to this rule were the scientific films of Jan Mol in Holland and

Jean Painlevé in France, whose microscopic views of sea life coincided with ideas about a new mechanical vision and were thus popular with avant-garde cinema clubs, allowing their very empiricism to be co-opted by the modernist project.

What connected American avant-garde filmmakers to Romanticism, however, was their interest not only in depicting nature, however abstracted, but, more importantly, in utilizing nature as a visual metaphor for the expression of human (mostly male) subjectivity. Henwar Rodakiewicz's supremely romantic *Portrait of a Young Man* (1932) indicates in its very title that this nature film is a reflection of the filmmaker's inner consciousness. There is little interest in documenting nature objectively; rather, it is the abstraction of nature that fascinates the eye, its formal play in an infinite variety of patterns of form, movement, light.

Ralph Steiner's H_2O is a perfect case in point. This twelve-minute film of water, rain, raindrops, pools, brooks, streams, rivers, and oceans moves from very concrete images of water in all its manifestations to extremely abstract images of the way water reflects and refracts light.[81] For Steiner it is in fact the ability of the camera to capture the play of light in water that becomes the film's text. Steiner's *Surf and Seaweed* (1931) is a continuation of his exploration of water and light, with its montage of closeup images of the ocean, low-angle shots of waves crashing against the rocks, and extreme closeups of the swirling patterns of seaweed.

Very similar in terms of its construction, but closer to the modernist project in terms of its thematic concerns, is Steiner's *Mechanical Principles* (1933). Like H_2O and *Surf and Seaweed*, the film's images of reality are iconic. In this case moving engine parts create highly abstract geometric designs, their sense of composition heightened by movement. In the 1960s this kind of film would be called structural, but in the 1930s it was considered an attempt to find the abstract beauty of nature, invisible to the human eye, but accessible to the camera lens. *Mechanical Principles*'s machine parts are imbued with a strong sense of the anthropomorphic, romantic endeavor to reintegrate technology with the realm of nature.

Much the same can be said for Artkino's *Oil—A Symphony in Motion*, which postulates an even more radical synthesis of nature and technology by discovering the origins of the latter in the former.[82] The film utilizes a first-person monologue (intertitles), spoken by the oil underground: "I am the pulse beat of green jungles stored in the ground beneath your farms." The monologue in intertitles continues throughout the film, as oil narrates its own rise to power as the force behind technological development. The images, mostly held in heroic high-angle shots with objects shot against the open sky, and strongly influenced by Soviet aesthetics, begin with a pastoral landscape of farms, cows, and farmers, slowly giving way (thankfully, since the soil is exhausted) to oil derricks. Yet these derricks are presented almost as natural phenomena willed into existence by the narrating oil, since they, too, are anthropomorphic, functioning with few exceptions independently of humans and sprouting from the ground like the corn that preceded them. The final third of the film is a paean to technology and the speed of modern transportation, as the filmmakers juxtapose antiquated horse-drawn buggies to motor cars, trains, and planes. A closeup of a turning auto tire, superimpositions in criss-cross patterns of fast-moving railroad cars, and high-angle shots of the oil derrick silhouetted against the evening sky become metonymies for a functioning technology in harmony with nature. With its optimistic view of technology and, by extension, economic expansion, it is also very much an expression of male desire in the early twentieth century.

Henwar Rodakiewicz's *Portrait of a Young Man* is, likewise, an intensely romantic film, communicating a desire for union with nature. The young man of the title in fact never appears in the film; instead, the film presents an abstract montage of the sea, clouds, smoke, trees, and man-made machinery, mostly in closeup. The camera eye as an extension of the filmmaker's body constructs male subjectivity. According to Rodakiewicz, the meaning of the whole arises from the sum of its parts: "In creating a film of nature that represents the cameraman's individuality, the importance of selection cannot be overestimated."[83] Divided into three movements, the film's construction and rhythm are modeled on that of a symphony: an adagio layered between two faster-paced sequences.

Another subjective view of the natural environment was presented in Slavko Vorkapich and John Hoffman's *Moods of the Sea* (1942). Vorkapich was an early experimentalist who later made periodic forays into avant-garde film practice (*Millions of Us*, 1935, being a case in point) after establishing himself as a "montage specialist" in the Hollywood studios. Having collaborated with Robert Florey on *The Life and Death of 9413—A Hollywood Extra* (1928), Vorkapich in the 1930s and

1940s created "montages" in countless films, collapsing space and time into a matter of moments, thereby visually circumscribing the meteoric rise of a Broadway star, the cross-country tour of a boxer, or the simple passage of the seasons.[84] While such sequences soon degenerated from the experimental to the conventional, Vorkapich sought creative expression in the production of his own shorts.

Moods of the Sea, a pictorial fantasy, utilizes Felix Mendelssohn's *Fingal's Cave* as musical accompaniment to images of the ocean.[85] Opening with a view from a cave onto the ocean, the film orchestrates images of a powerful natural environment: giant waves breaking on the shore, cliffs towering above the surf, a sea gull in elegant flight, clouds gathering above the ocean, a sunset on the horizon. The images, true to Vorkapich's interest in montage, are cut precisely to the music, each image sequence reaching a rhythmic crescendo with the melodies. The romanticism of Mendelssohn's music contributes to the film's overall romantic quality, but it is both the framed image from the cave entrance at the film's beginning and the constantly moving camera that emphasize the subjective nature of the camera's point of view. Thus, like Rodak-iewicz's film, *Moods of the Sea* refers not so much to nature as to the human observer's experience of nature, the moods conjured up through a walk along the sea.[86]

Another film that seems to have existed between the commercial and the avant-garde was John Hoffman's *Prelude to Spring* (1946). Like many of the films discussed above, *Prelude to Spring* hoped to "not speak with words. It talks with images relating an eternal yet ever new story."[87] Presenting a series of shots of mountains, woods, and brooks, as the snow slowly melts, spring arrives, and a storm comes and goes, *Prelude's* images are composed for their formal beauty. Many of the shots tend toward the abstract, especially the images of flowing water, an effect heightened by high-contrast printing. Unfortunately, the soundtrack's clichéd use of Sergei Prokofiev's *Peter and the Wolf* gives the film a literalness that its often striking images contradict.

Reviewing the gamut of lyrical documentaries of nature, it seems evident that all of these experiments are motivated by a romantic subjectivity that is particularly American in terms of its aesthetics. The level of abstraction may vary, the correspondences established between images and music may be more or less direct, but these films are romantic in mood and seemingly far from the European modernist project.

PAINTING IN MOTION

The earliest known American experimental live-action and animated film, *The Enchanted City* (1922, fig. 2.6) is, like *Manhatta*, informed by romantic and modernist discourses. Made by Warren Newcombe,[88] the film treads an uneasy line between Hollywood kitsch and avant-garde abstraction.[89] Newcombe animates what are essentially a series of paintings, sandwiched between live-action images of a couple sitting at the sea shore.[90] The paintings are highly artificial, seemingly closer to Maxfield Parrish than to modern art. On the other hand, Newcombe's monumentalized spaces, devoid of human life, evidence a primacy of the architectural over the human form, recalling the metaphysical paintings of Giorgio de Chirico.

In its narrative of a quest down a river through an enchanted city, the film inscribes a male spectator looking at woman; it is a journey through dreams, through man's anxieties and fears in reference to female lack, as

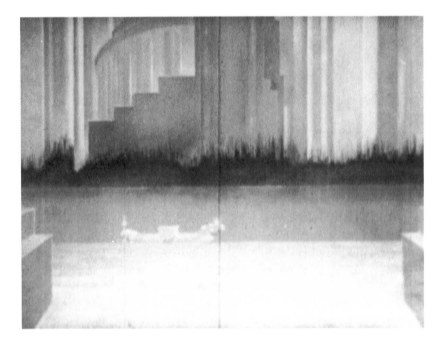

Figure 2.6.
Frame enlargement from *The Enchanted City* (1922), directed by Warren Newcombe

theorized by Freud. One of the earliest images of stairs, a tower, and a woman's face sets the tone by referencing Freud's conception of the phallic woman and man's fear of castration. This fear of castration is almost obsessively reworked in numerous other images, in shots of phalluses, and in the way views are restricted to a tunnel-like vision, culminating in the image of the voyager being engulfed in a giant waterfall, Freud's metaphor for man's disappearance into the gaping black hole of the womb. There is ultimately an irrationality to the sequencing of images, a narrative that does not so much resolve itself as come to a metaphysical halt, a formal *deus ex machina* dissolving the image of destruction into one of redemption. Thus, *The Enchanted City* too straddles romantic and modernist discourses, its narrative of romantic desire fraught with male *Angst* and unresolved conflicts, which the film's final images of nature cannot contain.

Francis Bruguière, who had collaborated on *Danse Macabre*, had by the late 1920s wandered to Europe, where he produced an abstract film, *Light Rhythms* (1930, fig. 2.7), in collaboration with *Close Up* editor Oswell Blakeston. In the film, Bruguière and Blakeston animated static forms solely through the manipulation of light.[91] Running eight minutes, the film presents a highly abstract meditation on the power of light to change perceptions of form. In this sense, the film can be compared to Lázló Moholy-Nagy's *Lichtspiel—Schwarz Weiss Grau* (1930), except that in the latter film, light is bounced off a moving object, whereas in this film the objects themselves never move.[92]

According to her own statements, Mary Ellen Bute began experimenting with abstract animated designs in order to visualize music. Like Oskar Fischinger in Germany, Bute was convinced of the formal possibilities of putting abstract forms to music. She joined forces with a young industrial film cameraman, Theodore Nemeth, to produce a whole series of abstract animated films. Through high-contrast lighting, color, and multiple exposures, Bute produced an effective method of creating animation in the third dimension, the length of the individual shots and their internal movement worked out with mathematical precision to visualize the accompanying music.[93]

Another pioneer of abstract animation was Francis Lee, who began his experimental work in 1939.[94] His *1941* is an emotionally powerful rendering of the Japanese attack on Pearl Harbor, presented in completely abstract form as an animated action painting:[95] an egg is smashed, red color dissolves over a globe floating in blue paint. Broken electric

Figure 2.7.
Frame enlargement from *Light Rhythms* (1930), directed by Francis Bruguière and Oswell Blakeston

light bulbs litter the phantasmagoric landscape. Lee painted directly on glass, shooting from underneath to a light source above, giving the film's color a strong vibrancy, which is heightened by the extreme saturation of the colors, an effect made possible through Lee's use of the then-new 16mm Kodachrome film stock. As the film progresses, the primary colors of the first images give way to grays, blacks, and browns, as the world is metaphorically turned into a desolate, ashen battlefield.

While this description may seem to give the film a narrative dimension, it must be underscored that all of Lee's early films are essentially abstract, their effect based on the emotional quality of their color and shape rather than any anthropomorphic reality. This also holds true for *Le Bijou* (1946) in which diamonds, red, blue, and gold crystals, and disks seem to move through a barren landscape. The three-dimensional quality of the objects nevertheless increases their anthropomorphic quality, creating an unspoken narrative of pure cinema. *Idyll* (1948) presents a phantasmagoric underwater landscape, using water and oil colors on glass, as in *1941*. Here nature seems to be abstracted, reducing animal and vegetable life to its spiritual essence, where color rather than shape predominates. The vibrant, saturated colors of *Le Bijou* give way in *Idyll* to more pastel hues like chalk colors, the whole underscored by romantic music.

Douglass Crockwell began his experiments at approximately the same time as Lee, and both indeed enjoyed a degree of favor with the second American avant-garde.[96] In 1938 and 1939 Crockwell, who was a well-known and highly paid commercial illustrator for the *Saturday Evening Post*, produced his first animated films. Working with paint on glass, Crockwell created a series of short animated abstractions, which he later compiled into what he called *The Glens Falls Sequence* (1946).[97]

Dwinell Grant began making abstract films in 1940, shortly after Lee and Crockwell.[98] His first film, *Composition 1 (Themis)* (1940), used wood, glass, and paper forms animated with a stop-motion camera. The lines, circles, and squares vary in their shape and movement, as well as in their color, which is limited to primary colors. In many respects this work resembles a constructivist painting in motion—Mondrian on the move. Yet, while the film gives a sense of objects in motion (time), they do not seem to move through anything but a two-dimensional space, and thus lack the kinetic force of other abstract animation.

In *Composition 2 (Contrathemis)* (1941), Grant increases the sense of movement, utilizing pulsating lines that move in circular patterns and seem to breathe as they grow thick or thin.[99] In his next two films, *Composition 3* (1942) and *Composition 4* (1945), Grant began moving into an exploration of three-dimensional space. In *Composition 3* this was accomplished by using three-dimensional media—clay, wooden objects, and such. In *Composition 4* the third dimension was actually created by developing a 3-D film, which used a beam-splitter and was viewed through polaroid glasses.[100]

It seems no accident that a number of the avant-garde filmmakers discussed here were later accepted into the pantheon of the second American avant-garde. Except for Newcombe and Bute, both of whom seemed to be tainted by commercialism, the work of these abstract animators could be subsumed under the aesthetics of Abstract Expressionism, while they simultaneously functioned as legitimate heirs to the European modernist traditions established by Hans Richter and others. For the producers of dance films, on the other hand, such a European modernist tradition was lacking.

TERPSICHORE ON FILM

One of America's earliest avant-garde films is *Danse Macabre*. Made in 1922, it was a collaboration between Francis Bruguière, film director Dudley Murphy,[101] and the dancer Adolph Bolm. While at first glance *Danse Macabre* seems to be a simple recording of a ballet set to Saint-Saëns' music, the use of animation in its first scene and of multiple exposures to visualize death's threatening presence bespeak its experimental intentions. At the same time, its final romantic image of love conquering death once again reflects male subjectivity.

Another American avant-garde filmmaker in Europe was Stella Simon. A photographer, Simon had studied with Clarence White in New York in the mid-1920s but, as a woman, was unable to receive any training in motion picture photography. She thus resolved to move to Berlin, where she entered the Technische Hochschule in 1926.[102] There she shot *Hände/Hands*, subtitled "the life and loves of the gentler sex."[103] Unlike Viktor Albrecht Blum's avant-garde documentary of 1928, which shows hands at work, Simon's film is a narrative of hands, dancing through expressionist-influenced miniature sets.[104] The film was successfully presented in Europe and in the United States, although its earnings were never enough to allow Simon to make another film.[105]

The film opens with hands waving in front of black velvet, the implication being that these hands and arms will be synecdoches for whole bodies.[106] In the highly abstracted scenes that follow, the viewer sees the mating of male and female, a "coquette" enticing a group of males, a wild party, an attempted suicide through drowning, and a final reconciliation and celebration of life—in short, a story of a *ménage à trois*. Utilizing abstract sets, which have been reduced to constructivist triangles, squares, and circles, the film's spaces are further limited by numerous variously shaped masks. The film's abstract quality is further strengthened by Marc Blitzstein's abstract twelve-tone music.

Yet, at the same time, the film presents a "melodrama" of female subjectivity and *Angst*. It is the drama of a woman who is afraid to lose her mate to another, more desirable woman, the melodrama of a woman who is continually playing out masochistic fantasies of defeat and self-mutilation, ever fearful that she is no longer the object of man's desire. The film's narrative closure, reproducing in its ballet of reunification a Hollywood ending, inscribes woman's desire for sexual harmony, and is indicative of Simon's romantic American approach.

While *Hands* can only be classified as a dance film in the widest sense, *Underground Printer* (1934) seems to have been more of a collaboration between filmmakers and dancers, although with a strong political intent. The film was directed by the photographer Thomas Bouchard in conjunction with the dancer/choreographer John Boving-ton, while Lewis Jacobs was responsible for photography and editing. Bouchard, who was best known for his photographic portraits of theater personalities, probably brought Jacobs and Bovington together. Boving-ton appeared in a solo dance in the film, while Jacobs took

> the grotesque movements and broke them up into their essences — mounting his sound and image with percussion shocks, throwing into startling relief the gyrations of the dancer as he spins and whirls as Goebbels, explodes as Goering, and exults as the Communist underground printer preparing his anti-Nazi leaflets.[107]

According to an ancient distribution catalogue, this was to be interpreted as "an artistic attack on the type of machine made thinking which produced the Nazi menace in Europe."[108]

Another early avant-garde filmmaker to attempt the motion picture visualization of dance was Sara Arledge. Like so many filmmakers in this period, Arledge had gone to art school and worked as a painter before beginning her film experiments. In 1936 she bought a 16mm Cine-Kodak Special, taught her husband how to use it, and began experiment-ing with multiple exposures, negative and positive images, fish-eye lenses, and colored filters.[109] Her first film, *Introspection*, was begun in 1941 but not completed until 1946.[110] It consisted of a series of multiple exposures of male dancers: their heads, legs, arms, moving in layered images.[111] In one sequence a body is wrapped in rags, much like a mummy, the body moving in a slow, dreamlike manner around its own axis. These images are intercut with negative images of hands reaching out and red-tinted images of a faceless body exercising. The repetition of movements, forms, and visual motifs makes the film almost structuralist in its concern with the cinema's formal applications. Unfortunately, as was often the case with avant-garde filmmakers, this beautifully conceived and mystical film was to remain Arledge's only completed film. A second film, *Phantasma-goria* (1946), shot on 16mm Kodachrome and "presenting some of the manifold possibilities of the motion picture as a medium for the dance," was apparently never completed.[112]

Ironically, none of these early dance films, except for the work of Sara Arledge, entered the canon of the second American avant-garde, even though the dance tradition would continue to have its supporters in the coming years, with many dancers (Maya Deren, Shirley Clarke, Kathy Rose) becoming avant-garde filmmakers. Again one might hypothesize that it was the lyrical and romantic elements in these earlier films that made them less fashionable. The same can be said for the experimental narratives produced by the first American avant-garde.

SHORT STORIES

Not all painters experimenting with avant-garde film made abstract animations. One painter at the edge of Hollywood, both geographically and spiritually, was Boris Deutsch, who in 1925 directed a one-reel experimental narrative film, *Lullaby*.[113] Shot in 35mm, *Lullaby* was apparently produced with the participation of the Russian exile community in Los Angeles, including Deutsch's wife, Riva, in the female lead, and the actor Michael Visaroff.[114] Opening on a painted miniature scene of Russian Orthodox church steeples, composed diagonally, almost abstractly, the film cuts to the sitting room of a Russian Kulak and family, drinking and eating happily. In a corner a (Jewish?) maid is rocking the baby of the family. The peasant patriarch mercilessly mistreats the maid, who, as a result, suffers from horrible dreams, including one in which she kills the child. After a brutal beating, the maid flees into the night. In the last image she is happily lying in the arms of an accordion player who had earlier shown her a moment of kindness.

This highly elliptical narrative, shot in two scenes on a very minimal set, is articulated without resorting to any intertitles, while its flashes of interior vision situate the film in the realm of the experimental. These very short shots consist of some of Deutsch's abstract paintings, which spin around their own central axis, denoting the subjective state of the female protagonist. In another scene, reminiscent of *Caligari*, Deutsch's high-contrast paintings of masks dissolve in and out in a subjective vision of paranoia (fig. 2.8). In fact, the power of the visions, and their stark abstraction and horrific anguish contrasted with the relative realism of the rest of the film, create a narrative excess that the film's final image of tranquility cannot contain.

Figure 2.8.
Frame enlargement from *Lullaby* (1925), directed by Boris Deutsch

One of the most important avant-garde filmmakers to come directly out of the Hollywood film industry was Robert Florey. In 1927 he produced *The Life and Death of 9413 — A Hollywood Extra* with Slavko Vorkapich. While simultaneously continuing to work on Hollywood film productions, Florey went on to produce *The Love of Zero* (1928) together with William Cameron Menzies, *Johann the Coffin Maker* (1928), and a city film, *Skyscraper Symphony* (1929).[115] The first two films in particular featured expressionistic sets (made almost exclusively in miniature and photographed with live actors through mirrors) and an elliptical narrative.

In 1928 Dr. James Sibley Watson, Jr., collaborated with Melville Webber on *The Fall of the House of Usher*, possibly one of the most highly regarded amateur film productions of its day: the chairman of the National Board of Review considered the film to be "the most outstanding contribution to motion pictures as an art form since *Caligari*."[116]

Watson's second avant-garde film, *It Never Happened/Tomatoes Another Day* (1930), is an unique example of dadaist aesthetics in early

Figure 2.9.
Frame enlargement from *It Never Happened/Tomatoes Another Day* (1930), directed by James Sibley Watson, Jr.

sound cinema: a minimalist and virtually expressionless acting style on a claustrophobic set characterizes the melodramatic love triangle. Although it seems extremely modern to today's eye, Watson considered the film a failure and suppressed its existence; it was recently discovered in the nitrate holdings of his estate (fig. 2.9).[117]

Another collaboration with Melville Webber, *Lot in Sodom*, was also shot in Watson's Prince Street studio, using a homemade optical printer.[118] It premiered at the Little Carnegie Theatre on 25 December 1933, along with Josef Berne's *Dawn to Dawn*, and continued to play in theaters throughout the 1930s and 1940s, becoming in the process probably the most commercially successful avant-garde film of the era.

Edgar Allan Poe was the inspiration for three major avant-garde works in 1928: "The Fall of the House of Usher" was adapted by both Watson and the French experimentalist Jean Epstein, while "The Tell-Tale Heart" was the literary source for an avant-garde short of the same name.

Charles Klein's *The Tell-Tale Heart* was another very low budget off-Hollywood production reprising German Expressionist cinema. It is considered one of the most successful art films of the period.[119]

The film opens with a closeup of a pair of eyes superimposed over a handwritten text from Poe's opening paragraph. The film relates an insane young man's killing of an old man, and his eventual mental breakdown and confession to a pair of detectives questioning him. Two particularly interesting devices are the use of words burned into the image (similar to *Caligari*), and the intercutting of single-frame images flashing back to the murder to illustrate the subjective state of the protagonist. Another expressionist device is the extremely distorted closeup of the killer, as seen through a magnifying glass by the detectives, hoping to discover "guilt in his eyes." It is in fact the closeup of the old man's eyes and the superimposition of an image of a beating hammer that become visual tropes for Poe's literary device of the victim's beating heart.

Another experimental narrative, produced by the Cinema Crafters of Philadelphia, Lewis Jacobs, Jo Gerson, and Louis Hirshman, was *Mobile Composition No. 1* (1928), a film that apparently has not survived. Jacobs describes it as a story about a love affair in which

> significant details, contrast lighting, double exposures, and large close-ups depicted the growing strain of disturbed emotions. In one of the scenes, in which the boy and girl were dancing together, the camera assumed a subjective viewpoint and showed the spinning walls and moving objects of the studio as seen by the boy, emphasizing a specific statuette to suggest the boy's inner disturbance.[120]

Gerson and Hirshman, who were both trained as painters,[121] apparently had a falling out with Jacobs over the conception of their film, because they decided to remake *Mobile Composition* without actors, calling it *The Story of a Nobody* (1930). In the film they attempted to recreate the subjective views of the two lovers, defining them metaphorically through objects, rather than actions. Utilizing a symphonic structure, the film consisted of numerous closeups, which were edited together through dissolves, laps, and quick cutting, depending on the rhythm of the scene.[122] Thus, as in *Portrait of a Young Man*, the camera's gaze becomes its own text, a direct articulation of the filmmaker's male subjectivity.

Charles Vidor's *The Bridge* was an adaptation of Ambrose Bierce's short story "An Occurrence at Owl Creek Bridge." Vidor's film uses a flash-forward technique to visualize the escape fantasy of a World War I Austrian deserter condemned to hang, which metamorphoses into a "life-before-one's-eyes" construction, similar to Fejos' *Last Moment*. Making use of real locations and nonprofessional actors without makeup, the film's quick cutting style, a montage of fantasy and grim reality, effectively created a mixture of objectivity and inner subjectivity, stretching a few moments into a one-reel film.[123]

Adapted by Seymour Stern,[124] Josef Berne's *Dawn to Dawn* (1933), at thirty-five minutes in length, was thought to be an "arty" featurette. It told the story of a young farm girl who comes into conflict with her authoritarian father over a young drifter, leading to the father's death of a stroke after the young man leaves. Presented in only a few scenes with a cast of unknowns without makeup, and virtually silent except for a musical score, the film's strength lay in its lyrical realism, its pastoral scenes on a real farm, which did not suppress the harsh reality of American agriculture before the age of electricity and machinery, and its explicit seduction scene. The film's central narrative conceit, the fear of strangers in a rural environment, struck a chord in the American psyche while almost self-consciously developing a lyrical realist aesthetic that nevertheless incorporated flashes of Expressionism. Eric Knight called the film "one of the most remarkable attempts at independent cinematography in America."[125]

Finally, the Hollywood stills photographer Roman Freulich directed a first short, *Prisoner*, which is apparently lost, although a complete script survives.[126] *Prisoner* opened at the Filmarte in Hollywood in July 1934, and was shown successfully in various little theaters, including Baltimore's.[127] Taking its cue from the last scene of Erich von Stroheim's *Greed*, the film concerns a prisoner (played by George Sari), lost in the desert and chained to a sheriff (Jack Rockwell). He dreams of escape as his captor sleeps, then awakes to find him dead, making freedom possible, although it is clear that the desert will not allow him to escape alive. Shot in an expressionistic style, with subjective images preventing any differentiation between dream and reality, Herman Weinberg rhapsodized about the film: "The world cinema at large can only justify itself to historians when it will give imaginative young men like Freulich a chance to put their theories into practice and, perhaps, help their bit to found an authentic film language."[128]

A remarkable one-reel short, *Broken Earth*, was Freulich's second experimental short narrative. The producer was Edward Spitz, who had produced Fejos' *The Last Moment* and who now planned a whole series of shorts on "Negro life" with Freulich and the African-American actor Clarence Muse.[129] *Broken Earth* related the story of a black sharecropper whose son miraculously recovers from a fever through the father's fervent prayer. Shot on a farm in the South with nonprofessional actors (except for Clarence Muse), the film's early scenes focused in a highly realistic manner on the incredible hardship of black farmers, with plowing scenes as powerful as those in *Dawn to Dawn*. The latter half demonstrated the centrality of the religious experience for a rural African-American population.[130]

It seems to be no coincidence that the experimental narratives discussed here not only attempted to expand aesthetically beyond the narrow confines of Hollywood classical narrative, but were also produced by amateurs or film technicians at the fringes of the film industry who were European-born or educated. Ironically, in the cases of Deutsch, Florey, Klein, Vidor, Berne, and Freulich, their European background and extremely low budgets conspired against what was probably their primary goal—breaking into the commercial film industry—and led them inadvertently to produce experimental narratives that would be valorized in the "art cinema" market. At the same time, these films, like those of the Europhile James Sibley Watson, are not simply copies of European art films. Their thematic concerns are for the most part American, their stylistic sensibilities a mixture of sophistication and naiveté, their aesthetics against the grain of Hollywood narrative. In contrast to these serious narratives, the first American avant-garde also developed a more satirical form of narrative.

PARODIES AS AVANT-GARDE CRITIQUE

While the American avant-garde film of the 1920s seemed to focus more on abstract and formalist experimentation, moving from the modernist vision of Strand and Sheeler's *Manhatta* to the new realist abstraction of Steiner's *H$_2$O*, and from Newcombe's animated dreamscapes in *The Enchanted City* to Florey's expressionist *The Love of Zero*, the 1930s avant-garde seemed, in general, to gravitate toward metaphor and parody, possibly a sign of increasingly difficult times.

In contrast to the earnest metaphors of Watson, Webber, and others, parody was the preferred genre of Theodore Huff, another prominent ACL member, who in the early 1930s directed 16mm spoofs of Hollywood genre films. His first two productions, *Hearts of the West* (1931) and *Little Geezer* (1932), starred children, giving the films an ambiguous sexuality and implicating the subject in the director's slightly perverse gaze, although ostensibly both films merely imitated the conventions, stereotypical characters, and naive plots of silent film.

Mr. Motorboat's Last Stand (1933), Theodore Huff and John Flory's 16mm silent Depression comedy, is a much less self-conscious work, an ironic comment on America's inability to deal with the economic catastrophe of the 1930s. *Mr. Motorboat* is, in fact, a humorous allegory on America's economic rise and fall, employing visual metaphor in the manner of medieval morality plays. Images communicate their meaning quite literally, like the bursting bubble that refers to the "exploding prosperity bubble" of the 1920s. After working as a film curator at the Museum of Modern Art, Huff returned to filmmaking in the late 1940s to produce, in collaboration with Kent Munson, *The Stone Children* (1948) and *The Uncomfortable Man* (1948).[131]

The photographer Ralph Steiner, who had made abstract avant-garde films in the late 1920s, contributed his own parody of American economic life with *Panther Woman of the Needle Trades, or The Lovely Life of Little Lisa* (1931), made in collaboration with John Flory.[132] The film opens with Jehovah creating the world out of a test tube and proceeds to present a short history of the universe. The birth of Elizabeth Hawes (1903) introduces the real-life heroine, whose career from child seamstress to Parisian designer of *haute couture*, via a Vassar education, is recounted.[133] Reminiscent of Robert Florey's *Life and Death of 9413 — A Hollywood Extra* in terms of its art direction and elliptical narrative style, *Panther Woman* is a parody of the all-American success story, a young woman's fantasy of a glamorous career in an age of diminishing possibilities. Steiner also collaborated on *Pie in the Sky* with Elia Kazan, Irving Lerner, and Molly Day Thatcher.

While most avant-garde films discussed in this section are parodies of mainstream commercial cinema, two films can be seen as parodies of the avant-garde itself. William Vance's *Hearts of the Age* (1934) was, according to Orson Welles, a parody of *Blood of a Poet*.[134] Vance shot the film on 16mm reversal, after completing a parody of *Dr. Jekyll and Mr. Hyde* in 1932. The film opens with a positive and negative image of a bell ringing in a bell-tower. There follows a series of visual non-sequiturs: an old woman ringing a bell, an angel carrying a globe, Death stalking corridors, a Keystone-like cop, a hanged man, a hand beckoning from the grave. Like earlier avant-garde films, *Hearts of the Age* privileges obtuse camera angles, expressionist lighting, and narrative ellipses, utilizing these avant-garde techniques both seriously and with tongue in cheek.[135]

Near the end of the 1930s, Roger Barlow, Harry Hay, and LeRoy Robbins produced their own parody of the avant-garde, *Even As You and I*. The film was shot for the most part in Robbins' home, using leftover film scrounged from the film studios.[136] The three filmmakers began the project after *Liberty* magazine announced a short film contest sponsored by MGM's "Pete Smith Specialties" series. The contest in fact became the frame for the film's narrative.[137] Playfully ironic, almost dadaist in construction, the film narrated the attempts of three unemployed young men to make a film for an amateur film contest. After rejecting numerous "boy meets girl" script ideas, the three discover an article on Surrealism and proceed to construct a script randomly out of paper scraps. The film within a film is an anarchistic montage of images, which acknowledges its debt to Surrealism, Eugene Atget, Donald Duck, Luis Buñuel's *Un Chien Andalou*, Hans Richter's *Ghosts Before Breakfast*, Sergei Eisenstein's *Potemkin*, René Clair's *Entr'acte*, and Leni Riefenstahl's *Triumph of the Will*. It ends with the three would-be film artists realizing they have missed the deadline for the contest, and then attempting to invent a useful gadget for another competition. Shot silent, the film was performed with selections from George Gershwin's *An American in Paris* and, in the second half, Sergei Prokofiev's *Love for Three Oranges*.[138] Almost postmodern in its use of quotation, *Even As You and I* comments on the pressure of originality when a canon of avant-garde works has already been established, and to the difficulty of becoming a filmmaker and surviving economically in a Depression economy.

As is not surprising in a worldwide Depression, most of these satires have a political dimension, an implicit or explicit critique of social relations in American society and the inability of the economy to meet even the most basic needs. Like their spiritual predecessor, *Entr'acte*, they also question the role of the artist and the intellectual in a society geared toward profit. Unlike European models, though, they are willing to use metaphor overtly, almost naively, in the interest of social critique, their signifiers unambiguously literal. For the surrealist wing of the early American avant-garde, on the other hand, ambiguity is a virtue.

THE SYMBOLIC AND THE SURREALIST

Best known as a painter and sculptor, Joseph Cornell produced his first film, *Rose Hobart*, in 1936.[139] A nineteen-minute (at silent speed) re-editing of images from Universal Pictures' fiction feature *East of Borneo* (1931), with a few snippets from scientific instructional films thrown in, Cornell's film, like his famous collage boxes, is essentially a creation out of *objets trouvés*. Completely eliminating any semblance of plot and dialogue, Cornell's montage of the ostensible heroine, hero, and villain has them moving in slow motion through empty rooms, caressing curtains, reacting to unseen events, never meeting. Their looks lead nowhere, their erotic desires careen into a void, while the audience is left with a mystery, as the film's purple-tinted eroticism masks unfulfilled desire. In keeping with the surrealist creed, Cornell subverts not only the standard conventions of Hollywood filmmaking, but also viewer identification, draining the gaze of meaning.

Jerome Hill,[140] later known for his film animation, began his career in the late 1920s, when he purchased a 16mm Cine-Kodak Special to shoot *The Fortune Teller* (1932)[141] in a village in southern France. True to the title, the film has mystical overtones, its narrative constructed from seemingly unconnected images: a young woman hanging wash, a walk in the surf, a consultation with a gypsy fortune teller, a man rising up out of the sea. Apart from their pictorial beauty, the film's images seem to hold some primordial meaning connected to fertility rites, to mystical love and romantic fate, yet they remain ambiguous, like the old gypsy's fortune as visualized in the cards. The film's visual text thus constructs romantically imbued riddles that remain unsolved, the stuff of dreams.

Born in Merion, Pennsylvania, in 1905, the painter and avant-garde filmmaker Emlen Etting graduated from St. George's School and Harvard (1928), then moved to Paris to study painting with André Lhote. He returned to Pennsylvania in 1932, where he started teaching art at the Tyler School of Temple University and making films, including *Oramunde* (1933), *Poem 8* (1933), and *Laureate* (1940), the last a Kodachrome film in collaboration with his wife, Gloria.

Being also a sometime poet and translator of verse by Paul Valéry, Etting combined his visual and literary senses in his films, creating film poems "wherein the picture, their sequence and development are used as in a poem as opposed to the customary story form. . . . In the film poem, music, the dance, the theater and the artist will all work together."[142] Accompanied by Alexander Scriabin's *Poem of Fire* and Gustav Holst's *Saturn* cycle, *Oramunde* presents (mostly in operatic long shots) a mythological Melissande dancing/walking through woods and ocean grottos, searching for her dead lover, Pelleas, and the lost wedding ring of her king and husband, eventually crossing the river Styx in a rowboat with a black-hooded man. *Poem 8* uses a moving, reeling "subjective camera" to signify a male gaze, erotically enticed by several women. The viewer ultimately participates in the murder of a seductress before fleeing through city streets.[143] *Laureate* demonstrates the hand of the painter in its spectacular use of still-lifes and complementary colors, as it metaphorically visualizes a writer's struggle to create poetry by having him (Etting himself) chase and confront various muses (played in classical Greek garb by Gloria Etting and friends of the couple) before receiving his laurels.

Christopher Baughman Young, the son of the landscape artist Charles Morris Young, made his first avant-garde film, *Object Lesson*, in 1941. An avid skier, explorer, and mountain climber, Young was apparently wealthy enough, like Jerome Hill, to finance the film himself. Billing it as "America's first surrealist film," he took over his own distribution after having "most unsatisfactory" dealings with a business partner.[144]

Shot in 35mm, *Object Lesson* begins with the statement: "Let us consider objects. For they tell the story of life. There is nothing without meaning—and the combination of things make new meanings that are too complicated to explain." The film itself opens with a series of natural landscapes in which there appear various objects: the heads and masks of Greek statues, swords, shields, violins, tennis rackets. These objects have been strewn about, out of place in the lush vegetation, creating a surrealist image of incongruence: nature and the detritus of man. In the next sequence, Young presents documentary images of the Empire State Building, hydroelectric plants, and garbage, followed by a metaphorical rendering of war. There is no dialogue or commentary, just an array of musical excerpts, including liturgical music, industrial sounds, Eastern European folksongs, and electronic music.

Virtually all the images are static and extremely well composed, like photographs. This lack of motion or action heightens the film's surrealistic aspect, allowing the viewer to contemplate both the incongruence of the moment and the juxtaposition of images in a syntactical construction. According to Young, "the objects must first be looked at as objects before they can be thought of as symbols," allowing viewers "to imagine their own story."[145] The filmmaker interprets the film's ending, where statues and objects "just have a good time being themselves and not representing anything," as a state where destruction and war have given way to objects and nature without meaning. Thus, Young wants to have the film read two ways: as a surrealist construct (*sans raison*), and as a metaphorical and poetic vision. His film also stresses the conflict between man and nature, articulating ultimately its belief in nature as a dominant and abiding force.

Lacking any kind of narrative cohesion, these seemingly diverse films nevertheless are evidence of authorial voices that foreground the subjectivity of the artist. There seems to be in the works of Hill, Etting, and Young a romantic urge to understand the mysteries of nature, and possibly to escape into a universe in which a natural order once again holds sway. In such a world the role of the artist is productively defined, his creation not a throwaway object of civilization, as in *Object Lesson*. Even Cornell's conscious deconstruction of narrative in the interest of subverting classical modes of address creates a new narrative out of the void, one in which the artist is central. The subtext in all of these surrealist films is avant-garde practice itself.

A NEW GENERATION

The reception of *Object Lesson* coincides with the birth of what this book calls the "second American avant-garde." By the late 1940s a new generation of filmmakers was about to burst onto the scene. Exhibiting that new energy were new programs at Cinema 16 and the San Francisco Museum of Modern Art. Avant-garde film would now increasingly be embraced by the cultural institutions of the mainstream, as exemplified by Maya Deren, who was able to show her work immediately at the Museum of Modern Art. While the commercial industry, of course, continued to marginalize the avant-garde, these filmmakers were indeed able to professionalize their status, working within academia, museums, and other nonprofit arts organizations, earning Guggenheim and other foundation grants. The avant-garde thus entered the institutional if not the commercial mainstream.

NOTES

1. A first, admittedly incomplete bio-filmography of American avant-garde cinema before Maya Deren (1943) can be found at the back of this volume.

2. Jonas Mekas, "The Experimental Film in America," *Film Culture* 1, no. 3 May–June 1955): 16.

3. Arthur L. Gale, "Amateur Clubs," *Amateur Movie Makers* 3, no. 2 (February 1928): 100.

4. Herman Weinberg, *A Manhattan Odyssey: A Memoir* (New York: Anthology Film Archives, 1982), p. 28.

5. Roy W. Winton, "For the Love of It," *National Board of Review Magazine* 3, no. 7 (July 1927): 4.

6. Herman Weinberg, "A Paradox of the Photoplay," *Amateur Movie Makers* 4, no. 1 (January 1929): 866.

7. Hans Richter provides a perfect case in point. While his early "avant-garde" films were initially produced as advertising films or prologues to commercial features, they were later exhibited and discussed by Richter and others as pure art films. See Jan-Christopher Horak, "Discovering Pure Cinema: Avant-garde Film in the 1920s," *Afterimage* 8, nos. 1–2 (Summer 1980): 4–7.

8. See Patricia Zimmermann, "The Amateur, the Avant-Garde, and Ideologies of Art," *Journal of Film and Video* 38, nos. 3–4 (Summer/Fall 1986).

9. C. Adolph Glassgold, "THE FILMS: Amateur or Professional?" *The Arts* 15, no. 1 (January 1929): 56.

10. See review of *The Life and Death of 9413—A Hollywood Extra*, *Variety*, 20 June 1928; see also Weinberg, "A Paradox of the Photoplay," 866; *Close Up* 2, no. 6 (June 1928): 76.

11. See *Close Up* 7, no. 6 (December 1930): 454.

12. See "Honor Without Peace in Hollywood," *New York Times*, 5 April 1936, Sec. X.

13. Sheldon Renan, *An Introduction to the American Underground Film* (New York: Dutton, 1967), p. 220.

14. "Cranking Your Own," *National Board of Review Magazine* 2, no. 6 (June 1927): 3.

15. See letter, Arthur Gale (Amateur Cinema League consultant) to Marion Gleason, 21 November 1928, Gleason file, George Eastman House (GEH), Rochester, N.Y.

16. The film was shown at the Cameo Theatre in New York. See *New York Times*, 26 January 1927, review of *Slums of Berlin*. No print or negative is known to survive.

17. See Arthur Gale, "Oil Film," *Amateur Movie Makers* 5, no. 10 (October 1930): 640; see also "Homemade Locale," *Amateur Movie Makers* 4, no. 12 (December 1929): 797. No trace of the filmmakers has surfaced.

18. Founded by the playwright Lajos N. Egri, Herman Weinberg, the stage designer Robert van Rosen, and the amateur cameraman Merle Johnson, the group failed actually to produce a film, although Weinberg's *City Symphony* (working title *Cosmopolis*) was apparently scheduled for release through Eccentric. See "Expressionism," *Amateur Movie Makers* 4, no. 8 (August 1929): 526; see also *Close Up* 5, no. 4 (October 1929): 338–339.

19. *Amateur Movie Makers* 3, no. 2 (February 1929): 100.

20. Frederick Kiesler, "100 Per Cent Cinema," *Close Up* 3, no. 2 (August 1928): 39–40.

21. *Amateur Movie Makers* 3, no. 2 (February 1928): 100.

22. See O. Spearing, "A Valuable Service," *Exceptional Photoplays* 2 (March 1922); John Hutchins, "L'Enfant Terrible: The Little Cinema Movement," *Theatre Arts Monthly* 13, no. 9 (September 1929): 696. See also Michael Budd, "The National Board of Review and the Early Art Cinema in New York: *The Cabinet of Dr. Caligari* as Affirmative Culture," *Cinema Journal* 26, no. 1 (Fall 1986): 7–8.

23. Quoted in Hutchins, "L'Enfant Terrible," p. 697.

24. See Marguerite Tazelaar, "The Story of the First Little Film Theatre," *Amateur Movie Makers* 3, no. 7 (July 1928): 441.

25. Alfred B. Kuttner, "The Little Motion Picture Theatre," *National Board of Review Magazine* 1, no. 2 (May–June 1926): 3.

26. The full text of Gould's speech was published as "The Little Theatre Movement in the Cinema," *National Board of Review Magazine* 1, no. 5 (September–October 1926): 4–5. See also a report on the speech in "Special Theatres Urged for Artistic Pictures," *New York Times*, 10 October 1926, Sec. VIII.

27. "The Little Cinema Marches On," *New York Times*, 6 February 1938.

28. "The Fifth Avenue Playhouse," *National Board of Review Magazine* 1, no. 6 (November 1926): 4. According to Weinberg, the day-to-day operations of the 5th Avenue Playhouse were handled by Ed Sullivan, Joe Balaben, and Jean Dubarry, with Weinberg serving as publicity director. See Weinberg, *Manhattan Odyssey*, p. 28.

29. *New York Times*, 6 February 1938.

30. "More About the Little Theatre," *National Board of Review Magazine* 2, no. 11 (November 1927): 5.

31. "Hollywood Notes," *Close Up* 3, no. 1 (July 1928): 74. While there were reports of the closure of the Filmarte in April 1929, the theater did continue screenings. See "Hollywood Notes," *Close Up* 6, no. 4 (April 1929): 78.

32. The Baltimore "Little Theatre" was founded by the management of the 5th Avenue Playhouse, and Weinberg was sent down to Baltimore to become the new manager. See Weinberg, *Manhattan Odyssey*, pp. 35–36, 47.

33. Letter, Arthur Gale to Marion Gleason, 21 November 1928, Gleason file, GEH.

34. Kiesler, "100 Per Cent Cinema," pp. 35–38; see also "Four Screen Theatre Being Built Here," *New York Times*, 9 December 1928, Sec. II.

35. "The Motion Picture: A Calendar of Progress," *Theatre Arts Monthly* 13, no. 9 (September 1929): 644.

36. See program brochure for twentieth anniversary of the Little Theatre (1929–1949), published by the Civic Association of Rochester, vertical file, GEH.

37. See inaugural program of the Eighth Street Film Guild Cinema, 1 February 1929, vertical file, New York Public Library, Performing Arts Library at Lincoln Center, New York.

38. Brian Taves gives an extensive listing of the playdates of Florey's avant-garde films in Chapter 4 in this volume.

39. Harry A. Potamkin, *Close Up* 6, no. 2 (February 1930): 111.

40. *Close Up* 7, no. 6 (December 1930): 454.

41. Hutchins, "L'Enfant Terrible," p. 694.

42. Lincoln Kirstein, "Experimental Films," *Arts Weekly* 1, no. 3 (25 March 1932): 52.

43. See "Close-Ups," *Amateur Movie Makers* 7, no. 4 (April 1932): 179. See also Elena Pinto Simon and David Stirk, *Jay Leyda: A Chronology*, published in honor of Leyda's memory by the Tisch School of the Arts, New York University, December 1987.

44. Russell Campbell, "Radical Cinema in the 1930s: The Film and Photo League," reprinted in *Jump Cut: Hollywood, Politics and Counter Cinema*, ed. Peter Steven (New York: Praeger, 1985), p. 131.

45. Interview with Florence LeRoy and Harry Hay, 24 May 1991, Escandido, Calif.

46. See William Alexander, *Film on the Left: American Documentary Film from 1931 to 1942* (Princeton: Princeton University Press, 1981), pp. 36–38.

47. Letter, Arthur Gale to Marion Gleason, 10 December 1927, Gleason file, GEH.

48. Letter, James W. Moore to Frank Stauffacher, 28 January 1947, "Art in Cinema" files, Pacific Film Archives (PFA), Berkeley, Calif.

49. The panel of judges for the contest was made up of industry members and private individuals, including King Vidor, James R. Quirk (*Photoplay*), George Pierce Baker (Yale), and Wilton A. Barrett (National Board of Review). See "H_2O," *National Board of Review Magazine* 4, no. 10 (December 1929): 12.

50. Letter, Robert Florey to Frank Stauffacher, 27 February 1947, "Art in Cinema" files, PFA.

51. Letter, Symon Gould to Frank Stauffacher, 1 March 1950, "Art in Cinema" files, PFA. Even in the late 1940s, the field of avant-garde film distribution had not changed substantially. Thus, Stauffacher and Amos Vogel at Cinema 16 in New York could not fall back on established distribution outlets for avant-garde film, but were dependent on personal contacts to find films and filmmakers, usually borrowing directly from the makers for about ten dollars per film.

52. Kenneth MacPherson, "As Is," *Close Up* 2, no. 6 (June 1928): 5.

53. "Experimental Film in America," *Experimental Cinema* 1, no. 5 (1934): 54.

54. See e.g. review of *Lot in Sodom* by James Shelley Hamilton, *National Board of Review Magazine* 9, no. 2 (February 1934): 14–15.

55. Louis Hirshman, a.k.a. Hershell Louis, donated an original nitrate print to the museum in 1947. It was destroyed through decomposition by 1956.

56. Kirk Bond, "*Lot in Sodom*," *Film Art* 1, no. 4 (Summer 1934): 69.

57. See Richard Abel, *French Cinema: The First Wave 1915–1929* (Princeton: Princeton University Press, 1984).

58. See *Film und Foto der zwanziger Jahre*, ed. Ute Eskildsen and Jan-Christopher Horak (Stuttgart: Verlag Gerd Hatje, 1979). See also Horak, "Discovering Pure Cinema," pp. 4–7.

59. Hans Richter, *Filmgegner von heute, Filmfreunde von morgen* (Halle/Saale: Verlag Wilhelm Knapp, 1929).

60. Mekas, "Experimental Film in America," p. 15.

61. P. Adams Sitney, *Visionary Film: The American Avant-Garde 1943–1978* (New York: Oxford University Press, 1979).

62. Dana Polan, *The Political Language of Film and the Avant-Garde* (Ann Arbor: UMI Research Press, 1985), p. 64.

63. Ibid.

64. Bart Testa, *Back and Forth: Early Cinema and the Avant-Garde* (Toronto: Art Gallery of Ontario, 1992), p. 19.

65. Long considered lost, a print survives at MOMA, but this version of Flaherty's seems to have been seriously compromised by re-editing. Directed and photographed by Flaherty, originally in two reels, the film was cut down to one reel by John D. Pearmain, the business manager of the film's financiers, Mrs. Ada de Acosta Root and Col. Breckenridge, for its New York release at the Roxy Theatre. See Herman G. Weinberg, *Film Index Series, No. 6 — Robert Flaherty* (London: British Film Institute, 1946).

66. See Arthur Calder-Marshall, *The Innocent Eye: The Life of Robert Flaherty* (London: Penguin Books, 1970), p. 122.

67. Quoted in Lewis Jacobs, "Experimental Film in America (Part 1)," *Hollywood Quarterly* 3, no. 2 (Winter 1947–48): 116. See also Wolfgang Klaue and Jay Leyda, eds., *Robert Flaherty* (East Berlin: Henschelverlag, 1964), pp. 210–211.

68. Before he began production of *A Bronx Morning*, Jay Leyda articulated his ideas on filming urban landscapes in "Tips on Topicals," *Amateur Movie Makers* 6, no. 1 (January 1931): 13–14, 39.

69. MOMA has preserved the original negative, which was a full-aperture silent negative, indicating that Browning had originally intended the film to be silent. See *Travelling* 56 (Fall 1979).

70. A still from the film was reproduced in *Amateur Movie Makers* 7, no. 3 (March 1932): 103.

71. *City Symphony* was first shown at the Little Theatre in Philadelphia in June 1930. See Weinberg biographical file at MOMA, New York.

72. *Autumn Fire* premiered at the Europa Theatre in Baltimore in December 1931. See Weinberg biographical file, MOMA. See also Robert Haller, "Autumn Fire," in *Field of Vision* (Spring 1980), who claims that Weinberg cut

up *City Symphony* for his next film. There is some reason to doubt this assertion, whose source may be Weinberg himself, since the former film was shown publicly and it is hard to imagine that a future film historian would intentionally destroy his own film a mere year after its first public screening. On the other hand, William Uricchio in Chapter 12 in this volume quotes Harry Potamkin, who may have been the impetus for Weinberg to destroy the film. The 35mm negative of *Autumn Fire* was discovered in 1993 and has been preserved at George Eastman House. MOMA has a 16mm negative and reference print.

73. See FIAF notes by Weinberg in *Travelling* 56 (Fall 1979). Given Weinberg's penchant for generating publicity about the production of *City Symphony*, this seems unlikely. In a letter to Frank Stauffacher, 7 March 1947, Weinberg does note that the film was shown throughout Europe and America in the early and mid-1930s, "although it was never intended for public showing, having been made primarily as a personal exercise in cutting." See "Art in Cinema" files, PFA; compare *Close Up* 5, no. 4 (Oct. 1929): 339; *Amateur Movie Makers* 5, no. 6 (June 1930): 377.

74. Weinberg apparently planned a sound film remake, *Rhapsody*: "A poem in picture and sound . . . the rushing emotions of two young people very much in love . . . the parallel in nature . . . the flowering of this romance to an exuberant climax." See note in *Film Art* 1, no. 4 (Summer 1934): 83.

75. See "Comment," *Film Art* 1, no. 3 (Spring 1934): 34.

76. See Robert Allen, "Cine Experimenter," *Home Movies* (1940), clipping in possession of Lewis Jacobs. Thanks to Mr. Jacobs to making his files available to me.

77. Letter, Lewis Jacobs to Frank Stauffacher, 12 November 1946, "Art in Cinema" files, PFA. See also Manuel Komroff, "Lewis Jacobs—Explorer," *Direction* (September 1936): 8.

78. Jacobs described *Case History* as follows: "Most of the sound was to be INNER MONOLOGUE. . . . Realistic street sounds, remembered phrases and thoughts—all exaggerated and distorted to emphasize the stream of consciousness of one's inner—but disturbed—logic." See *Competition du Film Experimental 21–27.IV.1958*, ed. Jacques Ledoux (Brussels: Cinémathèque de Belgique, 1958), p. 71.

79. Henwar Rodakiewicz describes the film's construction in some detail in "Treatment of Sound in *The City*," in *The Movies as Medium*, ed. Lewis Jacobs (New York: Farrar, Straus & Giroux, 1970), pp. 278–288.

80. Burckhardt went on to make numerous other portraits of his city, including *The Climate of New York* (1948), *Under the Brooklyn Bridge* (1953), *Eastside Summer* (1959), and *Default Averted* (1975).

81. Photographed and composed by Ralph Steiner, 16mm black and white, silent, 330 feet. Print preserved at MOMA.

82. A 35mm negative of this film (without a soundtrack) was recently discovered and has been preserved by the UCLA Film and Television Archives. Producer: Artkino; camera and editing: Jean D. Michelson; direction: M. G. MacPherson; music: Lee Zahler; special effects: Leon M. Leon; black and white, 945 feet.

83. Henwar Rodakiewicz, "Something More Than a Scenic," *Amateur Movie Makers* 7, no. 6 (June 1932): 249.

84. For Vorkapich's own discussion of his pioneering work in the montage field, see "Montage: A Look Into the Future with Slavko Vorkapich," *Cinema Progress* 2, no. 5 (Dec./Jan. 1937–38): 18–22.

85. Originally shot in 35mm: a 16mm print (black and white, 340 feet) is available at MOMA.

86. Slavko Vorkapich made a second nature film, illustrating woods and wildlife in the style of *Moods of the Sea*, and utilizing Richard Wagner's *Forest Murmurs*. The film was apparently produced for Metro-Goldwyn-Mayer, but probably never distributed. See letter, Slavko Vorkapich to Stauffacher, 29 October 1950, "Art in Cinema" files, PFA.

87. *Prelude to Spring* (1946). Conceived, photographed, and produced by John Hoffman. Production associates: Bror Lansing, Ray Olsen; optical printing: Howard Anderson. 35mm print, 610 feet, at MOMA.

88. Using the same "Newcombe process," Newcombe shot a second film, *The Sea of Dreams* (1923). Born in Waltham, Mass., in 1894, Warren Newcombe worked for over thirty years as head of the special-effects department at MGM, but also had a career as a painter with a series of one-man exhibitions in the late 1920s and 1930s. See Newcombe entry in *Who Was Who in American Art*, ed. Peter Hastings Falk (Madison, Conn.: Soundview Press, 1985), p. 447; see also *The 1938–1939 Motion Picture Almanac* (New York: Quigley Publishing, 1938), p. 561; William Moritz, "Visual Music and Film-As-An-Art in California Before 1950," in *On the Edge of America: California Modernist Art, 1900–1950*, Paul Karlstrom and Ann Karlstrom, eds. (Berkeley: University of California Press, 1996).

89. The film was distributed by the Educational Film Exchange. A print of the film survives at MOMA, and a nitrate original was recently discovered in Argentina, where it was apparently also distributed. According to the credits, the film was presented by E. W. Hammons and produced by Newcombe, "by special arrangement with Howard Estabrook."

90. For a contemporary review see Myron M. Stearns, "The Art of Suggested Motion," *Arts and Decoration* 12, no. 3 (July 1922): 191, 221.

91. See James L. Enyeart, *Bruguière: His Photographs and His Life* (New York: Alfred A. Knopf, 1977), pp. 85–93.

92. Stills from the film were published by Bruguière and Mercurius in *Architectural Review* (March 1930). A 35mm print has been preserved at MOMA.

93. For a general introduction to Bute's work, see *Experimental Animation: An Illustrated Anthology*, ed. Robert Russett and Cecile Starr (New York: Van Nostrand Reinhold, 1976), pp. 102–105.

94. A student of Hans Hoffman at the National Academy of Design, Lee finished his first film, *1941*, shortly after Pearl Harbor. After spending the next four years in uniform as a combat motion picture photographer, Lee completed *Le Bijou* in 1946, followed by *Idyll* (1948). See Russett and Starr, eds., *Experimental Animation*, pp. 114–115.

95. Completed on 16mm Kodachrome in December 1941, the four-minute film has been preserved by Anthology Film Archives.

96. See Arthur Knight, "Self-Expression," *Saturday Review of Literature*, 27 May 1950, pp. 38–40.

97. The films were acquired by MOMA and shown at the "Art in Cinema" series in 1946, at which time, having just moved to Glens Falls, New York, he christened one group of animations *The Glens Falls Sequence*, "in lieu of any better name." See letter, Douglass Crockwell to Frank Stauffacher, 31 August 1946, "Art in Cinema" files, PFA.

98. Educated at the Dayton Art Institute and the National Academy of Design in New York (like Crockwell), Grant had been an abstract painter since 1933. See Russett and Starr, eds., *Experimental Animation*, p. 111.

99. All of Grant's films are available at Anthology Film Archives.

100. See Dwinell Grant, "Film Notes to Compositions 1–5," in Russett and Starr, eds., *Experimental Animation*, p. 112.

101. Murphy went on to make *Ballet Mécanique* in Paris with Fernand Léger, before eventually returning to the United States to work at the fringes of Hollywood, where he produced off-beat, if not exactly experimental, work. See William Moritz's chapter in this volume (Chapter 5). A 35mm print has been preserved at GEH.

102. Louis M. Simon, "Stella Simon and Her Film, *Hands*," manuscript (1989), Simon files, MOMA.

103. The official credits list Miklós Bándy as director, Leopold Kutzleb (photographer), and the composer, Marc Blitzstein. The film's original length was 609 meters. A 16mm print is preserved at MOMA. See also Simon file, MOMA, which includes letter from Louis Simon (Stella's son) to Ron Magliozzi.

104. According to Louis Simon his mother was aware of but never saw the Blum film. Letter, L. Simon to J. -C. Horak, 16 October 1989.

105. First shown in Berlin in September 1927, the film was later screened at an all-night soire of the "Novembergruppe" (16 February 1929), which included Man Ray's *Emak Bakia*, music by George Antheil, a performance of Negro spirituals, and a boxing match.

106. See Oswell Blakeston, *"Hands," Close Up* 5, no. 2 (August 1929): 137. Four stills from the film were published in *Close Up* 5, no. 1 (July 1929).

107. See *"Underground Printer," Film Art* 3, no. 9 (Autumn 1936): 28.

108. Film Classic Exchange, *16mm ART FILMS*, catalogue, no date (presumably from the late 1940s), vertical file, GEH. Bovington, who apparently financed the film, had a falling out with the two filmmakers, because it was taken out of their hands and re-edited by him. Interview, Lewis Jacobs with J. -C. Horak, New York City, September 1989. See also letter, Eli Willis to Frank Stauffacher, 9 February 1947, "Art in Cinema" files, PFA. Prints of the film are for sale through a distributor, but were too expensive for this project.

109. Barbara Hammer, "Sara Kathryn Arledge," *Cinemanews* 1, no. 6 (1981): 3.

110. Arledge had shot three minutes in 1941, but lacked the funds to complete the film. In the summer of 1946 she shot additional footage, and premiered the film in November 1946 in Hollywood. Letter, Sara Arledge to Richard B. Foster, 9 October 1946, "Art in Film" files, PFA.

111. *Introspection* was planned and directed by Sara Kathryn Arledge; photography by Clyde B. Smith, Don Sykes; dancers: James Mitchell, Bill Martin, Joe Riccard, John R. Baxter; technicians: Don Littlepage, Ida Shapiro. 222 feet, 16mm, color, sound. Available through Canyon Cinema, Berkeley, Calif.

112. Letter, Arledge to Foster, 9 October 1946. A handwritten letter from Arledge to Frank Stauffacher, 25 August 1947, suggests that George Barrati was to write the music for her second film. "Art in Cinema" files, PFA.

113. Born in Lithuania in 1892, Deutsch emigrated to Los Angeles in 1919, via Berlin and Seattle, after breaking off his studies for the rabbinate. See Ralph Flint, "Boris Deutsch," *Creative Art* 8 (June 1931): 430–432; see also *Who Was Who in American Art*, 1985, p. 162.

114. *Lullaby*'s credits list Boris Deutsch for "direction and special effects." No distributor is listed in the print. A 16mm print is stored at GEH. The film can be purchased from Murray Glass Films, Los Angeles, Calif.

115. A still from *Skyscraper Symphony* was reproduced in *Theatre Arts Monthly* 13, no. 9 (September 1929). No print is known to have survived in this country, although it is rumored to exist in Moscow.

116. See "Club Library," *Amateur Movie Makers* 4, no. 7 (July 1929).

117. All the films of James Sibley Watson have been preserved in 35mm from the original nitrate negatives at GEH.

118. The optical printer, as well as Dr. Watson's papers, can be viewed at GEH.

119. See "Hollywood Notes," *Close Up* 3, no. 2 (August 1928): 54. Three stills from the film are reproduced in the same issue. *The Tell-Tale Heart*, 35mm print, black and white, 1,825 feet, is housed at GEH. Klein was a German

cameraman and director who trained at UFA (Berlin) and Emelka (Munich), before coming to America with Lee DeForest in 1923. He would go on to a short and undistinguished career in Hollywood before returning in the early 1930s to Germany, where he continued his rather mediocre filmmaking activities in the Nazified film industry. This film is somewhat of an anomaly in his *ouvre*.

120. Lewis Jacobs, *The Rise of the American Film*, 2d ed. (New York: Teachers College Press, 1968), p. 555.

121. Gerson studied art at the University of Pennsylvania in the late 1920s and became an instructor there for a few years. He later worked as a puppeteer with his wife, Mary Gerson. Hirshman studied at the Academy of Fine Arts in Philadelphia, and began his career as a painter, but eventually gravitated to three-dimensional caricatures, which have been widely exhibited.

122. See Harry A. Potamkin in *Close Up* 6, no. 2 (Feb. 1930): 111; see also "Modernist Film by Local Makers," *Philadelphia Inquirer*, 23 February 1930, and unidentified clippings in Gerson file, Theatre Collection, Free Library of Philadelphia.

123. For a shot-by-shot analysis see *From Fiction to Film: Ambrose Bierce's "An Occurrence at Owl Creek Bridge,"* ed. Gerald R. Barrett and Thomas L. Erskine (Encino, Calif.: Dickenson Publishing Co., 1973), pp. 87–106. Vidor apparently tried unsuccessfully to get his film released for some time; finally, in 1931, it was distributed to great acclaim under a new title, *The Spy*. See Moritz, "Visual Music and Film-As-An-Art," p. 10. A negative without the original soundtrack has been preserved at GEH.

124. Seymour Stern, who later made a "career" out of writing about D. W. Griffith, was not only an editor for *Experimental Cinema*, but was also apparently involved in a number of avant-garde projects with leftist tendencies. Prior to 1932, Stern had worked for a while in Hollywood as a script doctor and second-unit director at Universal. Between 1932 and 1936, Stern worked at MGM. He directed the documentary *Imperial Valley* in 1932. See Ira H. Gallen, "Notes on a Film Historian: Seymour Stern," manuscript (1979), Stern file, MOMA, p. 2.

125. Quoted in *Audio-Brandon Film Catalogue* (1971), p. 444. This film, like *Lot in Sodom* and *The Spy*, was distributed by Brandon from the 1930s through the 1970s.

126. In the mid-1920s Freulich had joined his brother Jack Freulich as a stills photographer at Universal and remained there until 1944, when he became head of the stills department at Republic. See Judith Freulich Caditz, "Roman Freulich — Hollywood's Golden Age Portraitist," *The Rangefinder* (July 1991): 46. Thanks to Ms. Caditz for making a copy of the script for *Prisoner* available to me.

127. See "Notes from the Hollywood Studios," *New York Times*, 5 August 1934; *the Little magazine* 1, no. 5 (14 October 1934), program brochure for Baltimore Little Theatre, vertical files, GEH.

128. Herman Weinberg, *"The Prisoner," Film Art* 2, no. 5 (Winter 1934): 39.

129. Freulich noted that in Hollywood blacks were treated as an inferior race, useful only as "comedy relief," while he (not completely free of his own subconscious racism) perceived them to offer a "rich vein of cinematic material. Here is a race with a tragic background, though primitive and elemental, rich especially in folklore and music." See "Herman Weinberg Interviews Roman Freulich," *Film Art* 3, no. 8 (Summer 1936): 41.

130. The film is not mentioned by any of the standard histories of black film, and is misdated by Henry T. Sampson, *Blacks in Black and White: A Source Book on Black Films* (Metuchen, N.J.: Scarecrow Press, 1977), p. 272. A short review appeared in *Motion Picture Daily*, 30 March 1936. The film has been preserved by the Southwest Film/Video Archives at Southern Methodist University.

131. See letter, Ted Huff to Frank Stauffacher, 20 June 1949, in which Huff apologizes that his film was "not up to your standard" and demands that it be air-freighted back immediately. "Art in Cinema" files, PFA. All of Huff's films are being preserved at GEH.

132. The cast included Morris Carnovsky (Jehovah), Elizabeth Hawes, Julian Whittlesey, Alice Shepard, and F. Day Tuttle. 16mm print at MOMA.

133. Elizabeth Hawes was in fact the first American *couturière* to have collections shown in Paris. She later married Joseph Losey. See Michel Ciment, *Conversations with Losey* (New York: Methuen, 1985), p. 39.

134. Quoted in Joseph McBride, *Welles* (New York: Viking Press, 1972), p. 26.

135. A 16mm print, black and white, 222 feet, can be viewed at MOMA.

136. See Renan, *Introduction to the American Underground Film*, p. 220. Robbins was a photographer on a Works Progress Administration (WPA) Project in California that included Edward, Brett and Chan Weston, Roger Barlow, and Hy Hirsch. In some sources Hy Hirsch is listed in the credits, but the film was produced by Barlow, Hay, and Robbins, with Hirsch only appearing as an actor in two shots. Interview with Florence Robbins and Harry Hay, 23 May 1991, Escadido, Calif. See also letter, Harry Hay to J. -C. Horak, 14 September 1990. 16mm print available at MOMA.

137. *Even As You and I* failed to win any prizes, although it was shown at the Los Angeles Carpenters' Local Hall, along with Paul Strand's *Redes*, and screened by Fred Zinnemann for MGM executives. Interview with F. Robbins and H. Hay, 23 May 1991.

138. Letter, Harry Hay to Frank Stauffacher, 16 September 1949, "Art in Cinema" files, PFA. Robbins, who left a second avant-garde film uncompleted (*Suicide*, 1935–1937), and Barlow both went on to make documentaries after the demise of the WPA photography project in 1939, while Hay later worked as a trade union organizer and gay activist.

139. A 16mm print is preserved at Anthology Film Archives.

140. Born into a wealthy St. Paul family, Hill moved to Europe in 1927, where he was inspired by French surrealist films. See Jerome Hill, "Some Notes on Painting and Filmmaking," *Film Culture* 32 (Spring 1964): 31–32.

141. *The Fortune Teller* and *The Magic Umbrella* were incorporated *in toto* into Jerome Hill's autobiographical compilation/meditation, *Film Portrait* (1972), available through Filmmakers' Coop.

142. Letter, Emlen Etting to Frank Stauffacher, 26 March 1947, "Art in Cinema" files, PFA. After Etting's death, all of his films were donated to George Eastman House, where they are being preserved. For further biographical details, see obituary, *Philadelphia Inquirer*, 18 July 1993.

143. According to Amos Vogel, *Poem 8* "retained a certain poetic vitality and verve" through its early use of the subjective camera. See letter, Amos Vogel to Frank Stauffacher, 7 June 1949, "Art in Cinema" files, PFA.

144. See letter, Rosland Kossoff to Frank Stauffacher, 13 August 1949. See also letter, Christopher Young to Frank Stauffacher, 28 July 1949, "Art in Cinema" files, PFA. The film was screened in the series in 1950, won a prize for best avant-garde film at the Venice Film Festival that same year, and was eventually added to Cinema 16's distribution catalogue. See obituary, Christopher B. Young, *Philadelphia Evening Bulletin*, 2 December 1975, Young file, MOMA.

145. "*Object Lesson*—A Motion Picture by Christopher Young," unpublished program notes to be read before (part 1) and after (part 2) the screening, "Art in Cinema" files, PFA.

3

The Limits of Experimentation in Hollywood

KRISTIN THOMPSON

Traditionally, historians have created an opposition between the commercial Hollywood cinema and the American avant-garde. One goal of the International Congress of Independent Cinema held at La Sarraz, Switzerland, in 1929 was to define the "independent" cinema, a term that was preferred to "avant-garde" or "experimental." The implication was that independent filmmakers worked outside commercial cinema industries. By the 1940s, Lewis Jacobs found the independently made shorts of Paul Strand, Robert Flaherty, Robert Florey, Charles Klein, and James Sibley Watson and Melville Webber to exemplify a cinema solely concerned with "motion pictures as a medium of artistic expression."[1]

The distinction between commercial cinema and the avant-garde is, in general, valid. Certainly many separate institutions have grown up to support avant-garde filmmaking, and virtually any spectator would perceive a vast difference between, say, Watson and Webber's *The Fall of the House of Usher* and King Vidor's *The Big Parade* (1925). Other films, however, escape easy categorization. Paul Fejos' experimental, feature-length *The Last Moment*, for example, was produced independently of the Hollywood studio system. Critical praise brought the film to the attention of Charles Chaplin, who arranged its premiere; its success on that occasion led to its being picked up for distribution by Zakoro Films.[2] Similarly, Florey's shorts had commercial distribution and played in regular theaters as well as art houses.[3]

Beyond such tangential commercial links between a few avant-garde films and the mainstream, a small number of silent films made by the Hollywood studios themselves were perceived as unusual by critics, audiences, or exhibitors. They might be described as highbrow, arty, obscure, box-office poison, novel, or technically sophisticated, depending on the source.

Most of these films are not "experimental" by the standards of the avant-garde films discussed elsewhere in this book, but occupy a fuzzy middle ground between commercial and experimental work. By examining their unusual traits, we can get a better sense of the limits of experimentation within the classical studio system. Those limits were relatively narrow, and violation of them often caused important films to fail and major directors to leave Hollywood.

Early films of the pre-1909 "primitive" era often contain anomalous, even bizarre, devices that fascinate many modern viewers, including avant-garde filmmakers and film historians. Yet such devices usually resulted from the exploration of a new medium rather than from an effort to set up an alternative to the commercial cinema. It seems to me that it is only after the formulation of classical Hollywood norms was well advanced that we can meaningfully speak of an avant-garde alternative. The earliest set of films I have been able to identify as overturning established norms in some way came in 1916, a point at which the classical cinema was approaching its complete formulation.

What counted as avant-garde for Hollywood between 1916 and 1930? In order to investigate this question, I have chosen to survey a number of films that were initially perceived as unusual.[4] These choices are based primarily upon a survey of trade journals of the period and on viewings of surviving films that these journals identified as exceptional. Some of these films were produced by major studios like Famous Players–Lasky. Others were made on a shoestring with private money, and some of these were distributed to regular theaters.

The films also present a wide range of stylistic traits. Some, like *The Last Moment*, which borrowed heavily from contemporary European avant-garde movements, were highly experimental by Hollywood's standards. Others, like *The Old Swimmin' Hole* (1921), a Charles Ray film that used no intertitles, would probably be perceived as close to a normal classical film by modern viewers. This range of "experiment" across the films should give us a sense of the possibilities that existed in mainstream American cinema. I cannot discuss each film in detail, so I shall analyze a few and refer to others briefly.

How can we compare the types of experimentation in films so different from each other? David Bordwell offers one solution in *The Classical Hollywood Cinema*, where he distinguishes among three levels of Hollywood's style: *devices, systems,* and *relations among systems.* Devices are isolated techniques, such as editing or camera movement. Clearly films may experiment with these, as when *The Old Swimmin' Hole* eliminates intertitles. The next level up, systems, consists of the functions that individual devices perform and the relations among the devices and their functions. Fiction films, the type we are dealing with here, can be considered to have three basic systems: narrative logic, cinematic time, and cinematic space. Devices are motivated by their relationships to one or more of these systems. One device may replace another, as long as the function remains virtually the same; for example, a track-back beginning on a close framing may establish a room's space as well as a static long shot would. The third level, as noted, involves the relations among systems—here, the relationships between narrative logic, cinematic time, and cinematic space.

In *The Classical Hollywood Cinema,* Bordwell argues that in the classical style, the spatial and temporal systems remain subordinate to the narrative logic; that is, individual devices that function to create time and space should also aid in making the ongoing action clear. At the same time, the narrative logic is likely to make unusual individual devices serve familiar functions, as when disjunctive cutting conveys a character's perception of an unsettling event.[5] The systematic quality of the classical cinema allows Hollywood to experiment in a limited way with new techniques and functions, and to assimilate those which prove useful into its overall filmmaking style.

The classical style was standardized during the 1910s. Its systems and relations among systems have changed relatively little since, and even many of its devices, like shot/reverse shot, have changed only slightly. Why would the Hollywood studios want to experiment? As Janet Staiger argues, the Hollywood system built into itself a need to balance standardization and differentiation. Unless films could be distinguished from each other, it would be hard to publicize them: "Examples of appeals to *novelty* manifest themselves continually in the catalogues and later newspaper advertising. The words 'novelty' and 'innovation' become so common as to be clichés: 'one of the genuine motion picture novelties,' 'an innovation in picture making.' " Staiger points out that the need for differentiation had two effects on style and production practices: "an encouragement of the innovative work and the cyclical innovation of styles and genres." Various "innovative workers," such as John Ford, Cecil B. De Mille, and Gregg Toland, throve within the Hollywood system:

"The promotion of the innovative worker who might push the boundaries of the standard was part of Hollywood's practices. Normally, furthermore, innovations were justified as 'improvements' on the standards of verisimilitude, spectacle, narrative coherence, and continuity."[6] Of course, not all innovations pleased the public, and some directors of the experimental films under discussion here had short careers in Hollywood, or, as with Josef Von Sternberg, adopted a more conventional style.

Hollywood could thus, in a limited way, risk assimilating avant-garde art. During the 1920s, for example, the German cinema influenced the work of the American studios, but, as Bordwell points out, the borrowings were selective. The moving camera, bizarre camera angles, and special effects to convey subjectivity were picked up freely. "Other formal traits of Expressionist cinema—the more episodic and open-ended narrative, the entirely subjective film, or the slower tempo of story events—were not imitated by Hollywood; the classical style took only what could extend and elaborate its principles without challenging them."[7]

EXPERIMENTATION IN THE EARLY CLASSICAL ERA

Most early experimentation in Hollywood seems to have resulted from influences entering the cinema from the other arts. Modern trends in painting and theatrical design, derived in particular from Art Nouveau and Art Deco and typified by the stage designs of Edward Gordon Craig, led to mildly avant-garde mise-en-scène in a few films during the second half of the teens and the beginning of the 1920s. In some cases, such experimentation affected the films only on the level of devices, primarily those of set design and costume. In rare instances, the stylization also extended to changes in the narrative system.

An early example of modernist design in films comes with *Madame Cubist* (1916), a two-reel film starring Mary Fuller. No print is known to survive, but a contemporary synopsis makes the plot seem quite conventional. The hero bets that he can win the love of a society woman nicknamed "Madame Cubist" for her striking clothes; he does so but falls in love with her. After a tiff resulting from her discovery of the bet, the couple reconciles. According to the *Motion Picture News*, "It was eccentric in many ways, being an eccentric drama, with eccentric settings and Miss Fuller wore very eccentric and sensational gowns."[8] The *Moving Picture Weekly* ran a fashion-oriented two-page spread;

photographs of the star in "cubist" gowns accompanied a brief rundown on the Armory Show and current art trends, including Futurism, Cubism, Vorticism, and Synchronism: "If you can't visit a New Art exhibition, then go to see Miss Mary Fuller in 'Madame Cubist.'" Clearly, however, the excesses of modernism had been tamed for American consumption. The article's conclusion begins:

> Perhaps it is as well for our sartorial peace that the Cubist-Futurist, and other "ist" movements, had spent its [sic] first force before it reached our shores. Maybe there is a disadvantage to living where the new things start, after all. We escape some of the wildest vagaries in that way.[9]

The attention accorded this short film made by a minor production company suggests that novelty had a publicity value.

Madame Cubist apparently motivates its modernist mise-en-scène by presenting a heroine interested in the latest fashion or art style. A few American directors, however, used modern style to create the entire diegetic world of their films. A remarkable 1915 Vitagraph one-reeler, *The Yellow Girl*, seems at first to motivate its stylized costumes and decors through the characters' participation in the New York art scene. The hero is a painter; his model is a dancer in an arty stage show; his jealous girlfriend works in an ultra-modern boutique where the model buys her clothes. Later, however, the characters walk through a "real" park represented by the same kind of modernist decor (fig. 3.1: the incongruous blob of white at the lower right is a live rabbit). Here the realistic "chic" motivation outruns the plot: the artist's studio and the dancer's stage performance are no more stylized than are the landscapes. The *Moving Picture World* considered the costumes and settings "a pleasing novelty": "They are inspired by the futuristic school of art and are faithful copies of the odd figures and scenes that are produced by the followers of this method."[10] Again, however, the experiment appeared in a relatively minor one-reel film. More extensive exploration in this direction soon followed from one of the era's major filmmakers.

Maurice Tourneur gained fame for experimentation, and some of his films departed from the norms of mise-en-scène that were being established in Hollywood. In 1918 he made two ambitious films that used stylized decor extensively. The sets in both *The Blue Bird* and *Prunella* displayed strong influence from simplified, fantasy-oriented stage design, and, indeed, both were adaptations of successful plays. *The Blue Bird,*

Figure 3.1.
Frame enlargement from *The Yellow Girl* (1915), directed by Edgar M. Keller, with Corinne Griffith and Florence Vidor

Maurice Maeterlinck's allegorical fantasy, had been a phenomenal stage success in the United States. (Reviews of the film often refer to the universal familiarity of the story and characters.) Tourneur's version used spectacular special effects, and the sets often incorporated spare, almost cartoonlike backdrops typical of contemporary stage productions (fig. 3.2). It also moved away from the typical narrative pattern of the classical cinema by stressing allegory; several of the characters visible in the illustration are personified objects (sugar, milk, and so on), and the goal of the central fantasy is to find the bluebird of happiness.

Reviewers loved the film for its innovativeness and pictorial beauty. The *New York Dramatic Mirror* stressed how the obscure qualities of the narrative were smoothed over by the technical innovations: "All thoughts of symbolism, however, are forgotten in recalling the colossal splendor and magnitude of the production. Famous Players–Lasky Corporation have achieved a triumph in artistic and technical effects. In fact, since seeing the screen 'Blue Bird,' we believe in magic—for only magic could

Figure 3.2.
Frame enlargement from *The Blue Bird* (1918), directed by Maurice Tourneur

have conjured such spectacles of fact and fancy."[11] The *Moving Picture World* advised exhibitors on phrases to use in publicizing the film: "Great Stage Success Exceeded in Beautiful Photoplay," "Pictorially Beautiful Reproduction of Famous Classic," and "Mammoth Phot-Dramatic Spectacle of Lavish Splendor."[12] It is interesting to note, however, that Artcraft's trade advertisements for *The Blue Bird* featured photographs of the two lead child actors, with little suggestion of the stylized sets or the oddly costumed allegorical characters.[13] It was promoted partly as a children's or family film (just as the initial Broadway run included a special 10:00 A.M. matinee for children).[14] Even so, it was not a commercial success.

Only fragments of Tourneur's next film, *Prunella*, survive. They suggest that the odd settings were not limited to a fantasy scene, as in the earlier film. The story was not allegorical; it was based upon a recently successful symbolist play by Granville Barker, and its star, Marguerite Clark, originated the title role on Broadway. The press found it an experiment in high art, "best appreciated by persons of culture and taste."[15] Indeed, this film engendered a sort of commentary that I have not encountered in earlier American film reviewing. Several writers praised the film while regretfully suggesting that its unusual qualities might harm its box-office potential. *Variety* remarked, " 'Prunella' may not break any b.o. records nor call forth any great outburst of hard applause, but it is refreshingly sweet when compared with the deluge of sickly, sentimental and maudlin romantic subjects that have swept the photoplay of late."[16] While the *New York Times* opined that most people would be "delightfully entertained," its reviewer added: "Those who do not like fanciful poetry, costumes, and people of the imagination will probably be helplessly bored. But that won't be 'Prunella's' fault."[17] Such fears proved realistic, and the film did poorly. Many exhibitors thought it too highbrow.[18]

Tourneur's main contributions to the Hollywood cinema arguably came in his less avant-garde films, such as *The Wishing Ring* (1914), *Alias Jimmy Valentine* (1915), *A Girl's Folly* (1916), and *The Last of the Mohicans* (1920). Even here his artistry was recognized as distinctive, but in ways that did not draw so much attention away from the narrative. The cinematography in several of his films is strikingly beautiful, and he has become famous for using depth shots with framing elements in silhouette in the foreground.[19] At the level of production, however, Tourneur resisted the rise of the classical studio system in Hollywood, preferring to work autonomously.[20] In 1926 a dispute with MGM concerning *The Mysterious Island* caused Tourneur to return to Europe, the first of a string of major directors who abandoned Hollywood filmmaking.[21]

During these early years of experimentation within the classical system, one film played with all three levels of film form: devices, functions, and relations among systems. D. W. Griffith's *Intolerance* (1916) uses continuity editing within scenes, but several other devices break up the clear, linear flow of events. Most notably, parallel editing mixes four stories taking place in vastly different times and places; the function of such editing is to make conceptual, rather than causal, connections among events. Another device, the periodic use of nondiegetic inserts for the "Out of the cradle endlessly rocking" motif, also disrupts the causal flow, creating a symbolic pattern that holds the whole film together conceptually. Localized symbolic touches carry through this de-emphasis of narrative primacy: the allegorical ending, the huge, barren office of the financier, the dove cart. Although it is possible to follow the individual stories, their clarity is diminished in favor of a larger conceptual goal. Hence the normal use of the spatial and temporal systems primarily to enhance the narrative system is shifted in a radical way. (Indeed, it is possible to argue that Griffith has to a considerable degree failed to pull the four plots together into a unified whole.) A few years after the film's financial failure, Griffith tried to recoup his losses by releasing the Babylonian and Modern stories as separate, more conventionally structured films. Like other directors, Griffith was able to experiment until the rise of the studio system forced him to work in a more standard fashion, and eventually he was squeezed out of filmmaking prematurely.

THE EARLY 1920S

In the early 1920s, there was still little overt experimentation in Hollywood cinema. The slight trend toward innovative design that had begun around 1916 continued, and during the second half of the decade, a mild modernism was standardized as a major option for art directors and costume designers.

Two extreme cases were *Camille* (1921) and *Salome* (1923), both produced by and starring Alla Nazimova and designed by Natacha Rambova. Both women were thoroughly acquainted with modernist styles in theater and painting. *Camille*, an adaptation of Alexandre Dumas *fils*'s novel and play, employs interiors depicting sophisticated Paris. These were based primarily on Art Deco (fig. 3.3), though the opera staircase set seems to echo Hans Poelzig's expressionist Grosses Schauspielhaus in Berlin. Once Marguerite moves to the country to live a simple life with Armand, however, the design reverts to straightforward Hollywood sets. Stylization returns only late in the film, for Marguerite's feigned renunciation of Armand and her return to Paris.

Camille would seem to be a case where the novelty value of the unusual design counterbalanced the perception of the film as arty, highbrow, and hence potentially unpopular. The *Moving Picture World*'s review was reserved:

> There is no denying that the Nazimova production of *Camille* is interesting. It is filled with modern symbolism, which is expressed in the settings and the acting of the star and her supporting company. There are scenes

Figure 3.3.
Frame enlargement from *Camille* (1921), directed by Ray C. Smallwood

that suggest the lost souls in Dante's Inferno, and the human interest that gave the stage play its long life doesn't get much of a chance to make itself felt. In other words the story, in its present form, stands a good chance of shooting over the heads of the common mob.[22]

Camille, like *Salome*, seems to have succeeded mainly as a result of the star's popularity.[23]

Salome shifts the usual classical emphasis on the primacy of the narrative system. The stylized mise-en-scène lasts throughout the film, and both the spatial and temporal construction function as much to display the spectacle of the sets and costumes as to serve the narrative. These innovations are motivated largely by the simple and familiar story. Some of the editing functions mainly to show off portions of the single large set or the oddly costumed minor characters who stand about in exaggerated postures; Rambova based her designs on Aubrey Beardsley's drawings for the original edition of Oscar Wilde's play. The rhythm of the action is also slower than in the usual classical film. In combination with the sets and costumes, the stylized acting seeks to create an overall tone of decadence appropriate to the play, and this tone becomes at times more prominent than any narrative progression.

Rambova designed these two films in a situation that allowed her considerable control: they were independently produced by her friend Nazimova. By the same token, however, she had little impact on modernist style in Hollywood. It was at the major studios that outside influences entered the Hollywood cinema on a standardized basis. Most histories of set design credit Joseph Urban (a Ziegfeld Follies designer hired by William Randolph Hearst as art director of Cosmopolitan) with using the first realistically motivated modernist set, a Viennese Secession-ist room in *Enchantment* (1921). *Couturier* Paul Iribe did Art Nouveau sets for *The Affairs of Anatole* (1921), and William Cameron Menzies was influenced by the Ballet Russe when he designed *The Thief of Bagdad* (1924). A few films of the mid-1920s contained some Art Deco sets (e.g., *Fig Leaves*, 1926; *So This Is Paris*, 1927). By decade's end, Art Deco became the dominant modern style in the Hollywood cinema, with such films as *Our Dancing Daughters* (1928) and *The Kiss* (1929).[24] Except for *The Thief of Bagdad*, which was a fantasy, these films used modernism with a realistic motivation, to suggest a fashionable style appropriate to the characters' social situations. Similarly, Expressionism was convention-alized as appropriate to the horror genre, as in *The Cat and the Canary* (1927) and *The Old Dark House* (1932). In such cases modern design functioned within the classical system, supporting the narrative.

A very different approach to experimentation came in *The Old Swimmin' Hole* (1921), a star vehicle for Charles Ray, directed by Joseph De Grasse and produced by Ray's own company. Its only innovative element was its lack of intertitles. (At the time, it was taken to be the first titleless Hollywood feature.) Here we can see a clear case of play purely on the level of devices.

One might at first think it odd that this particular technique should be suppressed. After all, few silent-film devices promote narrative clarity more strongly than does the intertitle. In fact, however, the makers of *The Old Swimmin' Hole* balanced the novel elimination of intertitles by two simple tactics. On the level of devices, they introduced diegetic written texts into the mise-en-scène whenever vital narrative information could not be conveyed without language. On the systemic level, they used an extremely simple narrative with situations that would be recognizable to most audiences. Thus all the customary devices *besides* intertitles would suffice to convey the basic narrative information.

That the elimination of the intertitles created some difficulties for the filmmakers is evidenced by the clumsiness of their attempts to introduce written texts into the action. In the first scene we see the schoolboy hero fishing from a bridge. Some other boys join him, and one writes in chalk on the bridge's wooden surface: "Last in swimmin is a sissy." The motivation for this action is insufficient: any boy throwing out such a challenge would shout it and run immediately, not linger to write it out while his companions got the jump on him. Other written texts are somewhat better motivated, as when the hero, Ezra, writes in his diary that he will be going to a picnic on Tuesday (fig. 3.4) In general, the device of eliminating intertitles remains strangely artificial, since the scenes are shot in continuity style. Characters converse in shot/reverse shot, yet we never learn what they are saying. (By way of contrast, the German titleless films of this era adjust the plot to emphasize physical action, and the characters seldom speak.) Moreover, in order to make the

Figure 3.4.
Frame enlargement from *The Old Swimmin' Hole* (1921), directed by Joseph De Grasse

action clear, Ray has to play a caricature of his usual small-town-boy character.

The plot of *The Old Swimmin' Hole* is undoubtedly comprehensible, and the film as a whole remains classical. When it was released, several critics pointed out that the plot *had* to be simple and universal to make comprehension possible. The *Moving Picture World*'s reviewer pointed out, however, that "it might be termed a picture without a plot."[25] In Hollywood parlance, a "plotless" film is simply a film with a scant, rambling, or episodic plot. The film was also sometimes seen as mildly progressive. For *Variety*'s reviewer, the simplification of the plot vitiated any experimental value the lack of intertitles might have created (and note here that the author uses the term "experiment"):

> For years the film psychologists—principally those abroad—have claimed the day would come when it was possible to produce a full-length feature upon the screen without the aid of subtitles. The forthcoming Charles Ray release by First National, a film adaptation of James Whitcomb Riley's poem, "The Old Swimmin' Hole," is making the experiment, and the outcome should be watched with some interest. In some respects it is hardly a fair test, inasmuch as there is little or no story to the picture, merely a series of incidents in the life of a bucolic youth. . . .
>
> The proposition, therefore, is producing pictures and showing them without the assistance of subtitles, remains unsolved [sic], and if we never arrive at such a point in motion photography, we are at least moving closer and closer to it.[26]

Here Hollywood's claim to continual progress through innovation is invoked. The reviewer for the *New York Times*, however, was more enthusiastic about the film's progressive move, calling it "a unique work in kinetic photography. It is a signpost, and points a way sooner or later to be generally followed."[27] Here a description appropriate to the most avant-garde of European films is used of a classical work.

Did the lack of titles make any difference to exhibitors or audiences? It is difficult to judge, but some scraps of information suggest that it did. At about this time, *The Moving Picture World* began printing short reports from exhibitors on how various recent films had fared at their theaters. The manager of the Majestic Theatre in Greenfield, Tennessee, commended *The Old Swimmin' Hole*: "Pleases ninety-five per cent. The no-titles angle is novel. I worked the feature up with that alone," resulting in good attendance.[28] But a manager in Old Lyme, Connecticut, advised exhibitors: "Lay off this; did not please our audience. Nothing to it, no sub-titles."[29] Although *The Old Swimmin' Hole* seems to have had virtually no influence on the Hollywood cinema, its mild experimentation could generate some publicity as a novelty.

NATURALISM IN HOLLYWOOD

About 1924 a strain of naturalism surfaced in Hollywood cinema, spawning several films that were often regarded as stretching convention. Early cases included Griffith's *Isn't Life Wonderful?*, and the trend can be seen as continuing with Erich von Stroheim's *Greed*, von Sternberg's *The Salvation Hunters*, Karl Brown's *Stark Love* (1928), William K. Howard's *White Gold* (1929), Friedrich Wilhelm Murnau's *Sunrise* (1927), Paul Fejos's *Lonesome* (1929), Vidor's *The Crowd* (1928), and Victor Seastrom's *The Wind* (1928). Tame though the subject matter of these films may seem today, several of them were seen as sordid, gruesome, or, at best, obscure by contemporary reviewers and, perhaps, by audiences.

Greed, for example, began as a project for the independent Goldwyn Company in 1922. What the completed film would have looked like if released by Goldwyn must remain a matter for speculation. Shortly after Stroheim completed a twenty-two-reel version in early 1924, Goldwyn became part of the merger that created MGM, and the film was reduced to the truncated version we see today.[30] Despite the elimination of a considerable amount of symbolism and several emblematic subplots, *Greed* did poorly upon its initial release.[31]

Greed was perhaps the most gruesome of the naturalist films, involving as it did McTeague's biting Trina's fingers (which she subsequently loses to infection), her murder at his hands, and the climactic deadly confrontation between McTeague and Marcus in Death Valley. Violence and sordidness were commonly perceived as prominent features of naturalist films of this era, and despite the happy endings that graced most such films after *Greed*, reviewers seemed squeamish when faced with subject matter so far outside the Hollywood norm. In *White Gold*, the owner of a sheep farm tries to drive his son and new daughter-in-law apart; as a result, she is nearly raped (or perhaps really raped—the situation is left ambiguous) by a farmhand whom she kills. When the father claims *he* killed the man when he found the wife committing adultery, the son believes him. Disgusted at his lack of faith, the heroine walks away to start a new life.

The Wind presents a similar plot, as the heroine travels to the West, marries a naive young farmer, and then must kill her would-be rapist. In her nightmare, the ever-present wind uncovers the body she has buried in the sand, but the film ends with the prospect of a happy life with her husband (an ending imposed on Seastrom by MGM).

Other naturalist films of the era were less violent or sordid, but they often shared a propensity toward heavy symbolism. Even in its reduced form *Greed* retained some of the characters' visions of gold, and the finished film retained the symbolism associated with the sewer and the contrast of wedding banquet with funeral procession (fig. 3.5). The very titles of several "avant-garde" films of the 1920s—*Greed, The Salvation Hunters, Sunrise, The Crowd, The Wind*—are based on elemental, emblematic concepts. Weather often provided potent symbolism. In

Figure 3.5.
Frame enlargement from *Greed* (1925), directed by Erich von Stroheim

White Gold, the action occurs on a sheep farm during a drought, and the failure of the young couple's marriage is indicated by the heat and lack of water. An early intertitle puts it succinctly: "Heat . . . Drought . . . Nerves . . . Heat . . ." In *The Wind*, the elements represent the heroine's neurosis, and the wind is pictured as a white horse superimposed in the sky.

Perhaps the most controversial film among this group was *The Salvation Hunters*. Certainly it was the one made with the least assistance from the Hollywood establishment. According to von Sternberg, the film cost less than five thousand dollars, and he financed it with assistance from George K. Arthur. Arthur was apparently responsible for getting Charles Chaplin, Mary Pickford, and Douglas Fairbanks to view *The Salvation Hunters*, and their enthusiasm won it a release by United Artists.

The film has gained a reputation for being slow, even static. In fact, there is plenty of action. The protagonists are a shiftless young man and a woman who take under their wing a homeless boy; the heroine is lured by a pimp into prostitution to support them. Her first client takes pity on them and supplies money, and finally the pimp's abuse of the child galvanizes the hero into fighting him. The trio ends with a hopeful future.

Today the film may not seem revolutionary, yet at the time it stirred up extensive controversy. Under the subheadline "New Director Offers Symbolical Picture That Is Radically Different," the *Moving Picture World* published a revealing discussion of the film's originality:

> How is "The Salvation Hunters" different? In story, technique, acting and direction it gets away from commonly accepted standards. So radical is this departure that it is bound to provoke a variety of opinions, both pro and con, as to its artistic values, its effect on future production and its box office possibility.
>
> Just what has this new director, Josef von Sternberg, sought to do? According to the subtitles he has endeavored to present a picturization of a thought—that through unswerving faith we can eventually find the light and rise above the forces which tend to cast us down. . . .
>
> How does his treatment of this theme differ from accustomed handling? By the employment of symbolism, exceptional simplicity and straightforwardness in direction and unusual restraint in the acting of his players; by reducing his sets to the minimum, discarding the obvious as far as possible and avoiding the theatric [*sic*].

The review then debates whether the film succeeds. On the one hand, it is seen as too sordid and as involving uninteresting characters:

> As to Mr. von Sternberg's employment of symbolism. Much has been said about this. Some of this is obvious and hammered home with sledge-hammer blows by titles and repetition, such is the case with the dredge bringing up the mud from the darkness of the harbor bottom to the sunlight, doubly symbolical of the surroundings and the striving of the hero's struggle for the light. Also the fight which regenerates him culminates behind a real estate sign reading, "Here's where dreams come true." There are other symbolical touches, some so subtle that a great majority will not get them.[32]

The symbolism in *The Salvation Hunters* is indeed quite obvious. To be sure, many standard Hollywood films employ heavy-handed symbolism, as when the villainous German officer played by von Stroheim in *The Heart of Humanity* (1918, director Allen Hollubar) is equated with a spider by means of a cut-in to a (diegetic) arachnid. This remains an isolated moment within a largely nonsymbolic narrative, however, whereas *The Salvation Hunters* frequently employs overt symbolism, as when some game-trophy horns behind the pimp are lined up so as to render him diabolic.

The *Moving Picture World* reviewer concluded:

> While Mr. von Sternberg does not appear to have achieved his ideal goal, he has succeeded in traveling a long way toward it. Certainly he has a picture that will interest the student of the motion picture and the intelligent patron, for it will make them think and cause a diversity of opinion. So radical a departure is it that its box-office effect is problematical. Its appeal to the average theatregoer is doubtful but its very "difference," if sufficiently exploited may serve to bring them in.[33]

Despite considerable advance publicity and a record-breaking premiere at the California Theatre in San Francisco,[34] the few big-city runs recorded by *Variety* were disastrous. The reasons given for its failure in New York suggest that its naturalism disturbed some spectators: "Although this picture was lauded heavily by the daily papers it failed to pull at the box office. In some quarters it was stated this production was disgusting. The business proved that the public wants to be entertained rather than shown life in its sordidness."[35] It was not until von Sternberg mixed "sordidness" with the gangster genre in *Underworld* (1927) that he found success.

Few naturalistic films did well at the box office. Some directors made deliberately pared-down tales of typical or everyday couples: *Sunrise, Stark Love, Lonesome, The Crowd.* Most involved romances and happy endings. *Lonesome* was financially successful, and *The Crowd* made a modest profit. While *Sunrise* did not realize Fox's high hopes, it was not a disaster.

The "poetic" or symbolic aspirations of Hollywood naturalism in this era can be seen in several attempts to universalize a film by giving characters no names or very common ones. *The Salvation Hunters* involves The Boy, The Girl, The Child, The Man, and so on. In *Sunrise,* the triangle involves the Wife, the Man, and the "woman from the city." The *American Film Institute Catalogue* gives names for the characters in *White Gold,* but these come from the original play; they are not used in the film itself. The silent version of *City Girl* (1929) has no named characters. The central couple in *The Crowd* are simply John and Mary. This practice found its archetypal usage in the "Modern Story" of *Intolerance,* where the main characters are the Dear One, the Boy, the Musketeer of the Slums, and the Friendless One. Similarly, the filmmakers often sought to de-glamorize their characters by choosing relatively minor actors (e.g., Gibson Gowland in *Greed,* Barbara Kent and Glen Tryon in *Lonesome*), unknown aspiring actors (James Morrison in *The Crowd*), or even nonactors (the cast of *Stark Love*).

In general, naturalism or a variant of it that might be called poetic realism remained a minor trend within Hollywood, fostering films that were often considered unconventional. It is interesting to note that with the coming of sound, some directors who had worked in this vein turned to more glamorous projects (as did Sternberg); others had already been forced out of Hollywood (von Stroheim, Seastrom). Despite exceptions like *Our Daily Bread* (1930), naturalism diminished during the 1930s.

EUROPEAN AVANT-GARDE INFLUENCES

Although a few European avant-garde films like Abel Gance's *J'Accuse* and Robert Wiene's *Das Cabinet des Dr. Caligari* reached the United States by 1921, it took some years before any direct influence became apparent. *Beggar on Horseback* (1925) was widely seen as the first major

Hollywood film influenced by German Expressionism. Produced by Famous Players–Lasky, it was an adaptation of George S. Kaufman and Marc Connelly's successful 1924 play about a composer who gives music lessons while trying to write a symphony. Since he is too poor to marry, his selfless girlfriend suggests that he marry one of his pupils, Miss Cady, a *nouveau-riche* businessman's daughter. The composer falls asleep and dreams of such a marriage. In the dream, the grotesquely stylized mise-en-scène represents the hideous traits of his wife and in-laws: his sedentary mother-in-law has a rocking chair tied to her body; the women wear clothes emblazoned with dollar signs; the millionaire smokes a huge cigar and speaks into oversized phones. After the hero kills the Cadys in disgust, he is tried before a jury garbed as undertakers; when he asks that his case be taken to a higher court, the judge cranks his bench up several feet. (This gag presumably imitates the town clerk's tall stool in *Caligari*.)

Sadly, only a portion of *Beggar on Horseback*, comprising the opening and about five minutes of the crucial dream, survives. This segment, along with contemporary descriptions and photographs, allows us to draw only provisional conclusions.

The lengthy opening portion, set primarily in the hero's shabby apartment where he teaches piano, is shot in the lustrous big-studio style of the mid-1920s, with perfect continuity. As the overworked hero falls asleep, a change in the lighting signals the beginning of the dream. A stop-action effect transports him to a grotesque, though nonexpressionistic, wedding scene. During the ceremony, everyone dances to a jazz band. The attendants carry bouquets of dollar signs, and a pattern of the same signs appears on the altar. In the next scene, the honeymoon departure at a train station, the set is stylized (fig. 3.6).

These few scenes, in addition to publicity stills from the rest of the dream, suggest that this portion of *Beggar on Horseback* was grotesque and caricatural, but hardly obscure or challenging—or expressionistic. To many modern viewers, the opening sequences would seem to provide thorough preparation for the dream, and its comic qualities motivate the dream's stylized mise-en-scène. As a result one might also assume that the film would be popular (especially since the young Edward Everett Horton was widely praised for his performance as the composer).

Nevertheless, some reviewers viewed the film as European-influenced or highbrow. The *Moving Picture World* referred to its "futurist courtroom" set.[36] *Variety* praised the film's quality ("a fine production made

Figure 3.6.
Frame enlargement from *Beggar on Horseback* (1925), directed by James Cruze

with much intelligence and insight") but predicted dire box-office con-sequences ("miles over the head of picture audiences").[37] The prophecy was accurate. Since the film was distributed by Paramount, it played widely, and no "avant-garde" film was so widely commented upon in the exhibitors' column of The *Moving Picture World*. The manager of a small Iowa theater was sympathetic but complained, "It was so deep that some could not follow it. It was a money loser here. Good only for those who grasp the director's idea."[38] An exhibitor in a small town in Texas was more adamant: "I didn't get to see this one, but my people didn't fail to tell me they thought it 'a piece of cheese.' "[39] From a modern perspective, *Beggar on Horseback* would seem to be trying to balance Hollywood-style narra-tive motivation and stylization of individual devices. The fact that such an apparently playful film failed suggests that by 1925 the Hollywood distri-bution system and publicity institutions (including reviewers) could not market such an anomalous film.

The increasing influence of European cinema over the next few years improved Hollywood's tactics for exploiting stylization. The expressionist nightclub set and vast craning camera movements in *Broadway* (1929) and the opening montage sequence in Paul Leni's *The Last Warning* (1929) exemplify devices adopted from the European avant-garde into mainstream films.

Fejos's *The Last Moment* may have been the most radically experimental American-made feature film released within the commercial American distribution network during this era. Unfortunately, no prints are known to exist, but descriptions make it sound distinctive both stylistically and narratively. Lewis Jacobs has provided us with an extensive outline of its action:

> The story was "a study in subjectivity" based on the theory that at a moment of crisis before a person loses consciousness, he may see a panorama of pictures summarizing the memories of a lifetime. The film opens with a shot of troubled water. A struggling figure and a hand reach up, "as if in entreaty." This is followed by a rapid sequence of shots: the head of a Pierrot, faces of women, flashing headlights, spinning wheels, a star shower, an explosion which climaxes in a shot of a children's book.
>
> From the book, the camera flashes back to summarize the drowning man's life. Impressions of schooldays, a fond mother, an unsympathetic father, a birthday party, reading Shakespeare, a first visit to the theatre, the boy scrawling love notes, an adolescent affair with a carnival dancer, quarrelling at home, leaving for the city, stowing away on a ship, manhandled by a drunken captain, stumbling into a tavern, acting to amuse a circle of revellers, reeling in drunken stupor and run over by a car, attended by a sympathetic nurse, winning a reputation as an actor, marrying, quarrelling, divorcing, gambling, acting, attending his mother's funeral, enlisting in the army, the battle-front. No attempt was made to probe into these actions but to give them as a series of narrative impressions.
>
> The concluding portions of the film were likewise told in the same impressionistic manner. The soldier returns to civilian life and resumes his acting career, falls in love with his leading lady, marries her, is informed of her accidental death, becomes distraught, finally is impelled to suicide. Wearing his Pierrot costume, the actor wades out into the lake at night.
>
> Now the camera repeats the opening summary: the troubled waters, the faces, the lights, the wheels, the star shower, the explosion. The outstretched hand gradually sinks from view. A few bubbles rise to the surface. The film ends.[40]

Contemporary reviews make it clear that the "rapid sequence of shots" that introduces the central flashback and returns at the end must have consisted of very fast montage: "The flashing summary of a lifetime first shown is mere meaningless phantasma, but when it is repeated, it does take on some significance, and the whole business, although merely a theatrical device, has a kick, even if the subject matter and mode of telling is [sic] morbid."[41] It would seem that Fejos was influenced by French Impressionism, with its use of rapid bursts of shots for subjective purposes. Gance had used the "life flashing before one's eyes" device in *La Roue* (1918), in the scene of Elie hanging above an abyss and recalling his life with Norma just before he falls; there the shots accelerate to a series of single-frame images. Working in Paris from 1921 to 1923, Fejos very probably saw *La Roue* and other Impressionist films.

The Last Moment was experimental in other ways. Its only intertitle appeared at the beginning, setting forth the premise of a life flashing before one's eyes in moments of crisis.[42] As with *The Old Swimmin' Hole*, this lack of intertitles meant that the narrative had to be simple, stressing obvious, recognizable points in the hero's life. In addition, *The Last Moment* apparently used all the tricks of contemporary European camerawork, including superimpositions and a rapidly moving camera.

The film, however, went beyond experimenting at the level of individual devices. Descriptions suggest that it was structured as a series of chronologically presented impressionistic scenes rather than as a linear, causally linked progression. Jacobs hints that this difference was, in my terms here, a downplaying of narrative logic in favor of a play with time and space:

> For America it was a radical departure in structure, deliberately ignoring narrative conventions of storytelling and striving for a cinematic form of narrative. Instead of subduing the camera and using the instrument solely as a recording device, the director boldly emphasized the camera's role and utilized all of its narrative devices. The significant use of dissolves, multiple exposures, irises, mobility, split screen, created a style which though indebted to the Germans, was better integrated in terms of visual movement and rhythm and overshadowed the shallowness of the film's content.[43]

Any final judgment must be reserved until a print of the film is found. It does seem, however, that *The Last Moment* may have involved experimentation even on the level of the relations among the film's formal systems.

Not surprisingly, the film was made independently. Fejos has described how, when he was trying to get work in Hollywood, he was offered a ride by a rich man's son while hitchhiking. After hearing a description of Fejos' project, the young man provided five thousand dollars, and Fejos wangled the rest on credit. Georgia Hale, a star since *The Gold Rush* (1925), agreed to defer her salary; the Du Pont company was persuaded to furnish free raw stock in return for acknowledgment at the film's beginning and end; and the Fine Arts Studio let Fejos rent bits and pieces of filming time in the standing sets from other productions. Fejos claimed that he wrote the script day by day, depending on the sets available to him. Some of the film's experimental techniques served to cover time lapses. A marriage's drift toward divorce was shown through shots of a bird cage with doves dissolving to two crows fighting, a sink with dirty dishes, and the like: "The whole film was made this way. The aim was to make it in kaleidoscope-like speed, as it might seem in actuality to the hero when he was dying."[44] Fejos' description raises the intriguing possibility that *The Last Moment* was essentially a series of montage sequences.

The finished film seems to have gone through a process similar to that which won *The Salvation Hunters* a distributor. Two prominent Hollywood critics, Welford Beaton and Tamar Lane, agreed to see it. Both wrote rave reviews and arranged for Chaplin to view it privately. After a preview at the Beverly Theatre, with Chaplin in attendance, the Zakaro Film Corporation took over the film's distribution.[45] This was an unusual way of handling a film; *Variety* remarked on the lack of a trade showing when the film had its world premiere in Boston in January 1928. Handled as an art film, it played at Symphony Hall for two dollars[46] and, apparently, did relatively well.[47]

The reviews were mostly positive. The *New York Times* commented:

> It is a film that is said to have cost $13,000, but this is in its favor, for the result is infinitely more absorbing than many pictures on which twenty times that amount has been expended. The impressionistic theme is one that brings to mind Guy de Maupassant's works, and, although the beginning and end of the narrative are far from cheerful, the events that are brought out in the meantime are so stirring and so artistically pictured that it is not depressing.[48]

The Last Moment was among the runners-up in the 1928 *Film Daily* survey of critics on the "Ten Best Pictures of 1928."[49]

CONCLUSIONS

This chapter serves mainly to confirm the longstanding belief that Hollywood has only a very limited tolerance for unconventional filmmaking. Avant-garde filmmakers may gain recognition through experiment, but if they hope to keep working within a commercial system, they must soon learn to accommodate their work, whether on the level of devices, systemic functions of devices, or relationships among systems, to the prevailing norms. In our own era we can see this same process at work, as when John Waters moves from *Pink Flamingos* to *Hairspray,* or David Lynch from *Eraserhead* to *Wild at Heart.*

Hollywood experimentation largely died out with the introduction of sound in the late 1920s. Odd camera angles, superimpositions, and nondiegetic symbolism could serve the narrative flow within the context of montage sequences. Theater programs included short films, and while these were usually newsreels and studio cartoons, they occasionally included such items as Oskar Fischinger's abstract *An Optical Poem,* released as a regular MGM animated one-reeler in 1937. Government documentaries like Pare Lorentz's *The River* (1937) also appeared on regular theatrical bills. The presence of such films within the mainstream system should remind us that the avant-garde and the commercial cinemas are not as widely separated as we might believe. The reasons for this propinquity are not that the avant-garde can subvert the mainstream cinema. Most probably the reverse is usually true: the commercial cinema can turn *almost* anything to its own uses. In that "almost" lies the survival of the avant-garde.

NOTES

I would like to thank David Bordwell, Jan-Christopher Horak, Bruce Jenkins, and Lea Jacobs for their comments on drafts of this article. Thanks also to the staffs of the Cinémathèque Royale de Belgique, the Library of Congress, the National Film Archive, and George Eastman House for help in the research.

1. Lewis Jacobs, "Avant-Garde Production in America," in *Experiment in the Film,* ed. Roger Manvell (London: Grey Walls Press, 1949), p. 113.

2. John W. Dodds, *The Several Lives of Paul Fejos: A Hungarian-American Odyssey* (New York: Wenner-Gren Foundation, 1973), pp. 33–36.

3. See Chapter 4, by Brian Taves, in this volume.

4. The films analyzed or mentioned include only films that were produced or distributed by a regular commercial company and that could thus be

considered acceptable to at least some elements of the mainstream American film institutions.

5. David Bordwell, Janet Staiger, and Kristin Thompson, *The Classical Hollywood Cinema: Film Style and Mode of Production to 1960* (New York: Columbia University Press, 1985), p. 3.

6. Ibid., pp. 99, 109–110.

7. Ibid., pp. 70, 72–73.

8. " 'Madame Cubist' Is Eccentric Play for Mary Fuller," *Motion Picture News* 13, no. 3 (22 January 1916): 377.

9. Mlle. Chic, "Mary Fuller's Eccentric Gowns," *Moving Picture Weekly*, 12 February 1916, pp. 18–19. My thanks to Richard Koszarski for giving me this source.

10. "Comments on the Films," *Moving Picture World* 29, no. 11 (9 September 1916): 1688.

11. H. O. R., " 'The Blue Bird,' " *New York Dramatic Mirror*, no. 2051 (13 April 1918): 522.

12. "Advertising Aids for Busy Managers," *Moving Picture World* 36, no. 1 (6 April 1918): 134.

13. See, for example, advertisements in *New York Dramatic Mirror*, no. 2050 (6 April 1918): 2; *Moving Picture World* 35, no. 12 (23 March 1918): 1591–1592.

14. " 'The Blue Bird' a Hit on Screen," in *New York Times Film Reviews*, vol. 1 (New York: New York Times/Arno, 1970), p. 34.

15. Edward Weitzel, "Prunella," *Moving Picture World*, 36, no. 10 (8 June 1918): 1472.

16. Mork., "*Prunella*" (7 June 1918), in *Variety Film Reviews*, vol. 1 (New York: Garland, 1983), n.p.

17. "Crowd Gets Thrills in 'Stolen Orders,' " in *New York Times Film Reviews*, 1:37.

18. Jan-Christopher Horak, "Maurice Tourneur and the Rise of the Studio System," in *Sulla via di Hollywood: 1911–1920*, ed. Paolo Cherchi Usai and Lorenzo Codelli (Pordenone: Edizioni Biblioteca dell'Immagine, 1988), p. 278.

19. In 1921 Burns Mantle wrote: "Tourneur differs from most of the directors in his class in that he can achieve great beauty of background without sacrifice of story value, and while he does permit a certain repetition of his favorite shots, the views from a darkened cave through to the blazing firelight or sunlight or moonlight beyond, for example, with silhouetted figures against the light, they seldom interfere with the spectator's interest in the tale." See Burns Mantle, "The Shadow Stage," *Photoplay* 19, no. 5 (April 1921), reprinted in George C. Pratt, in *Spellbound in Darkness: A History of the Silent Film* (Greenwich, Conn.: New York Graphic Society, 1966), p. 281. Here we find the critic acknowledging that the director's stylistic experimentation does not deflect from the primacy of story logic.

20. Horak, "Tourneur and the Rise of the Studio System," pp. 288–290.

21. Rex Ingram moved his Metro production unit to France after the 1924 merger that formed MGM, but he continued to produce through that company for several years. MGM also caused problems for eccentric directors like von Stroheim and Seastrom.

22. Edward Weitzel, "Camille," *Moving Picture World* 25, no. 4 (24 September 1921): 446.

23. For example, *Variety*'s review of *Camille* dwelt primarily on Nazimova's performance and failed to mention the design at all. Samuel., "*Camille*" (16 September 1921), in *Variety Film Reviews*, vol. 1, n.p.

24. See Léon Barsacq, *Caligari's Cabinet and Other Grand Illusions: A History of Film Design* (New York: New American Library, 1978), p. 55; Donald Albrecht, *Designing Dreams: Modern Architecture in the Movies* (New York: Harper & Row/Museum of Modern Art, 1986), pp. 39, 43; Mary Corliss and Carlos Clarens, "Designed for Film: The Hollywood Art Director," *Film Comment* 14, no. 3 (May–June 1978): 29; Howard Mandelbaum and Eric Myers, *Screen Deco* (New York: St. Martin's Press, 1985), pp. 7–8, 10, 48–49, 85.

25. Robert C. McElravy, "The Old Swimmin' Hole," *Moving Picture World* 49, no. 1 (5 March 1921): 44.

26. Jolo., "*Old Swimmin' Hole*" (25 February 1921), in *Variety Film Reviews*, vol. 1, n.p.

27. The same reviewer also described why the film remains thoroughly classical: "And it is entirely pictorial, cinematographic. It has no subtitles, or captions. It uses words only in a few inserts, which are integral parts of its story. Its moving pictures follow one another in logical sequence and the story comes directly from them. This is something new and important. In addition to giving pleasure to those seeking only to be entertained, this photoplay sheds a great deal of light on what may be done in pure cinematography. To this some may reply that the story in question is exceedingly simple. It may be said that it sticks so close to common human experience that its action might be autobiographical for almost any one. It may be pointed out that a story more complex in plot and characterization would not lend itself to wordless treatment as "The Old Swimmin' Hole" does. And this is all true." "The Screen," in *New York Times Film Reviews*, 1:90.

28. "Straight from the Shoulder Reports," *Moving Picture World* 60, no. 3 (20 January 1923): 244.

29. "Straight from the Shoulder Reports," *Moving Picture World* 55, no. 9 (29 April 1921): 965.

30. Richard Koszarski, *The Man You Loved to Hate: Erich von Stroheim and Hollywood* (New York: Oxford University Press, 1983), pp. 115, 142.

31. See "Chi. Takes Dive; McVicker's $19,000; Chicago, $40,300," *Variety* 78, no. 2 (25 February 1925): 26; "$20,000 at Fox's, Philly, with Big and Imposing Program," *Variety* 78, no. 2 (25 February 1925): 27; "$50 Separates L.A. Leaders; 'Devil's Cargo' at $26,550 Tops," *Variety* 78, no. 1 (18 February

1925): 26; "Straight from the Shoulder Reports," *Moving Picture World* 76, no. 4 (26 September 1925): 317.

32. C. S. Sewell, "The Salvation Hunters," *Moving Picture World* 72, no. 7 (14 February 1925): 701.

33. Ibid. *Variety* took a far less charitable approach to the film's artistic pretensions: "Word came a month or so ago from the west that 'The Salvation Hunters' was the work of a new cinema genius, that it was a revolutionary picture, that its theme was original and the treatment masterful. On top of that Charlie Chaplin, Doug. Fairbanks and Mary Pickford endorsed it as being the ultra-ultra in picture production. Applesauce. "The Salvation Hunters" is nothing more nor less than another short cast picture to express an apparently Teutonic theory of fatalism." Sisk., *"The Salvation Hunters"* (4 February 1925), in *Variety Film Reviews*, vol. 2 (New York: Garland, 1983), n.p. The term "short cast" here apparently means that the film contained no stars.

34. " 'Salvation Hunters' Has Big Premiere at the California," *Moving Picture World* 72, no. 7 (14 February 1925): 708.

35. "Super-Specials Begin Spring Battle; 'Salvation Hunters' Flop at Strand," *Variety* 77, no. 13 (11 February 1925): 27.

36. C. S. Sewell, *"Beggar on Horseback,"* *Moving Picture World* 74, no. 8 (20 June 1925): 859.

37. *"Beggar on Horseback"* (10 June 1925), in *Variety Film Reviews*, vol. 2, n.p.

38. "Straight from the Shoulder Reports," *Moving Picture World* 76, no. 4 (26 September 1925): 318.

39. "Straight from the Shoulder Reports," *Moving Picture World* 76, no. 6 (10 October 1925): 504.

40. Jacobs, "Avant-Garde Production in America," pp. 119–120.

41. Rush., *"Last Moment"* (14 March 1928), in *Variety Film Reviews*, in vol. 3 (New York: Garland, 1983), n.p.

42. "Exceptional Photoplays: *The Last Moment,"* *National Board of Review Magazine* 3, no. 2 (February 1928), reprinted in *Spellbound in Darkness*, p. 502.

43. *Spellbound in Darkness*, p. 502.

44. Information from a 1962 interview with Fejos, quoted in Dodds, *Several Lives of Paul Fejos*, pp. 28–33.

45. Ibid., pp. 33–38.

46. "Foreign [sic] $2 Film Starts in Boston," *Variety* 90, no. 1 (18 January 1928): 4.

47. Jacobs states, "Exhibited in many theatres throughout the country, *The Last Moment* aroused more widespread critical attention than any American picture of the year." Jacobs, "Avant-Garde Production in America," pp. 120–121.

48. Mordaunt Hall, "The Screen: An Impressionistic Study," in *New York Times Film Reviews*, 1: 430.

49. "Ten Best Pictures of 1928," in *Film Daily 1929 Year Book* (New York: John W. Alicoate, 1929), p. 9.

4

Robert Florey and the Hollywood Avant-Garde

Brian Taves

The avant-garde and Hollywood studio production are generally considered opposite poles of the filmmaking spectrum. Their respective goals seem mutually exclusive, the one devoted to the search for art, the other to profit. In the past, however, a unique compatibility existed; the first popular American avant-garde films were created not by independents, but by individuals from within Hollywood who would continue working there. Not only did their avant-garde pictures have a basis in commercial filmmaking, but they would apply their experimental techniques during their subsequent careers. Between 1927 and 1929, William Cameron Menzies, Slavko Vorkapich, and Robert Florey combined to create such avant-garde landmarks as the *The Life and Death of 9413—A Hollywood Extra* and *The Love of Zero*. These films, while made in opposition to the classical style, were embraced by Hollywood, and as a result all three men won even more prestigious assignments within the industry. Robert Florey (1900–1979) is the central figure in this group, since his work most fully exemplified this temporary harmony between Hollywood and the avant-garde. Unlike most avant-garde films, which emphasize moods and emotions rather than a storyline, Florey fully merged representationalism into his plots to allow abstraction and narrative to become co-equal, thereby gaining a mainstream audience. He successfully brought this avant-garde style into his later studio productions, and in one case even remade one of his experimental films into a feature.

Florey's fifty-year career as a writer-director included more than 65 features and 220 filmed television dramas. Born in Paris, he grew up near the studio of film pioneer Georges Méliès, and later moved to Switzerland, where he became active in motion pictures at the age of sixteen. Returning to France four years later, he served as assistant to Louis

Feuillade before his enthusiasm for Hollywood product led him to America in September 1921.[1] Initially a journalist and publicist, he soon advanced to technical and assistant director. Most prominently, he was assistant to Josef von Sternberg, from whom he learned the use of light and shadow in photography—ironically on two pictures later re-shot by other directors. Working for many lesser directors, however, often left Florey frustrated with the conventions of the seamless Hollywood technique:

> The rules didn't have to be followed—was it necessary to spend a lot of money to express an idea?—why should a sequence always be shot in the same order: establishing long shot—medium shot—close ups—over the shoulder shots and reverse shots? Why not express certain things, feelings or sentiments with an insert or a simple single cut—why did we need so many subtitles? Was it not permissible to cut from an extreme long shot to an extreme close up without using intermediary shots?[2]

Florey's goal was to become a full-fledged director, and so in 1923 he wrote and directed an independent two-reel comedy, *Fifty–Fifty*, which found limited distribution. Two years later, he decided to venture toward the avant-garde. He photographed short strips of film showing the bizarre patterns of light and shade produced by the abstract appearance of a hand in motion, using nothing more than a milk bottle, a flashlight, and screens to direct the light. In 1926 he shot tests for a proposed production entitled *The Mad Doctor*, revealing actor Michael Visaroff in a costume, pose, and lighting distinctively reminiscent of *Das Cabinet des Dr. Caligari* (1919). Neither of these experiments was shown publicly, and none of his early shorts survive today. Simultaneously, he directed several low-budget features, to be discussed later in this chapter.

Meanwhile, Florey's reporting on Hollywood had given him the idea for a short picture based on the impressions of an "Everyman" actor who dreams of becoming a star, only to have his hopes crumble.[3] After attending a performance of George Gershwin's *Rhapsody in Blue*, Florey was inspired to write a "continuity in musical rhythm of the adventures of my extra in Hollywood, the movements and attitudes of which appeared to synchronize themselves with Gershwin's notes."[4] The script was worked out in precise detail, shot by shot: "I figure out my scenes—so many scenes, so many feet. You see? Long shot—ten feet. Close-up, four feet. So. I want 1,200 feet and no waste."[5] This planning was necessary because of the high cost of film stock, given that the budget was coming entirely out of Florey's pocket.[6] The final and biggest obstacle, acquiring the use of a camera, was overcome when Florey met Slavko Vorkapich in a restaurant.

> He has a little amateur camera—what they sell for "toy" cameras. It has one lens—a DeVry; I say to Slav, "Slav, I have an idea but not much money—you have a camera and you are a clever painter. Let's make the picture in collaboration and we will split the benefit."[7]

Final preparations and shooting took place over a period of three weeks in late 1927.

Only three professional performers appeared, with the title role enacted by Jules Raucourt, a former leading man who by then was unemployed and nearly forgotten. The vapid star was portrayed by Voya George, a Romanian friend of Vorkapich, and the starlet was played by Adriane Marsh, an authentic extra. The story of *A Hollywood Extra* concerns John Jones, who comes to Hollywood to become a motion picture player. Presenting himself to the representative of the studio establishment, Mr. Almighty, Jones gets a number (9413) inscribed on his forehead. Other performers audition at the same time. One of these (George) has a completely bland, expressionless face, contrasting with Raucourt's evident sincerity. George dons a series of masks, mimicking other well-known actors in an effort to compensate for his own lack of personality. George's vapid "blah-blahs" are greeted with enthusiasm by the studio chiefs and the public, and a star instead of a number is inscribed on his forehead.

When Raucourt appears in a scene opposite George, he is treated with disdain. Even his mask appears dingy in comparison with that of the superficial celebrity. Success eludes Raucourt as he is daily faced with the dreaded sign, "No casting today." Whether auditioning or unemployed, the actors become automata under the direction of a large, pointing hand in the foreground of many shots. Finally, Raucourt dies of privation, his death represented by the cutting of a film strip. He is buried in an expressionist cemetery full of distorted tombstones; one next to his own repeats the omnipresent "No casting today." Despite the mockery of Raucourt's fellow performers, he ascends to Heaven (depicted as located in the opposite direction from Hollywood), where the offensive number is erased and he becomes an angel. The denouement is intended as both a fitting cap to the melodramatic story and a satire on Hollywood's traditional happy endings.[8]

A *Hollywood Extra* has a surreal story rendered in an expressionist manner. Shapes, angles, and disorientation are its visual hallmarks, with three basic types of compositions: miniatures, closeups with live actors, and newsreel-type scenes of Hollywood and the studios. The faces of the three performers are often kept in partial shadow, blocking off part of their features and depriving them of wholeness. A casting director is mocked with an extreme closeup revealing only his mouth stuffed with a cigar, one hand holding a phone and the other shaking a pointed finger. The acting has an overwrought, tormented tone that complements the expressionistic visuals. Miniature sets were constructed out of paper cubes, cigar boxes, tin cans, children's toys, and other odds and ends. They represent buildings and geometric designs, and are characterized by distortion and superimposition, quivering and reflecting light in a myriad of directions according to the mood.

In contrast to the artificial scenes of the city are newsreel-type shots of the streets and local sights of Hollywood. Filmmaking is symbolized by scenes of previews, spotlights criss-crossing the night sky, and moving cameras, reels, and dangling celluloid strips. While authentic in content, these scenes are often shot from a wildly moving or tilted camera, and edited into rapid juxtapositions. This relative objectivity is the false surface of Hollywood: the city, the glitter, and the ceremonies at which the extra marvels. Reversing expectations, these views are announced by the subtitle "Dreams." (The spectacle of this splendor is voraciously and almost literally consumed by the extra, an idea conveyed through a closeup of his face going through exaggerated eating motions.) The purer expressionism of miniatures and closeups is used, not for the dream mode, but to tell a realistic narrative of disillusionment. The reality of Raucourt's experiences is told expressionistically; the glamour and success that turn out to be only the material of dreams are portrayed more objectively.

A *Hollywood Extra* is highly cinematic, without subtitles; even the two captions, "Dreams" and "Success," are created by moving cardboard cutouts with light flashing through and spreading shadows, a fully integrated and visual element. Sound is approximated through the vigorous motions of a hand playing a trombone and closeups looking into the horn of the instrument. Most of the camerawork was done by Florey and Vorkapich, with some additional work by the twenty-eight-year-old Paul Ivano, noted for his cinematography with von Sternberg. All the lighting in the picture was provided by a single 400-watt bulb, with which Vorkapich spectacularly illuminated the miniatures. The actors often had to function as their own lighting men, passing the light from one hand to the other. Gregg Toland, then twenty-three and assistant to George Barnes, had use of a Mitchell camera, which allowed some shots that would have been impossible with the DeVry. These scenes included some three hundred feet of closeups and what Florey called "trick stuff—four or five exposures on one plate."[9]

A *Hollywood Extra* was edited to a one-reel length of 1,200 feet, with special attention to tempo and rhythm. All shots, moods, players' movements, and repetitions of scenes were to be synchronized with *Rhapsody in Blue*. (Sadly, most of this original lyrical quality has been lost in the shortened and mutilated versions still extant, one of which was made from an incomplete negative containing hundreds of splices.) While Vorkapich's famous montage work of later years is foreshadowed, so is Florey's preference for breaking continuity with unanticipated changes in angle, lighting, or distance. For instance, he memorably juxtaposed a suicide to organ music through a series of closeups and contrasting angles when directing the Edgar Wallace gangster melodrama *Dangerous to Know* (Paramount, 1938). The shots alternate between Akim Tamiroff, completely absorbed in playing Tchaikovsky on a pipe organ, and his discarded mistress (Anna May Wong) standing behind him; she haltingly considers reaching out to Tamiroff, then instead plunges a knife into herself.[10]

Upon the completion of A *Hollywood Extra*, Florey showed the film to his friend Charles Chaplin (in 1946, the two would co-direct *Monsieur Verdoux*). Chaplin watched A *Hollywood Extra* five times and then invited the elite of Hollywood to a screening at his home. The audience merely expected one of the comedian's gags, and Florey feared they would not be receptive to his satire. To his surprise, however, "the producers and stars present were vitally interested in this new technique and at the unexpected angles of the shots."[11] The enthusiasm was echoed by Henry King, whom Florey had already served as first assistant on *The Magic Flame* (Goldwyn, 1927). King vividly recalled the event over fifty years later: "Everybody went wild over it. . . . It was way ahead of its time. . . . a stroke of genius. . . . it was the most original thought I ever saw."[12] Florey was cheered, and Douglas Fairbanks offered his facilities to prepare A *Hollywood Extra* for public exhibition. Also among those present was Joseph Schenck, who arranged for the picture to be shown at the new United Artists theater on Broadway, where it was given the presentation that usually accompanies a "big" picture. A special musical score, prepared by Dr. Hugo Riesenfeld and based on *Rhapsody in Blue*, was played by a live orchestra. Starting 21 March 1928, *A Hollywood Extra* played twice nightly for a week with Gloria Swanson in *Sadie Thompson* and was advertised as "the first of the *impressionistic* photoplays to be made in America!" Assorted reviews indicate that *A Hollywood Extra* was shown not only in New York and the Hollywood area, but also in Montreal, Washington, D.C., Philadelphia, and Cleveland. Eventually *A Hollywood Extra* was released by F.B.O. to more than seven hundred theaters in America alone.[13]

A Hollywood Extra, although clearly an avant-garde film, was not only welcomed by Hollywood, but was later remade as a feature. *Hollywood Boulevard* (Paramount, 1936), co-authored and directed by Florey, expanded the central premise of *A Hollywood Extra*. In *Hollywood Boulevard*, the central figure is again an actor, looking for a job amidst the cruel splendors of movieland, dependent on the whims of public fancy and the vagaries of producers. The theme, and Jules Raucourt's appearance as the lead in *A Hollywood Extra*, was echoed in *Hollywood Boulevard* through the appearance of more than two dozen former stars in supporting and cameo roles. Stylistically, *Hollywood Boulevard* opens with an extraordinary credits sequence. Over a jazzy introductory score is a fast-paced montage of streets and buildings, shadows of swinging legs, and the street signs framed crosswise. Credit portraits emerge out of quadruple images, and the entire sequence is shot with a preponderance of diagonals. (The startling angles reflect the disordered and askew nature of movie life, described as "crazy, senseless and exciting.") It ends on a slanted shot of a boulevard street sign as the traffic signal clangs to read "GO" as the story commences; the picture concludes with the sign changing to read "STOP. The movie is a self-conscious historical document, displaying landmarks of the city, capturing its flavor as dreamland and harsh reality, and using locations from nightclubs to the main thoroughfare itself. The city is portrayed as a place of broken dreams and false pretenses, ready to exploit, consume, and discard those who offer themselves to it. As in *A Hollywood Extra*, the direction both makes light of, and pays lip service to, the conventional excesses of such cinematic self-portraits. Florey himself maintained this cynical and affectionate view of the motion picture capital. His lifelong fascination with Hollywood was also shown in *The Preview Murder Mystery* (Paramount, 1936), and such television shows as *The Hollywood Story* and *This Is a Love Story* for the 1953

Loretta Young series, *A Letter to Loretta*, as well as his voluminous writing on filmmaking history.[14]

Following the success of *A Hollywood Extra*, William Cameron Menzies suggested to Florey a collaboration on a new avant-garde work. Menzies, then thirty-one, was set designer on Henry King's *The Woman Disputed* (Goldwyn, 1928), on which Florey was first assistant director; the two had known each other for several years, and would remain lifelong friends. Florey and Menzies co-authored the scenario of *The Love of Zero* (often mistakenly called "The Loves of Zero"). Florey directed, with Nate Stein assisting, and Menzies designed the sets and staging. Made in March 1928 on a budget of two hundred dollars, under the auspices of United Artists, *The Love of Zero* had a 1,200-foot, twelve-minute length.[15] Two Russians were given the leads: Joseph Marievsky, a dancer with Nikita Balieff's popular "Chauve-Souris" panto-mime artists, and Tamara Shavrova; Anielka and Marco Elter and Arthur Hurni completed the cast. (fig. 4.1). Unlike *A Hollywood Extra*, *The Love of Zero* survives in complete form, preserving the original editing.

Noticing the accessibility of the story and style of *A Hollywood Extra*, Florey and Menzies decided this time to film in a considerably more complex manner. The principals, Zero and Beatrix, are patterned after Harlequin and Columbine, but the acting style is even more formal, and the roles are far more vague, than those of the movieland types in *A Hollywood Extra*. Beatrix's clothes resemble the fashions of eighteenth-century Europe, and Zero's curled moustache and elongated top hat complement the architecture of the settings. Like the satirical, numbered Hollywood extra, Zero is an aspiring artist, but Zero's bizarre, ornate appearance makes him even more of a caricature. Taking advantage of the cast's background in ballet, patterns of rhythmic movement are created that utilize and exaggerate nearly every step, emphasizing Zero's contortions and jerky gestures as a way to express his internal emotions.

Since *The Love of Zero* is seldom revived, a plot analysis is in order. *The Love of Zero* opens on a Sunday as Zero, a sensitive, isolated musician, plays a trombone. The closeups of the instrument, amplified through multiple exposures, compensate for the absent sound, a tech-nique reminiscent of *A Hollywood Extra*. As a member of the elite of art, Zero is high above the world, safely viewing it from his balcony. To his surprise and delight, the demure Beatrix admires his music from the courtyard below. As she stands against a wall, next to enormous cutout

Figure 4.1.
Production shot on the set of *The Love of Zero* (1928). *Left to right:* Robert Florey (director),
Tamara Shavrova, Joseph Marievsky, William Cameron Menzies (sets), Edward Fitzgerald
(cameraman)

sunflowers, Zero and Beatrix exchange furtive but rapturous glances. Zero
must wait with eager anticipation for their next rendezvous, becoming giddy
in his expectant hope, the excited movement of his hands echoed by the
shaking of his frilly, lacy cuffs. The "next Sunday" (the days of the week are
shown in a modernistic stained-glass design), Zero comes down from his
apartment to the street, where he and Beatrix meet. While heart-shaped
silhouettes mask the screen, Zero offers Beatrix his heart—a literal valentine
cutout—and she responds in kind as the two hearts become one.

From January through September, Beatrix remains enthralled as Zero
again plays the trombone, this time from high atop a platform. Then a
surprising scroll arrives. Although lovely and loving, Beatrix is a woman
of the world, a woman with a past. She is summoned back to the palace
of the Grand Vizier, Abdul of Afghanistan, and ordered never to see Zero
again. Reading Zero the missive, she looks up at him, as the camera
adopts their contrasting viewpoints. Split screens then unite the two

grief-stricken faces and project their mutual sadness. Just as the two hearts had literally become one, this conjunction of faces indicates that the couple now think and feel as one. They slowly walk to the railroad, past a giant wheel on a street with machines, their two small figures occupying the bottom half of the screen. The mechanical realm proceeds busily above them in a cold, uncaring world.

At this point, the film's plot becomes increasingly surreal, unlike the more concrete externalization of the consciousness of A *Hollywood Extra*. Despairing, Zero returns to his home via "Di Stasse Blotz," where his figure dwarfs the residences. He pauses to read his future in a mammoth book of destiny filled with grotesque and discouraging words. Outside, an organ-grinder begins to play the inexorable tune of fate to which Zero must dance. The organ-grinder is also Zero's musical opposite, representing art in its lowest, most commercial form.

Scenes at the palace follow, and its grandeur is shown through a simple trick shot of candlestick-type objects placed over three sides of the frame, with sound implied through brief shots of a drum beating. The heartbroken Beatrix cannot bear to dance with the other concubines. Meanwhile, the despairing Zero sees another woman loitering invitingly in the street below his balcony and calculatingly hopes she is another Beatrix, but the meeting is not the innocent and ideal coincidence the first encounter had been. The sunflowers are gone, and Zero has not played the trombone to attract her. On bended knee, Zero again offers his heart, but this woman merely laughs, her derision amplified by rapid cutting back and forth between closeups of each party, then multiple exposures of her sneering face, eyes, and mouth. (During Zero's first meeting with Beatrix, the camera gave her an angelic look by multiplying the images of her face.) The humiliated Zero crouches as she marches off in a clipped, businesslike lockstep with two men with whom she strikes up an easy alliance. Zero returns to his miserable loneliness, climbing atop his platform and caressing the bonnet Beatrix had worn when they first met. No longer do the grief-stricken halves of Zero's face match or coincide in size. Then, as candles are extinguished and drums punctuate the final palace scene, Beatrix appears on a catafalque. Her death is announced by the only major intertitle, in order to emphasize the shock of the news.

Zero is despondent. The insistent, merciless organ-grinder returns with ever more labored effort, now switching 90 degrees from a normal, upright stance to a nearly horizontal angle. The camera moves to a closer, darker shot, as the noise becomes deafening to Zero. Having once experienced love, Zero cannot live without it, and he begins to foresee his own death. His union with Beatrix has inevitably led to a fatal and failed mingling with the outside world. Indeed, Zero is wraithlike rather than fully human, entering a room by passing through the door. His life becomes a perpetual nightmare, surrounded by giant, deformed ghouls who leer, laugh, mutter, and point as they surround and overwhelm him (fig. 4.2). Zero sees them filing past him, as if he were already in a coffin; finally a huge hand closes around him, ending his wretched existence. In the end, as Zero's name implies, his music, life, and love count for nothing.

In style as well as narrative, *The Love of Zero* is technically superior to *A Hollywood Extra*. In contrast to the many miniatures and location shots in *A Hollywood Extra*, the sets in *The Love of Zero* are usually of a size commensurate with the actors. Distorted window frames, which even appear in the sky above the organ-grinder, are reminiscent of *Caligari*, a

Figure 4.2.
Still from *The Love of Zero* (1928), directed by Robert Florey, with Joseph Marievsky

characteristic to be repeated in Florey's 1929 Paramount feature *The Hole in the Wall*. The streets and costumes of *The Love of Zero* are echoed in Florey's *Murders in the Rue Morgue* (1932). Apart from its expressionistic lighting and decor, *The Love of Zero* is actually more impressionistic, as a title description correctly announces. For instance, the railroad station is simply expressed by puffs of smoke emerging from an overhead train model, accompanied by the initials "RR" and a conductor's repeated arm gestures. Nearly every shot or scene takes advantage of an oblique angle, a split screen, or distortion created through superimpositions. Often the inmost thoughts of the characters are revealed through multiple, prismatic, and revolving exposures of their face. Larger or smaller portions of the faces of Zero and Beatrix may be grafted together in a single shot. Though variations on these effects are used again and again, the intricacy of their arrangement and combination avoids the impression of repetition.

Whereas *A Hollywood Extra* can be grasped in an initial screening, *The Love of Zero* requires repeated, attentive viewing to absorb the intense abstraction that the technique exercises upon the theme. While *A Hollywood Extra* has a straightforward narrative, with the expressionism serving the plot, *The Love of Zero* is less concerned about the clarity of the effects and the story. Critics reacted with interest and encouragement, but found *The Love of Zero* confusing and lacking the clarity of *A Hollywood Extra*. As Louella Parsons remarked, *The Love of Zero* "certainly carried out the 'arty' idea. It was so impressionistic that most of us had to stand on our heads to understand it. However, Robert Florey deserves a pat on the back for his courage and perhaps his next contribution will be less elusive."[16]

Yet even the abstract visuals were soon incorporated into at least some studio productions. Shots like the superimposed clapping hands in *A Hollywood Extra* were quickly becoming a standard device in Hollywood films. In Menzies' short, *Glorious Vamps* (Joseph Schenck, 1929), the heroine's concluding song appears over a pan of chorus girls as the camera divides them in half, with the halves moving horizontally in opposite directions. Enormous male faces are superimposed, apparently at random. Over a skyscraper set, two more lines of girls are split at cross angles and superimposed to attain an abstraction that would exceed even Busby Berkeley. Simultaneously at Paramount, Florey directed shorts, often showing multiple reflections in musical instruments, or placing white figures against black backdrops, as in the Helen Morgan sequence in *Glorifying the American Girl* (1929). Even an otherwise stage-bound comedy like the feature *The Cocoanuts* (Paramount, 1929) offers such surprising visual touches as credits shot in negative, approximated practical split-screen effects, and shots of musical numbers revealing new perspectives on their movements from high, low, and even overhead angles.

While *The Love of Zero* is unable to match the thematic power of *A Hollywood Extra*, in many ways the narrative, especially during its first half, utilizes the format of the love story. The genre was a favorite of Florey's, and in future years he directed such love stories as *Le Blanc et le Noir* (Braunberger-Richebé, 1931) in France, and in Hollywood *The Man Called Back* (Tiffany, 1932), *Those We Love* (Tiffany, 1932), *Ex-Lady* (Warner Bros., 1933), *The House on 56th Street* (Warner Bros., 1933), and *The Woman in Red* (Warner Bros., 1935). Although the offbeat rendering of the love story form is the crux of *The Love of Zero*, this approach was foreshadowed in Florey's first tries for creative freedom, undertaken in 1926 and 1927. The skill with low budgets and fast shooting that facilitated avant-garde efforts had allowed him to direct and edit four features for poverty-row studios: *That Model from Paris*, which he took over from Louis Gasnier, and *One Hour of Love* (both Tiffany, 1927), *The Romantic Age* (Columbia, 1927), and *Face Value* (Sterling, 1927). *The Romantic Age* and *Face Value* were each made in about ten days for under twenty thousand dollars, and both survive today. They provided the groundwork and practice for his avant-garde work, revealing his penchant for innovation and much of the experimental style, technique, and approach exhibited in *The Love of Zero*. Although shadows, unusual and angled compositions, and the subjective camera were inimical to the classical style, Florey had startling success integrating experimental techniques into the studio system, despite its constraints. Indeed, Florey's real goal from the outset was to mix expressionism and avant-garde methods into studio-made features: "The ideal thing," he wrote early in 1929, "would be to combine artistic ideas, technique, and treatment with the scenarios produced for the general public."[17]

The Romantic Age was sold as a flapper comedy, and Columbia probably expected a directorial cynicism to match a trite script whose introductory title declares: "'Two thousand years ago, A. Sop [*sic*] said 'Romance is *personified* by lovers, *glorified* by an engagement, *petrified* by marriage, and *simplified* by divorce.'" Like many of Florey's studio pictures, *The Romantic Age* offered little substance and was made memorable only by his direction. He turned *The Romantic Age* into a serious love story, with more sentiment and sophistication than melodrama. At the same time, all the romantic scenes are treated with a European sensibility, a light yet knowing and distanced tone that revealed Florey's enormous admiration for the continental approach brought to the genre by Ernst Lubitsch. The plot concerns a flighty woman's maturation as she learns to appreciate the love of a dependable middle-aged man—although neither Alberta Vaughn nor Eugene O'Brien matched the respective youth or age of the characters they play. The danger supposedly inherent in her lifestyle erupts after an innocent flirtation with her suitor's irresponsible younger brother, who leaves her bonds in an unlocked safe where they will be menaced by a fire. Vaughn realizes her error, and the true lovers are reunited with a distinctly Lubitsch touch. She calls on the suitor, her clothes soaked, and after he looks up at the clear, starry sky, she explains that she encountered "a vulgar boatman." Moments later they share a lingering kiss as the camera pans down to reveal the growing puddle beneath her wet dress.

There are many such visuals in *The Romantic Age*. The isolation of objects from their context, breaking them into fragments, reflects the influence of the Russian montage school. In the opening shots, the girl remains unseen as she dresses, the camera focusing first on her feet, then on the application of makeup, then on the roses she lifts. Finally, the heroine is introduced in a closeup via a mirror, followed by the title noting her name and the first full shot of her standing. Later, shots of dancing feet indicate O'Brien's inability to follow her fast steps. The faces of Vaughn's girlfriends, arrested in a speakeasy and taken to jail in a wagon, are scanned by a camera moving alongside at a slightly slower speed. A nearly subjective moving camera photographs the couple's car going downhill, out of control, descending at the same speed until both come to rest at a gas station. One intertitle offers the girl berating her betrothed's brother with a series of oaths, while onscreen one exclamation follows another in shots taken from various angles and directions.

Face Value is a less polished but still interesting film, notable for its careful construction and visual expression of the narrative. Like *The Romantic Age*, *Face Value* is an emotional love story, but it is less traditional, encompassing broken faces as well as broken hearts, and laden with the type of symbolism that would appear in Florey's avant-garde work. *Face Value* is structured around questions of seeing and who sees what, the "face value" or the person behind. Such questions as how the disfigured hero views himself, and how he is perceived by others, are expressed by mirror shots at pivotal moments in the narrative. Another device is the alternation between long shots and closeups to emphasize the protagonist's face or the reactions of others, and his face further serves as an externalization of his anguish. As an intertitle asks, "In a world that takes everything at 'face value,' is there any affliction more cruel than a disfigured face?" Like many of Florey's films, *Face Value* is not only a precursor of the style and excesses of melodramatic film noir, but also contains the themes of torment, love, and empathy that figure in both his features and his experimental work.

The opening battle scenes and parade of the wounded cut to a pan of the pitiful faces of the "Société des Gueules Cassees," whose lonely members find solace only with similarly disabled veterans. They drink to themselves, "To the Broken Faces—may their spirit be unbreakable!" believing that the fortunate ones among their ranks are the dead. The Society's sponsor (played by Gene Gowing) is the protagonist. The bleak story is concerned not with how he was wounded, but with the wounds' effects, asking whether love can withstand such scars. While Gowing wonders whether to risk going home to discover if he is still loved, flashbacks of earlier, happier days are frequent. Daydreaming of the girl he left behind and the handsome man he used to be, Gowing is persuaded to return home after a three-year absence.

Numerous shots accentuate the theme and title, evidencing the German and Russian influence. Florey's touch is evident; Gowing's sympathetic father first sees his son's face through tear-laden eyes, shown almost subjectively, before the camera gradually shifts into focus. However, Gowing's worst fears are confirmed when he again meets his fiancée. She naively closes her eyes when he enters, so that she first happily sees his eyes, then scans down in alarm to the disfigured lower portion of his face. When Gowing initially meets his rival, the latter's eyes are highlighted in a reminder of the unblemished portion of Gowing's face. Editing builds the impact as Gowing overhears the rival tell his fiancée that any marriage would be based merely on pity. He sees the rival's arm around her. The film fades into a medium shot of the couple, then a closeup of the hand patting her shoulder; it then cuts to an extreme closeup of Gowing's jealous eyes, before returning to the closeup of the hand. The picture fades to the rival whispering into her ear, then cuts to a medium shot of Gowing and finally to a long shot of the entire room as he quietly leaves. Back in his room, Gowing looks into the mirror, the camera placed at a low angle, with a single, shaded lamp providing the shadowy illumination. As he reaches out his hands to cover his face, the other "Broken Faces" are superimposed, and his arms go out to embrace them, revealing that the camera is actually photographing the mirror's reflection, not Gowing himself. Seeking refuge in a seedy club, Gowing saves a girl from suicide and reunites her with her lover. The pair inspire Gowing to overcome his own tortured emotions, and he returns to France in a sacrificial gesture. The couple's reunion in France is shown as Gowing gazes sadly into the mirror. (Gowing had first decided to return home after viewing himself in the very same mirror, and looking into it was his first action after a reunion of the Society.) Now his face goes out of focus to reveal his fiancée entering in the background.

The use of another Hollywood genre that permitted experimentation governed Florey's choice of a more straightforward narrative for his third avant-garde film, initiated at the request of the Film Art Guild of New York. Florey worked without a major collaborator, although, as with *The Love of Zero*, Menzies designed some sets. Edward Fitzgerald again served as cameraman. Twenty-six years old, he had worked mainly on independent productions. The result was *Johann the Coffin Maker* (1928), the most ambitious effort so far, costing two hundred dollars. It lasted two and a half reels, it featured a cast of more than twenty, recruited from the set of *The Woman Disputed*, still in production. Filming took place, without any written script, from six o'clock on Saturday night through Sunday morning, with re-takes on Monday night.

Having received an order for a child's coffin on Christmas Eve, old Johann (Agostino Borgato) induces a few of the dead to return from their graves. He offers a bottle of wine to a murderous Apache, a soldier, and a prostitute, asking them to relate how they met their deaths. When they return to their homes beneath the sod, the coffin maker hears a knock at the door. It is his own bride—Death. Together they climb into a casket he built for himself. And he closes down the lid (fig. 4.3).[18]

It was "a Poe-like scenario" with "a dash of Baudelaire and Heine at their bitterest," according to Herman Weinberg, who was to become a close friend of Florey and a fellow member of the avant-garde.[19] *Johann the Coffin Maker* was warmly received by the press; today, despite occasional rumors, it appears to be lost.

Studied through reviews and Florey's stills and frame enlargements, *Johann the Coffin Maker* seems to expand on the surreal deaths in

Figure 4.3.
Still from lost film, *Johann the Coffin Maker* (1929), directed by Robert Florey, with Agostino Borgato

A *Hollywood Extra* and *The Love of Zero* to concentrate on the realm beyond. Its themes and technique have unmistakable echoes throughout Florey's subsequent work, adumbrating his relation to the horror genre. By the end of the very same year, he had directed his first such feature, *The Hole in the Wall.* Here he experimented with the use of sound to create a supernatural mood for scenes of spiritualism, embellished by strange decor, including looming ghosts and twisted windows. During 1931, Florey was adapting the techniques of the avant-garde to the burgeoning Universal horror cycle. He originated the treatment for *Frankenstein,* co-authored its script, and was also originally set to direct. His surviving continuity script reveals detailed plans for far more expressionist compositions, camera movements, setups, and lens, lighting, and special effects than were used in the final film. Florey was switched to the adaptation and direction of *Murders in the Rue Morgue* (1932), and he transformed Poe's story into a remake of *Das Cabinet des Dr. Caligari. Murders in the Rue Morgue* was popularized around the mad scientist theme, and seldom has a Hollywood film been so Germanic in treatment, amplifying the plot with artistic, dark, and expressionistic design and photography. Florey even parodied *Caligari* at Paramount in 1935 with a scene in *The Preview Murder Mystery* in which the makeup of the two ghouls almost precisely repeats that of the specters who haunted Zero to his death (fig. 4.4). Later Florey horror films were no less distinctive: *The Florentine Dagger* (Warner Bros., 1935), *The Face Behind the Mask* (Columbia, 1941), and especially *The Beast with Five Fingers* (Warner Bros., 1946), with its exploration of subjective states.

A year after *Johann the Coffin Maker,* the studios unexpectedly provided Florey with the opportunity for a fourth avant-garde movie. Monta Bell had been at the party where Chaplin first exhibited *A Hollywood Extra.* Appointed manager of Paramount's Astoria studio when it was reopened for sound, Bell was in search of fresh talent and promptly obtained a contract for Florey as a full-fledged director. Astoria became so busy that it was operated around the clock, and Florey was assigned to direct a Gertrude Lawrence musical, *The Battle of Paris* (1929), during the night shift. He took advantage of the unusual hours to make *Skyscraper Symphony,* also known as *Skyscrapers,* interpreting the metropolitan locations of New York City in the form of the popular "city symphony" genre. For three mornings he photographed, with a handheld DeVry, a montage of scenes emphasizing the geometric patterns made by buildings (fig. 4.5). Florey described the one-reeler as an

Figure 4.4.
Still from *The Preview Murder Mystery* (1936), directed by Robert Florey, with Henry Brandon, John George

architectural study of the skyscrapers, "seen from way high or from down shooting up, with wide and sometimes distorted angles, 24mm shots, and quick pan shots with fast editing."[20] One reviewer described *Skyscraper Symphony* as follows:

> Presently a tall, lean shadow flashed on the screen followed by varied shots of buildings, crevices in Wall Street, stone canyons with thin little shadows of sunlight trickling through them, Trinity Tower, a closeup of an office window set in stone like a gaping eye. The most fantastic effects were secured in shooting sheer heights, in a closeup of a detailed cornice, in the meeting of distant skyscrapers like gleaming needle points. Suddenly Times Square loomed ahead with Broadway narrowing in the distance like disappearing tracks. The Metropolitan tower flashed into view with its familiar clock-face. St. Patrick's steeples melted into girders of a steel skeleton rising grimly from the earth. The blank face of a new apartment

Figure 4.5.
Still from film, *Skyscraper Symphony* (1929), directed by Robert Florey

112

house gazed into the camera's eye like a soulless thing of stone gouged with holes that were windows.

It was partly the architectural wonder of New York that made the film so stirring, but, really, it was the artists's touch that moved one, the catching of mood, line, color and feeling in the strange walled city.[21]

Again, the relation to studio filmmaking was direct. Florey, a lifelong advocate of location shooting, had only a few months earlier written and directed a three-reel travelogue of New York City. The movie documented Maurice Chevalier's first days in the United States, and was shot with silent cameras for added mobility. The four-day tour encompassed Greenwich Village, the Bowery, Fifth Avenue, Wall Street, and the skyscrapers, and *Bonjour, New York!* proved very popular with its intended audience in France.

All of Florey's avant-garde films received phenomenal exhibition, both commercially and especially in the art house circuit. Critics heaped praise on *A Hollywood Extra, The Love of Zero, Johann the Coffin Maker, Skyscraper Symphony*, and their young director, giving his films the coverage attending major releases. Florey's own contacts in the industry gained him the attention of prominent individuals, and his background as a publicist had taught him how to marshal the support of journalists and reviewers. All these forces united to promote his films in a way that no outsider could achieve. His presence on both coasts (Hollywood up to 1928, thereafter New York) facilitated press access, and he gave numerous interviews and accounts of his avant-garde activity. He cultivated European interest when Pierre Braunberger, a foreign distributor of his experimental films, hired him to direct some of the earliest French talkies in 1929–1931. While overseas, Florey did another picture that is probably in an avant-garde vein: *Trees of England* (1929), alternately titled *Forests of England*. The film apparently does not survive, and nothing is known beyond Florey's description of it as "a lovely short."[22]

A Hollywood Extra, The Love of Zero, Johann the Coffin Maker, and *Skyscraper Symphony* became the first widely seen American avant-garde works, not only domestically, but also throughout Europe, including England, France, Germany, Italy, and even the Soviet Union. Their clear indebtedness to German Expressionism endowed them with the unmistakable aura of art needed for American avant-garde films of the time. A cynical reviewer for *Variety* even wondered whether *A Hollywood Extra* was "an unannounced foreign-made short."[23] By contrast, the 5th

Avenue Playhouse in New York advertised "A Marvellous Program for Jaded Movie-Lovers: The 'Caligarian' Works of a New Film Discovery—Robert Florey, Sponsored by Charles Chaplin!" The triple bill consisted of *The Life of 9413, The Love of Zero, The Coffin Maker,* and, in small print, "as an added attraction—Harold Lloyd in *The Freshman.*" In mid-June 1928, the Keith–Albee Cameo, at 42nd and Broadway, advertised the American premiere of Ivan Moskvin in *The Station Master,* "And In Addition—Remarkable Film made for $97—*Suicide of a Hollywood Extra,* An FBO Novelty Endorsed by Chaplin & Fairbanks." As the first of the four, *A Hollywood Extra* was something entirely new, in both style and substance; more than any other American film, it initiated the avant-garde in this country.

Florey could never have predicted this positive reception. Together, Florey, Menzies, and Vorkapich proved that it was possible to take a hiatus with the avant-garde and return to the studio system, where they were promoted for their experimental efforts and began to apply their innovations to mainstream filmmaking. Vorkapich became prominently associated with the artistry of montage sequences, contributing to a form of stylistic transition that became fashionable in the 1930s. These sequences facilitated experimental shots and editing, yet became fully integrated as a convention of Hollywood filmmaking. Vorkapich brought a theoretician's abstract approach to cinema, whereas both Florey and Menzies preferred the practical challenge of converting commercial production to artistic ends. While Menzies applied his genius for design and production to many great films, his directorial undertakings were usually in collaboration, and Florey was unique in achieving the comparative autonomy of a career as a director of features. Yet he always remained sympathetic to the avant-garde, and his own artistic frustration with the producer interference inherent in the studio system caused him to generally avoid long-term contracts. Others also found benefits in an association with the avant-garde. Gregg Toland soon became one of Hollywood's leading cinematographers. Although Paul Ivano and Edward Fitzgerald were identified with independent production rather than contract assignments, both ultimately became part of the industry. Only the actors in the shorts failed to achieve new prominence: Agostino Borgato remained a supporting player, Joseph Marievsky rarely rose above extra parts, and Jules Raucourt gradually left the industry.

Prior to *A Hollywood Extra, The Love of Zero,* and *Johann the Coffin Maker,* aspiring artists had regarded individual expression through the cinema as an impossible goal. In the industry, the structure of producers, the star system, and distribution presented seemingly insurmountable standardizing pressures. To avoid such conformity, the artist would have to make the film independently, and the costs of financing such a venture seemed prohibitive. Even von Sternberg's *The Salvation Hunters* (1925), whose $5,000 budget had appeared to approach the lower limit, was still well beyond the range of an ambitious single artist. However, the small cost of the pictures made by Florey, Menzies, and Vorkapich placed the potential for independent filmmaking in almost anyone's hands. Although they possessed advantages from the outset that were unavailable to true amateurs and outsiders, their success inspired a flood of experimental movies utilizing the expressionistic style. They succeeded in establishing a distinctly American avant-garde film, one that absorbed foreign styles, found an audience, and directly influenced studio production.

NOTES

1. Florey described these experiences in "Une saison dans la cage a mouches avec Feuillade," *Cinema 62* 67 (June 1962): 41–55.

2. Letter, Robert Florey to Don Shay, 12 August 1972.

3. "Young Director Here Describes His Impressionistic Film Drama," unidentified newspaper clipping (n.d.), Scrapbook 1928–29, Florey collection (private). Florey's scrapbooks provide hundreds of clippings from trades and newspapers, not all of which are accompanied by citations. The author wishes to thank Mrs. Virginia Florey for generously providing complete access to all of her late husband's papers.

4. Robert Florey, *Hollywood d'hier et d'aujourd'hui* (Paris: Editions Prisma, 1948), p. 145.

5. Kay Small, "He Made a Movie for $97!" *Hollywood Magazine*, 23 March 1928, p. 7.

6. A. L. Woolridge, "$97 Movie Made in Hollywood Kitchen," *Modern Mechanics*, n.d., p. 152, Scrapbook 1928–29, Florey collection.

7. Small, "He Made a Movie for $97!" p. 7.

8. Jack Spears, *Hollywood: The Golden Era* (New York: A. S. Barnes, 1971), p. 342.

9. Small, "He Made a Movie for $97!" p. 29.

10. Florey's skill in editing is also exhibited in the surviving two reels of silent 16mm film he shot during his 1937 trip to Asia. One sequence of the

embarkation of a steamer—beginning with Florey and fellow director Nick Grinde waving and ending on a child and a bouquet—provides a virtuoso demonstration of this ability. The mood of farewell is captured in a flurry of activity, the crowd waving flags and thousands of light streamers connecting boat and dock. They flutter in the wind, with departure foretold by their decreasing density and buoyancy. In between these shots numerous changes of camera angle take place, first from one end of the ship, then the other, as Florey reveals the visual poetry inherent in this ritual. Isolated details are picked out from the mass of humanity: a girl choking back tears and dabbing them from her face; one man with a camera and another lighting a pipe; a mounted life preserver with the ship's name and home port; a saddened old man and a sleeping baby.

Vorkapich had no role in either the scenario or the direction of *A Hollywood Extra*, his contribution being limited to the set design and miniature lighting. However, Florey generously insisted on sharing equal credit for "realizing" the picture, using the French term for filmmaking. Vorkapich's name was later written into the F.B.O. distribution contract by Florey's own hand. While Vorkapich did nothing to promote the film at the time, in subsequent years, when it became recognized as a classic, he tried to claim more and more responsibility, fabricating accounts of the film's production. A few later critics regrettably accepted Vorkapich's word, although contemporary accounts of the picture's production uniformly record Florey as the dominant artistic influence.

11. Florey, *Hollywood d'hier et d'aujourd'Hui*, p. 145.

12. Interview with Henry King, Los Angeles, 28 July 1981.

13. "As Is," *Close Up* 2 (June 1928): 5.

14. Florey had an early appreciation of the cinema's heritage and a passion for film lore, becoming known as one of the outstanding chroniclers of Hollywood and movie history, for which he won the Legion of Honor from his native country in 1950. He wrote on the history of Hollywood, always in French, until his death; his last book, an illustrated history of the early studios entitled *Hollywood Village*, was published posthumously in 1986. See Brian Taves, "Robert Florey, Hollywood's Premier Director-Historian," in *Southern California Quarterly* 70 (Winter 1988): 427–449.

15. *The Love of Zero* was the only production at UA other than *The Woman Disputed*, according to the daily shooting schedule, as listed in the *Daily Screen World*, 31 March 1928, p. 4. The author is grateful to the British Film Institute for making a video copy of *The Love of Zero* available to Virginia Florey in 1988, which has permitted careful study of this scarce film. An identical copy is to be found at the Museum of Modern Art and at George Eastman House.

16. Louella O. Parsons, "Filmarte Theater Opened with Swedish production," *Los Angeles Examiner*, 11 May 1928.

17. See Robert Herring, "Art in the Cinema: The Work of Robert Florey," *Creative Art* 4 (1 May 1929): 360.

18. Irene Thirer, "Fifth Avenue Playhouse's Fine Program," unidentified newspaper clipping (n.d.), Scrapbook 1928–29, Florey collection.

19. Herman Weinberg, "A Trio of Thrillers," unidentified newspaper clipping (n.d.), Scrapbook 1928;nd29, Florey collection.

20. Letter, Robert Florey to Anthony Slide, n.d. *Skyscraper Symphony* may survive at the Gosfilmofond archive in Moscow, and would be a leading candidate for repatriation.

21. Marguerite Tazelaar, "Amateurs Point the Way," *Amateur Movie Makers* 6, no. 6 (September 1929): 599.

22. Robert Florey, Photoalbum I: 1900–31, Florey collection. In Hollywood, *The Love of Zero* played for a week at the Filmarte Theatre at 1228 Vine Street south of Sunset, on a bill headed by Gosta Ekman in *The Golden Clown*, preceded by *Moods of the Sea*, "A Filmarte-tone (our own invention) by Robert Bruce," and *News in Pictures*. In Philadelphia, *The Life and Death of 9413 — A Hollywood Extra* netted $32 in one week and was shown with *The Light of Asia*; Florey's short received considerably more praise than the main attraction. *The Love of Zero* netted $25 in New York; the French rights for it and *A Hollywood Extra* were sold for $390. *The Coffin Maker* later played the Filmarte, during late June and early July 1928, on a bill headed by *Salome*, in which Florey had played a bit as a Montmartre Bohemian at the request of Alla Nazimova, a friend. Rounding out the program were *News in Pictures* and *The Battle of Elderbush Gulch*. *The Life and Death of 9413*, *The Coffin Maker*, and *The Love of Zero* played together with Ivan Mosjoukine in *His Unknown Child* at the Russian-American Art Club at 5525 Harold Way in Hollywood on 22 June 1928.

Some sales figures are included in Symon Gould's Statement on Account of Distribution to Florey, 21 April 1929, Florey collection. Ironically, Florey never made a cent from the picture's distribution, and the original negatives were lost while in Gould's care during Florey's European sojourn in 1930. Gould had kept all profits on account against printing and storage costs.

23. *Variety*, 20 June 1928.

5

Americans in Paris
Man Ray and Dudley Murphy

WILLIAM MORITZ

Paris in the 1920s and the "Lost Generation" of American artists and writers who found satisfaction there in exile have become legendary. It should come as no surprise that this golden age of wild living and experimental creativity had an American filmmaking component, yet American experimental filmmakers are not commonly identified with this scene. Why?

Part of the problem may be misidentification. The American photographer Francis Bruguière (born in San Francisco on 16 October 1879) had belonged to the circle of experimental artists around Alfred Stieglitz at Gallery 291 in New York, and had been assigned to photograph Thomas Wilfred's 1921 experiments with his Clavilux color organ.[1] Wilfred's "lumia," fluid color projections, so impressed Bruguière that he began planning to make moving pictures that would extend his own photography into the realm of time. The results were an unfinished "surrealistic" film, *The Way* (1923), starring Sebastian Droste (partner of the notorious Anita Berber, dancer of vices) and, after he moved to London 1927, the abstract *Light Rhythms*, completed in 1931. In *An Introduction to the American Underground Film*, Sheldon Renan lists Bruguière as a "Belgian," following Hans Richter's error in the 1947 *Art in Cinema* catalogue.[2]

Some experimental films of this era seem to be lost: the opera diva Grace Moore recounts in her memoirs how the writers Charles MacArthur and F. Scott Fitzgerald (together with the eccentric American playboy Ben Finney) devised the scenario for a parody movie that was shot at Moore's villa in Cap d'Antibes in the summer of 1926.[3] Moore played Princess Alluria, the most wicked woman in Europe, and her friend Ruth Goldbeck played the farmer's daughter. MacArthur and

118

Fitzgerald painted the film's titles on the wall of Moore's villa, which proved embarrassing, since many of them contained obscene words. Jerome Hill remembered this film (which may have been entitled *Ob-Seen*) as "rather like a Kuchar brothers' film," but no print seems to have survived.

The most interesting case of Americans making experimental films in Europe is undoubtedly that of Man Ray and Dudley Murphy, whose role as primary filmmakers of the film known as *Ballet Mécanique* is usually ignored when this film is listed and discussed as a film by the French painter Fernand Léger—astonishingly so, since both Man Ray and Dudley Murphy can boast a filmography of several distinguished and interesting films, while Léger never learned the fundamental crafts of filmmaking and made no other film on his own.

Man Ray (born in Philadelphia, 27 August 1890) had made at least two experiments with film in New York before his first trip to France: an attempt to make a stereoscopic film of Marcel Duchamp's rotary discs, and a film in which he played a barber shaving off the pubic hair of Baroness Else von Freytag-Loringhoven.[4]

In Paris Man Ray created the wonderful three-minute film *Return to Reason* (*Le Retour à la Raison*) for the Dada "Soirée du Coeur à Barbe" on 6 July 1923. Some of the images in *Return to Reason* are made with his "rayograph" technique of laying objects on unexposed film and flashing them for an instant so that the objects produce their own images in pure light without any camera or lenses. Other imagery includes a variety of camerawork that also challenges the viewer to re-evaluate what a "movie" is: scenes of "moving" lights at night, a printed Dada poem by Man Ray (consisting only of dots and dashes) "set in motion" by jiggling it from side to side, a roll of paper "unreeling" before your eyes, the grid from an egg carton rotating on a string so that it "projects" moving shadows on a wall, and a textured window curtain that "projects" (both in positive and negative) light patterns on the moving torso of a nude woman. The editing further reinforces this reflexive contemplation: rayograph dust cuts to a field of daisies that is similar in texture. In the midst of a frenetic dance of pins and thumbtacks, the still image of Man Ray's painting *Danger/Dancer* is shockingly quiet except for a tendril of smoke swirling gently in front of it. As Elizabeth Hutton Turner pointed out,[5] it was the very "American tempo" that the French appreciated in Man Ray's film—which in fact shared the program with another American experimental film, Paul Strand and Charles Sheeler's *Manhatta*.

Man Ray also participated in another film project with a less favorable conclusion. At the Dada "Evening of the Bearded Heart," he was approached by a young French filmmaker, Henri Chomette (brother of René Clair), who told Man Ray that he was working on an abstract film not unlike *Return to Reason*, but had run out of money.[6] Chomette suggested that perhaps the Comte Etienne de Beaumont, a mutual friend, might fund them if they collaborated on a film project. De Beaumont agreed to put up the money, but insisted that the film should not be all abstract, but rather must contain some scenes of beautiful women comparable to the fine still photography of Man Ray. Chomette and Man Ray completed the film in 1924 and named it *À Quoi Rêvent les Jeunes Films* (*What Do Young Films Dream About?*), a parody of the popular question "What do young girls (*filles*) dream about?" De Beaumont was delighted with the film's madcap Dada nonsense and its mysterious "surreal" moods—and its "American tempo." He insisted on keeping the negative and distributed the film as a film by Comte Etienne de Beaumont, with camerawork by Chomette and Man Ray—much to the chagrin of the actual filmmakers. De Beaumont commissioned a score for the film, composed by Roger Desormière for a chamber ensemble. The film ran about twenty minutes when it was screened at the London Film Society on 20 December 1925 in the count's presence. But de Beaumont refused to send a print of the film to Germany for the historic "Absolute Film" screening of 3 May 1925 at the UFA Theatre in Berlin, in which for the first time the German avant-garde films of Viking Eggeling and Walter Ruttmann were shown together with *Ballet Mécanique* (1924) and *Entr'acte* (1924). Chomette and Man Ray's indignation now reached a boiling point: they arranged a supposed photo session at de Beaumont's home, and while the count was busy posing for Man Ray, Chomette stole the negative of *What Do Young Films Dream About?* The two filmmakers cut the film apart so each could exhibit his own contributions: Chomette's portions became *Cinq Minutes de Cinéma Pur* (1925), while Man Ray's sections were incorporated into his next film, *Emak Bakia* (1926; fig. 5.1), which closely resembled the overall structure of *What Do Young Films Dream About?*

Simultaneous with this debacle was the uncannily similar making of *Ballet Mécanique*. Dudley Murphy also met Man Ray as a result of the Dada "Evening of the Bearded Heart," and proposed that they collaborate on an experimental film. Murphy (born 10 July 1897) brought considerable film credits to the project. His father had been head of the art school

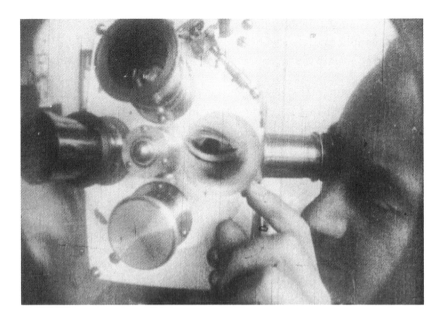

Figure 5.1.
Frame enlargement from *Emak Bakia* (1926), directed by Man Ray, with Man Ray

at Harvard University, and Dudley had attended the Massachusetts Institute of Technology and Cal Tech before becoming a pilot in World War I. Stationed in England, he flew bombing missions over Germany and ended up in Paris for a victory parade. After the war, he spent a year working as an art director and camera apprentice in Hollywood studios, as well as writing movie reviews for the *Los Angeles Evening Express*. He became involved with Theosophy, and decided to produce independent experimental shorts that would combine the best of music, dance, and visual arts into a "*Gesamtkunstwerk*"—and could, coincidentally, play in regular movie theaters as part of the live stage "prologues" that were very popular then. He shot three of these ten-minute "Visual Symphony" shorts during 1920 in California. The first, *The Soul of the Cypress*, was synchronized to Claude Debussy's *Prelude to the Afternoon of a Faun* and featured Murphy's new wife, Chase, being pursued among the picturesque trees on "the rock-bound coast" of Point Lobos.[7] The heroine of his second film, *Aphrodite*, was Katherine Hawley, a dancer from the Isadora Duncan and Ruth St. Denis schools, who became Dudley's wife two years later; she arose from the sea at the grottos of La Jolla and danced among the eucalyptus trees above the beaches of Los Angeles. The third Visual Symphony, *Anywhere out of the World* (following Baudelaire's prose poem), again starred Chase as a nymph bathing in the pools of the canyons near Palm Springs.

In September 1920 Murphy went to New York hoping to secure financial backing and get some of his films shown in the big first-run theaters, where they might be reviewed and attract the attention of distributors. In October he signed a contract with the Community Motion Picture Bureau to finance four artistic shorts, which he apparently completed even though Community ceased in December to pay the $500 monthly installments it had agreed to. Although Community seemed to consider the arrangement "dissolved," Murphy sued and in late June 1921 was awarded $2,500 in back payments.[8]

Two weeks later, *The Soul of the Cypress* premiered as part of the prologue to the feature *Conquest of Canaan* at the prestigious Rivoli Theatre on Broadway in New York. The prologue also included an orchestra playing *Scheherazade*, three dancers doing "Danse de Nymphes," and three opera singers—as well as a film comedy and some organ selections. But *The Soul of the Cypress* was the hit of the program. The *New York Globe* believed that it "points the way to a new field of motion picture theater entertainment," and *Film Daily* echoed that "it breaks away completely from the stuff that has been repeated so often, and makes a decided step forward both in an artistic sense, and in pictorial qualities."[9] The critic for the *New York Times* praised Murphy's "striking photographic works, distinctively composed and expressive," but complained that "the story of a dryad and a mortal . . . is too thin and broken to be effective"—which leaves open the question of whether this was really intended to be a "story" or merely a motif or metaphor in an essentially lyrical, abstract composition.[10] In any case, *The Soul of the Cypress* was repeated for a second week at the equally prestigious Rialto Theatre in New York (a rare achievement), and the *New York Times* cited it among the best pictures of the year, with the comment that "the camera can still charm by purely photographic effects" and that Murphy's film was a "picture with lyric quality."[11]

The fine quality of Murphy's camerawork was no accident; he was a dedicated professional. He spent the month of August 1921 at Dartmouth College, doing research in the Physics Department on lenses and camera technology.[12] Perhaps he developed there the faceted, beveled lenses that he would use later for *Ballet Mécanique* and *Black and Tan* (1929).

How many films did Murphy make at this time? In December 1921 the Community Motion Picture Bureau launched a counter-lawsuit against him, trying to recover either $3,000 (a sizable amount of money in that depression year) or the negatives to four short films that Murphy had supposedly made with monies it advanced: *Aphrodite, Anywhere out of the World, The Soul of the Cypress* (which we know he made in California), and *The Way of Love.*[13] Community claimed that Murphy had taken possession of these completed films. An earlier article notes that Murphy had finished two films synchronized with music by Beethoven and Debussy, and subsequent articles mention the use of the *Moonlight* Sonata and themes from *Peer Gynt* and *The Flying Dutchman* in Murphy films.[14] Another article lists the music used in all twelve Visual Symphonies in production, including Debussy's *Afternoon of a Faun*, Beethoven's *Pastoral* Symphony, Tchaikovsky's *Nutcracker* Suite and *Marche Slave*, Rimsky-Korsakoff's *Scheherazade*, Schumann's *Scenes from Childhood*, Mendelssohn's *Fingal's Cave*, and an excerpt from Gilbert and Sullivan's *Pirates of Penzance.*[15] Unfortunately, we can not tell which of the known film titles may have been synchronized with which music, and thereby establish how many films Murphy had actually completed. To compound the problem, just a few weeks later (29 January 1922), a film by Dudley Murphy called *The Romance of the White Chrysanthemum* opened at the Rialto Theatre in New York.[16] Was this a completely new film, or a re-named version of one of the earlier titles? Recall that 1921 was a year not only of financial depression, but also of drug, sex, and murder scandals (involving Wallace Reid, William Desmond Taylor, Fatty Arbuckle), which ultimately led to Hays Code censorship—so perhaps *Aphrodite* and *The Way of Love* were too risqué-sounding for 1922! If *The Romance of the White Chrysanthemum* was a new film, then Murphy would seem to have completed six of the Visual Symphonies.

That same month, Murphy was interviewed by *Moving Picture World* magazine about his Visual Symphonies.[17] He foresaw from his films a revolution comparable to the revolution in music appreciation that resulted from phonograph recording. The specific film he speaks about, *Danse Macabre*, was accompanied by the symphonic poem by Saint-Saëns and starred Adolph Bohm (a prominent Russian dancer who had performed in Diaghilev's company and the Metropolitan Opera ballet) as the young hero.[18] Ruth Page dances his lover, and Olin Howland lurks as a sinister Death. Bohm's choreography is lit in sensitive chiaroscuro by

Figure 5.2.
Frame enlargement of animation sequence of the Grim Reaper from *Danse Macabre* (1922), directed by Dudley Murphy. Courtesy of George Eastman House

Francis Bruguière, and follows the story of a couple fleeing the plague who take refuge in a remote castle, where Death still stalks them. Murphy takes considerable pains to give the otherwise somewhat stagey and conventional dancing a fresh envelope. He uses quite a bit of animation, which was rendered by F. A. A. Dahme, a commercial animation house that advertised in the trade papers that its staff could turn out titles in twenty-four hours (fig. 5.2). The title itself is composed of slim animated figures of Deaths and maidens that bend to form the letters of "Danse Macabre," delightfully recalling Erté's designer alphabets (fig. 5.3). The opening sequence establishing the locale—a clock in a church tower strikes midnight as bats expectantly look on, the Devil/Death seizes his violin and plays, the lovers scurry toward the deserted castle—is all rendered in animation. Once the lovers are inside the castle, the live dancers perform their pantomimes and choreogra-

Figure 5.3.
Frame enlargement of title animation from *Danse Macabre* (1922), directed by Dudley Murphy, animation by F. A. A. Dahme. Courtesy of George Eastman House

phies, neatly planned to synchronize with the musical score. Death now stalks them as a live-action Devil, but he is depicted in superimposition to give him an unnatural presence.

Danse Macabre (perhaps his only surviving early film) was certainly not typical of Murphy's filmmaking. We know from the reviews of *The Soul of the Cypress* that it contained superb lyrical landscape photography, and *Danse Macabre* is shot completely on a studio set. We also know that it was made rather quickly, and under the stress of a law suit. Furthermore, Bolm, as a ballet star who had danced the work on stage, may have exerted pressure to have his choreography recorded in a certain way. At first viewing, it may be hard to see the film as extremely avant-garde, but considering the prominent role that dance and musical interpretation would play in experimental film—from Walter Ruttmann's *In the Night* and Emlen Etting's *Oramunde* (1933) to Maya Deren and Sara Arledge—*Danse Macabre* must be seen as an unusual, adventurous "art film."

Before leaving New York, Murphy made a film for Pat Powers' Film Booking Office (probably a comedy short), a puppet animation film with the painter Jerome Brush, and a feature film, *High Speed Lee* (1923), based on J. P. Marquand's society story "Only a Few of Us Left."

Murphy's desire to ensure correct synchronization of music in his films led him to Europe, where experimental sound systems were being tested out in both Berlin and Paris. He also visited England, where he collaborated on an experimental film with the artist Will Dyson, and Italy, where he shot a Visual Symphony (starring Katherine Hawley Murphy) synchronized to "O Sole Mio." When he saw the more rigorous and imaginative work of Man Ray and Chomette in Paris, he was attracted to the idea of more radical filmmaking, and approached Man Ray as a possible collaborator. Murphy had brought with him the faceted, beveled lenses that could produce kaleidoscopic imagery on film. With Man Ray, Murphy shot "kaleidoscope" footage of still-life arrangements, a parrot, Murphy himself, and Man Ray's mistress, Kiki, in flat white mime makeup. They also walked the streets of Paris filming shop windows, traffic, sights in an amusement park (including a swinging statue of Uncle Sam), and arranged some mock-picture-postcard scenes of Katherine Murphy sniffing flowers and swinging. They also shot erotic footage of each other (Dudley and Katherine Murphy, Man Ray and Kiki), which was calculated to be intercut ironically between shots of pistons and other machine parts pumping up and down.

After shooting this considerable chunk of footage, carefully planned for a satirical Dada montage, they ran out of money. The American poet Ezra Pound had suggested that Fernand Léger could afford to finance a film and would gladly do so, since he was in the throes of cinephilia. Pound also suggested that the American heiress Natalie Barney, famous lesbian hostess and patron of the arts, would gladly underwrite a musical score by the young American prodigy George Antheil, which in fact she did. Man Ray, however, wanted nothing to do with such a diverse collaborative project (he was already beginning to have doubts about the Chomette/de Beaumont film), and particularly did not want to work with Léger, both because he knew Léger had no sense of humor (an area where the witty Man Ray and the jovial Murphy had gotten along fine), and because he suspected correctly that Léger would want to claim the film as his own. Man Ray warned Murphy and insisted that his own participation be kept secret, and so the name of one key collaborator disappeared from the film's credits. Within ten years, Murphy's name would disappear from the credits also.

This state of affairs is mirrored in the texts quoted by Judi Freeman in an article that presents the best account published so far of the film's making.[19] In *Self Portrait* Man Ray wrote: "Dudley realized *Ballet Mécanique*, which had a certain success, with Léger's name." This comes as close to the truth as one can without violating the agreement not to mention Man Ray's contribution (which Murphy carefully respected). Free-man assumed that Léger had in fact "made" *Ballet Mécanique*, as he claimed after the fact. Yet "making" a film requires equipment and skills that Léger did not have, while Man Ray and Murphy both did. Freeman tries to demonstrate that Léger had filmmaking expertise; she says, for example, that Léger's "first hands-on participation was in the making of Abel Gance's *La Roue* (The Wheel), in 1922," when in fact Léger merely observed some location shooting and wrote a publicity article about the film.[20]

Léger's actual role in creating *Ballet Mécanique* seems rather suspect. The title "Ballet Mécanique" was used by Man Ray's friend Francis Picabia on the cover of the August 1917 issue of his magazine, *391*, published in New York. The cover shows an assembly of mechanical parts that ironically resembles the capital of a classical Greek column.[21] In the July 1917 issue, Picabia had depicted "Américaine," the American girl, as a light bulb with the words "flirt" and "divorce" reflected right-side-up and upside-down in the curved surfaces of the glass, prefiguring the reflections in the swinging glass balls in *Ballet Méca-nique*. In the face of this, the claims that Antheil or Pound or Léger may have invented this title seem absurd.

In terms of the footage included in *Ballet Mécanique*, what might Léger have planned or had Murphy shoot? Man Ray was adamant that he and Murphy had shot all the footage using Kiki—"You don't loan out your mistress, do you?" he said—as well as all the open-air footage on the streets and in Luna Park. Murphy corroborates this in an interview given at the time of a New York screening of *Ballet Mécanique*.[22] Along with his discussion of "rhythmic and dynamic tempo," Murphy, who identifies himself as the key filmmaker (fig. 5.4), reproduces pictures of the stocking-model legs and kitchen utensils[23] mirrored in the kaleidoscopic lenses, as well as some machine parts, as examples of his ideas and work. In his unpublished memoir, "Murphy by Murphy," he further identifies the shot of the washerwoman climbing the stairs as his in idea and execution, including the looped editing, and also relates how he drove through the streets of Paris with the stocking legs over his shoulders, screaming—a scene one can hardly imagine Léger tolerating.[24] We know more plunging pistons were shot to be intercut with the pornographic footage of Man Ray and Murphy. What was left over for Léger to do—except possibly the pure geometric circles and triangles. Of all the supposedly preliminary sketches and plans by Léger, only the animation sequences of geometric forms seem to have been realized.[25] The wooden

Figure 5.4.
Still from *Ballet Mécanique* (1924), directed by Dudley Murphy, with Dudley Murphy.
Photograph by author

model for the animated "Cubist Charlie" is, of course, Léger's—but did Murphy shoot the animation, and did he, therefore, make the crucial decisions about gestures? It is not even certain that Léger had the idea of tinting, as seen in the prints at the Museum of Modern Art in New York and the Nederlands Filmmuseum in Amsterdam, although he colored the pure geometric forms in contrasting colors. In *Danse Macabre* the scenes are tinted night-time blue, but the eyes of the Devil/Death are hand-tinted red. The *Ballet Mécanique* print at Anthology Film Archives, which is supposedly the print screened at the film's premiere in Vienna in 1924, contains large sections that are copied in black-and-white from an edited original (probably Murphy's finished edit), and among those passages are frames that show signs of having been copied from a tinted original.[26]

In Léger's so-called preliminary plans, he mentions "showing a whole page of a newspaper advertising."[27] One might suggest that the mock "headline" reading, "Someone stole a pearl necklace worth 5 million" might be a realization of Léger's plan. But here we come to a crucial question of style. In the portions of *Ballet Mécanique* that we know originated with Man Ray and Murphy, an ironic spirit pokes Dada fun at the seriousness of Machine Modernism, at Futurist and Purist gravity and utopianism. Kiki's face is whitened like a clown's, and her exaggerated expressions, intercut with machinery, nonsense, and the washerwoman loop, serve to remind us that human emotions, the smiles and frowns we assume constitute profound signs of thought and feeling, are in fact predictable muscular functions, as perfunctory as the "work" of the pistons or the "mechanical work" of the washerwoman. The "pictorial" sentimental scenes of Katherine Murphy playing in the swing and smelling a flower that bracket the film convey a similar satirical perspective. And that sarcastic wit would certainly be quite pronounced in the scenes that intercut pistons with erotic activity—scenes that Léger hired someone to cut out of the original and virtually destroyed.[28] The "pearl necklace" sequence is injected with the same Dada irreverence, stringing out the zeros into absurd multiplications (which occasionally parody the abstract geometric circles), and forcing the puns on *collier* from "necklace" to "horse collar" to "guillotine," the necklace few wear gladly.

Léger's "Cubist Charlie Chaplin" is not very funny. The basic idea of the Tramp as a Cubist image might have been funny had the Cubists themselves not collaged many pop-culture, "low" images into their paintings. And the animation of Léger's Charlot sculpture (perhaps done by technicians at Gaumont, if not by Murphy) has no humorous direction, no gag: he just nods hello and goodbye. Even the Charlot graphic reproduced in the *Peinture Cinéma Peinture* catalogue along with Léger's so-called "Humor in Art" is not primarily funny.[29] Compared with the incisive wit of Duchamp's moustached Mona Lisa, Léger's labored tale (Mona Lisa loves Chaplin, he couldn't care less and leaves, she commits suicide, all the kings and emperors of the world attend her funeral) seems flat. Léger's painted nude women do not smile, but Kiki sparkles. Léger's painted machinery is glamorized and elegant; *Ballet Mécanique*'s machinery is peculiar and grotesque and menacing and finally (especially considering the twenty-minute running time of the earliest prints) oppressively aggressive. Léger loved machines; *Ballet Mécanique* does not.

There can be no doubt that *Ballet Mécanique* is a film made by committee, especially in the numerous revised versions that Léger had prepared later. There can be no doubt that Dudley Murphy was the primary filmmaker, even though the amateurs Pound and Léger hounded him in his editing room, demanding their share of the glory. Standish Lawder admits, "Henri Langlois believes Murphy's hand in *Ballet Mécanique* was considerable, particularly in the editing, where Léger would have had no practical experience,"[30] yet he continues to treat the film as if it were Léger's! Similarly, Freeman comes to the untenable conclusion that "Léger's evolving vision dominated that of Pound, Man Ray, and Murphy. . . . When Léger and Murphy sat down at the editing table, the rapid montage that Léger had learned by watching Abel Gance dominated his editing style"[31]—quite forgetting that Man Ray's films also show rapidly changing images and rhythmic intercutting, which was what attracted Murphy to him in the first place. And she quotes Murphy's claim that he developed the editing rhythms himself by trial and error.

Man Ray was right: without the glamour of Léger's name, *Ballet Mécanique* would probably not have been so successful or so long remembered. Murphy's own fortunes left much to be desired. He returned to America after completing the editing of *Ballet Mécanique*, having agreed with Léger that he would have the rights to the film there while Léger would have the rights in Europe. Although *Ballet Mécanique* was greeted with amazement in the United States (Murphy had a black percussionist accompany it at the U.S. premiere), it did not lead to offers of funding for further experimental work. Murphy was hired as assistant director to Rex Ingram for the feature *Mare Nostrum*, which was shot in France in 1925. During the 1920s and 1930s, he worked as writer or director on seventeen features for the whole range of Hollywood studios; he also shot two features in Mexico during the 1940s, one, *Yolanda*, about a Russian ballerina on tour in Mexico City. Many of these were overtly B pictures, but Murphy directed well and regularly injects imaginative and kinetic moments. In the 1932 *Sport Parade*, for example, he sets a key conversation in a Harlem nightclub where we see the distorted shadows of dancers fractured through kaleidoscopic lenses, and he makes dynamic scene transitions such as having an "exit" sign begin to whirl, then dissolve into a turning hubcap, then dissolve into a clock showing that Joel McCrea is late. Later in the same film he shoots a vital conversation with a long shot of the whole barroom, with the gossipers small against the right side of the frame; slowly (in an uncanny premonition of Michael Snow's *Wavelength*), the camera dollies forward until it shows only a photo of the villain pinned to the center of the back wall, and after a moment the photo comes to life as the next scene. In fact, Murphy was regarded as an "experimental," arty director: Mordaunt Hall bemoaned the fact that the author of *Ballet Mécanique* had his script for *Skyscraper* (1928) "twisted" by conventional Hollywood directors,[32] and Edgar Selwyn compared Murphy's "experimentations" to the German classics *Metropolis*, *Das Cabinet des Dr. Caligari*, and *Das Wachsfigurenkabinett*.[33]

In 1941 Murphy also shot at least ten Soundies—three-minute films of musical acts that were shown in jukeboxes on a small screen.[34] In *Alabamy Bound*, for example, he creates a deft and charming synoptic musical feature: dynamic montages of steam, locomotive and wheels shot close-up at dramatic angles establish the railroad journey, while aboard we watch a group of beautiful women performing a leggy ballet of getting undressed in their Pullman berths, the porters shining shoes in synch with the music, and the conductor, engineer, and sole male passenger lip-synching the words to the song—a perfect MTV video!

Murphy's most distinguished (or best-remembered) achievements were two short films about African-American musicians, and the feature-length film adaptation of Eugene O'Neill's *Emperor Jones* (1933) starring Paul Robeson.[35] The two musical shorts released by RKO in 1929 certainly continue the Visual Symphony of Murphy's earlier work. *St. Louis Blues*, Bessie Smith's only film appearance (fig. 5.5), is a conven-

Figure 5.5.
Frame enlargement from *St. Louis Blues* (1929), directed by Dudley Murphy, with Bessie Smith. Courtesy of George Eastman House

Figure 5.6.
Production still from *Black and Tan* (1929), directed by Dudley Murphy, with Dudley Murphy, Duke Ellington, Carl van Vechten, unidentified woman. Courtesy of George Eastman House

tional film (though nicely made, considering the low budget) that extrapolates a story to explain why Bessie has the blues. *Black and Tan*, starring Duke Ellington (fig. 5.6), uses the polished floor of the Cotton Club as a mirror to duplicate the dancers, and then, during an extended sequence representing the hallucinations of the dying heroine, expands these mirror reflections into dozens of facets in a dynamic composition, using the same sort of beveled lenses employed in *Ballet Mécanique*. Murphy's *Emperor Jones*, in the climactic sequence of the fugitive Jones's paranoid hallucinations, also utilizes the superimpositions and stylized dance movements and symbolism found in his earlier *Danse Macabre*.

After more than a decade of random access to the low end of the film industry (and of compromise, as he lamented),[36] Murphy opened a restaurant, Holiday House, in the Los Angeles beach area around Malibu and effectively retired from filmmaking, with a filmography of some forty-five items. Man Ray completed three stunning films after *Ballet Mécanique*: *Emak Bakia* (1926), *L' Étoile de Mer* (1928), and *Mystères du Château de Dés* (1929). By 1935 Fernand Léger had titles made for *Ballet Mécanique* that omitted Dudley Murphy's name and was distributing the film in America, but he never made a film of his own.

NOTES

1. James L. Enyeart, *Bruguière: His Photographs and His Life* (New York: Knopf, 1977).

2. Sheldon Renan, *An Introduction to the American Underground Film* (New York: Dutton, 1967), p. 71; see also Frank Stauffacher, *Art in Cinema* (San Francisco: San Francisco Museum of Art, 1947), p. 18.

3. Grace Moore, *You're Only Human Once* (New York: Doubleday, 1944), pp. 108–109; Arthur Mizener, *The Far Side of Paradise* (Boston: Houghton Mifflin, 1951), p. 199; interview with Jerome Hill, 1970, New York.

4. Man Ray describes these two films in his autobiography *Self Portrait* (Boston: Little Brown, 1963), pp. 99–100, 262–263 (pp. 86, 213 in the 1988 ed.). Although Man Ray claims that these experiments did not yield much film, he admits that enough of the stereo film survived to show in a stereopticon viewer, which demonstrated that the 3-D effect worked, and enough of the pubic hair movie survived for Man Ray to include clips from it

in a letter to Tristan Tzara from ca. June 1921, reproduced in *Perpetual Motif: The Art of Man Ray,* ed. Merry Foresta (New York: Abbeville Press, 1988), p. 150.

5. Elizabeth Hutton Turner, in Foresta, ed., *Perpetual Motif,* p. 151.

6. Man Ray tells something about this film in *Self Portrait,* p. 163, but with deliberate errors, including the use of *filles* ("girls") instead of *films* in the title. The correct details above were related to me by Man Ray during an interview at his studio on rue Ferou in Paris, 8 May 1972. He explained that he had often not told the full truth about certain episodes (including the collaborations with Chomette and Murphy) because he did not want to make enemies of the heirs of people like the Beaumonts or Léger. "I have plenty of credits to my name; let them have some crumbs, if they insist!" he said.

7. "Some Short Reels: 'The Soul of the Cypress'—Murphy Picture," *Wid's Daily,* 24 July 1921, p. 18.

8. "In the Courts," *Wid's Daily,* 2 July 1921, p. 2.

9. " 'The Soul of the Cypress' GLOBE," *Wid's Daily,* 12 July 1921, p. 4; " 'The Soul of the Cypress'—Murphy Picture," *Wid's Daily,* 24 July 1921 p. 18.

10. *New York Times,* 11 July 1921.

11. *New York Times,* 1 January 1922.

12. "Murphy Working on Camera," *Wid's Daily,* 6 August 1921, p. 3.

13. "Community Bureau Sues to Stop Murphy's Suit," *Moving Picture World* 54, no. 1 (7 January 1922): 50.

14. "Films from Music," *Wid's Daily,* 23 December 1921, p. 2; " 'Flying Dutchman' in Films," *Film Daily,* 20 January 1922, p. 2; "Offers Film to Supplant Prologue," *Exhibitors Herald* 14, no. 5 (28 January 1922): 46.

15. "Murphy and Macgowan Making One Reel 'Visual Symphonies,' " *Motion Picture News* 25, no. 5 (21 January 1922): 606.

16. "With First Run Theatres," *Motion Picture News* 25, no. 8 (11 February 1922): 986.

17. " 'Visual Symphonies' Find Recognition; New Short Subjects Replace Prologues," *Moving Picture World* 54, no. 4 (28 January 1922): 387.

18. A 35mm print of this film has been preserved at George Eastman House, Rochester.

19. *Dada and Surrealist Film,* ed. Rudolf E. Kuenzli (New York: Willis Locker & Owens, 1987), pp. 28–45.

20. Ibid.

21. This is reprinted in *391: Revue publiée de 1917 à 1924 par Francis Picabia, réédition intégrale presentée par Michel Sanouillet* (Paris: Terrain Vague, 1960), p. 53. The "Américaine" appears on p. 49, and the Man Ray Dada poem that was used in *Return to Reason* appears on p. 119 as part of the June 1924 issue.

22. William J. Reilly, "When Is It a Moving Picture? Dudley Murphy Helps to Answer the Question," *Moving Picture World* 80, no. 3 (15 May 1926): 209, 235.

23. Man Ray also made still photographs of kitchen utensils as early as 1918, and ironically, or cynically, labeled a pair "Man" and "Woman." See Foresta, ed., *Perpetual Motif,* pp. 78–79. Their sexual connotations ("egg-beater") and satirical comparison of human and mechanical parts fit right in with *Ballet Mécanique.*

24. See Dudley Murphy, "Murphy by Murphy, manuscript, p. 42. The manuscript was begun in 1966 and presumably left unfinished at page 87 (dealing with the author's experiences ca. 1939) at Murphy's death two years later. It belongs to his daughter Erin O'Hara, who kindly let me study it.

25. See Standish D. Lawder, *Cubist Cinema* (New York: New York University Press, 1975), pp. 122–123. Lawder never mentions that there are several differing prints of *Ballet Mécanique* in various film museums in Europe and America, that most if not all of these derived directly from Léger, and that several are hand-tinted.

26. Frederick Kiesler's widow donated this print to Anthology Film Archive, and since Kiesler had sponsored the 1924 world premiere of *Ballet Mécanique* in Vienna, it was assumed to be the "original" print. But Kiesler was involved in later screenings as well (his Theater Exhibition was presented in Paris in 1925 and New York in 1926), and he met Léger years later in America, so this might well be a "revised" print. The titles certainly derive from Murphy, since the word *mécanique* is misspelled *méchanique,* following the English word "mechanical" (and, ironically, the French *méchant,* "wicked").

27. Lawder, *Cubist Cinema,* pp. 120–121.

28. Murphy's own print of *Ballet Mécanique* still contained these erotic flashes, and he screened this print often in Los Angeles, where filmmakers like James Whitney and Man Ray remembered seeing it during the 1940s. Unfortunately, Murphy's copy burned in a nitrate fire, and none of the other known prints contains more than a single frame of a nude Kiki. In "Murphy on Murphy," the author also mentions a missing shot of Katherine's pregnant belly.

29. *Peinture Cinéma Peinture* (Paris: Hazan, 1989), pp. 141, 143, accompanying an article by Christian Derouet on "Léger and the Cinema," which also never seriously considers the fact that Léger had no filmmaking skills and therefore was most likely a minor participant in the making of *Ballet Mécanique.*

30. Lawder, p. 119.

31. Kuenzli, ed., *Dada and Surrealist Film,* p. 38.

32. Mordaunt Hall, "Iron Workers Aloft: *Skyscraper,*" *New York Times,* 11 April 1928.

33. Edgar Selwyn, "Apologia For Hollywood," *New York Times,* 25 February 1934.

34. The best published work on Soundies currently available is Maurice Terenzio, Scott MacGillivray, and Ted Okuda, *The Soundies Distribution*

Corporation of America (Jefferson, N.C.: McFarland, 1991). See Dudley Murphy entry, pp. 12, 54–57. The definitive data base and archive of actual prints, however, belongs to Mark Cantor of Woodland Hills, California, who is planning to publish an encyclopedia of Soundies. The University of California at Los Angeles Film Archive also contains a special collection of Soundies.

35. Murphy also made a musical short for Paramount, *Frankie and Johnnie* (1930, also released as *He Was Her Man*), starring Gilda Gray, a work that seems to be lost. To judge from a still, published together with a still from *Black and Tan*, an all-white cast in a Gold Rush–era saloon enacts the story implicit in the song's lyrics. See *Theatre Arts Monthly* 14, no. 3 (March 1930): 198.

36. Marguerite Tazelaar, "The Man Who Will Make *Emperor Jones* for Screen," *New York Herald Tribune*, 2 April 1933.

6

Startling Angles
Amateur Film and the Early Avant-Garde

Patricia R. Zimmermann

In 1923, the same year that Eastman Kodak and Bell and Howell standardized amateur film stock to 16mm, *Living Age* reprinted an article entitled "The Importance of Doing Things Badly." The author reasoned that the impoverishment of private pursuits and hobbies evolved from two sources. On the one hand, the practice of the arts demanded some skill; on the other hand, the higher, professional standards seemed unattainable for amateurs. By 1926, this sentiment of "doing things badly"—a concept that defined amateurism in terms of increased participation in all of the arts—reverberated as an argument against the constrictions of "professional" skill demanded by commerce. Art, then, would save American vision from the blinding efficiency of corporate capitalism. "The Amateur and the Dilettante," also published in *Living Age*, elaborated:

> If all men postponed engaging in any creative or recreative activity until they could do it expertly what would become of all the experimental vitality of human life? It takes a certain confidence in the value of experience, as such, to be a good amateur, and the modern world is probably too conscientiously utilitarian for that.[1]

Popular discourse on amateur moviemaking during the 1920s and 1930s expressed two competing definitions. In his 1927 statement to the meeting of the National Board of Review of Motion Pictures, reprinted in *Amateur Movie Makers* (fig. 6.1), Roy Winton warned that amateurs should not be derided; they could experiment and distinguish the cinema as an art, salvaging it from the crass commercialism of the talkie and the Hollywood movie studios. Amateurs, then, would serve as scouts

137

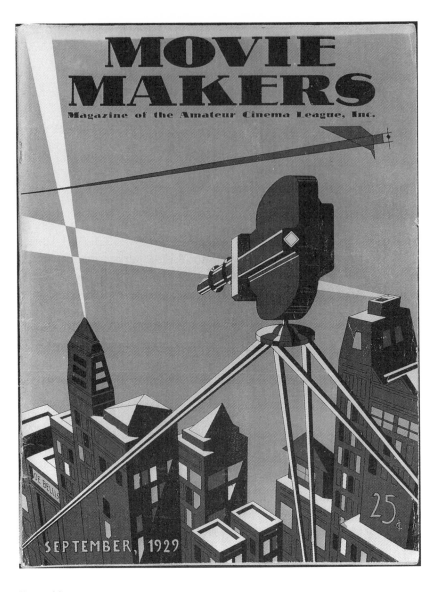

Figure 6.1.
Cover from *Amateur Movie Makers* (September 1929), journal of the Amateur Cinema League

for new cinematic horizons. His argument invokes nineteenth-century definitions of amateurism as a defense against commercialism and incorporation into commodity exchange:

> In the Amateur Cinema League we are trying to get back to the original meaning of the word "amateur." We are concerned about where this Eighth Art is going and we are concerned about it aesthetically as well as socially and ethically. We do not look on it as a means to an end only. We believe that, like every other art, it should be self-justified and that if it can present beauty to humanity it can stand on its own feet.[2]

Winton's proclamation clearly summoned idealized conceptions of amateurism that positioned freedom, creativity, experimentation, and art against the enervation of more industrialized and bureaucratized work. However, these somewhat utopian definitions were eclipsed by a more pervasive and popular idea about amateur film—that it was what Hollywood was not. Amateur film, whether reproducing Hollywood narrative style or experimenting with film form, was located within a discourse searching for a revival of artistic dignity through the integrity of individual filmmaking. *New York Times* writer Philip Sterling offered a succinct definition of amateur film in his 1937 article "Sowing the 16mm Field": "Because the 16mm world has always aimed to maintain cordial relations with the entertainment industry, the term amateur is applied indiscriminately to anyone who doesn't work in or for Hollywood."[3]

In the 1920s, the aesthetic discourse of popular and amateur film magazines demarcated amateur filmmaking on the basis of aesthetic skill. In general terms, it emphasized expertise and the perfect execution of Hollywood narrative paradigms. Hollywood was the cultural norm; imperfection or digression was therefore amateur and illegitimate. In a significant cultural and social reversal, this period also evidenced two strains of experimentation: professional cinematographers tested and created new visual effects with amateur cameras, and a small coterie of political and avant-garde filmmakers viewed this simple and inexpensive technology as a way to produce personally meaningful images. The amateur film movement of the 1920s and 1930s mapped out a discursive, production, and social space for experimentation.

Conventional film histories have generally ignored the importance of amateur filmmaking, even though amateur technologies and films were created as early as 1897. Histories of the avant-garde, as noted by Jan-Christopher Horak in the Introduction to this volume, have reiterated a pantheon of great artists but have generally ignored the social, political, and discursive relations within which they work.

The amateur film movement flourished in the 1920s because several historical modalities converged to create a discursive space for non-Hollywood production. The standardization of 16mm in 1923 dispensed with a plethora of competing technologies and formats designed by entrepreneurs. With the coming of sound in 1927, Hollywood style became stultified and thereby more vulnerable to critique from those who saw cinema as an art. The concentration and vertical integration of the Hollywood system imposed an effective barrier against independent producers, almost forcing "artistic" cinematic enthusiasts into amateur production. The rampant consumerism of the 1920s encouraged hobbies and a more expansive definition of leisure to include pursuit of the arts. The economic boom of the 1920s expanded the middle and upper-middle class, the major market for amateur equipment.

In its early years, the 1920s and 1930s, the amateur film movement was, in contrast to later years, much more expansive and inclusive of a wide range of filmmaking, serving as a kind of catch-all for various emerging forms of cinema excised from Hollywood: industrials, educational films, science films, travelogues, home movies, religious films, ethnographic and documentary film, time-motion studies, and avant-garde film. During this early period, these various forms, although operating within different production, distribution, and exhibition contexts, shared two traits. First, they functioned outside the Hollywood system and within various localized subcultural practices and reception sites. Second, as newly emerging genres, the very instability of their definitions and functions made it easy for the amateur film movement to serve as a discursive umbrella for film practices that did not have much in common except their difference from big-budget Hollywood productions.

The amateur film movement's fascination with avant-garde form and practice, then, does not simply stem from an opposition to the economic and artistic dominance of Hollywood. In general, amateur film magazines were dedicated to resurrecting the nineteenth-century ideal of amateurism as a pursuit unfettered by commerce and therefore able to promote the social and artistic improvement of individuals. This discourse did not entail collective political struggle to reorganize the structures of society or Hollywood, however. Amateurism was not in this sense a revolutionary practice (although it has that potential in modern mass-mediated society), but rather a practice of containment. The opposition between professional and amateur film—at least in magazines— maintained equilibrium and order in cultural practices. Amateurism salvaged individualism from capitalism, and then reinvested it with a form of spiritual artistry. Amateur film discourse, whether discussing the art of Hollywood filmmaking or the impact of the European avant-garde, emphasized that the goal of all amateur filmmakers was to restore artistry to filmmaking—to serve, as it were, as a moral and aesthetic conscience for a commercial film industry possessed by capitalist accumulation.

This celebration of the individual artist, and by extension bourgeois individualism, found many congruencies and resonances with the formal interventions of the avant-garde, which rejected consumer culture through aesthetic experimentation removed from commercial boundaries. Avant-garde interests, then, coincided with the ideological underpinnings of amateurism: experimentation, freedom, creativity, exploration, personal expansion, and self-improvement. Unlike today's theorizations positioning experimental film as an interrogative, oppositional text investigating politics, representation, and visual language, the amateur film movement saw avant-garde technique as an experimental vanguard that would invigorate and energize all of filmmaking, a sort of farm team for the big leagues of Hollywood. *Amateur Movie Makers* often printed articles on avant-garde film adjacent to articles on family movies, experimentation in Hollywood, and how-to technical pieces. Avant-garde discourse never dominated amateur film magazines, but instead popped up occasionally as a method for filmic exploration and artistry.

To understand the historical significance of the infusion of avant-garde discourse into amateurism, it is important to chart out two more pervasive modes: home movies and Hollywood. The persistent equation of amateur movies with the home had two important ideological consequences. First, popular discourse instructed filmmakers to exalt the everyday details of family living to matters of spectacle, wonder, and importance. In an unconscious homage to turn-of-the-century pictorialism, an article in a 1939 *Woman's Home Companion* exhorted women filmmakers to "remember that the simplest things are the best. . . . the things that happen in your own household everyday make the best moving pictures."[4] The writer further suggested such titles as "A Day in

Our Home," "The Sunday Motor Trip," and "The Saturday Afternoon Picnic." The writer uncritically assumed that narrative could control, maintain, and unify the activities of the home. For example, Herbert McKay cautioned in a 1926 *Photo Era* column that "action should not be meaningless motion. It should have a story to tell. . . . The usual patchwork of haphazard scenes is confusing and irritating."[5]

Second, aesthetic discourse emphasized action as an integral component of family memory, reinforcing the idea that philosophical, analytical thinking or spontaneity were not as critical as sequences, progression, and continuity development. "Pictorial Diary for a Lifetime: Home Movies for Christmas," which appeared in the December 1928 issue of *American Home*, exemplifies this attitude:

> Perhaps the greatest value of the home movie lies in its ability to record in close-up, semi-close-up, or long shot, the various members of his family and household, not in stiffly posed "still" pictures, but in action, just as they really are.[6]

This discourse on action articulated reality as observable. Although a bastardized version of empiricism and scientific management, it etched industrial concepts onto private life.

In this context, Hollywood technique functioned as a powerful management system to control and order reckless amateur home-movie production. An interesting example of this discourse was a 1929 "Amateur Movie Making" column in the professional film magazine *American Cinematographer*. William Stull advised:

> Look at your own latest cinematographic effort. Then in the theatre compare it with similar shots in the professional picture. It is not difficult. You shoot on the beach. You do not like it. Pick a picture that has beach shots in it. Look them over and see what the professional did to make his shots effective.[7]

This exaltation of technique camouflaged the material contradictions between the limited resources of the amateur and the corporate backing of a Hollywood spectacle.

As further evidence of this discursive colonization, Hollywood style was lionized as the pinnacle of cinematic perfection for amateurs. Professional cinematographers not only dispensed advice to amateurs in a special column in *American Cinematographer*, the trade journal for professional cinematographers, but also held seats on the majority of amateur movie-making societies.[8] Professionals touted tripods to stabilize "technique," limiting the hand-held, portable freedom of 16mm. Image stability and comprehensibility, foundations of the epistemology of Hollywood professional style, were equated with representational transcendence.

The proliferation of amateur moviemaking clubs in the 1930s indicated the extent of this concentration and institutionalization of amateur film as an adjunct and promoter of Hollywood. In 1934 the *New York Times* estimated that over two hundred clubs and research bureaus across the United States had been organized to help amateur movie makers.[9] The Amateur Cinema League (ACL) was the oldest of these organizations: founded in New York City in 1926, it published the magazine *Amateur Movie Makers,* and had 250 amateur cinema clubs on its rolls by 1937.[10] The *New York Times* speculated that there were more than a hundred thousand home-movie-makers in 1937 and 500 services for renting films for home viewing.[11] Normative, technical amateur advice books were part of this nationalization of amateur moviemaking discourse. Such books codified and popularized narrative norms. *Making Better Movies* was first published by the ACL in 1932 and went through three more editions.[12] *The ACL Movie Book: A Guide to Making Better Films*[13] described the range of activities in which the league was engaged: technical consultation on equipment, continuity and film-planning advice, reviews of members' work, publishing *Amateur Movie Makers,* and running film contests.[14] This text reiterated the requirements of good composition, a unified narrative theme, and rehearsals.[15] It conflated all other forms of non-Hollywood filmmaking with the amateur, and included a section on special-purpose films for business, religion, education, and scientific work.[16]

The league's yearly "Ten Best" contests for amateur films started in 1930.[17] Many other amateur film contests and competitive screenings evolved during the 1930s: a contest sponsored by the British Institute of Amateur Cinematographers that offered awards to professional films; screenings sponsored by members of the social elite in their homes; the Quebec Film Contest; the International Amateur Film Contest, sponsored by the Division of Film Study at Columbia University.[18] These contests and screenings pointed to two emergent trends in the popular discourse on amateur film: a nationalization of aesthetic norms, now rewarded in competition, and the concentration of amateur film technology and discourse within major institutions like corporations or magazines. Indeed, the publication of information relevant to these screenings and contests in the society and travel pages of the *New York Times* suggests an urban, upper-class constituency.

Hollywood was not the only cultural site to deploy 16mm technology for stylistic innovation. In the late 1920s and early 1930s, middle-class amateurs made experimental films that critiqued and challenged the more popular discourses on Hollywood style, compositional harmony, and pictorialism. A small group of photographic journalists interrogated films to see whether their approaches to style, content, and construction could be easily attained by the amateur. Experimentation was seen as the domain of the amateur. This emergent and sometimes resistant discourse surfaced in such disparate areas as film criticism, advocacy of expressionistic film techniques, and the Marxist film critic Harry Alan Potamkin's theories on amateurism.

Although at best only a diversion from the more pervasive emphasis on Hollywood style in amateur magazines, this linkage of an experimental disposition with amateur filmmaking was nonetheless significant. It suggests that the presentation of Hollywood aesthetic ideology was not a totalizing phenomenon. At least on the discursive level, magazine writers did not distinguish between amateurs who shot home movies and amateurs who produced "art" films. If anything, magazine writers considered amateur experimental filmmakers more ambitiously committed to amateurism than those who merely recorded their families, truly dedicated "artists" whose goal was to expand the possibilities of cinema.

Other historical factors may have contributed to this discussion of experimental technique in amateur film circles. The initial period of American avant-garde film (1928–1932) followed intense experimental film activity in Europe from 1924 to 1928. This spurt of experimental filmmaking maintained strong ties to professional film. Robert Florey, director of The *Life and Death of 9413 — A Hollywood Extra* (1928), for example, worked for the major studios as a director. In Hollywood, Paul Fejos directed *The Last Moment* (fig. 6.2), an experimental film using camera angles and shadowy lighting in the German Expressionist manner. It earned Fejos a job directing minor pictures at Universal. These filmmakers, along with Ralph Steiner, Herman Weinberg (director of *Autumn Fire* [1933] and contributor to *Amateur Movie Makers*), James Sibley Watson, Melville Webber, and others, produced their films as "leisure-time activities." However, unlike most amateur productions, their work could be distributed because it was shot in 35mm.

Figure 6.2.
Still from *The Last Moment* (1929), directed by Paul Fejos, with Otto Matiesen. Courtesy of George Eastman House

During the mid- to late 1920s, Robert Flaherty's *Nanook of the North* (1922) and *Moana* (1926), Sergei Eisenstein's *Battleship Potemkin* (USSR, 1925), Carl Dreyer's *The Passion of Joan of Arc* (France, 1928), Charles Chaplin's *The Gold Rush* (1925), and F. W. Murnau's *Sunrise* (1927)—all films praised for their artistry—established a place in major exhibition areas for films extending cinematic art.[19]

Conventional historical interpretations say that after the introduction of sound in 1927, Hollywood films forfeited some of the more innovative camera styles because sound equipment limited the camera's mobility. The interest of amateur magazines in silent experimental work during the following four to five years constituted a reaction to Hollywood's technological developments. Amateurs launched a major reconstruction project to save cinematic art. In fact, for a few months in 1930, the ACL and the American Film Arts Guild imported European-produced noncommercial films for distribution.[20] By 1931 the Workers International Relief, a leftist organization formed to assist strikers, was distributing many Soviet films noted for their artistic and political innovations, like Vsevolod Pudovkin's *Storm Over Asia*, Eisenstein's *Ten Days That Shook the World*, Dziga Vertov's *Man with a Movie Camera*, and Victor Turin's *Turksib*.[21]

The historian David Curtis contends that Hollywood studios were experimenting with optical printing, traveling mattes, rear screen projection, and camera movement by the early to mid-1930s. These effects created a larger cinematic cultural context for non-narrative visual experimentation.[22] Although these effects displayed and validated visual experimentation, however, the technology to produce them was, like sound, unavailable to amateurs.

Discussions about experimental or art films in the amateur film press may not represent a revolutionary rejection of Hollywood visual norms—that would be unlikely in magazines that so energetically embraced Hollywood. Rather, they suggest an effort to expand and strengthen cinema as an art. Given amateurism's historical role as the guardian of art uncontaminated by capitalism, it is not surprising that magazines like *Amateur Movie Makers* would promote experimental cinema.

Amateur movie magazines analyzed the formal techniques and different modes of production exhibited in such films as *Battleship Potemkin*, *The Last Laugh*, *Ten Days That Shook the World*, and French experimental shorts, emphasizing the low-budget opportunities they offered.

These writers did not attack Hollywood; rather, they promoted amateurism. George Hess praised Eisenstein's films in a 1933 review in *Personal Movies* because "all the directorial devices throughout the picture are simple; simple in that they are free from all evidence of pretentious artistry."[23] Eisenstein's *Thunder Over Mexico* (1934) garnered particularly high critical honors from Hess, who judged that amateurs could concoct nearly every stylistic device in it.[24]

Ideologically, these reviews severed amateur film from the Hollywood hierarchy to secure a more important goal: artistic freedom. Alfred Richman, in "Technique of the Russians" in *Amateur Movie Makers* (1929), underlined the similarities between Eisenstein and amateurs:

> Eisenstein, in *Ten Days That Shook the World*, uses virtually only amateur "actors," resorts to constructed sets as little as possible, studies profoundly the theory and experiments constantly with technique of the cinema and is interested, primarily, in the artistic integrity of his productions. We see how much he has in common with the aims of the amateur movement.[25]

These films offered a new, alternative paradigm for amateurs: simplicity and experimentation rather than complicated technical control by experts. C. W. Gibbs, writing in *American Movie Makers* in 1929, challenged Hollywood's compositional etiquette of not rankling the spectator by urging amateur filmmakers to "startle" their audiences through modernist effects: unusual camera angles, moving lights, extreme closeups, multiple images, distorting lenses, and use of flashbacks not connected logically to the previous scene.[26] One article even proposed that small movie houses (fig. 6.3) attack the inherent conservatism of commercial films by screening experimental shorts and amateur projects.[27] This sporadic articulation on artistic freedom and experimentation resisted the discourse on professional film in two ways: it defied the dominant conventions of narrative with formal experimentation, and it alerted amateurs to films produced outside the confines of Hollywood.

This advocacy of Soviet film technique was politically dangerous. The mainstream press diagnosed the perils of this counter-cinema. In a biting review of *Turksib*, satirically called "Home Movies in Excelsis" (1930), the *New Republic* de-legitimated the film by dubbing it a Russian "home movie" about a railroad.[28] Bruce Bliven, the author, complained about out-of-focus screenings:

the
little
magazine

IN THIS ISSUE:
Music in the Movies
by Gustav Klemm

Published by the

Little Theatre

Baltimore's Intimate Playhouse

Vol. 1 No. 5   Oct. 14, 1934

Circulation 5000 Copies Weekly

Figure 6.3.
Program brochure from the Little Theatre, Baltimore. Courtesy of George Eastman House

A few such sessions are enough to make anybody wish there might be a law restricting the use of motion picture cameras to professionals who work in studios and have discretion enough to let their mistakes die on the cutting room floor.[29]

During the late 1920s, many leftist critics and filmmakers envisioned the political and social possibilities of the Soviet cinema for mass mobilization and active spectatorship. Possibly in reaction to this discourse, the conservative *New Republic* praised as "professional" the films produced by the wealthy Pinchat family about their Caribbean and Pacific cruises, noting the films' natural beauty and good composition. The same article flailed away at *Turksib* for its excessive concentration on machinery and its short and disturbing scenes. This discourse mapped a cultural–class war between professionals and amateurs, and between the leisured class and workers. "Professionalism" was ascribed to the vacation films of the wealthy, whereas "amateurism" disenfranchised a film with social and political intentions.[30] Radical amateur columnists like Harry Alan Potamkin and other authors of amateur advice books took a positive view of the cheapness and flexibility of amateur cameras and discerned the populist potential of amateur film. According to a 1927 *Amateur Movie Makers* editorial, these cameras would "liberate the cinematic art from restrictions of commerce" and induce experimentation by thousands of amateur movie-equipment owners to whom profits and losses did not matter.[31] One extremely utopian anonymous writer in that journal even located experimental opportunities within the reaches of every family.[32] Indeed, some writers thought this inexpensive equipment could create an entirely new form of communication. A description of the purposes of the ACL, published in its journal in December 1926, illustrates this idealist position:

> Professional pictures must appeal to mass interest and mass interest does not always embrace things that ought to be known. On the other hand, the amateur has no necessity for appealing to mass interest. He is free to reproduce and record any action his fancy or the fancy of a friend might dictate.[33]

Leonard Hacker's *Cinematic Design* (1931), published by the American Photographic Publishing Company, also promoted amateurism as fertile ground for art. Dedicated to F. W. Murnau and stressing constructivist principles of geometric design, *Cinematic Design* explicated form, rhythm, color, and relativity in motion pictures. The book's final hundred pages featured avant-garde scenarios for amateur cinematographers. They reproduced the strategies of city symphony films produced in Europe in the late twenties: *Symphony Natural, Symphony Synthetic, Symphony Mechanique*, to name only a few. Hacker's "Preface" is fairly explicit about the purpose of amateur cinema: "Whereas the purpose of the professional film is to furnish cheap entertainment for the masses, the amateur will devote his attention to the development of cinematics as a highly original art form, eventually finding a market for small audiences of more cultural tastes."[34] Hacker's vision of aesthetic liberation linked amateurs with formal visual experimentation, but simultaneously concealed a latent elitism that assumed general audiences were ignorant of the complexities of personal art cinema. In the social context, these joyful exhortations to artistic expression not defined by commerce constituted a politically reactionary strategy. They invested leisure time with the illusion of control and the fiction of a residual nineteenth-century ethic of the individual craftsperson.

Sound production, as noted above, required enormous technological resources and deepened the divide between amateur and professional filmmaking. In a 1929 essay for the *New Republic* titled "Home Movies,"[35] Gilbert Seldes noted that several professional cinematographers and photographers produced films that rejected Hollywood style, such as Watson's *Fall of the House of Usher* (fig. 6.4) and Steiner's H_2O.[36] In *Amateur Movie Makers* Herman Weinberg touted Florey's *Life and Death of 9413—A Hollywood Extra* (1928) as a triumph of amateur experimentation, a work that imaginatively exploited limited resources. Florey's film visualizes Hollywood's abuse of actors by following an actor—No. 9413—through his hopes for success, his rejection, and subsequent death. Florey, a Hollywood director by trade, employed cutouts, Erector-set miniatures, and expressionistic lighting, rather than elaborate soundstages.[37] He was critiquing his own employer—the Hollywood studios—in this film. Its experimental style countered the logical organization of the dominant narrative style and turned diminished resources into an asset.

Perhaps the only theorist of amateurism during this period was Harry Alan Potamkin. A member of the leftist Workers Film and Photo League, he argued that cinema offered new positive tendencies "towards the compound, the reflective, and toward a new logic."[38] Cinema, he wrote, could initiate a new logic: it could break dependence on literalness

Figure 6.4.
Still from *The Fall of the House of Usher* (1928), directed by James Sibley Watson, Jr., and
Melville Webber. Courtesy of George Eastman House

through montage, a direct assault on Hollywood continuity. As a technique to reorganize film abstractly, rather than eternally, montage
decomposed and reconstructed continuity and natural pictorialism.

In his 1930 essay "The Montage Film," which first appeared in
Amateur Movie Makers, Potamkin advanced montage films such as
Walter Ruttman's *Berlin: Symphony of a City*, Alberto Cavalcanti's *Rien
Que les Heures* (fig. 6.5), and Vertov's *Man with a Movie Camera*.
Constructed according to abstract principles, these films were accessible
to the amateur.[39] As films about actual cities, these documentaries
presented a powerful strategy: amateurs were urged to film and critique
everyday aspects of American life or people—such as lunch hours and
transportation—outside the private confines of the home and the nuclear
family. It is significant that Potamkin cited examples of films about
public places; these examples attacked the amateur movie magazine
emphasis on private life and personal travel.

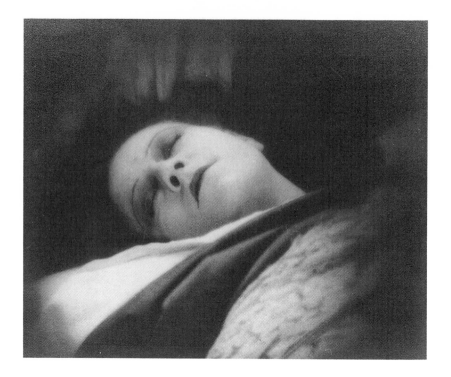

Figure 6.5.
Still from *Rien Que les Heures* (1925), directed by Alberto Cavalcanti. Courtesy of George
Eastman House

In a 1929 essay entitled "The Magic of Machine Films," also
published in *Amateur Movie Makers*, Potamkin reasoned that machines
had an impact on life on nearly every level. The amateur camera,
therefore, should force itself upon the machine and confront it, record it,
construct it visually, and examine its operation in detail. To accomplish
this, Potamkin advocated many formal interventions, such as slow, fast,
and stop action. He did not consider these aesthetic devices to heighten
emotion; instead, he saw them as instigating analysis of abstract principles in spectators.[40] On the surface, Potamkin's directives to amateurs
may resemble merely formal manipulations. However, within a social,
historical, and discursive context that exalted naturalism, emotionalism,
and beauty, these techniques constituted small acts of resistance to the
dominant ideology of Hollywood narrative.

In the late 1920s and early 1930s, the amateur film movement was
fleetingly paired with the early American avant-garde. Their allegiance to

each other, however, was tenuous, discursively hewn more than politically or artistically practiced. The availability of cheaper, small-format 16mm cameras offered the material conditions for a different imagining of the social relations of cinema. Both the amateur film movement and the avant-garde of this period shared the notion that Hollywood narrative film style had infected filmmaking with a crass commercialism that weakened its artistic potential. Both practices emphasized formal manipulation of the image as a form of visual exploration beyond narrative order. Both practices presumed that the role of an experimental cinema was to refashion the spectator from a passive consumer of entertainment into an active producer of meaning, and even images. If Hollywood cinematic style advocated harmonious compositions that would lull the spectator into the narrative flow, the advocates of an amateur avant-garde promoted "startling angles" that would force a new perception of the world.

NOTES

1. "The Amateur and the Dilettante," *Living Age*, 3 April 1926, p. 71.

2. Roy W. Winton, "The Amateur Cinema Camera Man," *Amateur Movie Makers* 2, no. 3 (March 1927): 28.

3. Philip Sterling, "Sowing the 16mm Field," *New York Times*, 25 July 1937, Sec. X.

4. Eleanor King, "Let's Make a Movie," *Woman's Home Companion*, April 1939, p. 48.

5. Herbert C. McKay, "Kinematography in the Home," *Photo Era* 54, no. 6 (June 1926): 343–344.

6. Gordon B. Wayne, "Pictorial Diary for a Lifetime: Home Movies for Christmas," *American Home*, December 1928, p. 266.

7. William Stull, "Amateur Movie Making," *American Cinematographer* (August 1929): 27.

8. Society of Amateur Cinematographers advertisement, *American Cinematographer*, January 1937, p. 23. The society's executive board included John Arnold, president of the A.S.C. and executive director of photography, MGM; Karl Struss, A.S.C., director of photography, Paramount; Fred Jackman, A.S.C.; Dan Clark, A.S.C., director of photography, 20th Century Fox; and David Abel, A.S.C., director of photography, Fred Astaire Productions and R.K.O. Studio.

9. Diana Rice, "Amateur Movies an Organized Sport," *New York Times*, 17 June 1934, Sec. VIII.

10. Sterling, "Sowing the 16mm Field," p. 3.

11. Ibid.

12. *The ACL Movie Book* (New York: Amateur Cinema League, 1932), p. vii.

13. Ibid.

14. Ibid., pp. 294–305.

15. Ibid., pp. 38–75.

16. Ibid., pp. 261–282.

17. John Markland, "Home Films Gain Scope," *New York Times*, 21 November 1937, Sec. XII.

18. "Coveted British Award Given for 'Sanders of the River,'" *New York Times*, 2 January 1926; "Amateurs Show Films," *New York Times*, 5 April 1926, Sec. II; "New Yorker Wins Film Prize," *New York Times*, 16 November 1936; Bosley Crowther, "Amateur Film Night," *New York Times*, 9 April 1939, Sec. X; Rice, "Amateur Movies an Organized Sport," p. 12.

19. Robert Sklar, *Movie-Made America: A Cultural History of the Movies* (New York: Vintage Books, 1976), pp. 86–100.

20. David Curtis, *Experimental Cinema* (New York: Universe Books, 1971), pp. 43–44.

21. William Alexander, *Film on the Left: American Documentary from 1931 to 1942* (Princeton: Princeton University Press, 1981), p. 9.

22. Curtis, *Experimental Cinema*, pp. 44–48.

23. George W. Hess, "The Cine Analyst: Thunder Over Mexico," *Personal Movies*, November 1933, p. 268.

24. Ibid.

25. Alfred Richman, "Technique of the Russians," *Amateur Movie Makers* 4, no. 9 September 1929): 56.

26. C. W. Gibbs, "Modernistic Movie Making," *Amateur Movie Makers* 4, no. 8 (August 1929): 505.

27. Gilbert Seldes, "The Intellectual Film," *Amateur Movie Makers*, March 1927, pp. 15, 38; also see Harry Alan Potamkin, "Tendencies in the Cinema," in *The Compound Cinema*, ed. Lewis Jacobs (New York: Teachers' College Press, 1977), pp. 43–46.

28. Bruce Bliven, "Home Movies in Excelsis," *New Republic* 61 (11 June 1930): 101.

29. Ibid.

30. Ibid., p. 102.

31. "Editorial," *Amateur Movie Makers*, January 1927, p. 5.

32. "The Little Movie Movement," *Amateur Movie Makers* 2, no. 12 (December 1926): 18.

33. "Amateur Cinema League: A Close-Up," *Amateur Movie Makers* 1, no. 12 (December 1926): 7.

34. Leonard Hacker, *Cinematic Design* (Boston: American Photographic Publishing Co., 1931), p. 3.

35. Gilbert Seldes, "Some Amateur Movies," *New Republic* 58 (6 March 1929): 71.

36. Ibid.

37. Herman Weinberg, "A Paradox of the Photoplay: A Professional Turns Amateur," *Amateur Movie Makers*, 4, no. 1 (January 1929): 866–867.

38. Potamkin, in Jacobs; ed., *The Compound Cinema*, pp. 43, 46.

39. Ibid., pp. 70–73.

40. Ibid., pp. 80–84.

7

U.S. Modernism and the Emergence of "The Right Wing of Film Art"

The Films of James Sibley Watson, Jr., and Melville Webber

LISA CARTWRIGHT

Despite their status as some of the earliest works of the U.S. film avant-garde, the films of James Sibley Watson, Jr., and Melville Folsom Webber remain virtually unconsidered in film scholarship. Watson and Webber's films include a 1928 experimental production loosely based on Edgar Allan Poe's "The Fall of the House of Usher"; the 1933 *Lot in Sodom*, an experimental sound film loosely based on the nineteenth chapter of Genesis and dealing with themes of gay male desire and heteronormative prohibition; a 1930 spoof on sound-film melodrama titled *It Never Happened* (also known as *What May Happen* and *Tomatoes Another Day*), and an unfinished film titled *The Dinner Party*, shot in 1925. The latter film and *The Fall of the House of Usher* were based in part on shooting scripts provided by the poet e. e. cummings. In addition to these collaborations with Webber and cummings, Watson produced two industrial films: *The Eyes of Science*, made in 1931 for the optical firm Bausch and Lomb, and *Highlights and Shadows*, made in 1937 for Eastman Kodak Research Laboratories. Finally, in conjunction with a team of radiologists working at the University of Rochester School of Medicine and Dentistry, Watson (who had received an M.D. degree in 1923) produced many studies in x-ray cinematography between 1946 and 1960. Showing interior processes such as blood circulation, respiration, and digestion, these studies might be considered works of modernist science.[1]

In one of the few historical considerations of the films of Watson and Webber, Lucy Fischer identifies three conditions contributing to their critical neglect.[2] First, in what might be called the definitive volume on the Anglo-American film avant-garde, P. Adams Sitney fails to acknowledge the importance of Watson and Webber and the German Expressionist tradition that influenced them.[3] Second, Fischer notes that Watson, the better-known figure of the filmmaking team, was modest to the point of self-effacement, and played down the importance of his own productions. A "literary bias" is the third condition Fischer specifies, and it is the nature and substance of this "bias" that I will address in my attempt to situate the films of Watson and Webber within the conservative climate of U.S. literary modernism in the 1920s and 1930s.

Watson and Webber's two completed avant-garde films exhibit a "literary bias" not so much because they originated in literary texts, but because they correspond structurally and aesthetically with theories of literary production with which the two were associated. Watson claims that he and Webber selected the Poe story as the basis for their first film collaboration precisely because they had not read it in ten or fifteen years, and therefore would be free of its influence.[4] This claim is supported by the film's scant reference to the story's narrative. The editor of the British journal *Cinema Quarterly* states in a review of *Lot in Sodom* that "to anyone unfamiliar with the Old Testament narrative the film is barely explicit."[5] The same could be said of *The Fall of the House of Usher*'s relationship to the Poe text. In the following pages, I briefly elaborate on Watson's and Webber's careers to ground a discussion of their films as texts critically informed by the specific conventions of U.S. literary modernism developed in the pages of *The Dial*, a journal published by Watson between 1920 and 1929. I read Watson's literary criticism as textual evidence of the views on modernism and aesthetic production that informed his collaborative filmwork. Finally, I consider the collaborative efforts of Watson and Webber as a process that also included a third figure—the writer e. e. cummings.

At stake in the study of the Watson and Webber films is not only the question of their absence from the Western avant-garde film canon, but the question of the place of film in general within U.S. modernism. In the United States, as elsewhere, avant-garde film production was closely tied to aesthetic developments in painting, poetry, and literary fiction and criticism. Fischer identifies Watson and Webber's stylistic debt to European-based movements such as Expressionism, Cubism, and Futurism. Her estimation of this influence is correct: Watson was an avid consumer of the European art and films that came to New York City, and he spent time in Europe, where he saw art and film. Webber traveled in France and Italy on scholarship in the early twenties,[6] and, while working on the distribution of *The Fall of the House of Usher*, he spent a significant amount of time at New York City screenings of new films from the United States and Europe. But Watson and Webber's approach to film emerged in response not only to European film modernism and the Soviet film avant-garde, but to more local aesthetic and political developments—specifically, the politics of modernism that took shape in the pages of Watson's literary journal and in Webber's writing.

Webber was an art historian and poet. His collaboration with Watson began in 1926 during his tenure as associate director of the Memorial Art Gallery in Rochester, New York, where he also taught art history and painting at the University of Rochester. Watson, as *The Dial's* co-owner, publisher, and critic, established close professional and personal ties with many of the writers associated with the twentieth-century U.S. literary avant-garde. He wielded great influence in the literary world through his monetary and intellectual support of particular authors, not only publishing but subsidizing the careers of the poets Marianne Moore and e. e. cummings and the critic Kenneth Burke. Watson and Webber's early experimental films, *The Fall of the House of Usher* and *Lot in Sodom*, were very much the product of this literary milieu, embodying the aesthetic conventions and cultural politics identified with *The Dial's* brand of literary modernism. The production and reception of these films were directly shaped by members of Watson and Webber's literary community, and the films remain unconsidered in no small part because many of the records relating to them (essays, notes, correspondence) are contained within literary, rather than film, publications and collections. *The Fall of the House of Usher* and *Lot in Sodom* cannot be understood, then, without considering Watson and Webber's place in the U.S. literary scene of the 1920s and 1930s.

THE DIAL AND ITS "RESPECTABLE" AVANT-GARDE

As literary figures, Watson and Webber were part of a tradition bent on upholding a North American liberal modernist tradition of separating art and politics. It is to this political ideal of aesthetic autonomy that the early film avant-garde is in some sense indebted. Watson, a medical student and intern in physiology until 1923, put medicine aside for two decades to pursue literary and arts criticism through *The Dial*. First published between 1840 and 1844, under the successive editorships of Margaret Fuller and Ralph Waldo Emerson, as a Transcendentalist quarterly of religion and the arts, *The Dial* did not simply embrace canonical views, but explored a conjuncture of mysticism and a progressive revision of Christian doctrine in the light of modern science—a modernist agenda in the historical sense.[7] Emerson's political agenda was to "emancipate the American imagination" in "an organ whereby the Free may speak." Though the review changed hands a number of times, its focus shifting from liberal social commentary toward literary criticism in 1916, its early modernist agenda withstood editorial and thematic shifts. Scofield Thayer, editor from 1919 until Marianne Moore's editorship in 1925, maintained the journal's ties to American intellectual liberalism and solidified the shift in focus from politics to literature. Thayer and Watson (an heir to the Western Union fortune) bought out stock in the journal, expanding its scope to include drawings and film, art, and theater criticism alongside poetry and literary criticism. Watson published work by authors considered unconventional— cummings' drawings and poems, drawings by Gaston Lachaise, Moore's poems, and Kenneth Burke's criticism. In part through *The Dial*, this work would come to be part of the canon of U.S. modernism, while Watson and Webber's own films would be relatively marginalized.

Watson's professed editorial policy of publishing "detached thinkers" threatened by "the persecutors of art" dovetailed with Emerson and Fuller's original policy, reasserted by the journal's editors in 1916, of an "experimental" approach "skeptical of inherited values."[8] It should be noted here that *The Dial's* "experimental approach" was quite distinct from the formal experimentalism described by some writers and filmmakers associated with European and Soviet modernism. Under Watson, the journal practiced what one historian has called a "more respectable" type of avant-gardism in which the theories and politics of arts movements in other national contexts were more apt to be discussed in terms of their formal strategies than in terms of their political agendas. The politics of *The Dial* of the 1920s is marked by the original journal's rhetoric of free speech and aesthetic autonomy, expressed in an adamant separation of aesthetics from politics. As James Longenbach has pointed out, "*The Dial* was precisely cutting edge in retreating from political concerns—it set the trend."[9] Watson and Thayer were aesthetically selective yet politically catholic in their editorial policies, conscientiously maintaining a stance of distanced, perhaps even disdainful, ambiguity on questions of politics.[10]

The conventions and strategies informing Watson's editorial policies and writings in *The Dial* carried through in his filmmaking practice with Webber. First, however, it is necessary to reconsider some of the claims made about the relationship of Watson and Webber's work to European and Soviet art movements.

WATSON, WEBBER, AND THEIR EUROPEAN AVANT-GARDE INFLUENCES

Fischer states that, in making *Usher* and *Lot in Sodom*, Watson and Webber drew from the work of European filmmakers associated with Expressionism, Surrealism, Futurism, and Cubism, as well as from Soviet Constructivism. I consider here the specific case of the influence of German Expressionism, not only because the Watson and Webber films bear unmistakable similarities to works such as Robert Wiene's film *Das Cabinet des Dr. Caligari* (which Watson viewed more than once during its successful 1921 run at the Capitol Theatre in New York City), but because this example allows me to suggest that Watson and Webber had some clear differences with this apparent source, and drew from some less obvious sources in their own work.

It has already been noted that *The Fall of the House of Usher* offers little in the way of a narrative. As Watson's scenario for the film accurately explains, "the plot is of little consequence."[11] Nevertheless, the Poe story is an important reference point for the film, since it was likely to be at least vaguely familiar to most viewers. The story centers on three characters: Roderick and Madeleine Usher, siblings (the last of their line) who occupy a crumbling family mansion; and a childhood friend of Roderick's who visits the Usher home. Madeleine falls into a catatonic state, and her brother temporarily entombs her in a vault in the cellar beneath the house in order to keep her body out of the hands of certain "obtrusive" medical men eager to investigate her malady. At the story's end, Madeleine rises up from her "region of horror" to "bear [her brother] to the ground a corpse" (fig. 7.1).[12]

Figure 7.1.
Still from *The Fall of the House of Usher* (1928), directed by James Sibley Watson, Jr., and Melville Webber. Courtesy of George Eastman House and the J. S. Watson estate

Framed by brief shots of the visitor entering and leaving, the fifteen-minute film takes place almost exclusively within the interior space of the house of Usher, a space constructed by Webber out of cardboard and paint in a barn behind Watson's Rochester home. Fischer observes that the sets constructed by Webber, "with their peculiar angles, their impossible spaces, their bizarrely decorated surfaces, and their discrepancies of scale," are "transpositions of Expressionist plastics to the cinema."[13] The set was, in Watson's words, "broken with moving prisms and tinted with light"[14]—a strategy also suggestive of an Expressionist use of light to fragment and destabilize conventional perspective and form. However, the disjunctive and optically fragmented space of the house also suggests a scene described quite explicitly in the Poe story itself. A painting executed by Roderick is described in the story as "a small picture representing the interior of an immensely long and rectangular vault or tunnel with low, smooth walls and no outlet or source of light; yet floods of light rays rolled throughout." Webber's published work on art history provides evidence of familiarity with a painterly scene that corresponds with this description. During his stay in France and Italy in 1922, Webber studied medieval frescoes. Watson's colleague and literary executor, Dale Davis, has noted that *Usher* bears striking similarities to the Tavant frescoes that Webber studied[15]—images that lined an immensely long and rectangular vault or tunnel with low, smooth walls, precisely the space described by Poe in the story that Webber himself purportedly selected.[16] It is undoubtedly this space, a primary object of Webber's teaching and writing throughout the 1920s, that was in some sense the model for the sets of the Usher house that he constructed for the film.

Optically fragmented and reduplicated, the house interior is a specular cave not unlike the scene described by Luce Irigaray as "the original matrix/womb which [the occupants of Plato's cave] cannot represent."[17] It is not surprising that the space of the home around which the film is organized is Madeleine's "region of horror"—the subterranean tomb to which Roderick relegates her body, a space rendered unrepresentable insofar as it is optically fractured, duplicated, and destabilized. It is to this region that Roderick descends on a montage of unstable and shifting stairs to beat upon his sister's coffin with a superimposed hammer, and it is here that a gloved, disembodied hand intrusively palpates Madeleine's catatonic body. Clearly, Madeleine's bearing "of her brother to the ground a corpse" is also a bearing of her brother's interests in a different sense.

Fischer also notes that the visitor to the house of Usher, played by Webber himself in a top hat, cape, and dramatic face makeup, is strongly reminiscent of the figure of Dr. Caligari. He also recalls Jean Epstein's top-hatted figure in *La Glace a Trois Faces* of 1927.[18] However, as Davis has noted, Webber is made up to resemble precisely the graphically drawn faces of the Tavant fresco figures. Clearly, while Webber may have been influenced by Expressionism, his more immediate source was the medieval art about which he was writing and teaching before and during the production of the film.

Watson and Webber's use of a combination of techniques including disjunctive narrative, psychological complexity and ambiguity graphically expressed, unusual architectural angles, dramatic lighting, anamorphic lens shots, and multiple exposure suggests that they were informed by a wide range of European and Soviet modernist conventions, as Fischer makes clear. How, then, can the viewer account for the specificity of Watson and Webber's productions in the U.S. context? What, precisely, did Watson and Webber take from these movements, and what meanings did these conventions take on within the specific context of U.S. modernism? By the late twenties, Watson was quite eager to distance himself from the European avant-gardes with which his films currently are contextualized. He wrote in 1928 that he saw his film in progress not as a modernist work, but as an amateur production wholly indebted to Hollywood technology and aesthetics—a production in which "the same old tricks" used in Hollywood film got put to a new use. Months before the completion of *Usher*, Watson expressed his retrospective disdain for the very visual, formal, and conceptual innovations that characterized 1920s European avant-garde film, embracing instead the special effects revived in the U.S. industry later in that decade. That revival was due in part to the popular reception of F. W. Murnau's 1924 *The Last Laugh*—a film that broke with the experimental style of *Caligari*, and seems to have been influenced by U.S. studio conventions. *Caligari* was released in New York City five years before Watson and Webber began work on *Usher*, and eight years before it was released. While both Watson and Webber saw Wiene's film a number of times during the following years (not only in New York but also in Rochester), Watson's correspondence with e. e. cummings on a planned film production during this period suggests that he was influenced most not by *Caligari* but by Murnau's film.

At least one film critic of the period saw Watson and Webber's films as markedly distinct from the films of the European avant-garde. Kirk Bond, in a 1934 *Film Art* review, sees in *Lot in Sodom* "neither the conditioned visual value of the German film, nor the free thematic development of the ideal film-poem or the absolute-abstract film, approached by [Hans] Richter and Germaine Dulac."[19] For Bond, critics who see in *Lot* the influence of European modernist conventions make a crucial error. Because they are unfamiliar with the specific conventions or vocabularies that make up the range of experimental films being produced, they fail to note the critical stylistic differences that separate works: "One of the greatest tasks of the cinemist of the future," Bond argues, "will be . . . to recognize the many diverse patterns in this and other films. . . . Only when the characteristics and scope of a given type [of film] are understood, will it be possible for anyone to express in it a true cinematic idea."[20]

In distinguishing Watson and Webber's work from that of European avant-garde filmmakers, Bond seems to be intent on emphasizing the use of apparently similar conventions in different contexts—a problem he refers to as "the unanswered question of filmic *meaning*."[21] This emphasis on the meaning of formal conventions in context is important because it provides a way to consider the transformations of meaning inherent in the transfer of formal and aesthetic conventions from Europe and the Soviet Union to Watson and Webber's particular history and culture. For example, Fischer notes that the motif of steps used in *Usher* evokes Eisenstein's well-known Odessa Steps sequence. But while Eisenstein's steps are the scene of political conflict and mass resistance restaged in graphic montage, the steps optically printed (fig. 7.2) and superimposed in the Usher mansion metaphorically lead the viewer, through the character of the visitor, into the interior life of an incestuous Oedipal family in decline. The film provides a bourgeois psychological portrait of individual psyches and decaying family ideology—a model that would not have had a primary place in Soviet constructivist film during this period.

Figure 7.2.
Still from *The Fall of the House of Usher* (1928), directed by James Sibley Watson, Jr., and Melville Webber. Courtesy of George Eastman House and the J. S. Watson estate

While in Eisenstein's film the steps are part of a public space, and the site of public resistance, in *Usher* the steps belong to a private family mansion, and are the site of a bourgeois Oedipal drama and prohibited intrafamilial desire—a theme also prevalent in *Lot in Sodom*, a tale of homosexual desire and pleasure flaunted publicly in defiance of familial heteronormativity (fig. 7.3).

While *Usher* offers pieces of a narrative about "perversions" of normative sexuality in the crumbling institution of the bourgeois family, *Lot* uses the tale of Sodom and Gomorrah to stage a more transgressive narrative about gay male desire as a challenge to the ideology of the heterosexual family as a cornerstone of community life. Lot, vexed by the tantalizing presence in the marketplace of the attractive, scantily clad, pleasure-seeking men of Sodom, delivers to this community of men a lecture extolling the virtues of womanhood and the pleasures of hetero-

Figure 7.3.
Still from *Lot in Sodom* (1933), directed by James Sibley Watson, Jr. Courtesy of George Eastman House and J. S. Watson estate

sexuality and reproduction—a speech in which the highly figurative birth of a child by his own daughter is the featured scene. The men of Sodom—who, as Marianne Moore notes, "do not look quite so responsibly sinister as they might"—are disgusted by Lot's evocation of normative sexuality; they stone him. In Moore's words, this civilization "is going to have pleasure, and is meting out justice to any man that interferes." (Lamentably, for Moore, this pleasure is a "strangling horror" represented in the shot of a phallic serpent "that thrusts forward rigid.") As Moore euphemistically indicates, homosexual desire in the film is ultimately punished: "we see gaiety waning into anguish, fire, ashes, dust."[22] As poetic evocations of illicit desire, Watson and Webber's films clearly are indebted not only to the focus on the psychological apparent in Expressionist films like *Caligari*, but to the French author and filmmaker Jean Cocteau's more conventionally shot and edited *Blood of a Poet* (1930), a film about gay male desire and power set in a prison.[23]

But for Bond in 1934, Watson and Webber are a part of what he calls "the visual, the Right wing of film art,"[24] composed of filmmakers and art theorists who, like Watson, advocated a radical separation of aesthetic concerns from their political milieu. The British journal *Film Art*'s editors and writers saw an avant-garde film movement coalescing around this approach roughly through the 1930s. Watson's critical writings show that his and Webber's own aesthetic affiliations fit in precisely with this conception of a politically conservative film avant-garde.

"THE RIGHT WING OF FILM ART": WATSON'S ANTI-MODERNISM

In 1924—a year before he began making films—Watson spoke out with vehemence against modernism, a term he identified with specific formal and aesthetic characteristics, arguing for a return to classical aesthetic standards. In his pseudonymously published critical writings, Watson condemned what some critics regarded as cummings' formal and visual innovation, calling these "modernist" tendencies part of a superficial and already outmoded trend. In a 1924 review of cummings' *Tulips and Chimneys* written under the pseudonym W. C. Blum, Watson attempts to reclaim cummings from his newly gained status as a "sort of extreme symbol of modernism" in order to cast him instead as a new lyric poet reworking classical forms in the tradition of Keats or Verlaine:

While extreme, [cummings] is only superficially "modern" and . . . he is quite content to sharpen some very well known tendencies of that fairly inclusive body of [literary] practice. With his typographical innovations, his extraordinary and ingenious appeal to the lust of the eye, he once led the fashion, or one of them. But it is rather the satisfaction which he offers to the lust of the ear and to other odd, often indecent, desires which poetry was supposed to gratify that I wish to emphasize; notably, the desire for rapid, unfailing lyric invention.[25]

Clearly Watson rejected the popular idea that cummings was part of a modernist wave of formal innovation, preferring to cast him as a student of classical form. This move is evident also in Watson's views on apparent formal innovation in avant-garde film. In an article written during *Usher*'s production, Watson dissociates his own project from what he perceives as an already outdated modernist agenda, linking it instead to what he sees as the everyday conventions of Hollywood cinema brought into the domain of the amateur filmmaker.

We suffered from the pseudo-scientific prejudice, the essence of modernism, which makes people believe that each medium of expression can and should be isolated and purified just as a chemical compound is isolated in the laboratory. You say to yourself that the cinema is not the theater or the dance and certainly not the novel, and then you begin to wonder what it is. You think of camera tricks as essential, of oppositions of movement, changes in size, changes in lighting and sharpness, accelerations and contrasts of speed, distortions of shape and perspectives. You decide to play any number of tricks on time and space. Then you remember that the worst picture you saw had all of this and nothing else; that every possible trick was invented the same year as the camera; that ideas have nothing to do with art and that there are too many ideas anyway.[26]

It is apparent from this quotation that the production of *Usher* was based not on the formal innovation of U.S. or European modernisms, but on the "old tricks" that were "invented the same year as the camera"—the cinematic strategies currently revived on the popular level, perhaps in part through the influence of *The Last Laugh*. Watson was not advocating full-scale Hollywood production, but a small-scale, selective use of some of the methods and techniques associated with the industry, in order to improve on popular industry products. In 1921 he commented on what he saw as the silent cinema's improvement on the conventions of the theater:

> [In watching a theater performance] there is something peculiarly humili-
> ating about the combined voice and facial expression of a good actor
> saying stupid lines or a bad actor saying good lines; and there are mighty
> few plays where one of these nefarious combinations is not kept before you
> most of the evening. The movie gives us the facial expression and
> eliminates the voice (just as the puppetshow gives us the voice and
> eliminates the expression) and we are grateful.[27]

The introduction of the sound film did not alter Watson's disdain for the
combined sound and image of theatrical performance. In Watson and
Webber's little-known 1930 sound-film spoof *It Never Happened*, bad
acting is combined with purposefully inane lines. The film is laced with
silly puns and metaphors made literal in a droll parody on the dramatic
talkie. The film centers on a love triangle in which a woman's lover is
discovered by her husband. "You are my husband," the woman asserts
impassively to a male character who enters the room a split second after
her lover departs. Later, her lover re-enters the frame to incriminate
himself with the question, "I underwear my shirt is." Handing the lover a
chisel, the husband flatly addresses him as "you who have chiseled your
way into my home." A shot of the husband firing a gun pointed off-screen,
presumably in the direction of his wife (fig. 7.4), is followed by a close-up
of the woman, unharmed, apparently reading her lines from a cigarette
package label: "Chester-field you in my arms again!"[28]

If *It Never Happened* draws on emerging sound-film narrative conventions only to mock them, how do *Usher* and *Lot* interpret and comment
on the conventions of modernism that they apparently incorporate—
conventions Watson had already derided? The correspondence on film
between cummings and Watson serves as an indicator of the meaning
and use in context of "modernist" conventions in Watson and Webber's
two avant-garde films.

If Watson and Webber's films were influenced by a literary bias, the
authors with whom Watson worked exhibited a reciprocal bias toward
visual and cinematic form. Cummings was a painter as well as a poet,
and took great interest in the graphic composition of his poems, or, as he
called them, his "poempictures." "What I care infinitely," he informed an
editor, "is that each poempicture should remain intact. Why? Possibly
because, with a few exceptions, my poems are essentially pictures."[29]
That he was also interested in the cinema is evident in his pseudonymously published farcical movie scripts and reviews—works that often

Figure 7.4.
Frame enlargement from *It Never Happened/Tomatoes Another Day* (1930), directed by
James Sibley Watson, Jr. Courtesy of George Eastman House

were deeply racist and anti-Semitic. One "prize movie scenario" that
mocks Hollywood themes and culture, published in *Vanity Fair* under
the pseudonym of C. E. Niltse (that is, nil T. S. E[lliot]), makes jokes at
the expense of Asians and Africans, the physically disabled, and hermaph-
rodites.[30] Another farce, an "ethnographic" study of an industry film set
titled "A Modern Gulliver Explores the Movies," casts the motion picture
industry as a society as "primitive" as the culture they construct in their
latest racist colonial fantasy of Africa. Cummings describes "blood-
drinking motion picture actors, scenic directors, camera men, forty-year-
old ingenues, and publicity artists at Astoria" during Famous Players–
Lasky Corporation's shooting of *Jungle Law*. The essay was credited to a
fictitious British explorer, Sir Arthur Catchpole.[31]

Clearly cummings shared with the Watson of *It Never Happened* an
interest in parody. However, his involvement with film also included
plans to engage in a collaborative rendering of some avant-garde
experiments with Watson. Their correspondence at the end of 1925

included the exchange of treatments and ideas for films that bore great similarity to cummings' own poetic form.[32] Unlike the *Vanity Fair* spoofs, these later film writings were taken very seriously by both Watson and cummings. The letters they exchanged just before the filming of *Usher* are perhaps the most important evidence of the meaning of Watson and Webber's avant-garde films. They address explicitly the search for what cummings called the "idiom," "language," or "aesthetic foundation of the 'moving picture' " (an entity cummings always set off in quotes). These letters, containing thumbnail sketches and diagrams with typed shooting directions followed by interpretive, analytical notes, provide concrete evidence of the perceived meaning and function of techniques and conventions associated with modernist art as taken up in U.S. avant-garde film.

Cummings' film scripts or "arrangements" lack narrative, characters, and anything but the most minimal of sets. The objective of each arrangement is to establish a variety of ostensibly "nonpictorial" means to represent in a range of patterns an object's movements through space.[33] For cummings, the abstract, nonnarrative, nonpictorial terms of dimensional form and circular motion constitute the basic idiom of the "moving picture." Clearly he considered his film treatments to be reflexive, formal works about representation and the conditions of cinematic illusionism:

> I should consider this "arrangement" a formula comparable to the "3 dimensions" formula in painting (i.e. to paint a subject so as to give the *illusion of behindness,*so as to make the spectator feel the a-little-less-than-half-of a subject (arm,woman,tree) which he does not see (in terms of paint)IS)—the camera formula being based,however,on NON-illusion, or better,on DISillusion.

On what theory or aesthetic does cummings base his own method? There is much in these formulas for "DISillusionment" to support an association of cummings' method with Cubist painting. Elsewhere in his notes cummings calls his technique for representing all perspectives on an object in a mobile shot "an idiom of seeingaround." His drawings (including those published in *The Dial*) have been described by critics and historians as exhibiting the influence of Cubism, and he was well-read in current writings on the movement.[34] The general recognition of alliances among poetic style, Cubism, and cinematic form is evident in the following review by Ezra Pound of Cocteau's poetry:

As the present reversed aim of literature, the literature from Cocteau to Rodker, we find a sort of writing which is sometimes incomprehensible if one does read every word and try to parse it in sequence. His contemporaries called Keats "incomprehensible." The life of a village is narrative. . . . In a city the visual impressions succeed each other, overlap, overcross, they are "cinematographic," but they are not a simple linear sequence. They are often a flood of nouns without verbal relations.[35]

Oddly, however, *The Dial* published no examples of Cubist works, and Watson makes no reference to Cubism in either his publications or his letters to cummings. I suggest that what appears to be an adaptation of Cubist conventions is perhaps more precisely the application of Pound's theories to the film medium. Pound's influence on cummings and Watson is important to acknowledge, not only because it is a more likely source for the aesthetic of Watson and Webber's filmwork, but because it suggests a very different cultural politics from that associated with Cubism.

Pound's Vorticism, and his use of science as a model for poetic language and production in general, was an important source for cummings' and Watson's film plans.[36] For Pound, "every concept, every emotion presents itself to the vivid consciousness in some primary form. . . . It is no more ridiculous that a person should receive or convey an emotion by an arrangement of shapes, or planes, or colours, than that they should receive or convey such emotion by an arrangement of musical notes."[37] Pound believed that geometry played a critical role in the production of meaning in any form. With geometry at its center, Pound's epistemological schema confers great stature on the role of the technician or the engineer who fabricates a work. Watson discussed the use of a wide range of devices to put cummings' systems into effect, and used a number of them in the shooting of *The Fall of the House of Usher*. Along with the dissolve, he mentions double exposure, tracking shots taken from a camera mounted to a ceiling track, the attachment of a gyroscope to the shutter, and the substitution of a prismatic ring in place of the shutter (the latter to be used with frameless roll film shot at a continuous rate, without intermittent stops). Fischer notes that a converted phonograph turntable was used in the filming of text to be superimposed in both films—an apparatus that cummings describes in detail in a letter to Watson. It would appear from these facts that Watson was to play the role of technical facilitator of cummings' geometric diagrams. However, the place of technical knowledge and form in

Pound's thinking cannot be underestimated. The following passage from Pound's *The Wisdom of Poetry* (1912) indicates one aspect of the nature of the relationship forged between geometry and poetic form in the literary context:

> What the analytical geometer does for space and form, the poet does for states of consciousness. . . . By the signs $a^2 + b^2 = c^2$, I imply the circle. By $(a-r)^2 + (b-r)^2 = (c-r)^2$, I imply the circle and its mode of birth. I am led from the consideration of the particular circles formed by my inkwell and my table-rim, to the contemplation of the circle absolute, its law; the circle free in all space, unbounded, loosed from the accidents of time and place. Is the formula nothing, or is it the cabala and the sign of unintelligible magic? The engineer, understanding and translating for the many, builds for the uninitiated bridges and devices. He speaks their language. For the initiated the signs are a door into eternity and into the boundless ether.
> *As the abstract mathematician is to science so is the poet to the world's consciousness.* Neither has direct contact with the many, neither of them is superhuman or arrives at his utility through occult and inexplicable ways. Both are scientifically demonstrable.[38]

Cummings was not the only one to associate experimental film form with geometry. In a 1934 review of *Lot in Sodom*, the critic Leonard Hacker commended Watson and Webber for their use of an effect resembling the lap-dissolve (an effect that was achieved through optical printing: fig. 7.5). A paean to the phenomenological event of the dissolve follows:

> In every film whether the device is used or not the Dissolve always takes place in the mind of the spectator, who by his own powers of mental alchemy, must transmute the images presented to him into intelligent patterns and concepts. . . . The Dissolve is a physio-chemical device where the Cut is but physical. It is only recently that the laws of chemistry and those of physics have been united in a single science with the realization that all life is both physical and chemical in constant interaction. The Dissolve naturally manifests this unity and thus becomes the true basis of the cinema.[39]

Cummings was immersed in similar phenomenological views about chemical and physical laws vis-à-vis cinematic movement (if not the specific device of the dissolve) when he asserted nine years earlier,

Figure 7.5.
Homemade optical printer, constructed from old lathe by James Sibley Watson, Jr., for *Lot in Sodom* (1933). Courtesy of George Eastman House

"Whereas, hitherto, 'moving' (pictures) has been used pictorially,to describe what things do(i.e. they move),I wish to employ 'moving' in a new
sense—as revealing the essential data of phenomena,the truth of Thing."
According to cummings' sketches, the analytical project of "seeingaround"
that he attributes to his cinema takes place within the geometrical laws of
the circle, as described by Pound (above). This approach to "Truth" of a
phenomenal "thing" via the laws of geometry and sensory perception
borrows from the language of Machist physics, in which "Truth" is no
longer located in an object apart from perception, but exists in the relation
between phenomena and sensation. For cummings, the moving picture
both illustrates and makes accessible this process of perception. Hence, the
geometrical film formula is "the strict idiom which seems to me to constitute
the 'aesthetic' foundation of the 'moving picture.' " However, cummings also
specifies that this scientific "idiom" is not without its psychological dimension. He indicates that this abstract language of geometrical film-poetics is
analogous to Freud's "language" of the unconscious:

> As to language which employs this idiom. The "language",as it seems to
> me,is concentric. It suggests Professor F's Repetition Compulsion.
>   I should think that,as the camera went around and around the
> track,shooting the heart which you [Watson] mention,the 3 background
> occurrences(flat;(flat–upright,bulging–fallingtoward,hollowing–falling
> away from)would give very much the same sensation as a good rollercoas-
> ter,or a lively Unconscious.

For cummings, the cinema materializes the movements of the unconscious conceived mechanistically. The moving picture is an analogue of
unconscious processes (fig. 7.6). However, cummings does not intend his
geometrical formulas to be mere models for mental phenomena; they are
prescriptions for patterns of movement which will trigger the spectator's
unconscious processes: the cinema also motors the unconscious. According to Watson, cummings' poems performed precisely this psychological
function:

> Suave, dangerous speed, dizzy falling, or veering in reverberating
> emptiness—always the appeal to the motor and visceral sensations, the
> sensations of effective effort, of change of position, of alarming passive
> motion (as in an elevator) and to the primitive emotions of power and
> helplessness which lie just behind.[40]

Figure 7.6.
Still from *Lot in Sodom* (1933), directed by James Sibley Watson, Jr. Courtesy of George Eastman House and J. S. Watson estate

The terms Watson uses to describe the sensation of reading a cummings poem closely match cummings' vision of film spectatorship for his own film schemes. The cinematic systems cummings describes are meant to act on the viewer like "a good rollercoaster" ride, evoking precisely the sensations of "speed," "dizzy falling," and "alarming passive motion" described by Watson. On some level, this interest in the physiological effects of mechanical propulsion and speed on the passive body can be linked quite easily to the militarized discourse of Futurism. Appearing in the context of Pound, cummings, and *The Dial*, these terms are drawn into a right-wing, liberal, purportedly apolitical modernism centered in England and the United States—a modernism that provides intellectual grounding for the "Right wing of film art" Bond advocates in *Film Art* in the thirties.

What are the implications for film history of the association of an American film avant-garde in the late twenties and thirties with the more conservative national trends in literary modernism? Of the renunciation of modernist production in favor of industry conventions—not after, but during, the production by its author of two of North America's earliest designated "modernist," "avant-garde" films? It might be easy to conclude, on the basis of Watson's writings and intellectual-political affiliations, that *The Fall of the House of Usher* and *Lot in Sodom* are improperly cast as modernist, and should instead be regarded as the amateur works that Watson insisted they were. I would suggest, however, that historians of U.S. film modernism need to use Watson's writings not to uncover some authorized take on the films, but to identify the nature of the influence of Pound and cummings on the film avant-garde before *and after* 1943. In *Visionary Film*, Sitney notes Pound's influence on two major figures of the post-1943 avant-garde: Stan Brakhage and Hollis Frampton. Brakhage himself has written about his use of Pound's theory of Vorticism in the production of *Dog Star Man* (1964).[41] However, neither Sitney nor Brakhage nor Frampton makes note of the relationship between Pound and early film modernists in the United States. My point is not, of course, that we need to look more closely for signs of a national avant-garde in order to construct an autonomous cultural history for film, but that it is important to take into consideration the specific ideologies that have informed U.S. film movements differently from those of Europe. Through an analysis of the place of Pound and cummings in the early film avant-garde, it is possible to situate the aesthetics and politics of filmmakers like Frampton and Brakhage not simply in light of general modernist literary influences (that of Pound, for example) and European film aesthetics, but in terms of a U.S. literary and visual-cinematic tradition formed out of a particular political and cultural context. Pound in the United States is the Pound of cummings, Watson, and the politically conservative *Dial*. It is this tradition, and not that of a Pound divorced from his place in the U.S. scene, that we need to consider in taking up Brakhage and Frampton's "use" of Pound.

What I have tried to suggest here is that it is not enough to read a virtually untheorized, unhistoricized body of films—the early U.S. film avant garde—in terms of their overseas aesthetic influences and sources. Such a strategy serves to strip aesthetic movements of their politics, history, and culture. In order to historicize the designated film avant-gardes of the pre- and post–World War II periods, it is critical that we begin to look outside the field of film history to locate the diverse but specific cultural and political factors that ground and shape film discourses and movements. Could the liberal, "apolitical" ideals of the literary avant-garde of *The Dial* have provided important intellectual support for the idealism and apoliticism that characterize much postwar U.S. independent and avant-garde cinema?

NOTES

1. Watson also structured this footage into humorous spoofs on popular cinema themes. For example, x-ray footage of animal locomotion is edited into a reel titled "Disney Animal Review"; and x-ray footage of male and female bodies becomes fodder for a seduction scene over which the narrator humorously identifies the physiological signs of sexual desire. On these films, see Lisa Cartwright, *Screening the Body: Tracing Medicine's Visual Culture* (Minneapolis: University of Minnesota Press, 1995). Prints of all of the nonscientific films are held at George Eastman House, Rochester, N.Y. The Eastman House collection also has some examples of the x-ray films: the bulk of these, however, are held at the University of Rochester School of Medicine and Dentistry, Department of Radiology. I thank Jan-Christopher Horak, (formerly of GEH) and Dr. John Wandtke and Mary Lou Bryant of the latter institution for access to prints.

2. Lucy Fischer, "The Films of James Sibley Watson, Jr., and Melville Webber: A Reconsideration," *Millennium Film Journal* 19 (Fall–Winter 1987– 88): 40–49.

3. P. Adams Sitney, *Visionary Film: The American Avant-Garde 1943–1978* (New York: Oxford University Press, 1974).

4. J. S. Watson, Jr., "An Amateur Studio Picture," *Transactions of the Society for Motion Picture Engineers* 12, no. 33 (April 1928): 216.

5. Norman Wilson, "*Lot in Sodom*," *Cinema Quarterly* 3, no. 1 (Autumn 1934).

6. His fellowship was for the purpose of studying the frescoes of Tavant— images that would inform his makeup design in the production of *The Fall of the House of Usher*. See his "The Frescoes of Tavant," *Art Studies* 23 (1925): 83–91.

7. The fact that the term "modernism" is historically based in Christian reform movements, and that modern science was a revolutionary force in these movements, is often overlooked in the consideration of modernist trends in cultural production. It is significant that Watson and Webber's 1933 *Lot in Sodom* is a revision of a biblical text. The film's visual-poetic birth sequence, used (unsuccessfully) to lure the men of Sodom toward heterosexuality, symbolizes precisely this agenda of historical modernism.

8. See Barbara Zingman, *The Dial: An Author Index* (Troy, N.Y.: Whitson, 1975), p. vi.

9. Personal correspondence with the author.

10. In his study of *The Dial*, Nicholas Joost confirms this common agenda: "Emerson was determined, like Thayer and Watson, to deny control of *The Dial* to the "Humanity and Reform Men," who trampled on letters and poetry; still, the activists were allowed their say in both magazines. Like the editors of the original *Dial*, Thayer and Watson were interested in "an organ whereby the Free may speak," though to be sure their organ ignored what another *Dial* advertising circular of 1920 termed "the fumy scene of contemporary politics." See Nicholas Joost, *Scofield Thayer and The Dial* (Carbondale and Edwardsville: Southern Illinois University Press, 1964), p. 26. See also pp. 25–29.

11. Watson, "Amateur Studio Picture."

12. Edgar Allan Poe, "The Fall of the House of Usher," in *The Portable Poe*, ed. Philip Van Doren Stern (New York: Viking, 1945), p. 257.

13. Fischer, "Films of Watson and Webber," p. 42.

14. Watson, "Amateur Studio Picture," p. 223.

15. This point was made in conversation and is elaborated in an excellent unpublished paper by Dale Davis, ". . . And Melville Webber" (1989, in author's possession). I am deeply indebted to Davis for generously sharing with me her expert knowledge and resources on Watson and Webber.

16. Davis, ". . . And Melville Webber," pp. 2–3. Her source is Hildegarde Lasell Watson, "Journals and Notes," n.d., n.p., Rosenbach Museum and Library, Philadelphia. Also see Hildegarde Lasell Watson, *The Edge of the Woods* (Rochester, N.Y.: n.p., 1979).

17. Luce Irigaray, "Plato's Hystera," in *Speculum of the Other Woman*, trans. Gillian C. Gill (Ithaca: Cornell University Press, 1985), p. 244.

18. Epstein released a film version of *The Fall of the House of Usher* in 1928, a few months before Watson and Webber's film was released. Watson claims to have begun work on his version in 1926.

19. Kirk Bond, "*Lot in Sodom*," *Film Art* 1, no. 4 (1934): 69.

20. Ibid., p. 69.

21. Ibid.

22. Marianne Moore, "*Lot in Sodom*," *Close Up* 10, no. 1 (1933).

23. *Lot in Sodom*, which shared the bill with Cocteau's film at New York City's 5th Avenue Playhouse, is an important example of the representation of gay sexuality and bisexuality in pre-1945 avant-garde cinema, resonating in important ways not only with *Blood of a Poet*, but with the post-1945 work of Willard Maas and Marie Mencken, Kenneth Anger, and Jack Smith. See O. C. Burritt, "*Lot in Sodom*," Toronto Film Society Program Notes (18 March 1968), in the files of the Museum of Modern Art Film Study Center, New York City.

24. Bond, "*Lot in Sodom*," p. 69.

25. W. C. Blum, "The Perfumed Paraphrase of Death," *The Dial* 76 (1924): 49.

26. Watson, "Amateur Studio Picture," p. 217.

27. W. C. Blum, "American Letter," *The Dial* 71 (1921): 347.

28. Watson's son Michael Watson has stated that Alec Wilder was the source of the film's verbal jokes. Phone conversation with the author, 17 October 1991.

29. Quoted in Rushworth M. Kidder, " 'Twin Obsessions': The Poetry and Painting of E. E. Cummings," in *Critical Essays on E. E. Cummings* (Boston: G. K. Hall, 1984), p. 244.

30. *Vanity Fair*, January 1925, p. 51.

31. *Vanity Fair*, March 1925, p. 49. Also see *Selected Letters*, pp. 107–108.

32. Letters held in a private collection.

33. Letters from cummings to Watson are in a private collection, copyright E. E. Cummings Trust, 1991, used with permission.

34. According to Kidder, " 'Twin Obsessions,' " p. 242. See cummings' drawing of Charlie Chaplin published in *The Dial* 26 (1924).

35. Ezra Pound, *The Dial* (January 1921): 110. I thank James Longenbach for providing me with this reference.

36. On Pound's relationship with science, see Ian F. A. Bell, *Critic As Scientist: The Modernist Poetics of Ezra Pound* (London: Methuen, 1981); and Martin A. Kayman, *The Modernism of Ezra Pound: The Science of Poetry* (London: Macmillan, 1986).

37. Ezra Pound, *Gaudier-Brzeska: A Memoir* (New York: New Directions, 1960), p. 81.

38. Ezra Pound, "The Wisdom of Poetry," *Forum* 47, no. 4 (April 1912): 500–501.

39. Leonard Hacker, "Lot in Sodom," *Film Art* 1, no. 3 (1934): 23, 27.

40. Blum, "Perfumed Paraphrase of Death," pp. 50, 52.

41. Sitney, *Visionary Film*, pp. 174, 182, 184, 195, 396.

8

Theodore Huff
Historian and Filmmaker

CHUCK KLEINHANS

Because the independent media artworld was still in the process of formation before the 1950s, we face several problems in trying to understand early avant-garde film. Today at least some formal institutions exist, however limited they may be, which carry on the financing, training, production, distribution, exhibition, preservation, and criticism of independent work. But before the 1950s, such structures cannot be taken for granted. The matrix of diverse institutions and individuals who create and sustain the specific works produced as well as artistic careers was characterized by uneven development.

Considered in terms of his various roles in an emerging film culture, Theodore Huff's life offers an instructive look into independent film and cinema studies as they were in the process of becoming institutionalized.[1] Huff's primary artistic contribution to early U.S. avant-garde cinema consisted of work on two major films: *Mr. Motorboat's Last Stand* (1933), made with John Flory, which mixed realism and fantasy in a comic satire of the Depression, and *The Uncomfortable Man* (1948), made with Kent Munson, a psychodrama of an alienated young man in New York City. As an amateur filmmaker he worked on several films in the 1930s and 1940s that are typical of independent cinema of the time, but he remains best remembered today for the Theodore Huff Memorial Film Society, organized by William K. Everson in the 1950s in New York, which continues regularly to screen classic film art. Professionally, Huff is remembered as a film historian whose examination of Chaplin's films, *Charlie Chaplin*,[2] was the first substantial and scholarly book-length study of a director written in the United States. It now appears that he was, in addition, instrumental in discovering and preserving the Library of Congress Paper Print Collection, which has given scholars an essential

180

archive of early U.S. silent film. Huff was also a collector, archivist, critic, silent-film accompanist, film society regular, college teacher, and acquaintance and friend of numerous people involved in creating and sustaining film culture.

The basic facts of his life and career provide a useful framework for understanding Huff's place in the film culture of his era. Born 20 December 1905, Edmund Newell Huff, Jr., was the first of three sons of a physician and his wife living in Englewood, New Jersey, a suburb of New York City. The father later deserted the family, and Junior changed his name to Theodore while in college. The boy grew up only a short distance from the Fort Lee, New Jersey, movie studios, which had their heyday during World War I. Fort Lee, across from upper Manhattan at the George Washington Bridge, provided outdoor locations, including bluffs overlooking the Hudson River and residential settings in Englewood. Although production there declined rapidly when most of the film industry moved to Hollywood after World War I, as a child and adolescent Huff saw films being made in his community and hung around the studios, catching glimpses of stars and seeing the production process.

The young man attended prep school at Phillips Exeter. Adolescent writings include a parody of the silent newsreel, "Passé News," and mock melodramas that exaggerate silent-film conventions: "The Strand Theatre Presents the Super-colossal Epic 'A Little Child Shall Lead Them' or 'The Pit Falls of a Big City,' Directed by D. W. de Reel." These parodies imitate comic features published in *Photoplay*, *Motion Picture World*, and other film periodicals that Huff collected. In the 1920s he provided piano accompaniment for silent films at summer theaters, a skill he also used later. He graduated from all-male Princeton in 1928, a year later than the rest of his entering class. There he participated in drama club activities, as he had in prep school. A revealing news photo shows him gathered with other students outdoors during the screen-test filming of some Princeton students by a Hollywood camera crew on a "talent search" promotion. His passion for cinema is clear in two English composition essays written at Princeton: one argues that Lillian Gish is the greatest actress of the day, and the other that D. W. Griffith is "the greatest artist of the Twentieth Century."

After graduation Huff spent several years working on Wall Street, according to a self-prepared promotional statement, but it can be surmised from some of his journals that he was unemployed or underemployed as the Great Depression proceeded. At this time he began making films and screening them at various Amateur Cinema League (ACL) meetings. For a short time he was involved with the left-wing Workers Film and Photo League, attending meetings and crewing for Ralph Steiner on documentary shoots. In December 1935 he joined the staff of the newly created Museum of Modern Art Film Library, the first museum archive, exhibition program, and noncommercial distribution service for film as an art form in the United States. He wrote to a friend, "My main job is arranging the musical accompaniment for the old silent pictures (I used to play in a summer theatre, have some of the old "movie" music, and was always interested in that field)."[3] He also seems to have put his own substantial collection of stills and other film materials at MOMA's service.

Huff was dismissed, officially because of a budget constriction, in May 1940, and began substantial work on his biography of Chaplin.[4] His next employment was with the Motion Picture and Sound Recordings Department of the National Archives in Washington, D.C., where, beginning in July 1942, he catalogued and described films, including captured German ones. This job ended in early 1946 with the demobilization. Two letters from this time refer to Huff's getting a position as "Director, Motion Picture Department, United Nations Headquarters," but that job fell through, as did a television job a few years later with the American Broadcasting Corporation, with no explanation in the available documents. He did some work in the late 1940s for the National Broadcasting Corporation, reviewing silent comedies, particularly the "Our Gang" films, for screening on the *Howdy Doody Show*. Huff examined them for broadcast suitability and apparently also edited out some offensive ethnic humor.

In the immediate postwar world, beginning in fall 1946, Huff began teaching film history and introduction to filmmaking on an adjunct basis in the Motion Picture Department at New York University. He also taught film history at the University of Southern California in the summer of 1948 and went on to the Film Institute at City College of New York that fall. During this time he also co-directed two films with his former NYU student Kent Munson, finally found a publisher for his Chaplin book, and wrote the *Sight and Sound* "indexes" for Chaplin and Ernst Lubitsch. These were scholarly historical listings of the works of major directors (dates of production, release, cast and crew lists, etc.) and involved considerable painstaking research.

He began the 1950s with a civil service job as a film reviewer (writing catalogue copy) and then became an assistant casting director for the U.S. Army Signal Corps, which made training films at studios in Astoria, Long Island. He continued to be active in film circles and to write; among other projects, he met and gathered materials on the emerging filmmaker Stanley Kubrick. The reviews of his Chaplin book were very favorable, and it was subsequently published in England and, in translation, in France and Italy. Encouraged, Huff said he hoped to write the definitive history of the movies. He died of a cerebral hemorrhage at his mother's house on Long Island on 15 March 1953. The bare facts of his professional life indicate the many different situations in which this figure in an emerging film culture found himself. Clearly some of this is to be expected in any inchoate field: refined division of labor usually comes after growth has produced a complexity that demands specialization.

In studying Huff, we see the situation of an emerging independent cinema in relation to a larger corporate capitalist industrial system, and in particular the situation of the individual intellectual worker within that system. The large-scale mass media systems of the modern era—the corporate and industrial production and diffusion of sound/image material—need intellectual workers, skilled specialists whose labor is primarily conceptual, who work within, around, and in relation to these systems. Today we experience these social formations and the intellectuals who fit into them in a fairly complex and articulated state: we understand and expect specialist division of labor. In looking at Huff's career, however, we see someone who does not occupy a simple or single position, but rather fits into several different positions at different times depending upon the evolution of the field. He is a "generalist," an intellectual handyman, who can fit into many different, changing, and evolving sites of the system as a whole. As an intellectual worker, much of the time he is part of the army of surplus labor. He can be brought into service when the evolving system needs certain key skills or types of knowledge, but as an individual he is never strong enough actually to command a premium for his specialized abilities.

Huff represents a permanent component of the independent filmmaking world: people who do not achieve high distinction in their own work, but whose talents are essential to the success of collaborative works. In particular, his expertise in the conventions of silent-film narration allowed him to provide highly accomplished camerawork and editing in the films he made with John Flory and Kent Munson. By considering his filmmaking in sequence, we can see the achievements and changing historical moments of the independent sector.

FIRST FILMS

Huff's notes indicate that he wrote the burlesque Western *Hearts of the West* for the First Lake Follies in August 1926, which would have been during his college years. There is no further information on this summer entertainment, but he indicates that he rewrote it in April 1929 and includes the information that he brought a second-hand projector at that time. Production began during summer 1929 with a cast of amateur child actors, dragged on into the fall with weekend shooting, and was revived in the spring. The first finished version was duplicated the next summer, but technical problems and additional shooting of titles and re-staging sequences delayed screening for the ACL until March 1931. According to his production diary, Huff continued to make changes, including re-staging, re-shooting, and tightening sequences, until January 1933: for example, "Aug. 9 [1931] changes in horses (after seeing *Birth of a Nation*)."

The juvenile movie announces its parody status from the opening titles:

> Ideal-Supreme Pictures presents D. W. DeReel's Hearts of the West. A D. W. DeReel Production with Rex Montague and Gloria Gishford. Copyright 1915 by Ideal-Supreme Pictures, Inc. Issac Ginsberg, President.
>
> This is a simple story of simple people. Down through the ages, since the beginning of Time, there has beaten in the hearts of all Mankind the Eternal yearning for Love. . . .

The children impersonating adult stars are well directed and maintain the illusion without mugging and breaking role. A barroom scene opens the film with a series of simple sight gags, such as blowing the foam off a beer onto someone else. When the villain paws a dance-hall girl, the sheriff kicks him out of the saloon, and he and the girl fall in love. The bad guy then kidnaps the dancer and takes her to his cabin. Duane, the sheriff, looks unsuccessfully for Nell, the barroom entertainer, until an Indian tells him where she is. Cross-cutting between the villain menacing the girl and the rescuer on his way heightens suspense. In a medium shot of Duane riding to the rescue, a moving cyclorama backdrop repeats the same scenery flowing behind the hero. A final fight on a cliff (the same Palisades used in Fort Lee productions fifteen years earlier) ends with the villain falling off and dying. The happy ending shows the couple living in a mansion. Huff wrote an original score for the accompaniment.

His production diary begins 6 July 1929: "went about trying to borrow money, to bank, etc. (had only $65)." This must have been a time of unemployment, since he notes that he "left Laidlaw's" on 20 June. He worked a few days a week on preproduction (scouting locations, building a set, arranging for horses, scouting talent, etc.) in July, and began almost daily production in August, once his camera, lights, and other equipment arrived (he found he could charge the purchase). The production diary reveals all the predictable problems of putting on a dramatic film with child amateur actors in the summer. Kids do not show up or are away on vacation; they get restless in the heat; a shoot is rained out; he rents horses that run away during the shoot; the boys fight with each other; doubles must be found for no-shows. In mid-September he goes job hunting at Chemical Bank and Chase Bank. Hired at Chase (he loses the job a year later), he then works on weekends to finish the project. "Sun. Oct. 20 — To Dean Street (double for Heffron) Plenty of trouble. A tough gang watched us — names, stole stuff — actors refused to ignore them. Police chased, but returned." Some of his principal talent gets tired of the project and does not want to participate in re-takes. Finally, in December, while shooting in the cold weather, he decides to start again in the spring. He begins again in April, working only on Sundays, and has to pay some of the boys five dollars to get additional shots. At one point he is arrested while scouting a location (fig. 8.1).

Hearts of the West is an extremely ambitious first film. A costume drama, it involved preparing barroom and log cabin sets and managing a cast of about thirty children for the crowd scenes. Nell was played by a ten-year-old boy, following the convention of Huff's prep school and Princeton theater days. While his previous experience in theater prepared Huff for organizing the production and his work as an accompanist gave him a sensitivity to editing, he was apparently self-taught as a cinematographer. It is a credit to his talent and perseverance that the film made the 1931 "Ten Best" list for the ACL's magazine *Amateur Movie Makers*. The award also marks the importance of an organization like the ACL in its time. For an aspiring young man, the ACL's recognition must

Figure 8.1.
Frame enlargement from *Hearts of the West* (1931), directed by Theodore Huff. Courtesy of George Eastman House

have been very important. Huff's production scrapbook includes letters from ACL officials praising the effort.

Huff's production diary lists some additional projects at this time. He developed a scenario for "The Prince and the Pauper" in summer 1931, but the project ended after an attempt to shoot test footage in and around a church was blocked. That fall he wrote "Little Miss Caesar" for a Methodist Church youth club, but apparently could not get any lasting interest from the mostly female group. In December 1931 and January 1932, he made a film commissioned for a hundred dollars by the Russell Sage Foundation.[5] This film, depicting the activities of the progressive social work organization and its staff, was shown at a retirement banquet for the director. Several people in the foundation or knowledgeable about film wrote letters praising it, and *Amateur Movie Makers* give it an honorable mention in its year-end "Ten Best" listing.[6] In December 1932 Huff began work on a "Riverside Church film," and shot several scenes that were shown in January; at a meeting in February, however, he "resigned" with no explanation. *What a Cook* was written in 1932 by Huff but photographed and directed by L. Wellender and shown at a party in April.

Huff's most substantial film from this period was in the same juvenile burlesque vein as *Hearts of the West. Little Geezer* (1932)[7] was a more modest effort in length, cast (all-boy), and sets. Originally written for a Methodist church club, Huff revised it and shot on weekends from February to May, then quickly cut it. It was mentioned in *Amateur Movie Makers* and received an honorable mention in the year-end list. Huff entered it, along with *Hearts of the West*, in an amateur contest run by *American Cinematographer*, a respected professional publication, where it placed in the top ten. A letter from the editors about the judging remarked:

> The acting of the players in *Little Geezer* seemed surer and more understanding. In entertainment value, the two pictures were closely matched—in fact, both of them were tremendously entertaining to the judges, all of whom had made many professional films of both of the types burlesqued—but the better tempo of *Little Geezer*, and its more succinct narration, gave it an appreciable edge.

This praise from Hollywood professionals must have been the high point of this phase of Huff's creative work. The correspondence indicates that he eagerly sought feedback from them. The ACL's magazine and letters to Huff often have a air of genteel clubiness, conveying a desire to encourage an earnest young man, as befits an organization promoting 16mm filmmaking, which was in numbers and economics largely an upper-middle-class recreation. (Its "Ten Best" lists always prominently include films that seem to be records of vacation trips to exotic locales.) The Hollywood judges are much more perceptive about technique and details. Amateur contests of all kinds are often ridiculed because they inevitably reveal a gap between ambition and accomplishment. This gap is easy to mock, especially in a competitive individualist culture where a large professional mass entertainment economy invites aspiration while rewarding excellence in conventional terms. For Huff, winning the contest and making the "Ten Best" list was national recognition, something not attainable in other ways. Thus, these amateur institutions provided validation that went beyond hobbyist amusement.

The letter from Hollywood explaining why his films were being returned must have been a disappointment:

> We were holding *Little Geezer* to show it to Hal Roach, producer of the "Our Gang" comedies. We felt he would be greatly interested in seeing these pictures because of the youngsters you use in them and the way in which they conducted themselves, especially the little fellow who played the part of the Big Shot. However Roach has been so very busy that we could not get an appointment with him as soon as we expected.

Many young filmmakers hope that a film will give them a toehold in Hollywood. John Flory recalled at a memorial meeting for Huff, " 'The one thing I can do best,' he used to tell me, 'is to direct kids. I'd like to make films like the "Our Gang" comedies.' "

MR. MOTORBOAT'S LAST STAND, 1933

In June 1933 Huff met John Flory, a twenty-four-year-old Yale graduate, and they began work on a satiric comedy of the Depression. Flory was interested in putting his available resources into a short film that he could use as a "calling card" to try to break into Hollywood. The credits for the film have always named Flory as writer and director, with Huff listed as "assistant in photography"; in the titles, Priscilla Peck is also credited as an assistant. Flory's experience in filmmaking at this point was limited, having previously only worked on Steiner's *Panther Woman of the Needle Trades* (1931), while Huff had four years of experience and had won awards the previous year. Huff's production diary supports the listed division of labor, but he was probably key in translating the script into shots and sequences, and he must have been essential to the editing, which tells the story with no intertitles. Flory and Huff spent about five days a week shooting in July and early August, did some additional shooting in September, and cut *Mr. Motorboat's Last Stand* in six days in October.

Subtitled "A Comedy of the Depression," the two-reel film begins with the hero, Mr. Motorboat (played by Leonard "Motorboat" Stirrup, a professional tapdancer), waking up at dawn in an auto junkyard. In a montage sequence marked by very effective closeups, he tunes in a radio program, does calisthenics, and puts on his clothes, with a series of sight gags on the theme of attempted dignity in the face of economic adversity. For example, he adds spats to his shoes, but a huge hole is evident in the sole of one (fig. 8.2). He shaves using a piece of tough rope for a brush, a knife for a razor, and an auto's rear-view mirror for a shaving glass. He then produces a frying pan and egg, makes breakfast, and feeds his pet rabbit. He places cigarette butts in a silver case, puts on a straw boater (with a hole in the top), adds a flower to his lapel, picks up an umbrella and a briefcase, and strides off, finding in a trash container a copy of the *New York Times* to carry. The scene is much in the mode of Chaplin, though the whole is carried by the effective shots and cutting, unlike Chaplin's typically static camera and long shots. The actor thus is not asked to reproduce the subtlety of Chaplin's whole-body mime, but instead is a plastic element within the fairly fast-paced montage. An African-American, Mr. Motorboat is seen as

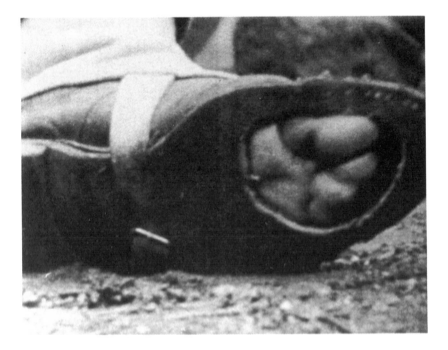

Figure 8.2.
Frame enlargement from Mr. *Motorboat's Last Stand* (1933), directed by Theodore Huff and John Flory. Courtesy of George Eastman House

comic but without Coon or Sambo stereotyping. The junkyard sequence is very effective and may well be the model for a similar opening in the Elia Kazan/Irving Lerner/Molly Day Thatcher satiric short *Pie in the Sky* a few years later.

Now that our hero is ready for the world, a junkyard vehicle beckons—literally, as, through the magic of editing, the door opens and closes to attract him. He appears to himself as a chauffeur, and enters the car to be driven by his double. Then follows a clever sequence in which the car seems to be moving, and cutaways of the passing scene and spectators give the impression of traveling. Arriving at his destination, Mr. Motorboat sets up his apple stand and prepares for business with the same tidy attention to detail we saw earlier: washing each piece of fruit, trimming, and polishing. His rival, a white roughneck, sets up a stand nearby, and the two sneer at each other when a passing woman stops for an apple. Mr. Motorboat tips his hat with smiling courtesy, while the rival puts up a misspelled sign, "Unemploid war veterin," and crudely polishes an apple on his clothes. The woman now sees that Mr. Motorboat offers, according to a newly produced sign, "sanitary apples," and has, moreover, magically acquired a spiffy white uniform.

Losing the sale, the rival goes off in disgust while Mr. Motorboat suddenly appears in Wall Street with his tiny capital. He "fishes" with his change-maker and reels in (the line is stock ticker tape) stock certificates. This montage is edited together with shots of balloons on which the years 1928, 1929, and so on are inflated, expanding tires, bubbles in a bubblepipe, and shots of the rival climbing a steep hill with a barrel and then taking aim at Mr. Motorboat's stand. Conceptually funny, this intellectual montage, which seems indebted to the Soviet silent-film editing style, comes to a climax when the barrel speeds downhill to knock apart the apple stand, as the balloons burst and apples go flying, finally raining from the sky on the unwary.

His stand a mess, Mr. Motorboat seems about to resign, when he spots his rival, who now has the coin-changer, and a chase ensues. The chase is well done. The two run about, and Mr. Motorboat assaults his opponent with a small popgun, resulting in several "x" marks on the other's body. Finally the rival escapes in a car (fig. 8.3) and Mr. Motorboat contemplates suicide (closeups with double exposures of a poison bottle, a hangman's noose, water: fig. 8.4). But then he is shown back at his old stand, where a group of white workers throw dollar bills at

Figure 8.3.
Frame enlargement from *Mr. Motorboat's Last Stand* (1933), directed by Theodore Huff and John Flory. Courtesy of George Eastman House

him while he performs the old magic trick of pulling his rabbit from a top hat.

Mr. Motorboat is shown as clever, resourceful, and quickwitted. The film is surprisingly free of racial stereotypes, while also avoiding the sentimentality often found in Chaplin. Its strength is in its wit, efficiency, and clever pacing. Showing the down-and-out as self-reliant was a progressive message during the Depression. As a project it worked for Flory, who quickly obtained a seven-year contract with Paramount.[8] The film brought Huff little success or recognition, however, although it made the ACL's "Ten Best" list, and was praised several times in *Amateur Movie Makers*. Huff finished one more film along with Mark Borgotte: *Ghost Town: The Story of Fort Lee* (1935), a short, undistinguished documentary shot in the abandoned Fort Lee studios, recalling their glory days through intertitles.[9]

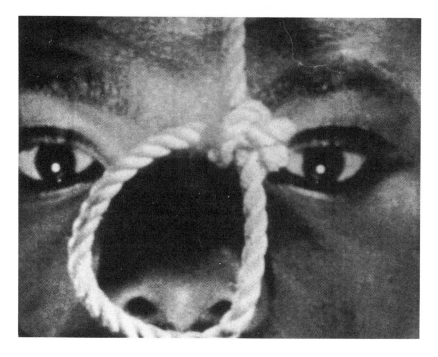

Figure 8.4.
Frame enlargement from *Mr. Motorboat's Last Stand* (1933), directed by Theodore Huff and John Flory. Courtesy of George Eastman House

LAST EXPERIMENTS

Huff made no films for the next twelve years. After he began teaching, he co-directed two projects with his former student Kent Munson. *The Uncomfortable Man*, a psychodrama about an alienated young man, is similar in conception, style, and mood to the work of Willard Maas and Curtis Harrington around this time. Jean Cocteau (especially his 1930 *Blood of a Poet*) and Maya Deren suggest themselves as inspirations (fig. 8.5). Its general direction is well captured in a program note written by Huff:

> This subjective documentary is a psychological study of a young man who lives in the chaos and confusion of a great city. The dividing line between reality and his dream identifications is very thin. Perplexed and frustrated, he retires to his underground room and ignores the world about him until the hero's schizophrenic personality splits. But eventually the forces of the city draw him into the Crowd, where he loses himself.

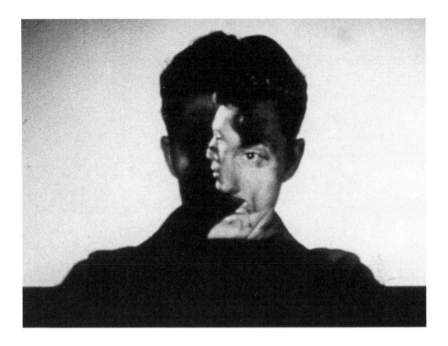

Figure 8.5.
Frame enlargement from *The Uncomfortable Man* (1948), directed by Theodore Huff and
Kent Munson. Courtesy of George Eastman House

Documentary shots of New York City are intercut with shots of a young
man in his room. Dream distortions appear in the interior sections with
shots such as an image projected on a face. These evocations of memory
and nightmare are contrasted with everyday shots of Washington Square
oratory, a Salvation Army band, kids at play, sidewalk vendors, people
being rousted out on the Bowery. The vision of personal alienation in the
city is much like Dostoevsky's underground man. Shots of movies on
42nd Street at night are cut with distorting mirrors, while repeated and
strongly canted shots in an Eisensteinian mode appear (fig. 8.6). The
available materials suggest that the work was written by Munson as a
longer dramatic piece and that only the first half of the script was actually
shot. Then the piece seems to have been drastically edited to fit the
images actually available rather than the original longer conception. It
also seems from the assorted materials of this time that Munson provided
the alienated young man theme (and played the lead) while Huff provided
the expert re-editing.

Figure 8.6.
Frame enlargement from *The Uncomfortable Man* (1948), directed by Theodore Huff and Kent Munson. Courtesy of George Eastman House

The Stone Children (1948), made by Munson and Huff in Hollywood the summer Huff taught at USC, is a less successful followup. As Huff described it:

> All sorts of tragedies and crimes go unnoticed beneath our very noses, from simple thefts to wars, but our increasingly artificial society places more importance in a fantasy-world than a world of reality, and because our minds are so drugged with the more-than-lifesize counterfeit of passion and violence (in movies, books, sports, music, etc.), we do not recognize the real things, or even worse, close our eyes to them. *The Stone Children* is an oblique allegory of an Exile's journey through the fantastic land of celluloid shadows. From his unsavory beginning to his psychotic end, he experiences in turn: anger, fear, pride, ambition, frustration, desire, remorse, confusion and madness. Played in counterpoint to the highly artificial shams of movieland, all these real emotions go unnoticed. Even his sardonic demise has ludicrous and theatrical overtones.

The film mixes black and white and color footage, and hand-held and tripod shooting, and prominently uses cross-cutting to demonstrate the contrasts of modern life. Again the alienated young man, played by Munson, appears cut against shots of Hollywood's presumed falsity. Yet the irony is thin and the statement seems forced because so much attention is paid to the interesting visual surface of Hollywood's glitter, and the young man's story seems overdramatized for a short narrative. Where *The Uncomfortable Man* used typical details of urban life to build its contrasts, *The Stone Children* uses Los Angeles details that are already encoded as exotic (Woodlawn Cemetery, Paramount Studios, Bel Air mansions, the Chinese Theatre, ocean piers, backlots, etc.), as well as celebrity moments (Louis B. Mayer, Sam Goldwyn, Chaplin, the Griffith funeral). The discrepancy between the ostensible message (this is all false and corrupt) and the obvious tourist fascination in the documentary material undermines the project. Sustained attempts to use amusement park images as metaphors of society's sham values seem pale clichés. Writing to Huff to explain why he had shown the New York film but not the Hollywood one at "Art in Cinema," the postwar avant-garde experimental showcase in San Francisco, Frank Stauffacher faulted Munson's acting and advised Huff that experimentalists were on shaky ground when trying to imitate what the industry could do so well.

The collaboration seems to have tried the patience and endurance of both Huff and Munson, and many notes attest to the frustrations on both sides. Munson is mentioned as active in New York City experimental film circles into the 1950s and then disappears from the scene. Huff made no more films.

HUFF AS FILM HISTORIAN AND TEACHER

Huff's Chaplin book, less biography than chronological discussion of the creative work, is his greatest achievement. It was definitive within its time and for years afterward. The first careful and substantial director study produced in the United States, it helped establish serious film studies, although it was done as a labor of love without institutional support. In a letter to Chaplin sent with a sample of his "handbook," Huff explained the research behind it:

In the year 1940–41 I managed in New York to see 54 of your total 76 films for the purpose of this book. On other pictures that have been withdrawn I had complete notes, taken down at the time. Instead of the usual drivel, etc. written by "highbrow" writers, I have tried to stick to facts and to turn out a practical guide and discussion of your pictures, one by one.[10]

He was unable to get it published immediately. It was turned down by several New York publishers; then he claimed (there is no record) that it was accepted for publication by the Academy of Motion Picture Arts and Sciences, but the war broke out and ended that plan. Attempts to interest Chaplin himself were rebuffed by the Chaplin Corporation, which wanted no "authorized" publication. (Unknown to Huff, Chaplin was anticipating writing his autobiography at the time.) It was not until the late forties that Huff found a publisher, a new small house that sought serious books.

Essentially a factual and descriptive study, the Chaplin book avoids making any strong evaluative statements or generating any overt analysis. The biography is constructed with sympathy to Chaplin's side in every dispute, professional, business, or personal, drawing on the existing journalism. But most of the book is a recapitulation of the plots of the various films with observations about changes or innovations in the Tramp persona, cast, or some other area.

Without academic training as a historian, Huff saw his mission as getting the facts correct. Among his papers is a list, unpublished but circulated in typescript, of "hundreds" of errors (mostly dates off by a year, as Huff marked with apparent anger) in Lewis Jacobs' pioneering and then-standard history of American film. While believing that history consisted primarily and essentially of "facts," Huff held that the cinema should have a canon based on aesthetic quality—a principle he apparently thought was self-evident. In an undated document, probably from the mid-1930s, he constructs a list of about a hundred "Films for a Permanent American Theatre (or Museum) of the Cinema." Today the list seems unexceptional, if one takes into account that it was constructed from knowledge of films actually available and thus omits entire national cinemas (e.g., Italian, Japanese) and major works then lost or unknown (e.g., many Soviet silent films), and assumes the dramatic narrative mode as the norm. In the mid-1940s, while working at the National Archives, Huff took sharp exception to Barbara Deming's argument that aesthetically inferior works could be given equal attention in preservation and archiving for purposes of later historical study.[11]

Among the papers are unpublished pieces in typescript, such as a complete shot-by-shot script of *Birth of a Nation*, including the length of each shot. This work was subsequently mimeographed on legal-sized paper with stiff covers and copyrighted, published, and sold by MOMA in 1961.[12] Other notes include descriptions of two German films of the Nazi era, *Ohm Krüger* (1941), set in the Boer War with British villains, and *Die goldene Stadt* (1942), an anti-Czech propaganda film. The papers also include what we might call applied history: lists of film music available from the Library of Congress, notes on the musical accompaniment for *Broken Blossoms* (1919), an arrangement for piano of the symphony orchestra score for *The Four Horsemen of the Apocalypse* (1921), done for a screening during the war at the Washington Workshop, a cinema society. And his papers include stray items like this apparent "fact": "Tom Mix never on screen smoke, drank, lied, or killed."

In one document from about 1950 Huff claimed, referring to himself in the third person, that "while in Washington, due to his persistence, the Library of Congress dug up their early 1896–1912 films which they had buried in the cellar." Credit for the discovery is in dispute, however. Patrick Loughney's dissertation credits a library clerk, Howard Lamarr Walls, for the discovery, and then-Librarian Archibald MacLeish for understanding its importance. Moreover, the discovery took place at least a year before Huff's arrival at the National Archives.[13] But Charles Turner's correspondence with Huff and memory of their conversations places him at the discovery.[14] According to this version, Huff moved to Washington in the summer of 1941 with the intention of tracking down the collection. He appealed to many librarians who were not responsive and finally recruited and trained Walls (both were active in the Library's film society). Doubtless Huff's expertise helped establish the importance of the find.

Huff apparently began collecting cinema materials at an early age and continued the practice throughout his life. Several trunks of papers that he put in storage in the 1930s were destroyed by a flood, but in the mid-1940s he estimates that he had 10,000 film stills ("said to be the most comprehensive private collection"), and in 1949 he estimates 15,000. Upon his death and the donation of his papers to the George Eastman House, it was announced that 30,000 stills were received. In addition, he had a large collection of silent film music and cue sheets, and apparently he first came to the notice of film curator Iris Barry at MOMA when he offered information about music for *Intolerance* and she responded by inviting him to screenings of early films.

As most collectors are, he was in touch with other collectors, although he does not seem to have been involved in extensive trading or buying and selling for a profit. When he worked for MOMA, he allowed the museum to duplicate many of his stills. MOMA then sold prints, apparently at some profit. As the uncredited and unpaid source for many stills in the MOMA collection, Huff was angry at what he saw as an exploitation of his original good will and carefully assembled personal resources. But Huff never had the business sense or merchandising acumen to make money for himself from the limited but definite market for his collection, which must have been the most substantial part of his estate. (Huff seems never to have owned any real property; he lived with his mother at various times, and most of his years in New York City stayed in YMCAs and residential hotels. That he took a very humble civil service job in 1950 seems evidence that he had few financial resources.)

During most of his professional life, Huff served as a critic working in a characteristic essay genre of the time: the informed program note for a film society or museum screening. These essays were about a thousand words long and fitted on two sides of a mimeographed sheet. A standard, virtually obligatory, item at nonprofit film screenings from the 1930s through the 1970s, the film notes format provided cast and credit information as well as an expository essay that typically provided pertinent information about production practices and a general aesthetic interpretation and evaluation of the work, and often placed the work in the director's career. In a time when serious and accurate reference books in cinema were rare, college classes in cinema virtually nonexistent, and thoughtful criticism unusual, film screening notes provided a valuable resource in an audience's self-education.

His files contain multiple versions of essays on the same classic films, slightly revised for each subsequent publication. These are evaluative essays on masterpieces, and Huff clearly explains each film's excellence in aesthetic terms applicable to the cinema. Everything else—the social and political significance of the work, how it relates to the society and historical moment in which it emerged, and so on—tends to be ignored. Huff painstakingly documented *Birth of a Nation*, to his mind a masterpiece, but never wrote a line about its racist content, and in the Chaplin book excused its use of blackface grotesques as a convention of the time.

Huff taught in three of the pioneer cinema studies programs in the United States as they were being established and expanded after World War II. At NYU he taught film production and film history; at USC and CCNY he taught film history. The records he kept were sparse, but from some syllabi, examinations, and a typescript of notes from his USC lectures prepared by one of his students, the courses seem conceptually unremarkable: history is again a collection of important facts organized in terms of conventional national cinemas and historical periods, with screenings of major works depending on which ones were in circulation. A USC lecture on sound results in a long, consecutive list of technological innovations from 1857 on but with no reflection on technological change in general or in relation to film aesthetics.

One USC lecture ends with the note: "DAVID WARK GRIFFITH DIED AT 8:25 A.M., JULY 23, 1948 IN HOLLYWOOD CALIFORNIA." This item captures what Huff thought was most important: the exact time of an event, its importance being affirmed without further reflection (the death of the Greatest Artist of the Twentieth Century, as his college essay put it), and assembled into a pre-existing framework.

Even without academic credentials, Huff might have secured a regular teaching position by offering equivalent professional experience (a fairly common practice in new academic disciplines and the arts in general). Certainly his Chaplin book would have supported his case. Huff was an awful teacher, however, and that was an insurmountable handicap. A long letter from department chair Robert Gessner, written after he visited Huff's NYU class, details the miserable quality of his classroom performance. And during an exchange of ideas about film history that took place in *Film Culture* in 1958, Hans Richter, who headed the CCNY program recalled:

> The late Theodore Huff was acknowledged as one of the most conscientious fact and date-finders in the realm of film history. He was quoted during his lifetime and is quoted today as the ideal film historian. On account of this quality, I engaged him to give a course in film history. His facts and dates were as exact as they could be. His success as an instructor, though, was negative. At the end of the term, there were few students left.[15]

It is hard to see Huff as a lasting success at anything, given his personality and the ample evidence that he was fairly neurotic. In correspondence, longtime friends setting up a meeting frequently add, "Don't fail me this time!" or similar phrases indicating that he did miss engagements. One undated note from a "Bob" or "Ben" left at the hotel where he lived in the 1940s and 1950s urges: "Ted—Don't just disappear. Let's talk. The atom bomb hasn't destroyed NYC yet!" His friend David

Bradley writes from Los Angeles in 1950 that the art house theater-owner Raymond Rohauer in conversation called Huff "a weak character." In remarks for a memorial program at George Eastman House, John Flory noted, "If Ted ever had a fault, it was his great and innate humility. Quick to appreciate ability in others, he regularly discounted his own unique talents."

Theodore Huff seems basically unable to imagine how others thought of him, or what others were thinking and feeling in a social situation—a skill necessary for good teaching and writing drama. Thus, he was unable, for example, to write dramatic screenplays except as parody of existing work. He is frequently insecure and underrates himself, characteristics for which his correspondents chide him. Most disagreeably, from my perspective, Huff exhibits a passive-aggressive syndrome in which he attacks people behind their back. In the early 1940s he writes to Mary Pickford and Chaplin, obsequiously praising them while decrying MOMA. His anger remained active, and in January 1952 he proposes writing an article on MOMA "films stolen (by them!)," films burned and ruined, left-wing political activities, and lack of scholarship.

In today's media culture Huff might have found a niche for his talents because the system as a whole is sufficiently specialized to validate and employ someone with his skills, and the institutions within it can teach an individual the related skills needed to hold down a job. Had he gotten a Ph.D. (none were offered in film at the time), he would have been socialized into the expectations, the manners, and the protocols of academe—the ideology of the system. He might have been a dull and fairly inept teacher, but he would have known how the system operated, worked as an apprentice teaching assistant, spent several years sitting in classes as an apprentice in the profession, and thus learned, on some level, to evaluate the process of teaching from the daily examples offered by his mentors. And he could probably have kept his job, or kept some kind of academic job in an expanding market for film scholarship. Or he could have come to the early realization that he was temperamentally unsuited to teaching and moved into a related position that did not call for it: working in a media library, an archive, a media art center, or some form of arts administration. In the still-developing media culture of the first half of the twentieth century, however, there were few such places, and those that existed were often tangential to the larger institutions that set the pace. The Amateur Cinema League, film societies like "Art In Cinema" and "Cinema 16," and the small-circulation serious film publications were started and kept going as labors of love, not as sponsored institutions. In Huff's time there was only one MOMA Film Library, and he burned his bridges when he left it. Huff did not have one place or one line of career development; as it turned out, he occupied several different sites at different times. Entering his mid-forties, when most professionals are well established in a career, and perhaps facing the luxury of a mid-life crisis, Huff achieved professional distinction with his Chaplin book. At the same time, he must have experienced personal humiliation when the only employment he was offered was the low-level clerical position of assistant casting director for the Signal Corps at Astoria.

There are two ways to look at Theodore Huff's professional and personal life. From the point of view of the overall system, of society in general, which accepts an ideology and practice of bourgeois individualism, Huff was a film nerd *avant le mot*. Underdeveloped socially, he was overinvested in film as an object of study. He knew almost everything there was to know about it, it seems, yet he was unable to capitalize on that knowledge. In the political economy of the intellectual labor market, he was a useful yet expendable item. Such a person, in our time, in our culture, is held responsible for his or her own failure: "Get a life!"—the slogan of the Reagan-Bush era.

From his own perspective, however, the same ideology of bourgeois individualism turned Huff into a self-validating person. He became a priest of the cinema—a low priest, to be sure, but a person devoted to service without regard for personal gain. Each humiliation validated his vocation. He was concerned with the ordering and arranging of cinema, with its proper interpretation and fixing its "facts" in the proper place. He was obsequious to the authorities he recognized, carefully learned the roles and rituals that needed to be carried out, attended to the proper procedures, and devoted himself to preserving the icon-photos of his saints. He preserved texts of all sorts like holy relics. He lived what seems, to an external viewer, a celibate life in extremely modest, one-room circumstances. Huff never traveled except for his one summer pilgrimage to Hollywood, bonded only with men, seems not to have socialized with married couples, single women, or any relatives except his widowed mother, and was in his own way blessed by being in this environment.

There are hints in his collected papers that Huff lived as a very closeted gay man. For example, as he turned forty, we find that a letter from his mother tells him to look for a "wife" (quotation marks in original) and settle down. It is tempting to "out" Huff in order to compare him with his contemporary Parker Tyler, a flamboyant dandy in the 1930s and a well-known homosexual writer and film critic (long overdue for recognition as a major gay intellectual figure). Both men published books on Chaplin at about the same time, but where Huff's is methodical and prosaic, Tyler's is witty, intellectually adventurous, and characterized by Tyler's trademark leaps of imagination and avant-garde style. Huff was part of a different movement, a different style. He was entranced by old films, especially by silent films, but he was unable to develop a larger analysis of them except to appreciate their technique (of which he had a great practical mastery). After the war, a younger generation used a slightly derisive term for his type—a "foof," a friend of old films. Theodore Huff probably would have accepted the label without hearing the sarcastic dismissal.

NOTES

The research for this article was supported in part by a Northwestern University Research Grant. Thanks to Associate Dean Kathleen Galvin and Professor Mimi White for their help. It was also supported by a summer fellowship at the Oregon Humanities Center of the University of Oregon, where the director, Professor John Stuhr, and the associate director, Robin M. Cochoran, provided a productive environment. For access to and assistance with the Huff papers I want to thank the George Eastman House, particularly the former Senior Curator, Jan-Christopher Horak, and Robin Blair Bolger. Patrick Loughney at the Motion Picture Department of the Library of Congress answered many questions about the discovery of the Paper Print Collection. Comments on an earlier draft by two anonymous reviewers for the University of Wisconsin Press were helpful. One reviewer directed me to recent research done by Ron Magliozzi at MOMA, who provided me with essential information based on his ongoing oral history interviews with people active in New York City film culture. One of those people, Huff's friend and correspondent Charles L. Turner, generously critiqued an earlier draft. The writing benefited from discussions with Chris Horak, Jack C. Ellis, Jim Schwoch, Kate Kane, Tom Gunning, and Julia Lesage.

1. This analysis is based on archival research in the Theodore Huff papers at George Eastman House, Rochester, N.Y. (GEH). My work there was limited in two significant ways. First, it turned out that the materials available were much more extensive than initially indicated, and my time was limited to three long

days. The full collection of Huff materials includes his extensive collection of at least 15,000 stills, mostly from Hollywood films; I did not examine that portion of the collection. While I was able to examine every single item in his personal papers, and make photocopies of the most important ones, I did not have the opportunity to carefully correlate all the material. I am reasonably sure that my conclusions do justice to the materials, but there are probably minor points that could be refined. The individual items in the Huff papers have not been arranged or separately indexed or catalogued. In numerous cases the papers include one or more draft versions of typed correspondence, with his own written emendations. I do not know what was actually sent, and I have had no opportunity to check the papers of his correspondents, even those documents that are known to exist (e.g., the Flory papers at Ohio State University are uncatalogued and unavailable; the Stauffacher papers are available at the Pacific Film Archive at the University of California, Berkeley). I have received summary information and comments on an earlier draft from Ron Magliozzi, assistant supervisor of the Film Study Center, MOMA, based on the letters from Huff to Charles L. Turner from 1942 to 1953 and interviews with Turner in the MOMA archives. Turner also provided ten pages of comments on an earlier draft of this chapter.

Second, of the various films available, only *Mr. Motorboat* had been restored at the time I was in Rochester. I was able to watch it numerous times, but in other cases I could only view the archival material once, taking notes while seeing films for the first time. *The Uncomfortable Man*, in particular, deserves a much closer and more detailed study than I could give it at that point. The most interesting discovery was a series of letters and scripts from Gregory Markopoulos from the late 1940s, which would be important for anyone researching the early career of that major independent filmmaker.

2. Theodore Huff, *Charlie Chaplin: A Biography* (New York: Henry Schuman, 1951).

3. Huff, 1933. All otherwise unreferenced quotes are from the Theodore Huff papers, GEH.

4. Ron Magliozzi's research suggests that Huff's dismissal from MOMA followed acrimonious inter-staff wrangling between him and the Soviet film expert Jay Leyda. Leyda was forced to resign from the Film Department following publication of an article smearing him as a leftist propagandist by Seymour Stern, "Film Library Notes Build 'CP Liberators' Myth," *New Leader* 23 (March 1940). Some context and details can be found in Janet Staiger, *Interpreting Films: Studies in the Historical Reception of American Cinema* (Princeton: Princeton University Press, 1992), chap. 7. Huff blamed "communist influence" for his departure from MOMA, with his strongest anger reserved for curator Iris Barry, who fired him.

5. The film was 900 feet in 16mm, but is apparently lost.

6. In all of these projects another person working on it with Huff is mentioned, but the creative roles are not clear. For the Russell Sage film a "Miss Perry" is mentioned, perhaps a foundation staff person.

7. 500 feet. The original 16mm reversal print has been preserved at GEH.

8. Flory left after a few years and a change in management, tried unsuccessfully to develop a script, and returned to the East. He worked in a film processing lab and eventually became the Eastman Kodak representative to the nontheatrical film market, a position that made him well known to the entire independent filmmaking sector.

9. This 16mm film (400 feet) is also preserved at GEH.

10. Letter, Theodore Huff to Charles Chaplin, 1942.

11. Deming wrote "The Library of Congress Film Project: Exposition of a Method," *L of C Quarterly Journal of Current Acquisitions* 2, no. 1 (July–September 1944): 3–36. Deming and others were employed in the project of determining which of the 1,400-odd films a year that were submitted for copyright should actually be archived. She and the research team worked at MOMA under a Rockefeller grant. Huff's response is in several heavily revised typescripts of his letter to the head of the Library of Congress, but it is not clear that a final copy was actually sent. Huff's vehement and personal attack on Deming is such that it would be easy to imagine that a friend reading it in draft form would counsel against sending it. Huff's letter dismisses her as a "college girl" (she had a master's degree), and includes a smear of Deming as a left sympathizer, a claim he also made about Iris Barry, head of the MOMA Film Library, after she fired him, and Siegfried Kracauer, the emigré film historian. The critical results of Deming's work are contained in her book on 1940s film, *Running Away From Myself* (New York: Grossman, 1969), somewhat similar to Kracauer's study of German Expressionism, which reads the films as symptoms of a general American social-political consciousness during the war. Films undistinguished in conventional aesthetic terms can be very important in such an analysis, a type of criticism quite different from Huff's values and practices.

12. The paper is described as "A Shot Analysis" done by Huff "circa 1939." Given his longstanding hatred of his former employer, Huff would have been outraged by this "exploitation."

13. *A Descriptive Analysis of the Library of Congress Paper Print Collection and Related Copyright Materials* (Ph.D. diss., George Washington University, 1988). Loughney's information is from LOC documents and phone interviews with Walls in the 1980s.

14. Huff–Turner letters and other materials, Film Study Center, MOMA. Author's personal correspondence with Magliozzi and Turner, November 1993.

15. Hans Richter, "Hans Richter on the Function of Film History Writing," *Film Culture* 4, no. 3 (April 1958): 26.

9

Ralph Steiner

Scott MacDonald

Like his predecessors on the American alternative filmmaking scene, Charles Sheeler and Paul Strand (*Manhatta*, 1921), Ralph Steiner was an accomplished photographer before he turned to film. His interest in motion pictures began as an extension of his still photographic work, though he gave up on his first film, the focus of which was funny road signs, when he "realized that . . . if you're making a film, what you were filming should move. Revelation!"[1] His first completed film, H_2O (1929), was a major contribution to independent cinema, as well as an audience pleaser. In a filmmaking career that spanned forty-six years, Steiner would produce or contribute to twenty-five films.

For purposes of this discussion, Steiner's filmmaking can be divided into three periods: an early period (from 1929 to approximately 1933) characterized by individual experimentation and exploration; a second, "political" period (from 1934 to 1942) during which he collaborated in a variety of ways with other filmmakers and with film production groups; and a final period (from 1960 to 1975) during which he returned to explore the cinematic terrain he had discovered in his first films. In all three periods, Steiner's contributions to North American independent cinema are noteworthy.

EARLY EXPERIMENTS

In an article co-written with Leo Hurwitz in 1935 as a means of clarifying their new approach to filmmaking, Steiner described the sense of film history from which his early experiments had developed:

> During the twenties we grew disgusted with the philistinism of the commercial film product, its superficial approach, trivial themes, and its

standardization of film treatment: the straight-line story progressing from event to event on a pure suspense basis, unmarred by any imaginative use of the camera, unmarred by any freshness in editing or any human or formal sensitivity. Our reaction, which we shared with the young generation of experimental film makers, was a more or less aesthetic revolt from the current manner of film production. The important thing, we felt, was to do those things which the film was capable of, but which the commercial film didn't and couldn't possibly do. There seemed unbounded possibilities for the use of the film as a visual poetry of formal beauty.[2]

As of 1935, Steiner and Hurwitz were inclined to see the experiments of the twenties as both a success and a failure:

Much was learned and explored about the technical resources of cinematography and montage, but the whole emphasis was on the beauty, the shock, the effectiveness of OBJECTS, THINGS—with no analysis of the effect on the audience. . . . It could lead to nothing else but ivory tower aesthetic films, unrelated to contemporary life. The film had been depersonalized, inhuman; the THING, technique and formal problems were supreme.[3]

Their disavowal of the experiments of the twenties, however, ignored dimensions of Steiner's early films that seem more apparent now than they must have in the middle of the Depression.

While it is true that Steiner's first films were unrelated to the political developments and issues so central to his concerns in 1935, these films are anything but irrelevant and inhuman. To recognize their achievements—and especially the achievements of H_2O, easily the most interesting of the three films—one must ignore not only Steiner's mid-thirties reassessment, but the tendency ever since to see his early films as simple: the prints of H_2O currently distributed by the Museum of Modern Art (MOMA) include a rolling textual introduction that describes Steiner's first film as "A simple study of the patterns of light and shadow on water." H_2O might legitimately be called "simple" if one is referring to Steiner's decision to ignore nearly all the conventional elements of the commercial cinema (obviously H_2O includes no plot or characters), but it is precisely because of the complex visual experience Steiner is able to create with his simple means that H_2O remains interesting and accessible.[4]

To explore the visual complexities of H_2O, one must approach it, not as a short, but as a mini-encyclopedia of visual explorations, related to the kinds of visual explorations that characterize Steiner's still photography. In 1984 the Smith College Museum exhibited a large collection of photographs of clouds Steiner had made over the last fifteen years. These images were subsequently reproduced in the book *In Pursuit of Clouds,*[5] where they are grouped according to various "topics": "The Big Sky," "Creatures," "Celebrations," "Signs and Portents," "Magic," and "Dreams." The likelihood of recognizing the full visual potential of the cloud images is enhanced by the set of "captions" that follows each section of the book: for each cloud image, Steiner provides several "readings" offered by visitors to the Smith Museum show (Steiner had suggested a competition in which people would "write titles or verbal parallels—metaphors—to fit the cloud pictures"; almost five hundred people responded).[6]

One could say that *In Pursuit of Clouds* is a "simple" catalogue of cloud images, but the moment one begins to explore this catalogue using the guidelines Steiner himself provided, one discovers that the point of these images is precisely their fertility, the pleasure of discovering the many ways in which *each* image, among the dozens Steiner printed, can be understood. Because H_2O is a film, viewers usually have no opportunity for exploring Steiner's images of water in any detail. The more one sees H_2O, however, the more apparent is the film's similarity to Steiner's cloud photographs. H_2O divides into a series of sections, each focusing on particular visual elements; and within the individual section, every image offers its own particular set of visual concerns and developments. Together, the sections provide an encyclopedia of one person's visual exploration of water in motion.

H_2O opens with a mini-prologue, which is followed by six roughly distinguishable sections, each longer, but made up of fewer individual shots per minute, than previous sections. This would seem to suggest that the film's pace slows down, but in fact, because of Steiner's use of composition, there is no relationship between the length of shots and the excitement of the visual experience he creates. The prologue of H_2O is made up of shots that suggest elements of the visual terrain the remainder of the film will explore in increasingly complex ways. The opening shot is, apparently, a closeup of a waterfall: a wall of water falls vertically through the frame. It is followed by a shot of the surface of a pond or lake, with raindrops making concentric circles, and by a shot of rainfall through the window of some sort of structure. These opening images announce a number of visual concerns (H_2O is a silent film, projected at 18 frames per second), relating to both the water itself and Steiner's presentation of it. We see water in various forms, both in a natural state and as controlled by human beings. And we see Steiner using the process of filmmaking to articulate distinctions between the flatness of the screen (shot 1) and its ability to create the illusion of three-dimensional spaces by manipulating planes of imagery in relation to the plane of the screen (shots 2, 3).

The opening shots are followed by a brief (twenty-four frames), upside-down shot of water flowing out of a pipe that simultaneously challenges the viewer's alertness (the combination of the upside-down image and the brevity of the shot confounds the expectations the slower-paced earlier images have begun to develop),[7] and introduces a twenty-nine-second passage focusing on the technological control of water. As is true of all the sections that follow, even this brief passage is clearly divided into subsections. The first three shots reveal water gushing out of pipes; in the second three, water is released in regular spurts by different sorts of pump mechanisms. The increasing involvement with rhythm within the shots in this passage is emphasized by the way in which Steiner has composed the sequence.[8] In the final and most dramatic shots, the foamy white water released by the pump mechanisms tends to white out the image, a fact Steiner uses to surprise the viewer, by cutting from the fifth to the sixth shot at the moment of maximum whiteness. The rhythm of these last two pumps, both of which move almost precisely in time with the mechanism of the projector moving at 18 frames per second, echoes the rhythm of the editing. Steiner seems to be suggesting that, as a mechanical technology, film has much in common with the pump mechanisms: like the pumps, the camera and projector redirect the flow of a natural element (light) and imagery of natural elements, concentrating and modulating them. In the completed film the strip of images captured in the emulsion flows through the projector, as the water "flows" through the pipes and pumps.

The sequence of six images, combined with the prologue, seems to announce not only a general recognition that motion pictures need to be about movement (and that "movement" involves both what happens within individual shots and what develops from shot to shot), but a specific awareness of the principles of montage explored by the Soviets. In "The Cinematic Principle and the Ideogram," Sergei Eisenstein sees montage as a mechanical process comparable "to the series of explosions of an internal combustion engine,"[9] and while that essay was not translated into English until after Steiner had completed H_2O, the American seems to have been aware of Eisenstein's thinking, which was much discussed in the late twenties and early thirties, as Soviet films and cinematic principles made their way west. Indeed, one could argue that the increasing focus on composition, rather than on montage, during the remainder of H_2O demonstrates what Steiner may have seen as the perceptual limitations inherent in the dependence on editing that characterized Eisenstein's work.

The transition to the more visually dramatic sequences that follow is emphasized by two shots, each of which seems metaphorically suggestive in terms of Steiner's organization of H_2O. In the first, a tiny rivulet courses through a little canal—as if suggesting a passage from one kind of experience to another—and in the second, a pipe sticking out of the water and the pipe's reflection create what looks to be a question mark. The "question mark" is suggestive, and in tune with Steiner's earlier film and photographic work: one of the earliest of his better-known photographs, *Typewriter Keys* (c. 1921), is a closeup of typewriter keys with punctuation marks; and many of his photographs of the 1920s, as well as the film project he abandoned just before beginning H_2O, focus on visual texts. And, of course, the title H_2O is a textual symbol. Steiner seems always to have been conscious of how his work might appear to "average viewers," and the "question mark" in H_2O might have been his way of empathizing with viewer response to his first experimental film: the question mark seems to ask, "Is *this* a movie?" Given Steiner's complex exploration of the surfaces of water/movie screen during the remainder of the film, the question mark might also imply, "Where *is* the surface?"

The last nine minutes of H_2O are a visual phantasmagoria rendered all the more remarkable by the less spectacular imagery included in the early sequences. As is true in the earlier sections of the film, Steiner's exploration of the visual potential of surfaces is roughly organized into passages that create a variety of perceptual/conceptual experiences for viewers (fig. 9.1). The eighty-seven-second passage that immediately follows the "question mark" is, in my view, the most beautiful in the film, and it seems one of the earliest instances in film history of a filmmaker's devoting his efforts directly to the production of exquisite imagery.[10]

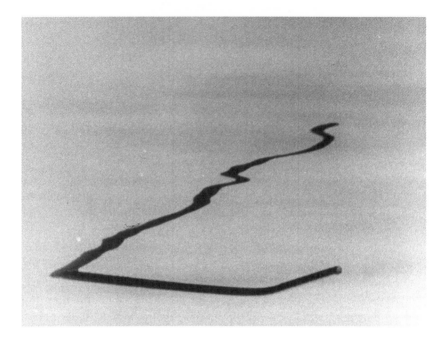

Figure 9.1.
Frame enlargement from H_2O (1929), directed by Ralph Steiner. Courtesy of George Eastman House

Steiner reveals a variety of reflections on the moving surface of the water, all of which have in common that we can see or deduce the nature of what is making the reflections. In some cases, the reflections are made by the posts supporting a pier or dock; in others by weeds along the edge of a pond; and at still others, by trees. The reflections of the posts are beautiful because of the chiaroscuro of black, white, and gray—and fascinating because of the way the reflections create figure–ground relationships that defy our understanding of what we are seeing: the reflections of light between the darker posts and reflections of posts seem more substantial than the posts themselves. The reflections of the weeds have a lacy delicacy. And the water's geometric distortions of the trees are reminiscent of Mondrian paintings of trees made during the same years. This passage of beautiful but recognizable reflections is followed by a shot of some kind of pool, and then by a series of sequences in which the precise nature of what is reflected in the water is increasingly obscure.

The MOMA rolling text that precedes H_2O indicates that the film "approaches the abstract in its climax as the camera becomes increasingly absorbed with texture and design"—a description that misconstrues the nature of what Steiner accomplishes. It is true that after the sequence I have just described, when the objects reflected become more obscure, the reflections are frequently reminiscent of abstract painting and of such abstract films as Oskar Fischinger's wax experiments of the mid- and late 1920s. And it is also true that in the second half of H_2O, Steiner's compositional eye discovers increasingly complex designs and textures of considerable variety (fig. 9.2). Often, in fact, we seem to see multiple and varied layers of light and dark reflections simultaneously. And yet these images are never abstract in the conventional meaning of the term, since one of the layers of imagery we are *always* aware of is the literal surface of the water the reflections are occurring in/on. As a result we are always aware that the phantasmagoria of "abstract" shapes, designs, and textures is a literal, everyday, observable reality, that the miraculous visuals

Figure 9.2.
Frame enlargement from H_2O (1929), directed by Ralph Steiner. Courtesy of George Eastman House

Steiner presents are the results of careful observation and thoughtful composition *and nothing more.*[11] "Effects" that some independent and industry filmmakers labor years to create, often developing complex technologies to produce, are, Steiner proves, available to anyone willing to look more carefully at the world.

In the introductory essay to *Ralph Steiner: A Point of View,* Steiner describes his

> almost lifelong interest in the enjoyment of seeing and in trying to help other people toward it. . . . My "theory of education" is that enjoyment can be learned but not taught as such. I think that the ability to enjoy can be gained only out of experience in enjoyment, and so I say that my films are based on education through inebriation—that is, drunkenness of the eye."[12]

H_2O is full of visual play. The most obvious dimension of this, as has been suggested, is Steiner's pleasure in presenting us with seemingly almost endless variations on the theme of reflections in water, and, more particularly, with superimposed kinds of reality that tease our perceptual and conceptual faculties. There are also instances when Steiner uses reverse imagery: the concentric circles made by the raindrops get smaller and disappear. Other effects are produced by variations in how near or far from the surface Steiner positions the camera, and in at least one sequence by the use of a dark filter that causes the water to look like molten metal.[13] H_2O concludes with a series of particularly complex shots, which sing the perceptual pleasures of the physical world while reminding us that the nature of what we see is a function of how willing we are to "play with" our senses and to learn from those technological aids to visual perception—the still and motion picture cameras—at our disposal.

For the Steiner of H_2O, the world *is* a motion picture, and the central responsibility of the artist is to help people enjoy this "movie" as fully as possible. Filmmaking is not so much an end in itself—though clearly it *is* a pleasure—as an aid to vision and to Vision. Ultimately, the film's title must be seen as ironic. We may generally think of water, in everyday life and in film, as merely two parts hydrogen, one part oxygen, but for Steiner water includes infinite visual possibilities that render any schematic description of it laughable.

Though they have much in common with H_2O, and each has interesting dimensions, the two films that followed it—*Surf and Seaweed*

(1930) and *Mechanical Principles* (1933)—are much less interesting. *Surf and Seaweed* seems an extension of the brief passage early in H_2O during which the flow and surface of a stream is defined by the plants growing in the water. The film is divided into sequences that focus on specific kinds of imagery in and around ocean surf. It is particularly involved with texture, with the grain of beach sand, with the intricate density of seaweed growing in tide pools, and with reflections of light on sand, seaweed, and surf.[14]

While *Surf and Seaweed* is a good bit less impressive now than H_2O, it does confirm the attitude toward vision, and the relationship of vision and film, that Steiner demonstrates in his first film. Steiner is interested in the film experience's capability to invigorate everyday sight, to alert viewers to the simple, magical visual pleasures available in nearly any circumstance. As in H_2O, in *Surf and Seaweed* Steiner uses no complex camera technology or editing: composition within the shot is everything. The frame of the image becomes simply a window through which we learn to see more carefully, and the only dynamic dimension to Steiner's imagery is created by his frequent framing so that the surf, or a less dramatic flow of ocean water, moves in and out of the frame. The very continuity and variation of these forces, Steiner seems to suggest, are what make the potentials of vision so extensive and so important. The physical world offers us so much visual fascination and pleasure that to ignore it—either in our daily lives or by restricting our film-going to the conventional, sight-limited experiences provided by commercial theaters—is nearly criminal.

In many ways, *Mechanical Principles* is of a piece with H_2O and *Surf and Seaweed*, though it reveals an added dimension to Steiner's attitude toward vision.[15] Steiner's third film was inspired by an exhibition at the Science Museum in New York City, consisting, according to Joel Zukor, of "various displays of small wooden machine parts (gears, shafts, levers, wheels, and pistons). These wooden models were called 'eccentrics.' "[16] As is true in H_2O and *Surf and Seaweed*, Steiner uses the film frame to help us focus on dimensions of the motion of these "machines" that might not be visually appreciated were we to see the models themselves. The seventy-two shots in the film are arranged into sequences, roughly according to subject matter: near the beginning, the focus is on pistons, arms, and wheels that combine vertical or horizontal with circular motion; later, the focus is on the meshing of teeth in various types of gears, first in a continuous flow, and later, in other mechanical circumstances, one gear tooth at a time (fig. 9.3). Near the end of the film, some of the images create optical illusions. Steiner's editing is, for all practical purposes, invisible: shot length varies according to Steiner's interest in the various movements and the length of time particular motions take. In general, shots are between 9 and 15 seconds, though from time to time a shot is closer to 5 or to 20 seconds. For the most part, each successive shot reveals a new configuration of machine parts, though here and there Steiner moves from a more distant to a closer view (all the shots are closeups), or vice versa. More fully than either of the earlier films, *Mechanical Principles* creates wry humor: at times the movement of various parts in relation to one another defies our expectations and our understanding: we know that in any machine one part makes another move, but it is difficult to see what is moving what in the models, and because of Steiner's consistent use of closeups, we never know why this movement is occurring.

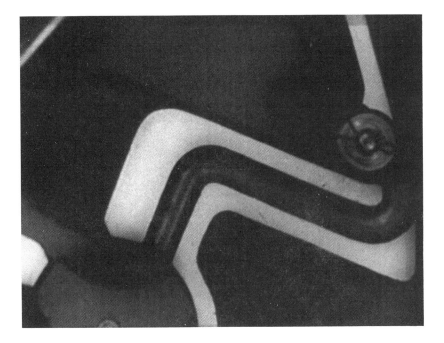

Figure 9.3.
Frame enlargement from *Mechanical Principles* (1933), directed by Ralph Steiner. Courtesy of George Eastman House

Mechanical Principles articulates Steiner's vision by revealing that his interest in sight is not simply in the service of nature, a conclusion that should be obvious anyway from his still photography. For Steiner, the natural world is merely one particularly useful arena within which we can explore our visual faculties. While H_2O and *Surf and Seaweed* may seem to connect Steiner with the long history of worship of nature explored by the Hudson River School of painting and by Steiner's contemporary, the photographer Ansel Adams, *Mechanical Principles* reveals that for Steiner any aspect of the visual world can fuel a fascination with sight. This is confirmed by the fact that Steiner is recording not real machines, but "eccentrics." Indeed, in 1931, when Steiner made *Mechanical Principles*, it may have been a reaction to the very different attitudes toward machinery evident in such well-known alternative films of the period as Dudley Murphy's *Ballet Mécanique* (1924, made in collaboration with Fernand Léger), Eisenstein's *Potemkin* (1925), and Dziga Vertov's *The Man with a Movie Camera* (1929). In these other films, machinery is beautiful and fascinating, not simply in itself but because of what it means: for Murphy/Léger it is the essence of modern life; for Eisenstein, the embodiment of dialectic materialism; for Vertov, the heart of a new egalitarian society. Steiner's "machinery," however, is entirely detached from such ideas: not only is there nothing in *Mechanical Principles* that relates, in any ideological sense, to Modern Society, but, as has been mentioned, these are not real machines: Steiner's imagery does not even convey the more restricted kinds of meaning that would have been suggested had he filmed specific machines functioning to produce a particular product. One can only conclude that the pistons, gears, and arms in *Mechanical Principles* are of interest to Steiner precisely *because* they are meaningless (fig. 9.4). By being detached from larger mechanical or political functions, they become available to Steiner's interest in looking at their simple but visually intriguing movements *as movements*, as pleasures and fascinations *for the eye*.

In one instance, *Mechanical Principles* does seem consciously to provide a single reference for the gears, pistons, and arms Steiner records. In the film's final four-second shot, two ovular gears stop, creating an implicit parallel between the machinery Steiner has filmed and the machine responsible for the illusion we are watching: the projector. Actually, this parallel has been implicit throughout *Mechanical Principles*, in the 18-frames-per-second projection speed: the flicker

Figure 9.4.
Frame enlargement from *Mechanical Principles* (1933), directed by Ralph Steiner. Courtesy of George Eastman House

created by silent speed and the sound of the projector (almost inevitably audible during a silent film—at least when operating in any but a large commercial theater) are indices of the sorts of motion Steiner is fascinated with. It may be that Steiner felt that in his third film, he had discovered not only that "what you were filming should move," but that some forms of movement are, quite precisely, filmic.[17]

COLLABORATIVE FILMS

Steiner's avoidance of overt political ideology in his early films was not a function of any basic lack of interest in people—far from it: the rigorousness of his focus on the faculty of sight was evidence of his commitment to use filmmaking as a means of enriching the daily lives of people who had allowed their visual sensibilities to atrophy. The arrival

Figure 9.5.
Frame enlargement from *Panther Woman of the Needle Trades, or The Lovely Life of Little Lisa* (1931), directed by Ralph Steiner. Courtesy of George Eastman House

and development of the Depression forced a change in Steiner's filmmaking: the human devastation around him was so compelling, so much a part of what everyone was *seeing* during these years, that Steiner quickly came to feel that a new kind of film had become necessary: film that would plead the case of the economically disenfranchised and assist them in collaborating to bring about a revolution within the economic system that had wrought such havoc. This goal of bringing the masses of workers together affected not only the subject matter Steiner felt was appropriate for film, but the means that would be used in what he was later to call "revolutionary movie production": those interested in forging a new cinema formed collaborative groups within which the labor of making movies was shared. Steiner's career as an individual experimental filmmaker in control of all aspects of his films was put on hold, and for all practical purposes did not resume until he began the series of films called "The Joy of Seeing" nearly thirty years later.

Steiner's first important political involvement was his membership in the Workers Film and Photo League. While continuing to support himself by doing advertising photography for mass market periodicals (the *Ladies Home Journal*, for example), Steiner documented the Depression and politicized responses to it, beginning with the 1931 May Day demonstration in New York. The Workers Film and Photo League was a reasonably diverse group politically: some members were devoted to the goal of communist revolution; others were less doctrinaire. In *Film on the Left*, William Alexander argues that Steiner was one of the latter: "Like some others in the League, he was responding much more to the human suffering caused by the desperate Depression winters than he was to any specific ideology, and as a result his commitment to the Party program had its limitations."[18]

Whatever his limitations as a political person, Steiner threw himself into the process of documenting the suffering he witnessed, and seems to have committed himself, in particular, to the idea that those who had been disenfranchised by political and economic developments must not also be disenfranchised cinematically by being represented in ineffective films. Soon Steiner was pushing the Workers Film and Photo League to move away from the quickly shot newsreels of suffering and responses to it, and to produce films that might develop a more sophisticated viewership and have more longevity than newsreels devoted to the events of the day. As far as Steiner was concerned, the potential audience for a new, more socially involved cinema was considerable:

> The present size [he writes in 1934] of the organized audience which now sees Soviet and other working class films turns that potential importance [of film] into a very real and exciting fact. Last year in 1,580 theaters, workers' groups and organizations in the United States, Canada, Mexico, Cuba, and South America, 400,000 people were entertained by, excited by, educated by, and strengthened by seeing revolutionary films. This great audience should not only be a great inspiration to film makers but also a definite responsibility.[19]

For Steiner the responsibility was not simply to produce films that revealed that the filmmakers had the correct Marxist ideology, but to respect his viewers' perceptual capacities and aesthetic sensibilities, as well as their politics. His experiences with the Workers Film and Photo League convinced him that too rigid an adherence to ideology constricted people's ability to see reality with clarity and understanding.

By the end of 1934, Steiner was so frustrated by the League's rigidity that he and fellow League members Leo Hurwitz and Irving Lerner founded their own group, Nykino, a collaborative production organization that soon became entirely independent of the League. During this transitional moment, Steiner was at work on several films, including *Pie in the Sky* (1934) and *Cafe Universal* (1934), the latter a now-lost antiwar film inspired by George Grosz's drawings, and using actors from the Group Theatre, including Elia Kazan and Clifford Odets.[20] *Pie in the Sky*, a satire of religious pretension in an age of widespread starvation, remains in distribution. It was produced collaboratively, as the opening credits indicate, by Elia "Gadget" Kazan, Molly Day Thatcher, Elman Koolish, Russell Collins, Irving Lerner—all members of the Group Theatre—and Steiner. Steiner is credited with the camerawork; since he was the only accomplished filmmaker in the group, I have assumed that decisions about editing and composition were largely his as well.

Pie in the Sky is a silent film, complete with intertitles. It focuses on two men (played by Kazan and Koolish) who have stopped at a Catholic mission house in the hopes of getting some food. After a long, boring sermon, the priest cuts up a single pie for the assembled men. The two central characters are too far back in line to receive the narrow wedges of pie the priest has dished out; he tells them not to despair and points to a sign: "The Lord Will Provide." Frustrated, they leave and are next seen at a dump where they enact a series of amusing skits relating to their predicament.[21] The film concludes with two presentations of the lyrics of the chorus of Joe Hill's song, "Pie in the Sky" ("You will eat/Bye and bye/In the glorious/Land above the Sky/Work and pray/Live on hay/You'll get pie/In the sky/When you die"), the second accompanied by funny tableaux.

Pie in the Sky is interesting and suggestive on several levels. It is reasonably effective both as comedy and as satire. Kazan and Koolish are credible actors, and their moments of physical comedy are often amusing. The ability of the characters to respond imaginatively, and with considerable good humor, to the pangs of hunger that periodically interrupt their play or resurface within the fantasy situations they create recalls early Chaplin, as does their cynicism about religious pretension and the openness of Kazan's fondling of the "Mae West" mannequin. And the interchange between the two men suggests both Samuel Beckett's *Waiting for Godot* (1952) and Robert Frank's *Pull My Daisy* (1959). While the film's satire is much too general to have pleased the more ideologically doctrinaire members of the Workers Film and Photo League, within the context of conventional film of the day, *Pie in the Sky* is "political," most obviously in the filmmakers' refusal to pretend that the problem of hunger is on its way toward resolution at the end of the film. *Pie in the Sky* is an entertainment, but it is an entertainment in touch with the reality of the Depression.

Pie in the Sky makes the filmmakers' solidarity with the hungry explicit through a variety of self-reflexive gestures. The fact that the first junk item we see is a film can, and that the film can looks like the empty pie plate we have just seen, is suggestive: from the point of view of the makers of *Pie in the Sky*, organized religion and the film industry, at least in America, have offered nothing to those in need of essentials. Both have ignored the realities of hunger and poverty in favor of empty illusionism.

The skits Kazan and Koolish perform are filmed so that we are always aware of their fantasies *as* fantasies: we laugh with them at their ingenuity at mimicking scenes that suggest mainstream movies. When Kazan fondles the mannequin, we do not become part of his fantasy the way we often do in conventional movies. We laugh at his ingenuity in dramatizing his feelings for "Mae West"—his redirection of one kind of hunger into another, perhaps—while remaining consistently aware of his impoverished surroundings: his fantasy may seem to take *him* somewhere else, but *we* can see where he really is. Similarly, during the chariot/automobile race, as Koolish "whips his horses to a frenzy," we see objects flying past him through the frame, as if he is moving at breakneck speed; then the camera pans left and we see Kazan throwing things (fig. 9.6). If we stay entirely within the narrative level of the film, we might assume that Kazan is merely throwing things at Koolish and that the composition of the shot has momentarily disguised what is happening. But it is equally true to say that Kazan is simultaneously functioning within the diegesis of the story *and* helping to create an effect for the camera. We are amused by the effect of an illusion which is then revealed as an illusion that *all* of us—viewers, cameraperson, actors—have consciously collaborated to fabricate.

In two instances late in *Pie in the Sky*, when the characters cover their eyes, the lens of the camera is covered up: subjective camera images become self-reflexive moments. One of these gestures occurs after Kazan hands his companion a cross made of two sticks: when Koolish takes hold of the sticks, they come apart and he pretends they are eating utensils. While Kazan gestures toward Heaven and the "pie in the sky" Koolish will have to wait for, Koolish covers his eyes in frustration and hands

Figure 9.6.
Frame enlargement from *Pie in the Sky* (1935), directed by Ralph Steiner et al., with Elia Kazan and Elman Koolish. Courtesy of George Eastman House

cover the lens. If we assume that *Pie in the Sky* was made for an audience that included not only those generally empathic with hunger, but those who knew hunger firsthand—and surely this is a fair assumption—the characters' frustration within the skit is not only an expression of their recent experiences at the mission, but extends to those members of the audience who, having also known the reality of hunger, might well be "covering their eyes" in the movie theater at seeing their own experiences, and their own frustrations with empty rhetoric, dramatized. The second covering of the lens has much the same impact.

The fact that *Pie in the Sky* creates characters whose story is largely made up of the "stories" they dramatize to entertain themselves in the middle of deprivation is implicitly a declaration of cinematic principles, a declaration that owes a good deal to Brecht's influence on the Group Theatre. Steiner and his Group Theatre collaborators, like the characters they create, are involved in the production of illusions that reflect experiences they have seen and endured. They are not capable of, or interested in, using these illusions to escape reality; rather, they wish to entertain themselves and each other as they live through a difficult and frustrating period. Indeed, the film's creation of self-reflexive illusion within illusion distinguishes it not only from the commercial cinema of the time, but from the various arenas of experimental and revolutionary film that had developed by 1934. If a work is "modern" by virtue of its use of tactics that become more popular at a later period, *Pie in the Sky* is a remarkably modern film: its tactics seem prescient of such films as Robert Nelson's *Blue Shut* (1970) and Yvonne Rainer's *Lives of Performers* (1974).

The same year saw the completion of a third Steiner film. *Hands* is more in keeping with the triad of early experimental films, both formally and (since it seems a *Steiner* film) in terms of how it was produced. *Hands* was one of a series of films sponsored by the Work Projects Administration (WPA) during the early 1930s in the hope of stimulating the American economy. It is a silent film, just under four minutes long, that focuses on human hands as a synecdoche for workers.[22] At the beginning of the film, pairs of idle hands, photographed in closeup against a dark background, move vertically downward through the image. While the hands enact gestures related to the frustration and deprivation that come from not having remunerative work to do, and while their consistent movement through the frame may suggest their instability and/or their transience, the hands are lit and filmed so that their essential loveliness and potential strength are obvious. The sequence of idle hands moving through the image is suddenly interrupted by a dynamic shot of hands pulling on a rope. The interruption is emphasized by a very different lighting: these working hands—and the hands in the shots that follow—are photographed against a lighted background. While the opening sequence appears to be a single continuous shot during which the hands merely pass through the image (it may be a sequence of ten shots edited invisibly), the sequence of brighter, more active hands that follows is dynamically edited: in thirty-eight seconds, we see seventeen shots; there is movement within each shot. This sequence is followed by a shot of a U.S. Treasury Department check—the camera pulls back so we see hands holding it. Presumably, the interchange of labor and government paycheck re-energizes the economy, for the next sequence is organized differently: individual shots of hands performing various kinds of labor are intercut with individual shots in which financial transactions are taking place.

As *Hands* develops, the density of its implications increases: within the general tactic of focusing on hands, Steiner creates many particular synecdochic images. In the passage of intercutting between individual moments of labor and financial transaction, each shot of labor is a metaphor for the economy at large. A shot of a key turning in an ignition simultaneously suggests what the money earned by labor will buy and the idea of the economy "getting started"; a shot of a doctor taking a child's temperature suggests both the medical care these government checks make possible and the national economic "recovery" that is underway. In the final minutes of *Hands* the intercutting continues, but more loosely. Clusters of shots of hands at work are intercut with shots of financial transactions presented as multiple-image composite shots: first a pair of transactions, then three, four. The focus of the hands' activities develops, too. Soon the hands are involved with luxuries: toys for children, trips (a hand gases up a car), a night at a hotel (a hand gives a tip to a bellboy), art (in a sequence of three brief shots, one pair of hands directs a second in positioning a picture on a wall). *Hands* concludes with images of hands making financial plans for the future—investing, buying insurance—and with the most complex composite image in the film. The frame is divided into quadrants within which we see images of hands doing labor. In the center of this composite image is an iris, within which one image of financial transaction follows another, each replacing the previous one with an iris wipe. The final image in the circle is a Treasury Department check that expands to fill the screen, as the other images fade out.

Hands is government propaganda: its goal is to sing the praises of the program that financed it and other related programs. But it is an ingenious piece of propaganda that, like the great Soviet films of the 1920s, communicates not only through the polemical thrust of its content (which is both obvious and subtle), but through the very unconventionality of its "experimental" structure: the film suggests that the government that has produced it is imaginative and inventive, open to new possibilities, supportive of forms of free expression that respect both the laboring person's efforts and the artist's imagination. *Hands* is also very much a Steiner film: it uses the general strategy of clusters of shots that explore variations on a visual theme, so evident in *H₂O*, *Surf and Seaweed*, and *Mechanical Principles*. And like these earlier films, it demands that viewers look more carefully at the details of their everyday fields of vision than is normally expected in cinema, or in life.

Between 1934 and 1942, Steiner was known and respected not so much as an independent, experimental filmmaker, but for his contributions as cinematographer on a series of documentaries,[23] several of which remain among the most distinguished American nonfiction films: *The Plow That Broke the Plains* (1936), *People of Cumberland* (1938), *The City* (1939), *New Hampshire Heritage* (1940), *Youth Gets a Break* (1941), and *Troop Train* (1942).

The City—"the biggest film I ever worked on"[24]—includes the most exuberantly Steineresque imagery of any of the documentary projects he contributed to. Steiner and Willard Van Dyke share credits as directors and photographers; each was in charge of specific sequences. Van Dyke filmed the opening New England village segment and the long, closing segment that explores the "ideal city" envisioned by the American Institute of Planners, the urban-planning organization that saw the 1939 World's Fair as an opportunity for presenting members' ideas to a large audience and thus produced *The City*. Steiner was in charge of three sections of the film: an early passage dealing with the impact of the Pittsburgh steel industry on the everyday lives of steelworkers, a segment on the oppressive nature of big-city life, and a passage about highway traffic jams. The three sections reveal a variety of skills. The Pittsburgh sequences are powerful, both in their rendering of the energy and excitement of industry and in their documentation of the grim environment the factories create for the workers who live nearby.[25] The big-city sequences seem much of a piece with early Steiner photographs (and at times reminiscent of *Manhatta*), especially in their frequent observational wit. And the traffic jams are amusing. The final shape of *The City* was the result of negotiations with the American Institute of Planners Civic Films Committee (which originally wanted a less artistic, more straightforward film than the witty, artistically impressive one Van Dyke and Steiner made).

The City was a popular and critical success. Not only are nearly all the sections visually compelling (the one exception, ironically, is the overly long final section on the ideal city, demanded by the urban planners), but Aaron Copland's score is poignant and memorable.[26] And, of course, as other commentators have suggested, the film's idea that the quality of life in modern cities can be improved, and its upbeat conclusion (the implication that such improvements are just around the corner), were appealing to a generation of World's Fair patrons at the end of a grueling Depression. The overall organization of *The City* and many of its particular sequences reveal remarkable visual and conceptual parallels to Godfrey Reggio's *Koyaanisqatsi* (1983), a film that, like the Steiner/Van Dyke collaboration, interprets modern industrialization in a manner that has attracted a mass audience to an apparently noncommercial form of film. Both *The City* and *Koyaanisqatsi* appeal to their audiences' desire for fundamental changes in the relationship of human society and the environment, while assuaging audience hunger for a film experience that provides sophisticated, sensual (and guiltless) entertainment.

CODA: THE JOY OF SEEING

The final period of Steiner's film production is not, strictly speaking, within the historical purview of this volume: the films involved were made from 1960 to 1975. And yet I am emboldened to discuss them here, at least briefly, because they are so obviously the culmination of the filmmaking approach Steiner developed in the late 1920s—and because film history has so thoroughly ignored them. One can imagine that the eight films that make up what Steiner called "The Joy of Seeing" are the sorts of work he might have done after *H₂O*, *Surf and Seaweed*, and *Mechanical Principles*, had the tragedy of the Depression not intervened or, to put it in more Steineresque terms, caught his eye. Steiner conceived of "The Joy of Seeing" series as "exactly the opposite of the typical didactic teaching films in which rules of perception are spelled out, and a voice tells the audience what is on the screen, what its meaning is, and why enjoyment should be derived from it."[27] *Seaweed, a Seduction* (1960), *One Man's Island* (1969), *Glory, Glory* (1971), *A Look at Laundry* (1971), *Beyond Niagara* (1973), *Look Park* (1974), *Hooray for Light!* (1975), and *Slowdown* (1975) contain much of Steiner's most beautiful and memorable imagery—indeed, some of the loveliest imagery any American independent filmmaker has produced. And yet, not only are the films not in distribution; they are not mentioned in extensive listings of important films of the period,[28] and, to my knowledge, have never been acknowledged by any of the major avant-garde screening spaces.

The two earliest films vividly reveal the strengths and flaws of the series. *Seaweed, a Seduction* is a continuation of the visual exploration conducted in *Surf and Seaweed*, using a very similar approach to very similar imagery, though the later film is more effective in communicating the magic of the everyday. *One Man's Island* explores more extensive terrain. It begins with a distant shot of Mohegan Island, Maine (where Steiner had a summer home), and a superimposed text ("Why go to an island in Maine?/Why go anywhere?/To see what everyone else sees?/Or to see with your own eyes?"), and then explores various visual "topics": the wake of the boat taking Steiner to the island, the birds hovering in the wind, grasses waving in the breeze, a tide pool, foam created by the surf, a particular type of weed that grows there, reflections on water (this sequence is reminiscent of H_2O), birds following a boat dumping garbage. The film concludes with another superimposed text: "See for yourself./Take time to see for yourself." To find work of comparable visual beauty made during the same period, one must go to Bruce Baillie, Larry Gottheim, Andrew Noren, Peter Hutton, and Nathaniel Dorsky (who edited Steiner's *A Look at Laundry, Beyond Niagara,* and *Look Park*).[29]

Unlike Steiner's early films, the "Joy of Seeing" films have soundtracks. Steiner seems always to have assumed that his films could be enhanced by music. Even the early experimental films were, on at least one occasion, screened to the accompaniment of scores written specifically for them by Colin McPhee and Marc Blitzstein. The scores were performed with the films on Broadway in connection with the Copland/Sessions Concerts, though they were never recorded.[30] Steiner came to maturity as a filmmaker during an era when sound seemed almost inevitable. Apparently, it never occurred to him that his films *required* silence, practically and philosophically, even though by the sixties there was a distinguished tradition of North American avant-garde films that were committed to silence because of the filmmakers' belief in the essential visuality of cinema.

To the extent that the "Joy of Seeing" films are about *seeing*, they are consistently strong. But to the extent that they incorporate the music Steiner saw fit to use, they undercut the filmmaker's own central commitment: they make it difficult to *see* the imagery he captured. One could argue that these soundtracks are consistent with Steiner's interest in "reading" visual imagery, that the composers interpret his visuals in much the way visitors to the Smith College show of cloud photographs interpreted those images. But the point of the interpretations of the cloud images is precisely their variety: each photograph can be seen in many ways. With a single exception, each of the soundtracks of the "Joy of Seeing" series imposes *one* way of seeing Steiner's imagery, and destroys viewers' chances of exploring the imagery in their own ways.

In *Glory, Glory* alone, Steiner confronted this issue directly by juxtaposing the same sequence of images of irrigation with very different soundtracks: excerpts from François Couperin's *Fountains of the French Kings*, Anestos Athenasiou's "Let Her Rip," Jon Appleton's "Computer Assisted Hydraulics," Scott Joplin's "Ragtime Squirts," a bit of a schoolteachery lecture on irrigation, and an excerpt from Vivaldi's *Gloria*. Though it came near the end of Steiner's career, *Glory, Glory* was surprisingly in tune with the explorations of cinema and perception in such films as Tony Conrad's *The Flicker* (1966), Taka Iimura's *Models* (1972), and J. J. Murphy's *Print Generation* (1974). The particular experiment Steiner conducts in *Glory, Glory* has most in common with Larry Gottheim's *Mouches Volantes* (1976) and *Four Shadows* (1978); indeed, it could be said to prefigure Gottheim's work, though Steiner's juxtapositions are relatively straightforward. At most, viewers are engaged with the general idea of what such juxtapositions reveal, rather than (as in Gottheim's films) with an intricate, subtle network of intersections between visuals and sounds.

While *Glory, Glory* reveals a consciousness of the importance of the soundtrack that seems altogether absent in the other "Joy of Seeing" films, it also demonstrates a second flaw in Steiner's later films: their tendency to contradict Steiner's stated intentions for them. The obvious assumption of *Glory, Glory* is that each change in sound will alter our understanding of the imagery, and while the film does bear this out to some degree, the impact of the experiment is rather less than the final text seems to assume it has been. Further, there is some unwitting irony in the fact that even in *Glory, Glory*, where the nature of his experiment is obvious, Steiner feels compelled to begin with a teaching text that states the obvious as clearly as any pedagogue could: "Your feelings, your mood have a lot to do with what you see. Music changes your mood. Music can change what you see."[31]

Hooray for Light! is the most controlled and accomplished of the "Joy of Seeing" films I have had the opportunity to see (I have not been able to find *Slowdown*). The credits are tacky and the music distracting,[32] but the imagery itself is consistently beautiful. Again, Steiner has organized the film into suites of particular kinds of material: the film opens with shots of the ocean—of the sun rising or setting and of reflections on the surface of water—then continues with closeup images of fire, with shots of a mountainous tropical landscape, a waterfall, grass and trees blowing in the breeze, ferns deep within a forest, a winter scene and a snowbank, and finally mountains covered in mist. In all instances, Steiner begins with long-shot "generalities," then zooms or cuts to details that, de-contextualized, are magical in a manner reminiscent of the latter sections of H_2O. The editing is straightforward and entirely in the service of Steiner's sense of composition, though when he explores the snowbank closeup, he dissolves between shots in a manner that enhances the rather fantastic quality of the tiny ice and snow "sculptures" he discovers. Especially if seen silent, *Hooray for Light* is a remarkable film, an impressive conclusion to Steiner's career and a stunning reconfirmation of the filmmaking approach he discovered in H_2O.

As a teacher, programmer, and writer, I have always assumed that films should be shown in precisely the manner in which filmmakers release them. For me, Steiner's later films are the single exception. The "Joy of Seeing" films deserve recognition, but it seems obvious that they will never receive it as sound films. I did not know Steiner, but I would guess that his essential commitment was always to motion picture photography, not filmmaking, and that, as a result, all dimensions of the filmmaking process other than composing, shooting, and then arranging visual imagery were accepted grudgingly, as external requirements, rather than internal necessities. Judging from what others said about him, he may have felt that it would be pretentious to take a stand for silent film or to reject the music supplied by the composers he chose to work with. But the pleasure of contemporary audiences in Steiner's work need not be constricted by his unpretentiousness—at least insofar as sound is concerned. Steiner's motion picture photography deserves an audience; and audiences deserve the pleasure Steiner offers. My hope is that at least some independent programmers will liberate the "Joy of Seeing" films from the accoutrements of conventional cinematic presentation and allow a distinctive American cinematic vision to be appreciated.

NOTES

1. Steiner quoted in Joel Stewart Zukor, *Ralph Steiner: Filmmaker and Still Photographer* (Ph.D. diss., New York University, 1976), pp. 120–121. Zukor's dissertation discusses Steiner's career in detail on the basis of research and extensive interviews with Steiner.

H₂O, Surf and Seaweed, Mechanical Principles, Panther Woman of the Needle Trades, Pie in the Sky, The Plow That Broke the Plains, People of Cumberland,

and *The City* are available from the Museum of Modern Art (MOMA). *Hands, Youth Gets a Break*, and *Troop Train* are available on VHS from the Motion Picture Division of the National Archives (NNSM, Room 2W, Washington, D.C., 20408), under numbers 69.47, 119.32, and 208.139 respectively. *New Hampshire Heritage* is available from Dartmouth College. *Earth and Fire, Seaweed, a Seduction, One Man's Island, Glory, Glory, A Look at Laundry, Beyond Niagara, Look Park*, and *Hooray for Light!* are available from Michael Thomas, September Films, 535 East 6th St., New York 10009 (212–460–8888). *Dance Film, The Quarry, Harbor Scenes, G3*, and *Slowdown* exist, apparently, though I have not been able to locate them. *Cafe Universal* is lost.

2. Ralph Steiner and Leo Hurwitz, "A New Approach to Film Making," *New Theatre*, September 1935, p. 22.

3. Steiner and Hurwitz, "New Approach to Film Making," p. 22.

4. In his later years, Steiner pooh-poohed the early experiments, even H_2O: "Not long ago I saw that film for the first time in almost forty years, and I thought that Aaron [Copland] and I did not do too well in organization. I saw that Aaron, in choosing a career of composing rather than film editing, showed splendid judgement. . . . Except for some innovative photography these films now seem primitive and inept." Steiner, "Introduction," in *Ralph Steiner: A Point of View* (Middleton, Conn.: Wesleyan University Press, 1978), pp. 12–13.

5. Ralph Steiner, *In Pursuit of Clouds* (Albuquerque: University of New Mexico Press, 1985).

6. For the first image of "The Big Sky" section, for example, Steiner provides six "readings": "The big doubt. *Man's doom*. Giant pillow. *Inflated ego*. Heavy ceiling. *Threatened land*. Weight." *In Pursuit of Clouds*, p. 27. Steiner describes the competition in his introduction to *In Pursuit of Clouds*, "Is the World Worn Out?" p. 13.

7. I assume this fourth shot is in reverse, like later upside-down shots; but it is so brief that one cannot be sure.

8. Steiner's use of "composed" in the credits—"Photographed and Composed by Ralph Steiner"—is an allusion to music composition that places H_2O within the tradition of "visual music" explored by Hans Richter, Viking Eggeling, Oskar Fischinger, Len Lye, and others. Indeed, Steiner had asked composer Aaron Copland to work with him on the editing of H_2O: "I persuaded him that a composer should know about unity and progression, and that these had to be important to film editing." Steiner, "Introduction," in *Ralph Steiner: A Point of View*, p. 12.

9. "The Cinematic Principle and the Ideogram" was subsequently edited and translated by Jay Leyda, and included in *Film Form* (New York: Harcourt, Brace & world, 1949). In "A New Approach to Filmmaking," Steiner and Hurwitz discuss the impact of Soviet montage theory and practice, particularly of Pudovkin. the influence of the Soviets, and particularly of Eisenstein's films, is also apparent in Steiner's "Revolutionary Movie Production," *New Theatre* (September 1934), pp. 22–23.

10. The slightly earlier work of Henri Chomette, *Jeux des Reflets et la Vitesse* (1923–1925) and *Cinq Minutes de Cinéma Pur* (1925), seems particularly close to Steiner's *H₂O*, as does some of the 1920s work of the German Walter Ruttman. In more recent years, the tradition Steiner helped establish includes Bruce Baillie, Andrew Noren, Larry Gottheim, Nathaniel Dorsky, and Peter Hutton, among others.

11. Our experience of flipping from "abstraction" to documentation—both of the water itself and self-reflexively (at least by implication) of the means by which it is being recorded—prefigures Robert Breer's work, which, like H_2O, relentlessly toys with our sense of what we see and how we understand it.

12. *Ralph Steiner: A Point of View*, p. 32.

13. Zukor mentions the use of the filter in his discussion of H_2O. I assume the filter was mentioned by Steiner in one of his extensive conversations with Zukor. See Zukor, *Ralph Steiner*, p. 130.

14. My guess is that because of the particular nature of Steiner's textural concerns, *Surf and Seaweed* loses even more than the other early films by being seen in current 16mm prints. That this is the case is suggested by the later 16mm film, *Seaweed, a Seduction* (1960), in which the general subject is much the same as in *Surf and Seaweed* (indeed, many shots from the later film are almost identical to shots in the earlier film). Even though current prints of *Seaweed, a Seduction* have probably faded to some degree in the thirty years since the film was finished, the imagery is a good bit more crisp and scintillating than the imagery in *Surf and Seaweed*, and the film as a whole is quite lovely to look at.

15. Zukor argues that there is a logical continuity in Steiner's first three films: "in this last film of his early experimental investigations, Steiner shows how man took what he learned from nature and put it to work." Zukor, *Ralph Steiner*, p. 140. Since, as Zukor himself emphasizes, the "machines" filmed in *Mechanical Principles* do no work—indeed, as "eccentrics," they are a subversion of conventional machinery—Zukor's contention is not convincing, though it is true, as he points out, that the motion of the "machines," especially as it is emphasized by Steiner's closeups, does echo the pulsing motion of the ocean in *Surf and Seaweed*.

16. Zukor, *Ralph Steiner*, pp. 135–136. No source is specified for Zukor's information about the show at the Science Museum. I assume his description is derived from conversations with Steiner.

17. In 1931, Steiner also completed *Panther Woman of the Needle Trades, or the Lovely Life of Little Lisa* (current listings read "Lonely Life"—an understandable error, since the title moves from right to left across the screen too quickly for the viewer to be sure of individual letters), a playful biography of the American wunderkind clothing designer Elizabeth Hawes, who, according to the film, was "God-marked for greatness." In a series of heavily edited sequences, director/cinematographer Steiner traces Hawes's life from before conception—Jehovah (Morris Carnovsky) creates the Earth, sets it spinning on its axis, then creates Hawes. We see her as a child in a crib, played by Hawes herself, dressed up in

baby clothes (Hawes plays herself throughout the film), then as a child growing up (resisting all temptations to distract her from her "gift"), then as a Vassar College student, then as a young and increasingly successful professional designer who finally takes Paris by storm. Steiner uses playful tableaux to create his affectionate homage to Hawes: perhaps the film's most amusing moment happens before Hawes's conception, when Jehovah falls asleep reading the Bible. Though *Panther Woman of the Needle Trades* is distinctly apolitical, Steiner's approach—especially his use of anti-illusionary techniques to develop character and plot—foreshadows *Pie in the Sky*, made three years later.

I have not been able to locate four other films from the early thirties: *Dance Film* (1931, 1.5 minutes), *The Quarry* (1932, 9 minutes), *Harbor Scenes* (1932, 10 minutes); G-3 (1933, 10 minutes).

18. William Alexander, *Film on the Left: American Documentary Film from 1931 to 1942* (Princeton: Princeton University Press, 1981), p. 15. Zukor concurs with Alexander's judgment.

19. Ralph Steiner, "Revolutionary Movie Production," *New Theatre*, September 1934, p. 22.

20. The Group Theatre was organized in 1931. Zukor discusses at length the background of *Cafe Universal* and the film itself, based on a reconstruction from stills that remain, and that Zukor reproduces in an appendix. See Zukor, *Steiner*, chap. IV.

21. The film's division between the indoor mission sequences and the material shot in the Brooklyn dump recalls an incident that got Steiner fired as an instructor with the Workers Film and Photo League. As Zukor suggests in his shot-by-shot study of the film (appendix I), "The regimented and antiseptic feeling of the mission house has been replaced by an ambience of freedom and openness in the deserted dump" (p. 402). That Steiner can see something positive in a big city dump may seem to defy the requirements of serious political ideology, but it is consistent with his fascination with using sight to uncover what is worth seeing even in seemingly unpromising circumstances.

22. Zukor indicates that according to Steiner, the film "was edited by someone he never saw" (p. 240)—a statement that Steiner must have made to Zukor in one of their interviews (since no other source is cited). Whether Steiner meant that the organization of the film was decided by someone else, or merely that the process of assembling it fell to someone else, is unclear. In his filmography, Zukor lists Steiner as director and credits the photography to Steiner and Willard Van Dyke. I have assumed that Steiner designed the film and either conducted or oversaw all the photography.

23. This situation of becoming at least as well known for one's contributions to films directed by others as for one's own directorial efforts has occurred a number of times in the history of American independent film. Babette Mangolte, for example, was, like Steiner, a still photographer before she was a filmmaker. She has made a series of interesting films—*What Maisie Knew* (1975), *The Cold Eye*

(*My Darling Be Careful*) (1980), *The Sky on Location* (1983)—though she remains best known as the cinematographer for a series of distinguished independent films, including Yvonne Rainer's *Lives of Performers* (1972) and *Film About A Woman Who . . .* (1974); Chantal Akerman's *Jeanne Dielman* (1975), Sally Potter's *The Gold Diggers* (1983), and Jean-Pierre Gorin's *Routine Pleasures* (1986). See Scott Mac-Donald, *A Critical Cinema* (Berkeley: University of California Press, 1988), pp. 279–296.

24. Steiner's opening comment in the section of *Ralph Steiner: A Point of View* devoted to *The City*.

25. Steiner's shots are reminiscent of Charles Sheeler's photographs of the Ford River Rouge plant, though they are both more dynamic and darker—at times almost hellish.

26. Copland credits Steiner with his involvement in *The City*, a project that opened the way for Copland's subsequent work in film: "*The City* started me as a film composer." See Aaron Copland and Vivian Perlis, *Copland 1900 through 1942* (New York: St. Martins's/Marek Press, 1984), pp. 288–291.

27. Steiner, *Ralph Steiner: A Point of View*, p. 32.

28. None of Steiner's films is included, for example, in the listing of avant-garde films in the American Federation of Arts, *A History of American Avant-Garde Cinema* (New York: American Federation of Arts, 1976)—a listing that, remarkably, begins in 1943. And none of Steiner's later films is mentioned in Sheldon Renan's *An Introduction to the American Underground Film* (New York: Dutton, 1967), a book that mentions hundreds of sixties and seventies films; in P. Adams Sitney's *Visionary Film: The American Avante-Garde 1943–1978* (New York: Oxford University Press, 1974); or in Malcolm Le Grice's *Abstract Film and Beyond* (Cambridge, Mass.: MIT Press, 1977).

29. Dorsky: "As far as Ralph Steiner is concerned let me tell you what I can off the top of my head. I was living in the country in northern New Jersey near Port Jervis New York. Somehow a woman from MOMA recommended me to Ralph as an editor based I'm not sure on what. . . . *Summerwind?* [Dorsky's lovely 1965 portrait of American small town life, available from Canyon Cinema] or else a film I did on four painters for some wealthy twins from New York a few years before that was shown at MOMA. The two of them came up and visited and I was honored to meet the man who had made H_2O and *The City*, in fact Ralph still had the converted 35mm B&H he had shot those films with and offered it to me for use. It seems that he had shot these three films but had lost all sense on how to cut the material as it had gotten too familiar. Basically he just gave me the footage for the three films and employed me for two weeks at which time I brought them down to him in the city and screened and he was very happy. With *Look Park* he had cut the park prelude and then said he wanted it to go from the ordinary to the more and more abstract. The same was true for the Niagara one. The Laundry one had the idea of cutting the sheet footage with Greek reliefs but I can't remember if I talked him out of the visualized metaphor

or we tried to make it work. He told me they would all have some baroque music as track, I believe. At any rate the last time I saw them it was in the form of the cut WP I delivered. I've never seen them finished in the sense of release print with sound. He was extremely warm and generous and always very friendly and grateful, but as many times as I asked to see the prints . . . it all never came about. At the time I showed him some of my own footage and his own philosophy was basically that he didn't want to make anything fancy but was an old man who appreciated life itself and wanted his film to simply show the special magic there was in our visual world in the most ordinary circumstances." Letter, Dorsky to the author, 7 September 1990.

30. The Copland/Sessions concert was presented at the Broadhurst Theatre on 15 March 1931. Aaron Copland and Roger Sessions had decided, in Copland's words, "to present something unusual." They presented H_2O, *Surf and Seaweed*, and *Mechanical Principles* along with Alberto Cavalcanti's *La Petite Lilie* (1928) with scores written specifically for the films by Marc Blitzstein, Colin McPhee, and Darius Milhaud, and performed by thirty members of the New York Philharmonic-Symphony Orchestra, conducted by Hugh Ross. According to Copland, "A funny thing happened during Steiner's film, *Mechanical Principles*. The film broke, and we had to switch the order of the program on the spot. It must have been handled smoothly, because the papers the following day assumed that *Mechanical Principles* was *meant* to be given in two parts with the Copland and Sessions music [Copland's *Music for the Theatre* and Sessions' *The Black Maskers* were also performed that evening] sandwiched between." See Copland and Perlis, *Copland*, pp. 184–187.

31. Steiner's hatred of pretension (a characteristic often evident in his writing and remarked about by those who knew him) seems also to have resulted in his use of ineffective graphics and generally banal titles. "More pretentious" film-makers of the seventies—Larry Gottheim and Andrew Noren, for example—refused even to include titles or credits on their films, for fear of compromising their imagery. Steiner was at least as fully committed to his cinematography as these other filmmakers; fortunately for us he was "pretentious" when he had the camera in his hand. His films suffer from his refusal to be as serious about the presentation of his imagery as he was in the filming of it.

32. The credits are superimposed over an image of the sun that one might expect to find in a children's book—a suggestion, perhaps, that Steiner continues to believe in direct, "childlike" vision that is open to the simple visual wonders of the world. One particular credit—"abetted by Caroline Neilson" (Steiner's second wife)— captures what strikes me as the cloying cuteness, the pretentious unpretension so at odds with the straightforward beauties of Steiner's imagery throughout the "Joy of Seeing" series. "Abetted" suggests that there is something criminal—cinematically radical, perhaps—in Steiner's effort, but in fact *Hooray for Light!* would obviously appeal to a very wide range of filmgoers and could offend or annoy almost no one.

10

Straight Shots and Crooked Plots

Social Documentary and the Avant-Garde in the 1930s

CHARLES WOLFE

> This concern of experimental photography for events close to our own time
> and society is not a fad, but a flowering.
> —Ben Belitt (1937)

> The documentary film has a constant hunger for new techniques.
> —Ben Maddow (1940)

Documentary cinema from the 1930s has come down to us largely as a genre of social reform: unambiguous in its rhetoric, didactic in its approach, at the service of organizations and agencies with programs to promote or defend. It may thus seem peculiar to link such a cinema to a history of the avant-garde, or at least the avant-garde of high modernism, with its tendencies toward abstraction, fragmentation, distortion, esoteric allusion, perceptual difficulty, and a destabilizing critique of bourgeois norms. Yet documentary and avant-garde filmmaking, if conventionally treated under separate rubrics, have a history of recurring affiliation, dating back to efforts in the 1920s and 1930s to define an "art cinema" distinct from the conventional practices of the commercial film industry.[1] Moreover, if we are willing to extend our notion of avant-garde cinema beyond the canonic movements of European modernism (Futurism, Expressionism, Cubism, Dada, Surrealism) to encompass more utilitarian and pragmatic strands of modernist thought, the impact of avant-garde experiments of the 1920s on documentary filmmaking in the United States in the 1930s comes more clearly into view.

This impact can be traced along several interconnected routes: an evolving critical discourse on film aesthetics in which the concept of documentary cinema took shape; the career trajectories of individual photographers and filmmakers who gravitated toward social documentary projects as the decade of the Great Depression advanced; the organizing of institutional spaces (workshops, exhibition sites) where films produced outside Hollywood could be showcased and discussed; and the variegated form and style of works to which the label "documentary" was applied. In this chapter I wish to clarify how these various paths hook up in a network of experimental social documentary practices. Social documentarists in the 1930s were above all future-oriented, committed to the prospect of a better world, whether forged at the anvil of a revolutionary proletariat, enacted through New Deal legislation, or projected upon a technological utopia, the "world of tomorrow", which was the theme of a major showcase for documentary films, the 1939 New York World's Fair. With this in mind, we might examine the films they produced as exercises in problem solving, the terms for which were set both by a tradition of formal experimentation in the arts and an ambition to contend with urgent social problems of the day.

In the 1930s, it is important to note, "documentary" was a highly provisional term, employed by critics and filmmakers to explain or advance varied trends in nonfiction filmmaking. Definitions in common circulation by the end of the decade—"the creative treatment of actuality" (John Grierson), "the creative presentation of facts as we find them in everyday life" (Paul Rotha), "the dramatization of facts" (Richard Griffith), "an emotional presentation of facts" (Joris Ivens), "factual photography with the impact of drama" (Arch Mercey)—shared a carefully crafted ambiguity.[2] Reference to the domain of the "factual" or "actual" marked only half of documentary's allure; no less crucial was its invitation to shape such material creatively. Phraseology of this kind loosened without severing the indexical bond of documentary images to their nonfictional referents, valorizing a surplus effect: beyond the presentation of mundane "facts," true documentaries were thought to alter or sharpen human perception (the domain of aesthetics), mount persuasive arguments (the domain of rhetoric), and tell compelling stories (the domain of narration). Filmmakers thus could approach work in documentary as an experimental process requiring—and giving expression to—personal or collective knowledge, belief, skill, ingenuity, or artistry. Spectators, in turn, were promised a heightened awareness or emotional experience of the everyday or commonplace. Critical discourse buttressing social documentary filmmaking in the 1930s thus sanctioned a double commitment by filmmaker and viewer alike: to a social sphere worthy of detailed documentation but also to a medium that might bring that world into perspective, structuring knowledge and stirring emotions through creative manipulation of filmic forms.[3]

This entailed less the codification of specific rules or procedures for documentary filmmaking than an eclectic reworking of existing models, including principles of continuity editing found in Hollywood fiction, elements of Stanislavskian performance technique, and the abstract, associative, or conceptual logic of montage experiments by filmmakers associated with the avant-garde. At the same time, social documentary filmmakers sought to distance themselves from antecedent forms of nonfiction found in industrials, educational films, and travelogues. Even Robert Flaherty's carefully staged narratives of life in distant locales, celebrated in art film circles in the 1920s, were critiqued as an adequate model for new social documentary work on both formal and political grounds, their poetic and dramatic effects reinterpreted as signs of an overly studied artfulness that deflected the attention of the spectator from the social turbulence of the day.[4]

At work here, we might surmise, was a process whereby documentary filmmaking was defined in relation not only to its most obvious alternative—the theatrical fiction of Hollywood—but also the very traditions out of which a loose sense of the genre had emerged. The referential appeal of documentary, its very status as a distinct mode of film practice with a privileged relation to the social world, was invigorated by novel claims to be made about the capacity of the medium to lay bare veiled or suppressed social truths. In support of these claims, filmmakers developed compositional styles that tended to be highly contingent, geared to specific projects. Documentary filmmaking was concurrently promoted as a discovery procedure, an artistic practice, and a social act.

FROM PHOTOGRAPHY TO FILM: ABSTRACTION, OBJECTIVITY, MONTAGE

A conceptual ground for the development of an experimental documentary aesthetic in the 1930s was staked out in the 1920s by artists and critics who found in the seeming mechanical objectivity of the camera a source of new ideas about visual perception in an age of mass, technological culture. These ideas were given varied but congruent expression in a cluster of European movements—French Purism, Russian Constructivism, German *Neue Sachlichkeit*—all of which emphasized the material properties of the medium employed, the precision and economy of mechanical processes, and the utility of mass-produced forms. In the pages of *Broom, The Dial,* and the *Little Review*; at the exhibitions of the New Art Circle, the Société Anonyme, and the Weyhe Gallery in New York; and at film screenings in art film houses in major cities or along the labor-left circuit developed by the Workers International Relief, American photographers and filmmakers had the opportunity to read and view the work of European painters and graphic designers who had responded to new industrial technologies with a call for an objectivist art in which the optical apparatus of the camera played a crucial part.

At the furthest reaches of abstraction were the photographic practices proposed by Lázló Moholy-Nagy, a Hungarian-born constructivist on the faculty of the German Bauhaus, and the French cubist painter Fernand Léger. In "Light: A Medium of Plastic Expression," published in *Broom* in 1923, and in more elaborated form in *Painting: Photography: Film,* translated into English in 1931, Moholy-Nagy outlined a scientific approach to photography that embraced the power of the camera to make visible a phenomenon that was otherwise imperceptible to the human eye and declared the "primary visual facts" of photography to be gradations of light/dark and color.[5]

In "A New Realism—The Object (Its Plastic and Cinematographic Value)," published in the *Little Review* in 1926, Léger extended this concern for the fundamental materials of photographic art to encompass the contours of an object placed before the camera's lens, arguing for the graphic and dramatic beauty of objects *as* objects as well as the unprecedented power of cinema to isolate, fragment, enlarge, mobilize, and juxtapose objects so as to heighten the viewer's contemplation of their shape and form.[6] One in a series of essays by Léger on machine aesthetics that appeared in the *Little Review* in the 1920s, his manifesto on cinema sketched a framework for a fuller political defense of the "realist" dimension to formal experimentation, a defense Léger would himself mount, amid the social upheaval of the Great Depression, in the pages of the American Artists Union publication *Art Front* in 1935 and 1937.[7] This new realism, claimed Léger, involved "scientific discoveries" of "pure sensibility" rather than deductive logic, and filled a need for a popular, nonhierarchical, reproducible art.[8]

The cross-breeding of this new formal emphasis on photographic abstraction and rhythmic editing with the subject matter of conventional nonfiction (actualités, travelogues, and newsreels) pointed toward a new documentary aesthetic. American filmmakers on the left in particular drew inspiration from the work of the Russian documentarists Victor Turin and Dziga Vertov, whose films, and on occasion writings, circulated in left film circles in the early 1930s.[9] Described by the French critic Leon Moussinac in the pages of Filmfront as constituting the "avant-garde of Soviet cinema,"[10] Vertov's "kino-eye" school of cinematography attracted the attention of newly politicized filmmakers in America for its complementary notions of the motion picture camera as a scientific instrument and of filmic montage as an aggressive, complex "language" of visual and acoustic "facts," commensurate with the demands of a revolutionary age. Screened at art film houses as well as smaller film societies, and reported on by the mainstream press, innovative feature-length "city films" like Walter Ruttman's Berlin: The Symphony of a City (1926) and Vertov's The Man with a Movie Camera (1929) provided perhaps the clearest and most conspicuous examples of how a documentary aesthetic might emerge at the point where commitments to social observation, abstraction, and rhythmic and conceptual montage converged.[11]

But there were also precedents closer to home. As early as the late teens, the American photographer Paul Strand and the painter-photographers Charles Sheeler and Morton Shamberg self-consciously developed a "straight" photography style that emphasized sharply focused, geometrically patterned images over and against diffused lighting or other "pictorialist" effects. Elaborated as an ethos as well as a working method, straight photography stressed equally a faith in the materiality and integrity of a pro-filmic field and the power of the photographic image to abstract from that field an acutely drawn, clarified image. In its mechanical registration of such an image, straight photography was to serve as a modern antidote to the enervating mannerism and pathos of studio photography. Hence the affinity of straight photography with the modern, "objectivist" poetry of William Carlos Williams and Marianne Moore, composed in reaction to genteel literary traditions, or with the Precisionist paintings of Sheeler, Shamberg, and Charles Demuth, who rejected impressionistic visual effects in favor of a hard-edged graphic style. For these artists, the optics of the camera offered a new metaphor for visual perception that was precise, uncluttered, focused upon the contours and textures of commonplace objects, viewed not as symbols but as *things*.[12]

Among these photographers, all habitués of Alfred Stieglitz's *salon*-style Photo-Secessionist Gallery at 291 Fifth Avenue in New York in the teens, Strand offered the fullest defense of "straight photography" as both compatible with American culture and an antidote to that culture's tendency toward crass materialism. In a series of essays beginning in 1917, Strand argued that the technology of photography, as employed by a cluster of American artists, bridged a now-obsolete gap in cultural thinking between the domains of science and art. If the *raison d'être* of photography was "absolute unqualified objectivity," the potential power of which was "dependent upon the purity of its use," the camera, employed by an artist, also constituted a powerful instrument of creative expression; in the very effort to grasp an object pictorially, the photographer's point of view inevitably was registered.[13] By 1922, these ideas had come to undergird a more fully elaborated notion of the contemporary photographer as experimenter, as purposeful and logical as the scientific observer, yet unencumbered by the reductive instrumentalism that increasingly had rendered scientists servants of "a new Trinity of God the Machine, Materialistic Empiricism the Son, and Science the Holy Ghost." At once celebrated and condemned in Europe, this new deity threatened to crush life in modern America, where the cult of the machine was driven by powerful economic imperatives. However, by approaching the act of picture-taking with a sensitivity to felt life, the photographer could join "the ranks of all true seekers of knowledge, be it intuitive and aesthetic or conceptual and scientific." Modern technologies of vision thus need not lead to the erasure of human perception and agency or a neurasthenic idolatry of the machine; rather, the camera could be placed in service of human need, reason, and design.[14]

Over the next decade, the implications of this approach for motion pictures were explored in commentary by various American critics and social thinkers concerned with the future fate of cinema as a socially useful art. To a certain extent, Strand's argument conformed to romantic conventions of artistic practice: an "objective" sphere was valued precisely to the extent that it yielded up an image to the discerning eye of the visionary photographer; in turn, the subjectivity of the artist was invested in the object perceived. In this regard, Strand's position statements on "straight photography" bore the impress of the teachings of

Stieglitz, especially Stieglitz's symbolist credo of photographic "equivalents," in which specific emotional or psychological meanings were attributed to visual forms. Yet in his call for photographic practices governed by human needs, Strand also signaled a crucial shift in emphasis from the sensibility of the artist to the well-being of the community, from the cult of the art object to its broader social function.[15]

In the early 1930s, efforts of this kind to articulate a join between mechanical objectivity and social intersubjectivity in cinema took on a new political cast. Given the economic turmoil of the era, David Platt argued in the inaugural issue of *Experimental Cinema* (1930; fig. 10.1), there was "exigent need of a *force* powerful enough to assist in the presentation of these problems, socially, politically, psychologically, and if possible to transform them to meet the realities of the time." The most appropriate such force was cinema, which penetrated "so deeply into the mystery of reality because of the *instantaneity of vision*."[16] Implicitly placing elements of Strand's earlier argument within a sweeping history of the machine, Lewis Mumford, in his influential 1934 study *Technics and Civilization*, likewise claimed that cinema was the unrivaled art form of the Neotechnic Age, a third phase of civilization in which machines, no longer "a substitute for God or for an orderly society," would serve "the organic and living."[17] Photography, Mumford proposed, was a form of historical note-taking, allowing the viewer to "grasp spatial relations which may otherwise defy observation." Moreover, the moving picture's shifting viewpoints registered the flux and variability of human perception and feeling. Hence cinema was "today the only art that can represent with any degree of concreteness the emergent world-view that differentiates our culture from every preceding one."[18]

Mumford's expansive argument for the organic uses of technology at the threshold of the Neotechnic Age—an era in which a Cartesian split between the dead, mechanical body and the vital, transcendent soul had been dissolved—would have a major impact on social reform initiatives in the 1930s, including those proposed in one of the most widely viewed documentary films of the period, *The City* (Ralph Steiner/Willard Van Dyke, 1939), for which Mumford served as consultant. Furthermore, Mumford's dauntingly exhaustive history of technology provided the intellectual framework for the widespread acceptance of documentary filmmaking as a progressive social activity. The tenets of straight photography thus were inflected by a new critical discourse on documentary cinema in which the political stakes seemed especially high.

Figure 10.1.
Cover from *Experimental Cinema* (June 1934). Courtesy of George Eastman House

This shift in emphasis from the aesthetics of perception to wider social and historical concerns can similarly be traced along the career trajectories of individual photographers who were central to the 1930s documentary movement. Prescient here again was Strand, who as early as 1921 collaborated with Sheeler on *Manhatta*, a "scenic" view of New York

City, pitched, as Jan-Christopher Horak perceptively notes, between Walt Whitman's romantic celebration of Manhattan as a primordial landscape and the abstraction and fragmentation of modernist pictorial arts.[19] Highly praised in art circles throughout the 1920s for the visual density of his deeply textured, sharply focused, platinum prints, Strand also supported himself financially as a freelance newsreel cameraman, honing his skills as a cinematographer in the process. In the 1930s, his circle of collaborators expanded as his film work then took an overtly political turn. Under Strand's supervision, *Redes/The Wave* (1934), an acted drama of a fishermen's strike, was filmed on location in rural Mexico in 1933–1934. For this project, he hired two young Austrian émigrés: Henwar Rodakiewicz, a photographer and filmmaker who had attracted attention in amateur circles for an experimental short, *Portrait of a Young Man* (1932); and Fred Zinnemann, a collaborator on the acclaimed German film *Menschen am Sonntag* (1929), who now worked in Hollywood. In 1936, Strand joined forces with Ralph Steiner and Leo Hurwitz to shoot Pare Lorentz's first New Deal documentary, *The Plow That Broke the Plains*, then assumed a leading role in the formation of Frontier Films, the leading labor-left documentary film unit of the decade, serving as its president until the organization's demise in 1942. Among projects at Frontier, he shot (and Hurwitz edited) the most ambitious left documentary of the period, a feature-length history of the violation of the rights of union workers, *Native Land* (1942).

Steiner, in turn, dated his own maturation as a photographer to his exposure to Strand's work in 1926 ("I was pole-axed; I had never seen prints so rich—with such real texture—and so glorious tonal values").[20] At the end of the decade, under the sponsorship of the Elmhurst Foundation, Steiner embarked on a series of short experimental works (*H₂O*, *Surf and Seaweed*, *Mechanical Principles*), similar to the abstract films of Viking Eggeling, Hans Richter, Ruttman, and Moholy-Nagy. He turned to documentary work in the 1930s, first briefly at the Workers Film and Photo League in New York, then joining Hurwitz to form an experimental splinter group, Nykino, where ideas about acting and film fiction were explored.[21] After shooting *The Plow That Broke the Plains* in 1936 (fig. 10.2), Steiner followed Hurwitz and Strand to Frontier; a rift eventually led to his departure to make *The City* with Van Dyke and Rodakiewicz in 1938. His influence, like Strand's, was widely felt: Irving Lerner and Jay Leyda, both a decade Steiner's junior, worked as his

Figure 10.2.
Production still from *The Plow That Broke the Plains* (1936), directed by Pare Lorentz, with Ralph Steiner (camera) and Paul Strand. Courtesy of George Eastman House

assistants prior to their involvement on major projects at Nykino and Frontier.

Social documentary cinema's debt to straight photography follows yet another route, commencing with the formation of Group f.64 in Oakland, California, in 1932. So named for the camera aperture best able to produce photographic images of sharp focus, f.64 included among its original members Van Dyke, Ansel Adams, Imogen Cunningham, and Edward Weston. Weston was the group's intellectual leader, and Van Dyke its chief organizer, but all members had been recently working in a style that focused on the surface texture and shape of closely viewed objects, cropped or tightly framed against the sky or other neutral background.[22] In commentary that echoed earlier position statements on modern photography, Group f.64's manifesto announced a commitment to "simple and direct presentation through purely photographic methods," a form of "pure photography" not derivative of any other art form.[23]

Although Group f.64 was short-lived, the photographers who came together to form it had an impact on social documentary filmmaking in varied ways. In 1931, for example, the bicoastal journal *Experimental Cinema* published a suite of Weston's photographs accompanied by his brief statement on the power of the photograph to attend to the "direct presentation of THINGS in THEMSELVES." For the journal editors, Weston's "honest eye" explicitly served as a useful counter-example to the "unhealthy artificialism of design" and "conventional technical sentimentalism" of cinematography in Hollywood; in this fashion, straight photography's great nemesis, pictorialism, was now linked to Hollywood's studio style.[24] Weston's son, Brett, an affiliate of Group f.64, also briefly served as a staff photographer for *Experimental Cinema*, providing illustrations for articles by David Platt on machine aesthetics and Lewis Jacobs on Sergei Eisenstein.[25] On the political front, East and West coasts connected again in 1934 when Film and Photo League veteran Lester Balog, having arrived in California to shoot and show documentary footage of migrant labor camps, collaborated with San Francisco Bay–area photographers in a "Photo Commentors" show at the Lilienthal Bookstore under the banner "Photographs of Social Significance."[26] In 1930, Strand met Adams in New Mexico and over the next several summers researched the terrain of the Southwest, honing an eye for horizontal landscapes that eventually shaped the look of his Mexican documentary, *The Wave*.[27] Meanwhile, Van Dyke, after a brief stint with the social documentary team of Dorothea Lange and Paul Taylor, crossed the continent in the opposite direction, joining Nykino in New York, then working as a cinematographer on Lorentz's second New Deal project, *The River* (1937). He also followed Steiner's path into independent documentary production with *The City* after a stint at Frontier.[28]

As first forays in filmmaking, "scenics" or pattern films allowed experimental photographers schooled in a straight style to explore the arrangement of mass, line, and volume temporally, through the orchestration of patterns of movement within and across individual shots. As Horak has shown, *Manhatta* is comprised in large measure of animated reconstructions of photographs by Strand and Stieglitz; in a sense, the film tests the aesthetic of an evolving New York school of photography against the possibilities of cinema, of regulated movement and kinetic design.[29] Likewise Steiner's shots of water, surf, and mechanical gears in his pattern films add movement to a series of abstract images, the clarity and tectonic precision of which strongly resemble his abstract photographs of the period. Cutting tends to follow and extend patterns of movement within adjacent shots, at times accelerating the pace of the action.

The temporal model for Steiner was music: the composer Aaron Copland assisted in the editing of all three films, and they subsequently were screened with musical accompaniment by Marc Blitzstein at a modern music concert in New York, where they shared the program with French avant-garde shorts. Analogies to music likewise mark Rodakiewicz's *Portrait of a Young Man*, where abstract patterns of waves, rocks, gears, trees, and clouds are explicitly divided into three separate "movements." Influenced perhaps by the title of Ruttman's *Berlin: The Symphony of a City*, this musical conceit was echoed in a host of projects suggested for amateurs in the early 1930s. In his 1931 guidebook *Cinematic Design*, Leonard Hacker proposed that "a film symphony of swaying trees and flowing water with man and animals as part of the surroundings is the finest type of picture that can be made," and presented seven short scenarios for amateurs, including "Symphony Natural," "Symphony Synthetic," and (with no acknowledgment to Léger) "Symphony Mechanique."[30] Leo Hurwitz, who like Steiner claimed to have been "bowled over" by Strand's photographs upon arriving in New York in 1930, referred to his first effort in filmmaking as "a channel of flow of the city" and a "dance film of the subways."[31] For these photographers turned filmmakers, the abstraction of the photographic image now acquired a rhythmic and choreographic dimension.

Social documentary projects, in turn, would offer manifold opportunities to refine and elaborate this style. Crisply focused, carefully composed images are the norm for these filmmakers throughout the 1930s, whether the subject is a western landscape (*The Plow That Broke the Plains*), a New England village (*The City*), or an intricate pattern of slatted tenement stairs (*The Fight for Life*, Lorentz, 1941). The sustained, rhythmic orchestration of edited shots, cut to music composed for the scene, also is a recurring, even virtuoso, set piece in these films, as when a stream of water gains speed and volume in time to Virgil Thomson's score to *The River*, urban traffic builds to a frenzy to Copland's score for *The City*, the movement of a tractor is cut to (and the sound of its engine integrated with) Paul Bowles's experimental music in *America's Disinherited* (Alan S. Hacker, 1937), or the harvesting of a corn crop is edited to a discordant, heavily cadenced verse chorus by Stephen Vincent Benét in *Power and the Land* (Ivens, 1940). The "conquest of a continent" sequence that opens *Native Land*—with its horizontal tracking shots, vertical counter-movements, and diagonally traced lines defining forces in conflict, accompanied by poet Ben Maddow's scripted commentary and Blitzstein's score—amply illustrates how the formal orchestration of complex patterns of movement, given direction and velocity through precise reframing and cutting, flourished under the rubric of social documentary practices.[32]

HOOKS AND CRANNIES: SOCIAL RECONSTRUCTION AND DOCUMENTARY FORMS

Experiments in the rhythmic patterning of sharply focused images, however, had limited value in advancing the central goals of social documentary filmmakers. Straight photography required alert, disciplined attention to a field of vision, a pro-filmic scene, which through selection and abstraction would yield up an image of reality that habitual ways of seeing masked. With social documentary projects, however, stress now fell on the links, pressure points, and relations of power in an invisible social system, residing, as it were, "behind" the world of physical objects, bound together in causal patterns that the social analyst had to work to reconstruct. The scientific analog for documentary inquiry of this kind was less biology or chemistry (recall Steiner's title for his abstract study of water, H_2O), where microscopic elements could be viewed through optical magnification, or patterns of movement invisible to the eye charted through time-lapse photography, but the *social* sciences, where analyses typically involved a mix of visual documentation, personal testimony, and statistics or charts. Or perhaps the analytical method of social documentary was less a science in any familiar sense than a form of conceptual grasping, closer to the humanistic notion of "understanding," unanchored by an agreed-upon set of logical principles or physical laws.

Indeed, social documentary seemed to bring to the fore another model of photographic practice, with roots in Jacob Riis's tenement photographs at the close of the nineteenth century, published in photo books that attacked the scandalous housing conditions of immigrants; or in the work of Lewis Hine (Strand's first instructor), whose photographs from 1908 through the early 1930s illustrated articles in the social reform journal *Survey* (later *Survey Graphic*), the massive, six-volume *Pittsburgh Survey,* and the brochures and pamphlets of the National Child Labor Committee.[33] Pattern films, in effect, de-historicized documentary photography, closing down the multiple temporal registers that a work of cinema might mobilize for an image, focusing attention on, and intensifying the spectator's sensation of, an immediate act of perception. City films, in contrast, often cued other temporal patterns by establishing, say, a time of day for the action (dawn to dusk was a typical formal structure), or alluding to economic tensions in a modern urban landscape. Leyda's *A Bronx Morning* (1931), for example, edges away from a strictly "symphonic" format for the city film by focusing on hand made signs ("fire sale," "prices down . . . the bottom") and incorporating a running series of intertitles ("The Bronx does business . . . and the Bronx lives . . . on the street") that cast the neighborhood as a public space marked by economic fluctuation and change. In a similar vein, Conrad Friberg in *Halsted Street* (1934) foregrounds economic and ethnic divisions along a city-spanning Chicago street in the era of the Great Depression. Opening with the laborious movement of a plow horse through farmland to the south, and closing with the leisurely gait of equestrian riders in park land to the north, *Halsted Street* reconstructs a dense social milieu through the juxtaposition of commercial billboards, movie marquees, ethnic storefronts, church missions, and political posters and placards, and caps the recurring image of a burly man walking briskly northward with his arrival at a solidarity march. In full-scale social documentaries, historical trajectories of this kind gain dominance. Thus, while straight photographers and social documentarists both rejected traditions of genteel refinement and decoration in the arts, new documentary film work relied on conceptual schema—social typing, social conflict, allegories of social transformation—that straight photographers had jettisoned in favor of strict attention to "the thing itself."

In 1940, the veteran documentarist Joris Ivens put the problem this way: "Films on wood-structure, or in the operation of a bridge should have no trouble in touching the reality of their subject. But films on larger, more important themes, require a deeper approach. In my opinion, it's necessary to find the social reality, then to find the essential drama of that reality."[34] Where precisely was *this* reality to be found? To a certain extent, the historical significance of social events was presupposed by the political or philanthropic organizations with which filmmakers often were aligned. The task of the documentarist was to invest these propositions with a sense of immediacy, density, lyricism, wit, or persuasive appeal. Yet the process of filmmaking itself could alter one's grasp of an inherited proposition about the world, complicating or even skewing any simple message a sponsor might wish to promote. For the ambitious practitioner, documentary filmmaking thus involved the dynamic interaction of inherited propositions, the specific social topic under scrutiny, and the properties of the medium through which social material was to be given dramatic force.

That this required the discovery or cobbling together of *new* forms of cinema was a widely shared view. On the left, the rhetoric of the Workers Film and Photo League easily absorbed the avant-garde's cultural critique of Hollywood cinema as philistine and dull, to which was added a sharpened economic critique of Hollywood's factory system of production and the money interests the film industry served. Organized two doors away from the old Biograph studios on East 14th Street, where D. W. Griffith had first risen to fame, and modestly funded by Workers International Relief, the New York Film and Photo League boldly sought to reclaim American cinema for the working class, announcing a program to expose "reactionary" films, champion "artistic and revolutionary Soviet productions," and "produce documentary films reflecting the lives and struggles of the American workers."[35] Harry Alan Potamkin, a vigorous advocate of avant-garde experiments of the 1920s, argued for the potential of films of "*montage* and document" to sharpen the technical skill, formal sensibility, and powers of political analysis of the amateur of modest means. "Bread lines and picket lines, demonstrations and police attacks," Potamkin proposed, were appropriate subject matter for aspiring working-class filmmakers. Workers' groups, moreover, were strategically placed to provide support for pioneering efforts of this kind.[36] At the League, Hurwitz later recalled, "the great mystique of craft was being dissipated" as filmmakers taught themselves in an ongoing workshop and loose apprentice system.[37] Experimental films from Europe and America, along with the work of Soviet filmmakers, were screened, discussed, and mined for ideas and techniques. To an excitement about new forms of spatio-temporal perception made possible by the modern medium of cinema, Marxist political theory added the promise of a revolution in historical consciousness, a theme sounded in the pages of *Experimental Cinema*, published by Lewis Jacobs and David Platt in association with their amateur film club, the Cinema Crafters of Philadelphia (see fig. 10.1), and echoed later in *Filmfront* and *New Theatre*, both of which were affiliated with the Film and Photo League. The infusion of amateur experimentation with new political commitments was for many young filmmakers a heady mix, as they envisioned the concurrent dawning of a new cinema and a new world. The 1920s amateur thus was recast as the 1930s cineaste-activist, with energies redirected to contemporary political concerns.[38]

As documentary production spread to other sites during the second half of the decade, rhetoric became more temperate. On the left, Popular Front politics muted calls for revolution, in cinema houses as well as in the streets. Meanwhile, social documentary was embraced as a defensible (if at times controversial) medium of persuasion by government agencies, labor unions, reform groups, and private foundations. The New Deal documentaries of Pare Lorentz, in particular, attracted wide acclaim for their forceful treatment of regional American themes. Yet even as debates concerning social documentary entered mainstream channels, the notion that documentary practices were necessarily experimental remained a recurring refrain. Over the horizon might reside an era of documentary guidebooks and manuals, but working filmmakers emphasized the contingent nature of their enterprise and, when opportunities arose, sought ways to expand the range of effects a documentary film might be thought able to achieve. "It was part essay, part poem, part political speech," Hurwitz later said of this new effort, "it was an attempt to create an emotional impact out of ideas, contradictions and conflicts."[39]

Viewed retrospectively, the principles governing experimentation by these filmmakers roughly match those David Bordwell has identified in the work of Soviet filmmakers of the 1920s.[40] American social documentary filmmakers, for example, considered the "art" of cinema a vital component of their work; debate centered on how aesthetic effects could best serve pragmatic ends. In these films, narration tends to be overt, foregrounding the relation of the film to an anticipated spectator, and often inviting that spectator to become one with a broader community the film posits and privileges. Causality is supraindividual, with the behavior of characters strongly marked according to social type. Abstract or associative patterns serve wider persuasive goals, as poetics and rhetoric converge. Social documentary projects, moreover, often draw on a prescribed set of argumentative commonplaces—the need for working-class solidarity, for restoring depleted soil, for fighting fascism at home and abroad—which filmmakers sought to render vivid through experimental techniques. Thus while an argument, in broad outline, might be highly familiar, its unfolding on film could be fresh, unpredictable; should a technique seem inappropriate, the effect also could be deemed peculiar or strange.

Indeed, we might say that the effort to restore a social and historical dimension to the representation of "things" encouraged documentarists in the 1930s to crook, torque, or detour an argument or narrative in an effort to invest it with greater social texture, open up an unpredictable line of inquiry, or achieve a particular dramatic effect. To make a direct assertion, a simple slogan might suffice. But to represent a plausible social world on film entailed dividing, stratifying, and recombining elements in complex forms. In social documentary, as in historiography more broadly conceived, the tensions generated by competing patterns of imagery, emplotment, and rhetoric could powerfully evoke a sense of the density and mutability of social experience and the associative pathways of memory. In raiding the storehouses of both avant-garde and classical narrative techniques, early social documentarists thus explored forms of comprehension not restricted to straightforward, transparent description, even as they sought to authenticate these accounts by treating the photographic image as empirical evidence.

Consider, for example, one recurring pattern in these films, the forceful juxtaposition of contrasting social elements: worker/capitalist, farmland/dustbowl, illiteracy/schooling, peace/war, and so on. At the local level, through rapid cutting, conceptual contrasts of this kind are sometimes invested with a brute perceptual force, as in the prologue to *Bonus March* (Workers Film and Photo League, 1932) when a series of peacetime military "travel" posters, swinging in the breeze, are abruptly intercut with newsreel footage of destruction and carnage from World War I. These contrasts may also underpin broader principles of construction, as in the five-part division of *The City*, based upon alternative patterns of social organization, each composed in a different style, with the final segment, a modern Greenbelt village, graphically linked to the first, an old New England town, and culminating in a series of summary cuts that distill the large-scale argument posed by the commentator: Urban slum or suburban utopia? "You take your choice" (fig. 10.3). More complex, and unique among films of the period, is the structure of *Native Land,* in which an elaborate detective plot is built up from discrete sequences arranged to foreground bold stylistic shifts: in musical tone (upbeat, downbeat), mise-en-scène (light, dark), and narrative style (verbal recounting, dramatic re-enactment) (fig. 10.4). The most wrenching transition, moreover, is reserved for the penultimate scene, when a holiday ride on a merry-go-round is ruptured without warning by a montage of still photographs, reconstructing from fragmentary evidence the slaying of workers at the Republic Steel factory in Chicago on Memorial Day, 1937. In this instance, stylistic contrasts at the local level hook up with a broader, cyclical pattern of victory and defeat, motion and

Figure 10.3.
Still from *The City* (1939), directed by Willard Van Dyke. Courtesy of George Eastman House

Figure 10.4.
Still from *Native Land* (1942), directed by Leo Hurwitz and Paul Strand, with Louis Grant.
Photo by Elinor Mayer. Courtesy of George Eastman House

stasis, celebration and mourning, that defines *Native Land*'s metahistorical ground.

Juxtapositions may also cut a different way, suggesting analogies or metaphors. In *The Plow That Broke the Plains*, tractors are likened to tanks, and grain spouts to cannons, as American agriculture goes to war. Later, flowing grain matches streaming ticker tape, and the quick hands of a jazz drummer are intercut with a vibrating ticker globe. A connection between economy and ecology is then sealed: the glass globe topples and shatters; fade out/fade in on parched, cracked, bone-strewn earth. *Men and Dust* (Dick, 1940) compares the diseased lungs of Ozark miners to eroded land by exploiting the overlapping term in "coal dust"/"dust bowl." As farmers dig irrigation ditches in *The Spanish Earth* (Ivens, 1937), soldiers dig trenches, linking civil war in Spain to land reform. Civilian and military life are bridged at the close of *The Heart of Spain* (Herbert Kline, 1937) through a metaphor for the body politic drawn from the film's title: as blood is extracted from the arms of donors, new recruits march boldly to the front, acts of common sacrifice by a people unified by war. Hands, at first seen idle, turn to labor, then to commerce, in *Hands* (Steiner/Van Dyke, 1934), a promotional short for the Work Projects Administration (WPA); isolated and multiplied in quadrants and prismatic frames, these gestures stand in synecdochically for a recovering U.S. economy. At the close of *People of Cumberland*, the outstretched arm of a young athlete, cross-cut with the flow of water through a Tennessee Valley Authority dam, is replayed as a gesture of solidarity and political optimism by backwoods youths about to come of age.

Efforts to invest social arguments with emotion also motivate striking stylistic strategies. Here, again, montage principles dating back to the silent era are in evidence. Lewis Jacobs' published notes for *Highway 66*, an unproduced documentary, consist of fragmentary descriptions of urban prowling, billboard slogans, and rural despair; readable as disjunctive poetry, this loose scenario suggests the degree to which the shock effects of a modernist aesthetic seemed an appropriate vehicle in the early 1930s to express the disorientation of the Great Depression across regional lines.[41] *Ford Massacre* (Detroit Film and Photo League, 1932) argues for worker solidarity by including footage of a police attack on Dearborn auto workers, viewed at ground level by participating filmmakers. Close-range, hand-held camerawork and abrupt, discontinuous cutting provide a visceral sense of violent disruption, of a struggle marked by high drama. Edited battle footage in *The Spanish Earth* (fig. 10.5), *China Strikes Back* (Frontier, 1937), and *Crisis* (Frontier, 1938) likewise emphasizes the percussive, disorienting force of attack and counterattack, adding a sense of urgency to partisan reportage and, in the process, establishing the model for many U.S. combat films of World War II.

Social documentary soundtracks often extend the range of these effects, in part through the sensory impact of sound effects and music, but also by way of the expressive function of the human voice. In the early 1930s, technological constraints limited sound recording, but lip-synchronized speech was on occasion employed to remarkably idiosyncratic effect. In *The Strange Case of Tom Mooney* (Los Angeles Film and Photo League, 1933) veteran Vitaphone director Bryan Foy withholds a lip-synchronized statement by Mooney until the closing moments of the film. With no more plot to be recounted, the incarcerated labor leader simply reminds his supporters that he is not getting any younger; his tremulous voice then yields to hauntingly silent footage shot

Figure 10.5.
Still from *The Spanish Earth* (1937), directed by Joris Ivens. Courtesy of George Eastman House

at the time of his arrival in prison seventeen years before. ("It is a moment," one reviewer noted, "which some centuries of Hollywood could not erase from my mind.")[42] In the opening, nonvocal section of *Millions of Us* (American Labor Film, 1935), Slavko Vorkapich's impressionistic montage establishes a transient's hallucinatory state of mind, as images of food are superimposed upon his sleeping body. Then, in the final segment, the unemployed worker joins a union, and his envisioned fantasies are replaced by lip-synchronized dialogue and his possession of a new collective, public voice.

By the late 1930s, thanks both to the critical success of Lorentz's poetic commentary for his New Deal documentaries and the greater resources documentarists had at their disposal, vocal patterns emerged as a carefully planned component of the formal design of these films. Beyond exposition and argument, voiceover narration often serves various expressive functions. Vocal commentators assume the voices of characters in *The Spanish Earth, Man and Dust, Power and the Land*, and *The Land* (Flaherty, 1942). Writer Ben Maddow and composer Marc Blitzstein designed the soundtrack to *Native Land* as an oratorio for the rich bass voice of Paul Robeson, who alternates between poetic commentary and songs. In his score for *Valley Town* (1940), Blitzstein included recitatives for an unemployed mill worker and his wife; sung as interior monologues, the music recalls Kurt Weill's for Bertolt Brecht— and was altered by *Valley Town's* disconcerted sponsor when the film was first released. Midway through *People of Cumberland*, exposition unexpectedly gives way to breathless, first-person narration, as we witness a re-enactment of the entrapment and slaying of a union organizer by antilabor thugs. A scored double heartbeat, maternal and fetal, establishes the pace of an ominous childbirth scene at the outset of *The Fight for Life*.[43] Later, as a doctor wanders the night streets of Chicago, his soliloquy is counterpointed by Joe Sullivan's jazz score. In this instance, social documentary cinema anticipates the stylistic effects of film noir.

It may be appropriate, then, to speak of a tension in social documentaries of the 1930s between the assertion of direct propositions concerning social reality and something more open-ended, eclectic, and loose-fitting in the way in which the social problems are recounted and future solutions set forth on the screen. Strand's early effort to locate in straight photography a human dimension—a way of thinking, an emotion felt—resurfaces in social documentary practices in patterns that are compound, oblique, and interlaced—in short, in a form that finally is anything but "straight." Even a film like *The River*, today often put forth as exemplary of a "classic" documentary style, achieves a sense of unity only through the strenuous orchestration of a wide range of diverse elements, across a series of discrete segments, incorporating natural, economic, and social histories of the Mississippi riverbed through intricate variations on visual, vocal, and musical themes. Moreover, even when efforts to generate a sense of human drama and emotion brought documentary filmmakers into close contact with the conservative dramaturgical conventions of Hollywood fiction and Socialist Realism, these films tend to foreground an exploratory or experimental dimension to performance. In neither of Nykino's extant works, for example, does the psychology of individuated characters principally structure the film: *Pie in the Sky* (1935; fig. 10.6) uses acting for improvisational satire; *The World Today* (1935) uses it to dramatize newsreel material, in the mixed

Figure 10.6.
Frame enlargement from *Pie in the Sky* (1935), directed by Ralph Steiner et al., with Elman Koolish. Courtesy of George Eastman House

format of *The March of Time*. Likewise, dramatic re-enactments in *People of Cumberland* and *Native Land* stress the localized, discrete effects the work of actors can achieve; within this context, performance functions as simply one among several ways in which history may be reconstructed, dramatized, and assessed.

These examples, moreover, argue against the commonly held view that documentary filmmakers, historically, have sought to perfect an invisible style. Rather, it seems plain, varied conceptions of realism underpin the use of different techniques, some of which are foregrounded, others masked. *Nanook of the North* (1922) surely gained a wide audience in part because of Flaherty's mastery of the conventions of seamless, continuity editing, but *Nanook*, *Moana* (1926), and *Man of Aran* (1934) also earned high marks from critics for their exceptional *compositional* beauty, which set the films apart from routine travelogue films. Moreover, in rejecting Flaherty's exotic imagery and domestic plots, a new generation of documentarists on the left in the 1930s privileged dynamic editing patterns that were highly pronounced, in search of perceptual effects and a conceptual logic that seemed commensurate with the acts of aggression, victimization, and resistance that these filmmakers took as their principal themes. Likewise, documentaries of liberal reform staked their claim to represent social reality in part on an exorbitant style; unexpected juxtapositions, dramatic set pieces, and odd transpositions in verbal diction or forms of address offer a more textured and conflicted view of social relations than do events more peaceably depicted or described.

To label social documentary in the 1930s a utopian project is to call attention to both the formal ambitions of the filmmakers and their faith, unparalleled perhaps in the history of documentary cinema in the United States, in new social compacts and the inextricable bond between political destiny and human design. Filmmakers, like the social theorists they sometimes quoted, were motivated by a passion to construct, with construction understood not as a mechanical or even necessarily efficient process but as a human activity involving dynamic experimentation with old and new forms. In these films, the power of social and technological innovation is repeatedly linked to the raw force and fecundity of nature, an image true to the organicist view of engineering articulated most fully by Mumford, whose Neotechnic Age was to be rational, not rationalized, inventive, not mechanized, cut to the measure of human hopes and desires, most especially the aspiration to make the world new.[44] Informed by a romantic streak that American modernism never fully shook off, these films are sometimes bleak but never nihilistic; even as scenes of poverty, disease, and despair are graphically rendered, future possibilities seem imminent. In part this is attributable to a recurring rhetorical trope: a closing call for commitment to a political program. But more persuasive than upbeat codas appended to frankly dark reports is a general commitment to problem-solving to which stylistic shifts themselves give evidence.[45] Uneven in execution, experiments in documentary composition convey, if nothing else, a sense of purposeful probing, a searching (and occasionally searing) quality that exceeds any simple effort to demonstrate a point. Like the picture of the Mississippi presented in *The River*—bent out of shape by failed social policies, but capable of alleviating social ills through better planning and design—the forked and twisted structures of these films exemplify both a sense of social disturbance and a human power to put things (back) together, drawing on past experience to order material in new and productive ways. Here formal experimentation seems part and parcel of social documentary's defense of the realm of social imagination, of the power to make palpable the corrosive effects of social ills and to plan and project a better world.

NOTES

1. For contemporary comment see Ben Belitt, "The Camera Reconnoiters," *The Nation*, 20 November 1937, pp. 557–558, reprinted in *The Documentary Tradition: From Nanook to Woodstock* ed. Lewis Jacobs (New York: W. W. Norton, 1971), pp. 141–145; and "David Wolff" [Ben Maddow], "Film Intensity: *Shors*," *Films*, Spring 1940, p. 57. Consider also the central role of Emile de Antonio, Lionel Rogosin, Shirley Clarke, and Robert Frank in the formation of the New American Cinema Group in the early 1960s; or in recent years the conscious blurring or effacing of any workable distinction between documentary and avant-garde practices in films by Agnes Varda, Chris Marker, Raoul Ruiz, Trinh T. Minh-ha, Yvonne Rainer, Su Friedrich, Marlon Riggs, James Benning, and Morgan Fisher, among others. On the ties between the avant-garde and political documentary filmmaking in the 1960s and 1970s, see Michael Renov, "Newsreel: Old and New—Towards an Historical Profile," *Film Quarterly* 41, no. 1 (Fall 1987): 20–33, and David E. James, *Allegories of Cinema: American Film in the Sixties* (Princeton: Princeton University Press, 1989), pp. 166–236.

2. John Grierson quoted by Paul Rotha in *Documentary Film* (London: Faber & Faber, 1939), p. 68; Paul Rotha, "The Documentary Method in British Films," *National Board of Review Magazine*, November 1937, p. 3; Richard Griffith, "A Note on Documentary Film," program note accompanying Museum of Modern Art retrospective, "The Non-fiction Film: From Uninterpreted Fact to Documentary," November 1939–January 1940, in File M257, Thomas J. Brandon Collection, Film Study Center, Museum of Modern Art (MOMA), New York City; Joris Ivens, "Notes on the Documentary Film," *Direction* 3, no. 4 (April 1940): 15; Arch Mercey, "New Frontiers for the Documentary Film," *Journal of the Society of Motion Picture Engineers*, November 1939, p. 525.

Film historians frequently have traced the foundation of a social documentary aesthetic to Grierson, but the impact of the work of Grierson and the British documentary school was not felt in the United States until later in the decade, thanks in large measure to Rotha, author of the first book-length study of documentary, who as a Rockefeller Fellow lectured on the topic and organized screenings at the Museum of Modern Art in 1937–1938. It might be more appropriate, then, to view Grierson's initiatives in Great Britain (and later Australia and Canada) as symptomatic of a more global effort to define, refine, and promote a documentary film aesthetic in an era of mounting interest in the power of nonfictional cinema to shape a sense of social reality for a community of spectators. For a discussion of some common patterns among radical documentary film groups in Germany, France, England, and the United States, see Jonathan Buchsbaum, "Left Political Film in the West: The Interwar Years," in *Resisting Images: Essays on Cinema and History*, ed. Robert Sklar and Charles Musser (Philadelphia: Temple University Press, 1990), pp. 126–148.

3. Efforts to recast documentary as a medium of filmic experiment also inspired a backlash. Oswell Blakeston, for example, argued that the power and lucidity of photographic observation had been spoiled by extravagant cinematic techniques: "We want documents which will show, with the clarity and logic of a scholar's thesis, the subjects they are supposed to tackle: we want no more filtered skies, 'Russian' montage and other vulgarities in our educational productions." See "Manifesto on the Documentary Film," *Close Up* 10, no. 4 (December 1933): 325–326.

4. See Irving Lerner, "Robert Flaherty's Escape," *New Theatre*, December 1934, reprinted in *New Theatre and Film, 1934 to 1937*, ed. Herbert Kline (New York: Harcourt, Brace, Jovanovich, 1985), pp. 307–310; E. K. [Ed Kennedy], "The Films Look at the Worker," *Filmfront*, 24 December 1934, p. 6; and Sidney Meyers, "An Event: *The Wave*," *New Theatre and Film*, November 1936, reprinted in Jacobs, ed., *The Documentary Tradition*, pp. 118–122. A similar critique of Flaherty was pursued in Great Britain; see David Schrire and John Grierson, "Evasive Documentary," *Cinema Quarterly* 3, no. 1 (Fall 1934): 7–9, followed by Grierson's qualified defense of Flaherty, pp. 10–11. Schrire's critique also included a polemic on how documentary was best to be defined, and excluded Flaherty's films from that definition.

As a consequence of these debates, Flaherty came to represent in early histories of documentary a certain romantic exoticism that hardly accounts for the full shape of his career as a filmmaker, which included work on an experimental "city film" (*Twenty-Four Dollar Island*, 1927) as well as a variety of unfinished projects. Locating Flaherty's films within a nexus of varied cinema practices—documentary, avant-garde, and commercial film fiction—might well serve to deepen our understanding of the historical conditions in which notions of an "art cinema" in America emerged during the 1920s and 1930s. For exemplary work in this direction, see Mark Langer, "*Tabu*: The Making of a Film," *Cinema Journal* 24, no. 3 (Spring 1985): 43–64.

5. Lázló Moholy-Nagy, "Light: A Medium of Plastic Expression," *Broom* 4, no. 4 (March 1923): 283–284; *Painting: Photography: Film* (Boston: American Photographic Publishing Co., 1931), first published as *Malerei, Fotografie, Film*, volume 8 in the Bauhaus book series (Munich: Albert Langen, 1925; rev. ed. 1927).

6. Fernand Léger, "A New Realism—The Object (Its Plastic and Cinematographic Value)," *Little Review* 11, no. 2 (Winter 1926): 7–8; reprinted in *An*

Introduction to the Art of the Movies, ed. Lewis Jacobs (New York: Noonday, 1960), pp. 96–98.

7. See Fernand Léger, "The Esthetic of the Machine: Manufactured Objects, Artisan, and Artist," *Little Review* 9, no. 3 (Spring 1923): 45–49, and continued in *Little Review* 9, no. 4 (Autumn–Winter 1923–1924): 55–58; "Film by Fernard Léger and Dudley Murphy," *Little Review* 10, no. 2 (Autumn–Winter 1924–1925): 42–44; see also "The New Realism," *Art Front* 2, no. 8 (December 1935): 10–11, reprinted in *Functions of Painting,* ed. Edward F. Frye (New York: Viking, 1973), pp. 109–113; and "The New Realism Goes On," *Art Front* 3, no. 1 (February 1937): 7–8.

8. Suggestively, Léger repeatedly insisted on the label "realism" over and against a term like "abstraction," perhaps because the latter undercut the concrete, worldly dimension of formal elements that he sought to promote. The theme endured in his writings over several decades. See "The Origin of Painting and Its Representational Values," *Montjoie* (1913), reprinted in Frye, *Functions of Painting,* p. 10.

9. See Victor Turin, "The Problem of a New Film Language," *Experimental Cinema* 1, no. 3 (1931): 11–12; Mikhail A. Kaufman, "Cine Analysis," *Experimental Cinema* 1, no. 4 (1932): 21–23; "Dziga Vertov on Kino-Eye: Excerpts from a Lecture Given in Paris in 1929," *Filmfront* 1, no. 2 (7 January 1935): 6–8; Leon Moussinac, "Dziga Vertov on Film Technique," *Filmfront* 1, no. 3 (28 January 1935): 7–9. For responses to Vertov's films in the United States, also see Simon Koster, "Dziga Vertoff," *Experimental Cinema* 1, no. 5 (1933): 27–28.

In his commentary on contemporary cinema for a wide range of publications in the early 1930s, Harry Alan Potamkin also drew the attention of U.S. readers to Soviet experiments in documentary, including Esther Shub's *The Last of the Romanoff Dynasty* (1927), Yakov Blok's *The Shanghai Document* (1928), and Mikhail Kalatozov's *Salt for Svanetia* (1930), as well as *Turksib* and *The Man with a Movie Camera.* See especially "The Montage Film," *Movie Makers* (February 1930), reprinted in *The Compound Cinema: The Film Writings of Harry Alan Potamkin,* ed. Lewis Jacobs (New York: Teachers College Press, 1977), pp. 70–73, as well as pp. 472–473, 59–65, 313–317. More generally on the distribution of, and critical response to, Soviet films in the United States during this period, see the "Hollywood Bulletin" column in *Experimental Cinema,* 1, no. 2 (1930): 12–14; 1, no. 3 (1931): 22–23; and 1, no. 4 (1932): 54–60; Herman J. Weinberg, "The Foreign Language Film in the U.S." *Close Up* 10, no. 2 (June 1933): 187–191; and Vlada Petric, *Soviet Revolutionary Film in America* (Ph.D diss., New York University, 1973).

10. Moussinac, "Dziga Vertov on Film Technique," p. 7.

11. Both *Berlin: The Symphony of a City* and *The Man with a Movie Camera* were reviewed by Mordaunt Hall in *The New York Times,* the latter film twice. See "The Soul of a City," 14 May 1928; " 'Moscow Today' Hailed," 13 May 1929;

and "Floating Glimpses of Russia," 17 September 1929. On *The Man with a Movie Camera*, also see Jere Abbott, "Notes on Movies," *Hound and Horn*, December 1929, pp. 159–162; and Evelyn Gerstein, "Three Russian Movies," *Theatre Guild Magazine* 6 (October 1929): 14–16. The crucial role of *Berlin* in establishing documentary as a different kind of experimental cinema is evident in Potamkin's suggestion in 1930 that among films where the "logic of images [is freed] from the logic of words ... the practices are, for the most, either documentary (as in the composite newsreel *Berlin*), or effetely fanciful, an *atelier* experiment, as in France." See Potamkin, *Compound Cinema*, pp. 45–46. In his discussions of Soviet documentary, Potamkin also frequently cites *Berlin* as precursor to Russian experiments.

12. On the relationship of straight photography to "objectivist" poetry, see Peter Schmidt, *William Carlos Williams, the Arts, and Literary Tradition* (Baton Rouge: Louisiana State University Press, 1989), pp. 10–47. On Precisionism, see Karen Tsujimoto, *Images of America: Precisionist Painting and Modern Photography* (San Francisco: San Francisco Museum of Modern Art, 1982). On the effort of twentieth-century photographers to reconcile science and art, see Peter Wollen, "Photography and Aesthetics," *Screen* 19, no. 5 (Winter 1978–1979): 9–28.

13. Paul Strand, "Photography," *Seven Arts*, August 1917, pp. 524–526; reprinted in *Photographers on Photography*, ed. Nathan Lyons (Englewood Cliffs, N.J.: Prentice-Hall, 1966), pp. 136–137.

14. Paul Strand, "Photography the New God," *Broom* 3, no. 4 (1922): 252–258, in Lyons, ed., *Photographers on Photography*, pp. 138–144.

15. On the social dimension of Strand's style of documentary portraiture, see John Berger, "Paul Strand," *New Society* (1972); reprinted in *About Looking* (New York: Pantheon, 1980), pp. 41–47. The placement of Strand's camera, Berger writes, "is not where something is about to happen, but where a number of happenings will be related. Thus, without any use of anecdote, he turns his subjects into narrators" (p. 43). On the relationship of Strand's work to traditional views of technology and nature in America, see Ulrich Keller, "An Art Historical View of Paul Strand," *Image* 17, no. 6 (December 1974): 1–11.

16. David Platt, "The New Cinema," *Experimental Cinema* 1, no. 1 (1930): 1–2.

17. Lewis Mumford, *Technics and Civilization* (New York: Harcourt Brace Jovanovich, 1934), p. 5.

18. Ibid., p. 342. In noting the current trend toward photographic objectivity, Mumford gave special credit to Stieglitz, retrospectively applying the by-then-common German term *Sachlichkeit* to a more deeply rooted American tradition. "Stieglitz's uniqueness," claimed Mumford, "was to embody this *Sachlichkeit* without losing his sense of the underlying human attitudes and emotions. He did not achieve objectivity by displacing humanity but by giving its peculiar virtues

and functions and interests the same place that he gives to steam engines, skyscrapers, or airplanes. . . . Spanning the period from the Brown Decades to our own, he has carried over in his own person and work some of the most precious parts of that earlier heritage." See Lewis Mumford, *The Brown Decades* (New York: Harcourt, Brace and Co., 1931; reprint ed. New York: Dover, 1971), p. 106.

19. Jan-Christopher Horak, "Modernist Perspectives and Romantic Desire: *Manhatta*," *Afterimage* 15, no. 4 (November 1987): 8–15.

20. Ralph Steiner, *A Point of View* (Middletown, Conn.: Wesleyan University Press, 1978), p. 10. John Grierson, in turn, would praise Steiner at the time of the release of *The City* "for a visual sense of things that must be one of the greatest influences in our observations today." See "Dramatizing Housing Needs and City Planning," *Films* 1, no. 1 (November 1939): 88.

21. An effort to reposition Steiner's photography within the framework of social documentary is evident in a four-page section devoted to his work in *Theatre Arts Monthly* 14 (January 1930): 77–81. Opening with strips of images from his recent films, the series proceeds to link Steiner's photographs in a logical sequence leading from "Nature's Own Design" (trees and clouds) through "Power from Nature" (electrical power lines) to "Nature Left Out" (a tattered poster for a Hollywood "talkie"). In short, the series is constructed as a proto-documentary montage on a theme central to social thought of the period.

22. Original members also included John Paul Edwards, Sonya Noskowiak, and Henry Swift. Invited to join the group for its first show at the De Young Museum in San Francisco in November 1932 were Consuela Kanaga, Alma Lavenson, Preston Holder, and Brett Weston. On the organization of the group, see *Seeing Straight: The Group f.64 Revolution in Photography*, ed. Therese Tauh Heyman (Oakland, Calif.: Oakland Art Gallery, 1992); and Michel Oren, "On the 'Impurity' of Group f/64 Photography," *History of Photography* 15, no. 2 (Summer 1991): 119–127.

23. "Group f.64 Manifesto, 1932," in Heyman, ed., *Seeing Straight*, p. 53. Direct lines of influence are not easy to trace, but Weston had seen the work of Stieglitz, Strand, and Sheeler in New York a decade before the formation of the group; Adams met with Strand in Taos, New Mexico, in 1930; and all members had the opportunity to view Bauhaus exhibits at the Oakland Art Gallery in 1930 and 1931. Reciprocally, photographs by Cunningham were included in the International Film und Foto Exposition in Stuttgart, Germany, in 1929. See Therese Thau Heyman, "Perspective on Seeing Straight," in *Seeing Straight*, pp. 19–31, and Naomi Rosenblum, "f.64 and Modernism," ibid., pp. 34–41. In an interview late in his career, Van Dyke claimed that Léger and Dutch *De Stijl* painter Piet Mondrian had been especially influential for his work: Oren, "On the 'Impurity,' " p. 126, n. 6.

24. "Edward Weston," *Experimental Cinema* 1, no. 3 (1931): 13–15. Initially edited by Platt and Jacobs in Philadelphia, *Experimental Cinema* had extensive coverage of Hollywood by Seymour Stern in Los Angeles. Potamkin originally served as New York editor, but split with the journal over a complicated dispute between *Experimental Cinema* and *Close Up* after the first two issues. See "Editor's Note," *Experimental Cinema* 1, no. 3 (1931): 34.

25. David Platt, "Focus and Mechanism," *Experimental Cinema* 1, no. 2 (1931): 2–3; Lewis Jacobs, "Eisenstein," *Experimental Cinema* 1, no. 4 (1931): 4. In its second issue, *Experimental Cinema* also listed among its staff photographers Lazlo Moholy-Nagy, Man Ray, El Lissitzky, George Grosz, Ralph Steiner, and Charles Sheeler. However, the work of none of these photographers was published in the journal.

26. According to Balog, other members included Imogen Cunningham, Ansel Adams, Otto Hegel, Consuela Kanaga, Peter Stackpole, and briefly Dorothea Lange. Although asked to join, Weston reportedly declined: Balog interview with Tom Brandon, 18 March 1974, File I158, Brandon Collection, MOMA.

27. Calvin Tomkins, "Profile," and "Excerpts from Correspondence, Interviews, and Other Documents," in *Paul Strand: Sixty Years of Photographs* (Millerton, N.Y.: Aperture, 1976), pp. 24–25, 152–153.

28. See Amalie R. Rothschild's 1981 documentary, *Conversations with Willard Van Dyke*; "Thirty Years of Social Inquiry: An Interview with Willard Van Dyke by Harrison Engle," *Film Comment* 3, No. 2 (Spring 1965): 23–37; interview by G. Roy Levin, in *Documentary Explorations: Fifteen Interviews with Filmmakers* ed. G. Roy Levin (Garden City, N.Y.: Doubleday, 1971), pp. 175–193; and interview by Tom Brandon, Brandon Collection, File K223, MOMA.

29. Horak, "Modernist Perspective and Romantic Desire," pp. 8–15; and see Chapter 11 in this volume.

30. Leonard Hacker, *Cinematic Design* (Boston: American Photographic Publishing Co., 1931), pp. 73–112, 149–158. Analogies to music are pervasive among amateur and avant-garde filmmakers during this period, especially as a way of distinguishing art cinema from the commercial films of Hollywood. Slavko Vorkapich, for example, observed in an address to the American Society of Cinematographers in 1926: "I should prefer to see the scenarios look more like musical scores, with their *andantes, largos, lentos, prestos,* etc., than like present apparent police records: No. 234, Long-shot of Mr. X coming through a french window (one can almost see the cross that 'marks the spot where the body fell'). So much for the physical motions." See "Motion and the Art of Cinematography," *American Cinematographer*, December 1926, p. 15. For a wide-ranging discussion of analogies between cinema and music in film theory, see David Bordwell, "The Musical Analogy," *Yale French Studies* 60 (1980): 141–156.

31. On Strand's influence, see Leo Hurwitz, "One Man's Journey: Ideas and Films in the 1930s," *Cinema Journal* 15, no. 1 (Fall 1975): 6. Hurwitz's first film is described in his interview with Tom Brandon, 8 November 1975, File I183, Brandon Collection, MOMA.

32. At a 1940 symposium on film music, with Copland, Thomson, Blitzstein, Bowles, Hanns Eisler, and Benjamin Britten participating, the consensus of the panelists was that documentaries fostered more innovative collaboration between filmmaker and composer than did commercial filmwork. See "Music in Films: A Symposium of Composers," *Films* 1, no. 4 (Winter 1940): 5–19. In response to a major documentary retrospective at MOMA in the winter of 1939–1940, and two programs at the American Music Festival organized by radio station WNYC, music critic Kurt London came to a similar judgment, noting: "In this era of commercialized entertainment, it is the documentary more than any other form that allows musical and sound experimentation. . . . The progressive documentary without a progressive use of sound or music is the exception and not the rule." See "Film Music of the Quarter," *Films* 1, no. 2 (Spring 1940): 45. Participants at an evening of film music in New York sponsored by the League of Composers, London later reported, "were pretty well agreed that experimentation was possible only in the documentary field." See "Film Music of the Quarter," *Films* 1, no. 4 (Winter 1940): 26.

33. Jacob Riis, *How the Other Half Lives: Studies Among the Tenements of New York* (New York: Charles Scribner's Sons, 1890; reprint ed., New York: Dover, 1971).

34. Joris Ivens, "Collaboration in Documentary," *Films* 1, no. 2 (Spring 1940): 32. Ivens speaks here from personal experience, having made an abstract study of a bridge (*De Brug*) while still in the Netherlands in 1928. For earlier commentary on the logical connection between avant-garde and documentary filmmaking, see Ivens, "Some Reflections on Avant-Garde Documentaries," originally published in *La Révue des Vivants* 10 (October 1931), and reprinted in *Joris Ivens: Fifty Years of Film-Making*, ed. Rosaline Delmar (London: British Film Institute, 1979), pp. 98–100.

35. "Workers Films in New York," *Experimental Cinema* 1, no. 3 (1931): 37.

36. Harry Alan Potamkin, "Workers Films," *Daily Worker*, 31 May 1930, p. 3. Also see *Potamkin, Compound Cinema*, pp. 397–398. As Patricia Zimmerman has argued, Potamkin helped to shift critical discourse on amateur filmmaking away from a preoccupation with domestic and leisure-time pursuits toward more public, political activity. See Patricia Zimmerman, "The Amateur, the Avant-Garde, and Ideologies of Art," *Journal of Film and Video* 38, nos. 3–4 (Summer–Fall 1986): 75–77, and Chapter 6 in this volume. Similar advice was offered to amateur filmmakers in Great Britain: see EMBFU [Empire Marketing Film Board], "A Working Plan for Sub-standard," *Cinema Quarterly* 2, no. 1 (Fall 1933): 19–25.

37. Hurwitz, "One Man's Journey," p. 10.

38. This sense of political urgency can be found in the evolution of an organization as innocently named as the Nature Friends Photo-Group in New York. In 1935, members reported that they had collaborated on their first 16mm film, a four-reel production contrasting scenes of crowding and breadlines in New York City with recreational activities in their rural campgrounds. "League News: Nature Friends Photo Group Challenges," *Filmfront*, 28 January 1935, pp. 14–15.

39. Hurwitz interview with Brandon, Brandon Collection, MOMA.

40. David Bordwell, *Narration in the Fiction Film* (Madison: University of Wisconsin Press, 1985), pp. 234–273.

41. Lewis Jacobs, "*Highway 66:* Montage Notes for a Documentary Film," *Experimental Cinema* 1, no. 4 (1932): 40–41. Scenarios of this kind bear a striking resemblance to experimental protest poetry of the period, which, as Cary Nelson has demonstrated, often was published side by side with more traditional, genteel poems in American magazines and literary anthologies. See Cary Nelson, *Repression and Recovery: Modern American Poetry and the Politics of Cultural Memory, 1910–1945* (Madison: University of Wisconsin Press, 1989).

42. Robert Littella, "Sound Without Fury," *New Republic* 71 (6 September 1933): 102.

43. For Pare Lorentz's conception of the soundtrack for this passage, as well as other instructions concerning the score, see Lorentz's notes to composer Louis Gruenberg, published in *The Best Film Plays*, vol. 2, ed. John Gassner and Dudley Nichols (New York: Garland, 1977), pp. 1082–1087.

44. Critics pursued organic metaphors as well. Consider the comment by Ben Belitt, quoted at the outset of this chapter. Belitt's image of experimental photography on social themes as "not a fad, but a flowering" suggests that innovative work by documentarists, instead of being chic or fashionable, was earthbound. However colorful, vivid, and varied, it was rooted in the land, where social experience (as so many documentaries of the period sought to make plain) properly began. So grounded, Belitt proposed, documentary films reconnected social actors with the drama of their historical moment, offering (in a phrase Belitt takes from Peter Quince in *A Midsummer's Night Dream*) "a marvelous convenient place for our rehearsal." See "The Camera Reconnoiters," p. 558.

45. In a forceful reinterpretation of three "moments" in American documentary history, Paul Arthur recently has proposed that distinctions among three occasions when documentary has penetrated mainstream, commercial distribution can be drawn in terms of the different view of technology offered by the films. Thus while New Deal documentaries in the 1930s identified filmmaking with the power of technology to rectify social ills, Arthur argues, *verité* documentaries in the 1960s incorporated and masked technology as the cognitive acuity of the filmmaker or spectator. Furthermore, a cluster of well-received "diaristic"

documentaries in the 1980s—*Sherman's March* (Ross McEllwee, 1986), *Lightning Over Braddock* (Tony Buba, 1988), *Roger and Me* (Michael Moore, 1990)—disavow technical proficiency, thus demonstrating the filmmaker's own sincerity and (feigned) inadequacy. If we expand this notion of technology to encompass a broader faith in rational problem-solving and technical skill, a link between filmmaking and "technics" seems pervasive in the 1930s, evident in the defense of radical programs to organize a new revolutionary class through the work of participant Film and Photo Leagues, as well of a broad spectrum of liberal social programs, consensus for which could be built through the wide circulation of well-crafted documentaries on these themes. On the process by which technology is linked to nature in New Deal documentaries, Arthur also has much of interest to say. See "Jargons of Authenticity (Three American Moments)," in *Theorizing Documentary*, ed. Michael Renov (New York: Routledge, 1993), pp. 108–134.

11

Paul Strand and
Charles Sheeler's *Manhatta*

Jan-Christopher Horak

Manhatta (1921), a seven-minute portrait of New York City, is acknowledged by many film and photo historians to be the first genuine avant-garde film produced in the United States.[1] Yet most published film histories give *Manhatta* short shrift, despite its acknowledged status, despite the fact that it is the most popular film in the Museum of Modern Art's circulating film library. Those critics who discuss *Manhatta* usually express only the faintest of praise, calling the film a "simple, poetic documentary," "a relatively colorless documentary," or "a series of static photographs."[2] Other historians recycle information from Lewis Jacobs' groundbreaking "Avant-Garde Production in America" (1949).[3] Less surprising, given the notorious indifference of photo historians toward film as a medium, is the cursory treatment *Manhatta* has received in books, catalogues, and monographs concerning Strand and Sheeler's work.[4]

Manhatta is in fact central to film modernism's project of deconstructing Renaissance perspective in favor of multiple, reflexive points of view. At the same time, Strand and Sheeler's commitment to modernism is mitigated by aesthetic concerns and philosophical premises that are archaic and antimodernist. In its conscious attempt to create an avant-garde, nonnarrative, and formally abstract cinematic experience in opposition to classical modes of address, *Manhatta* nevertheless never quite relinquishes those structures which manifest themselves most visibly in the tension between the image and verbal text, between its modernist perspectives and a romantic longing for a universe in which man remains in harmony with nature.

In this chapter I attempt to contextualize *Manhatta* in terms of the history of its production and distribution. *Manhatta* ultimately seems to

267

construct numerous, often conflicting texts, oscillating between modernism and a Whitmanesque romanticism, between fragmentation and narrative closure. As a result, the subject is positioned in the oblique perspectives of the modern skyscraper, but is simultaneously asked to view technology as an event ideally in tune with the natural environment.

In later years the widowed Katherine Sheeler claimed that her husband had been solely responsible for conceiving and photographing *Manhatta*, an assertion that should be corrected. In his memoirs, Sheeler makes no mention of *Manhatta*, or of Strand.[5] In fact, the two collaborators and friends apparently ended their six-year association in 1923, most probably over a review published by Sheeler that criticized Strand's mentor, Alfred Stieglitz.[6] Even before 1923, however, economic pressures had sent Strand and Sheeler in different directions to find work—Strand moving into cinematography, Sheeler working as a gallerist and advertising/fashion photographer. Naomi Rosenblum ventures the speculation that Strand also worried about the distribution of credit for their sole film adventure.[7] As early as September 1921, shortly after the film had its first run, Stieglitz in fact warned Strand:

> All I fear is that Paris will know the film as Sheeler's work, even if you are originally mentioned. It will be Sheeler and Strand. And then Sheeler . . . out of that, unless Sheeler requests De Zayas to be very particular always to mention the two names together. . . . It's one of those ticklish questions when one of two is an "artist" and the other only a "photographer."[8]

Stieglitz's prediction nearly came true: a London reviewer referred to the film as "a group of views by Charles Sheeler."[9]

Strand reckoned that he first met Sheeler in 1917, at Stieglitz's "291" Gallery, when Sheeler was still living in Philadelphia.[10] A common interest in abstraction and straight photography probably drew them together. Both had exhibited the same year at Marius de Zayas' Modern Gallery, and both were considered protégés of Stieglitz.[11] That year Strand won first prize in the Wanamaker competition, the "12th Annual Exhibition of Photography," with his photograph *Wall Street* (1916); Sheeler's *Bucks County House* (1915) and *Side of White Barn* (1915) won the first and fourth prizes, respectively, a year later. When Sheeler moved to New York in August 1919, the two artists became closer friends. Although Strand was seven years Sheeler's junior, the two struggling artists shared a fascination for cityscape architecture and its application to visual design. Then, according to Strand:

> One day I met him and he said, "You know I've just bought a motion picture camera. It's a beauty. It's a Debrie camera, a French camera. It cost $1600." I said, "Well that's certainly very exciting Sheeler. I'd like to see it." So we went to his place, as I recall, and saw this very handsome instrument. I don't remember any of the details, but the upshot of it was the idea of making a little film about New York. Who developed it, whether it was he or both of us together, I don't recall.[12]

Why and when Sheeler bought the Debrie Interview type E camera remains a mystery. According to Stebbins, Sheeler made at least two other films in this period. The photographer Morton Shamberg appeared with a parakeet in the first, which may have been shot as early as 1914 or 1915. The second, produced ca. 1918–1919, featured Katherine Baird Shaffer, Sheeler's future wife, in a series of closeup nude shots.[13]

In any case, Sheeler and Strand worked on the film from early 1920 until at least September of that same year. They shot it from a series of rooftops and streets in lower Manhattan. Sites, all within a five-block radius, included Battery Park, the Staten Island Ferry docks, Wall Street, Broadway, and Trinity Place. The film was probably edited in October, and apparently both artists took part.

Another question surrounds the film's original title. Shortly before his death Strand suggested in a letter to Richard Shales that Sheeler had "proposed that we might make a kind of experimental film about New York together—a silent film carried along by the titles which we took from Walt Whitman's poem."[14] None of the surviving correspondence mentions the title of the film, however, and Strand in later years alternately called the film *Manhatta* and *Mannahatta*, so its original title remains unknown. The film was released under the title *New York the Magnificent*, a title possibly chosen by the Rialto Theatre, the New York cinema where the film premiered commercially, to emphasize its position in the program as a "scenic." When the film was screened in Paris in 1922, the film's title had been changed to *Fumée de New York*. Finally, the film appeared at the London Film Society in 1927 displaying the title *Manhatta*.[15]

Manhatta opened commercially on 24 July 1921, at the Rialto on Broadway. The long delay between the film's completion and its public premiere surely indicates that Strand and Sheeler had difficulty finding an exhibitor. The film ran for one week.[16] American avant-garde filmmakers—unlike their European counterparts—could not at this early date rely on alternative, noncommercial distribution and exhibition organizations, such as film clubs and societies. Thus, neither the viewing context nor the expectations of the audience were really conducive to the reception of a film as an avant-garde, modernist work.

Nevertheless, Strand and Sheeler's press release and the film itself did not totally escape the notice of New York film reviewers. Six critics mentioned the film, and at least three of them devoted more than a line to the title, an extremely rare occurrence, given *Manhatta*'s status as an adjunct to the feature presentation.[17] Though praising the film, critics seemed at best perplexed by this "scenic." None of the critics dealt with the film's construction, its particular view of New York, or the fact that popular tunes and a sing-along were hardly appropriate to the reception of an avant-garde work.

Only one critic recognized *Manhatta*'s importance as a modernist work. Robert Allerton Parker's perceptive review, "The Art of the Camera: An Experimental Film," appeared in *Arts and Decoration* some weeks after the film's commercial run:

> In entering the field of the motion picture Sheeler and Strand sought to apply the technical knowledge gained from their experiments and achievements in still photography to the more complex problems of the motion picture. . . . The results have fully justified this daring adventure in a new art. . . . There was no heroine, no villain, no plot. Yet it was all thrilling, exciting, dramatic—but honestly, gloriously photographic, devoid of trickery and imitation. They used no artifice of diffusion. They did not resort to the aid of the soft-focus lens. They did not attempt to make pictures that looked like paintings.[18]

Parker distinguishes *Manhatta* from the kind of narrative commercial enterprise prevalent in the day, and the "soft-focus" pictorial photography that dominated contemporary photographic aesthetics, praising instead the values of the school of straight photography, associated with Alfred Stieglitz.

Unfortunately, the film died after its initial run, according to a letter from Strand to Stieglitz: "In spite of these [good reviews], I fear we will not be able to distribute it generally. Apparently everybody has been making a reel of New York."[19] As novices in the fields of filmmaking, distribution, and exhibition, Strand and Sheeler were possibly unaware that independently produced films, whether features or shorts, only rarely managed to break into the commercial market, since distribution and exhibition were rigidly controlled by film producers who supplied their own theaters with product. Even if *Manhatta* had been extremely successful, it would not have enjoyed an extended commercial run, because films rarely played more than a week, and because the film industry in any case could not allow an "amateur" to succeed. The exhibition histories of later avant-garde films, such as *The Life and Death of 9413—A Hollywood Extra* (1928), bear out this hypothesis.

Manhatta, although it did not meet the expectations of its makers, did eventually find an art house audience in New York (at the Film Guild), Paris, and London. In retrospect, the film probably enjoyed more public screenings than many European avant-garde films, and certainly more screenings than most American avant-garde film made before 1945. Given the economic structures of the commercial film industry, *Manhatta*'s reception was necessarily restricted to those institutions and audiences participating in a modernist discourse: art houses, galleries, film societies, all of which developed only in the mid- and late 1920s.

Like many American avant-garde works, *Manhatta* is both modernist and strangely romantic, even innocent, in its view of the world. Even before the film begins, *Manhatta*'s intertitles circumscribe its geographic space without inscribing its style. While the upper three-fourths of the image has been darkened to allow for the credits, the bottom of the frame presents an extreme long shot of the lower Manhattan skyline and the Hudson River, including (from left to right) City Hall and the Woolworth, Singer, Equitable, and Banker's Trust buildings. Though abstracted to a degree and flattened through high-contrast printing, the long shot of skyscrapers creates a unified space, positioning the viewer in relationship to the horizon in the manner of Renaissance perspective, and thus allowing him or her to establish spatial relationships among the individual skyscrapers jutting into the darkened sky (fig. 11.1). Nowhere in the film will this image be repeated, nor will spatial relationships be as clearly established. Nowhere in the film will a central perspective orient and position the viewer in the concrete and recognizable geographic space of the film's narrative. While the titles signify totality, inscribing the subject in a construction of a unified space and a centered point of view, the images of Sheeler and Strand's film signify (at first glance) discontinuity.

Figure 11.1.
Frame enlargement from *Manhatta* (1921), directed by Paul Strand and Charles Sheeler

Manhatta does on first viewing appear to be a random selection of images taken in lower Manhattan, images that emphasize abstract elements of visual design in a manner in keeping with the modernist project. As Strand noted in his press release:

> Restricting themselves to the towering geometry of lower Manhattan and its environs, the distinctive note, the photographers have tried to register directly the living forms in front of them and to reduce through the most rigid selection, volumes, lines and masses, to their intensest terms of expressiveness. Through these does the spirit manifest itself. They have tried to do in a scenic with natural objects what in "The Cabinet of Dr. Caligari" was attempted with painted sets.[20]

Invoking the expressionist abstraction of *Das Cabinet des Dr. Caligari* may have been a way of establishing the film's aesthetic credentials, but it also points to the film's use of oblique camera angles, collapsed space, and static compositions. Curiously, Strand does not mention the film's many references to his own photographic work, as well as that of his mentor, Stieglitz. Other images prefigure the paintings and drawings of

Figure 11.2.
Frame enlargement from *Manhatta* (1921), directed by Paul Strand and Charles Sheeler

Charles Sheeler, indicating that he, unlike Strand, would continue to draw inspiration from the project for many years.

Two Stieglitz photographs, *City of Ambition* (1910) and *The Ferry Boat* (1910), can almost be mistaken for frame enlargements from *Manhatta*, anticipating the shot/reverse-angle construction of the film's opening ferry boat sequence. In fact, both photographs were first published in issue number 36 of *Camera Work* (October 1911), which apparently offered Strand and Sheeler a blueprint for a number of other sequences. *Old and New York* (1910) and *Excavating New York* (1911), for example, presage the construction sequence (shots 17–20), while the railroad yard sequence (shots 37–39) recalls *Hand of Man* (1902) and *In the New York Central Yards* (1911).[21] The *Acquitania* steamship sequence likewise recalls Stieglitz's photograph *Mauritania* (1910), published in the same issue of *Camera Work* (fig. 11.2).

Strand also borrowed from his own work. His photograph *Wall Street* (1910), taken from the steps of the Sub-Treasury Building, is literally remade in *Manhatta* (shot 13), the blurred pedestrians of the original still dwarfed by the huge, dark windows of the Morgan Trust Company

Building. Strand's *Fifth Avenue* (1916) is echoed by a similar film image taken on Broadway, in both composition and its slightly low-angle perspective. Strand's *The Court* (1924), with its low-angle perspective, geometric construction of space, and rear view of buildings and rooftops, on the other hand, reprises an image in *Manhatta* (shot 29). Sheeler was more apt to reuse images from *Manhatta* in his photography and painting, as evidenced by an image (shot 15) taken from the Equitable Building and reproduced as a photograph in *Vanity Fair*,[22] as a pencil drawing, *New York* (1920), and as a painting, *Offices* (1922). Sheeler's painting *Church Street El* (1920) also was the product of a film image (shot 59; fig. 11.3) and a photograph published in *Vanity Fair*.[23] *Manhatta's* image of construction workers on geometrically arranged steel girders against a neutral sky appeared years later in Sheeler's painting *Totems of Steel* (1935), while the shots of the railroad yard and factory (shot 37) indicate Sheeler's growing interest in industrial landscapes, which manifested itself in his images of the Ford Motor Company River Rouge plant.[24]

These various cross-connections help to establish Sheeler's and Strand's artistic preoccupations and their willingness to translate imagery

Figure 11.3.
Frame enlargement from *Manhatta* (1921), directed by Paul Strand and Charles Sheeler

into different media, thereby commenting on the specific limitations and successes of each medium's formal practice, but they cannot definitively establish credit for *Manhatta's* individual scenes or images. Both artists seemed at this point in their careers to be interested in an abstract construction of space, in which lines, planes, and solids dominated composition, and both seemed to make extensive use of extreme perspectives in their photographs and paintings. Breaking down images into their basic geometric construction, privileging abstract and formal compositional elements over the image's iconic signifying functions, while at the same time positioning the subject through straight photography conventions to read those images as "reality," Sheeler and Strand created visual interest through dynamic compositional force. More than half of the images are either low-angle shots looking up at buildings or other objects, or high-angle shots looking down at the city from elevated places. In either case, these extreme perspectives tend to obscure spatial relationships, and thus contribute to the fragmentation of the subject's perception. As a result, a degree of disorientation occurs before recognition and cognition, forcing the spectating subject to become aware of his or her own position as spectator. *Manhatta's* extreme camera angles—and there are many more than in their paintings and photographs—thus contribute to the self-reflexivity of the audience's reception, a goal central to all modernist art. In this respect *Manhatta* is a seminal film, predating even the extreme perspectives of European avant-garde films, like *Berlin: The Symphony of a City* (1926) or Dziga Vertov's *The Man with a Movie Camera* (1929), as well as László Moholy-Nagy's Berlin Radio Tower photographs. In photography such perspectives were more common, and Strand and Sheeler had probably seen Alvin Langdon Coburn's photograph of Central Park, *The Octopus* (1912), taken from an extreme high angle.

These formal elements, though common to the modernist project as a whole, do little to clarify the syntagmatic structures ultimately governing the reading of motion pictures as a sequence of shots, rather than individual images. And because film images are embedded in a syntagmatic structure, *Manhatta's* images have been criticized as too static, and lacking in dynamism and movement.

Scott Hammen has correctly pointed out, though, that a number of individual shots do incorporate subtle movement.[25] The opening shot taken from the Staten Island Ferry, for example, moves slowly to the right, while within the frame a barge steams through the image to the left (shot 4). Sergei Eisenstein would later theoretically analyze the dynamic juxtaposition of movement within the frame in terms of a "montage of attractions."[26] A similar juxtaposition of movement, which, according to Eisenstein, increases the dynamic force of the contrasting movements, occurs later in the film when the *Acquitania* and a tugboat steam past each other in opposite directions (shot 41). More directly to the point of Eisenstein's theory of montage is another sequence of two shots in which the horizontal movements of a steam shovel and a crane are juxtaposed from shot to shot (shots 18, 19). In another sequence the filmmakers juxtapose the movements of a crowd toward and away from the camera, while the camera pans down with the movement of the crowd in the first shot, then remains static (shots 9–11).

Camera movement or movement within the frame, however, is only one aspect of cinematic dynamism. Another kind of dynamism, according to Eisenstein, can be achieved through formal contrasts from shot to shot. Strand and Sheeler juxtapose camera distances from shot to shot, increasing or decreasing the size of objects within the frame, establishing different sets of spatial relationships through varying focal lengths, as in the views of men on steel girders or the views of the Hudson River.

Finally, the film's rhythm, varying the length of the individual shots, indicates that the filmmakers were attempting to create another kind of dynamism through the temporal construction of images. Indeed, only two shots in the film last longer than twelve seconds, and both involve camera movement. Virtually every other shot in the film varies in length between four and twelve seconds, with shots usually alternating between shorter and longer images. These formal strategies of syntactical construction must however be contextualized within the film's overall narrative structure, if one is to make semantic sense of *Manhatta's* rhythm.

Although on first viewing the film seems to be nothing more than an impressionistic sequencing of images, *Manhatta's* overall narrative structure can actually be divided into four distinct movements of approximately equal length. Including intertitles, *Manhatta* consists of 65 shots with individual movements breaking down into sequences of 13, 15, 17, and 15 shots, respectively. Each movement focuses on a series of visual themes and motifs, while the four movements together resemble the structure of a symphony. The musical analogy, borrowed from Walter Pater, does not seem out of place here, given Stieglitz's exclamations that he wanted his later cloud photographs to recall "music! Man, why that is music."[27] The symphonic organization of visual images would indeed become overt in other European and American avant-garde films, most prominently in *Berlin: The Symphony of a City* and Herman Weinberg's *A City Symphony* (1930).

The first movement begins with the camera approaching Manhattan from the deck of the Staten Island Ferry, followed by a sequence involving commuters leaving the ferry and dispersing into the streets of the city. The second movement centers on the construction of skyscrapers and their architecture. Images of modern modes of transportation, specifically railroads and steamships, compose the third movement. Finally, the fourth movement returns to lower Broadway and images of the Hudson River. The striking similarity between the first and fourth movements implies that some kind of narrative closure may have been intended.

Strand and Sheeler take advantage of another means of creating an overall narrative structure by using intertitles at eleven points in the film. The intertitles have been lifted partially from Walt Whitman, although not only from his poem "Mannahatta" (1860), as one might suppose, given the film's title, nor are they all direct quotations from Whitman. In almost every case the intertitles introduce individual sections, though they are not purely descriptive, but rather form a lyric counter-point to the film's visual imagery. The first intertitle (shot 7) is taken from "A Broadway Pageant" (1860):[28] "When million footed Manhattan unpent, descends to its pavements," and inaugurates a sequence of shots in which commuters are seen leaving the Staten Island Ferry. The skyscraper sequence is inaugurated (shot 13) with a stanza from the poem "From Noon to Starry Night: Mannahatta": "High growths of iron, slender, strong, splendidly uprising toward clear skies . . ." It continues (shot 22) with another stanza from "A Broadway Pageant." The third movement, focusing on transportation, is introduced (shot 31) by the second to last stanza of "Mannahatta": "City of hurried and sparkling waters!" Finally, the second and the last intertitles are taken from "Crossing Brooklyn Ferry" (1856): "On the river the shadowy group" and "Gorgeous clouds of sunset! Drench with your splendor me and men and women generations after me."

The last intertitle is directly followed by two shots of the Hudson River bathed in light and clouds. As can be seen from these examples, as well as from other intertitles that may or may not be direct quotations from Whitman, but certainly have a Whitmanesque flavor in terms of themes and romantic exuberance, the intertitles do to a certain extent clarify the film's visuals, giving the narrative its cognitive structure. This doubling of verbal and visual content has offended most latter-day commentators, leading them to hypothesize that the intertitles were added by commercial interests against Sheeler and Strand's wishes. However, a number of factors addressing either internal evidence or biographical information speak in favor of the theory that Sheeler and Strand chose the stanzas from Whitman, and also decided on their placement within the film's text. First, the fact that the intertitles have been plucked from a number of different Whitman poems indicates a degree of concern that would have been extremely uncommon for a Broadway movie palace simply needing a short subject. Second, the close correspondence between Whitman's verbal imagery and the respective visual imagery with which it forms a syntagmatic unit creates a narrative structure that hardly seems the work of a lackey at the Rialto Theatre. Third, the poetic cadences of Whitman do seem to counterpoint the film's visual rhythm. Unlike later critics unaccustomed to viewing films with intertitles, contemporary silent film audiences would not have found them obtrusive.

The filmmakers' choice of Whitman must, of course, be addressed, and it is here that one might turn to external biographical evidence. As has been documented elsewhere, Sheeler belonged to the Arensberg Circle, as did the poet William Carlos Williams. The two became friends after meeting in 1925.[29] In the 1910s Williams was the unofficial spokesperson for a New York–based modernist avant-garde, which suffered something of a cultural inferiority complex in relation to the European avant-garde. In particular, Williams had severely criticized the Eurocentric cultural chauvinism of Ezra Pound, HD, and other Imagist poets who had become expatriates in Paris or London. The program of the New York avant-garde included the celebration of American values. Propagating the "independence of art in America," the newly founded and short-lived art magazine *The Blindman* (1917) invoked Whitman as its mentor: "May the spirit of Walt Whitman guide the Independents. Long live his memory and long live the Independents!"[30] Not surprisingly, Williams sought a positive reassessment of Whitman, the popular bard of nineteenth-century Americana, whose poetry had gone out of fashion even during Whitman's final years. Like Whitman, Williams wanted to create and propagate a specifically American—and simultaneously anti-European—perspective and aesthetic. Yet Whitman's hymns of praise to New York and America, constructed as a romantic discourse that repressed the conflicts of nineteenth-century industrial class relations in favor of a homogeneous melting pot of technology, art, science, nature, and man, were hardly comparable to the discourse of alienation and despair inscribed by twentieth-century poets of the city, whether European or American, like Williams. Whitman's view of New York, as expressed in "Sands at Seventy: Mannahatta" (1888), is a vision of the urban environment as a primordial landscape:

> My city's fit and noble name resumed
> Choice aboriginal name, with marvelous beauty, meaning,
> A rocky founded island—shores where ever gayly
> dash the coming,
> going, hurrying sea waves.

The urban cityscape, with its tenements and skyscrapers, its industrialization and technology, poverty and wealth, concrete pavements and steel bridges, disappears completely in Whitman's poem, subsumed by images of nature. Likewise, in "Crossing Brooklyn Ferry" Whitman writes: "Thrive cities—bring your freight, bring your shows." This transcendental view of the city as a natural phenomenon is also very much in evidence in the intertitles taken from Whitman's "From Noon to Starry Night: Mannahatta": "High growths of iron, slender, strong, splendidly uprising toward clear skies." Are not the film images themselves infected? Is not *Manhatta* something less than the modernist vision of the city? In fact, there is an anthropomorphic quality to many of Strand and Sheeler's images because the filmmakers have shown technology as independent of human control. Except for the early ferryboat sequence, with its teeming masses of commuters spilling out onto Broadway, and the later construction sequence, in which workers are actually seen in the act of production, *Manhatta* eschews images of human beings, substituting images of the city as a physical manifestation of social relations.

The inhabitants of the city, their interactions and communications, their production of labor, are reduced to antlike movements, insects crawling between skyscrapers. The metaphor also applies to ocean liners and trains, which likewise move through the cityscape like living creatures, their technology apparently independent of human control. In this scheme of things, the skyscrapers become natural formations of concrete and steel, mountain peaks and deep canyons, surrounded by the glistening waters of the Hudson and East rivers. Indeed, the film's final image is not of the cityscape, its man-made technological structure or urban squalor, but rather of natural elements: the river, clouds, the sun (fig. 11.4). This image of nature, like Whitman's "hurrying sea waves" in "Mannahatta," positions the subject in a transcendental reality, inscribed by the preceding intertitle: "Gorgeous clouds of sunset! Drench with your splendor me and men and women generations after me."

This yearning for a reunification with nature, inscribing technology, urbanization, and industrialization in mass society with naturalistic metaphors, seems to be a not uncommon feature of the "straight photography" advocates around Stieglitz, including Strand. While nineteenth-century pictorialism sought to exclude the economic and social discourses of American laissez-faire capitalism and manifest destiny with all their accompanying upheavals in class and social relations— retreating instead into subjectivity and individualism, privatized images of natural order, pastoral, idyllic landscapes, idealized historical and genre scenes, and harmonious family portraits of the *haute bourgeoisie*— *Manhatta* exemplified straight photography's desire to bridge the schism between city and country, nature and technology, man and mass society.

Steiglitz's description of how he came to make *The Steerage* (1907) expressed perfectly this perception of a possible synthesis, if only because

Figure 11.4.
Frame enlargement from *Manhatta* (1921), directed by Paul Strand and Charles Sheeler

his narrative articulates his desire, his own myth, rather than any historical reality:

> And as I was deciding, should I try to put down this seemingly new vision that held me — people, the common people, the feeling of ship and ocean and sky and the feeling of release that I was away from the mob called the rich — Rembrandt came into my mind and I wondered would he have felt as I was feeling.[31]

All the elements are here — mass society, technology, nature — but Stieglitz idealizes them in terms of a cosmic unity, so that the true condition of the urban proletariat dissolves into a vision of natural man, of genuine feelings, while the rich appear false, out of time, ironically denoted as a mob, the very term usually reserved for the working classes. As Abigail Solomon-Godeau has pointed out, Stieglitz was far from the revolutionary modernist that traditional photographic history texts have made him out to be.[32] And so it is with Strand, as he points out in "Photography the New God" (1922):

> We are not, as Natalie Curtis recently pointed out in *The Freeman*, particularly sympathetic to the somewhat hysterical attitude of the Futurists toward the machine. . . . We have it with us and upon us with a vengeance, and we will have to do something about it eventually.[33]

Is it any surprise, then, that Stieglitz should turn to the production of "Equivalents" and Strand forsake the city for pastoral landscapes once they realized that modernism would lead them into the quagmire of Dada/Futurism? Strand, at least, sought another exit in his politically committed filmmaking, but even here his realism contains antimodernist positions.

In this context the apparatus itself becomes for Strand a fact of nature, independent and anthropomorphic, rather than an instrument for the production of ideology. Strand's images of the Akeley movie camera (1921), the very camera with which he would earn his livelihood as a documentary and newsreel cameraman working for the mass media, concentrate on the sinuous curves and the roundness of the camera's metallic body.

Likewise, Strand's "Photography the New God" is not so much a tirade against the machine god, its empiricist son, and the scientific holy ghost as it is a call for a synthesis of nature and technology, with the camera acting as a catalytic force. According to Strand, pictorialism's crime was to deny photography's true nature, to obscure its technology, rather than embrace it: "At every turn the attempt is made to turn the camera into a brush, to make a photograph look like a painting, an etching, a charcoal drawing or what not, like anything but a photograph." The straight photograph, on the other hand, "has evolved through the conscious creative control of this particular phase of the machine a new method of perceiving the life of objectivity and of recording it."[34] Strand's idealist conception of the camera machine is thus that of the pencil of nature, able to capture human emotions through the science of optics and chemistry, able to overcome the schism between a dehumanizing technology and natural expression.

Paul Strand and Charles Sheeler's closing image in *Manhatta* is an image of nature, taken from high above the streets of Manhattan, that again raises the question of narrative closure. As stated above, *Manhatta*, far from being a nonnarrative film, demonstrates a narrative structure that can be dissected into four distinct movements, with the first and last movements demonstrating a strong similarity. A closer look at this structure reveals that a number of images or locales actually appear at both the beginning and the end of the film: for example, the image of the Brooklyn Bridge, taken from the Brooklyn bank of the East River (shot 6), finds its counterpart in an image from the Manhattan side of the Brooklyn Bridge (shot 52). This doubling—positioning the subject first on one side, then on the opposite side, inscribing the landscapes as the viewer/camera, both subject and object—is itself repeated a number of times, as in the mirror-image pairs of crowds coming and going on Broadway (shots 11, 61), and the low-angle views of Trinity Church Cemetery from opposite sides of the graveyard (fig. 11.5). Finally, and it is here that a sense of narrative closure comes most prominently into view, the first and last images of the film are mirror images of each other. In the first shot the viewer is positioned on the Staten Island Ferry as it approaches Manhattan; in the final image the camera is placed on the Equitable Building, looking over and down the Hudson River toward Staten Island. The subject has thus come full circle; the object of the subject's gaze has become the subject, the subject has become the object. The filmmakers have inscribed the subject in an actual and a metaphoric journey: in time from morning to evening, in space from Staten Island to Manhattan, in the gaze from an urban cityscape to an image of a natural

Figure 11.5.
Frame enlargement from *Manhatta* (1921), directed by Paul Strand and Charles Sheeler

landscape. A symbiotic relationship is thus established. The schism between city and country, technology and nature, "whose coming together might integrate a new religious impulse,"[35] is thus healed in an idealized universe of the camera's gaze. Strand's machine god is proved capable of achieving metaphysical unification.

Strand and Sheeler's visual equivalent of narrative closure violates tenets of modernism's discontinuous and nonnarrative aesthetic strategies. Yet *Manhatta*'s closure is only concretely realized in the gaze and seems hardly comparable to Hollywood's overdetermined narratives in which the subject is necessarily returned to a fetishistic world of order, harmony, and unity, regardless of the chaos that might have preceded it. *Manhatta*, on the other hand, merely approaches closure, implying a narrative that allows for the subject's inscription in the film's final transcendental image. This harmonious subtext is mitigated by and in conflict with the film's overall modernist design, its oblique and disorienting camera angles, its monolithic perspectives of urban architecture, and its dynamic juxtaposition of movement, light, and shadow. *Manhatta* is thus very much a heterogeneous text, both modernist and antimodernist. Its conflicting discourses never quite resolve themselves, as indeed they are never resolved within the discourse of twentieth-century American art.

NOTES

1. A much longer version of this essay was published in *Afterimage*. See "Modernist Perspectives and Romantic Desire: *Manhatta*," *Afterimage* 15, no. 4 (November 1987): 8–15.

2. Stephen Dwoskin, *Film Is . . .: The International Free Cinema* (Woodstock, N.Y.: Overlook Press, 1975), p. 34; Sheldon Renan, *An Introduction to the American Underground Film* (New York: Dutton, 1967), p. 75.

3. Lewis Jacobs, "Avant-Garde Film Production in America," in *Experiment in the Film*, ed. Roger Manvell (London: Grey Walls Press, 1949; New York: Arno Press, 1970), gives the film some significant attention. The only recent attempt to rescue the film from obscurity is Scott Hammen, "Sheeler and Strand's 'Manhatta': A Neglected Masterpiece," *Afterimage* 6, no. 6 (January 1979): 6–7, which provides a first descriptive analysis.

4. Nancy Newhall and Constance Rourke, two early biographers, devote no more than a paragraph (almost identical) to *Manhatta*, a pattern that has not been significantly altered by subsequent commentators. See Nancy Newhall, *Paul Strand: Photographs 1915–1945* (New York: Museum of Modern Art, 1945); Constance Rourke, *Charles Sheeler: Artist in the American Tradition* (New York: Harcourt, Brace & Co., 1938). Dickran Tashjian's discussion of the film in *Skyscraper Primitives* overestimates its modernist components: Dickran Tashjian, *Skyscraper Primitives: Dada and the American Avant-Garde* (Middletown, Conn.: Wesleyan University Press, 1975), pp. 221–223. An exception is Naomi Rosenblum's seminal but unpublished dissertation, *Paul Strand: The Early Years 1910–1932* (Ph.D. diss., City University of New York, 1978), which presents a credible account of *Manhatta's* genesis and Strand's relationship to Sheeler on pp. 96–105. Rosenblum, however, shies away from a close textual analysis and a contextual analysis, as it relates to the film avant-garde. Another exception is Theodore E. Stebbins, Jr.'s discussion of *Manhatta* in an exhibition catalogue that contributes valuable insights into Sheeler's participation in the project. See Theodore E. Stebbins, Jr., and Norman Keyes, Jr., *Charles Sheeler: The Photographs* (Boston: Museum of Fine Arts, 1987), pp. 17–21.

5. See unpublished manuscript, Charles Sheeler Papers (1883–1965), Archives of American Art, New York.

6. Rosenblum, *Strand: The Early Years*, p. 96.

7. Ibid., p. 102.

8. Letter, Alfred Stieglitz to Paul Strand, 21 September 1921, Stieglitz Archive, Center for Creative Photography (CCP), Tucson, Ariz. Copy in Beinecke Library, Yale University, New Haven.

9. See *Close Up* 2 (January 1928): 81.

10. Unpublished interview, Paul Strand with Milton Brown and Walter Rosenblum, November 1971, Paul Strand Archive, Archives of American Art, New York.

11. Stebbins and Keyes, *Sheeler: The Photographs*, p. 17.

12. Strand interview, pp. 8–9.

13. See Stebbins and Keyes, *Sheeler: The Photographs*, pp. 15–17. Neither film has survived; one still from the former and a series of stills from the latter film remain.

14. Letter, Paul Strand to Richard Shales, 31 March 1975, CCP.

15. The print shown in London was saved by Ivor Montague and eventually preserved by the British Film Institute; it became the master material, since all other American prints had disappeared. Like many other early American avant-garde films, including Robert Florey's *Love of Zero* and Charles Klein's *Tell-Tale Heart*, *Manhatta* owes its survival to Montague, who donated his collection to the BFI.

16. *Motion Picture News* 24, no. 7 (6 August 1921): 756.

17. *New York Evening Journal*, 25 July 1921; *New York American*, 25 July 1921; *New York Tribune*, 26 July 1921. The film was also mentioned in *Morning Telegraph*, 26 July 1921; *Brooklyn Daily Eagle*, 26 July 1921; and *New York Herald*, 25 July 1921.

18. Robert Allerton Parker, "The Art of the Camera: An Experimental Movie," *Arts and Decoration* 15, no. 6 (October 1921): 369.

19. Letter, Paul Strand to Alfred Stieglitz, 3 August 1921, CCP.

20. Naomi Rosenblum gave a copy of the press release to the MOMA Film Department in 1978.

21. In *Camera Work* 36 (October 1911); see also Hammen, "Sheeler and Strand's 'Manhatta,' " p. 6.

22. In *Vanity Fair*, January 1921, 72.

23. In *Vanity Fair*, April 1922, 51.

24. *Charles Sheeler: The Rouge: The Image of Industry in the Art of Charles Sheeler and Diego Rivera* (Detroit: Detroit Institute of Arts, 1978).

25. Hammen, "Sheeler and Strand's 'Manhatta,' " p. 7.

26. Sergei Eisenstein, "A Dialectic Approach to Film Form" (1929), in *Film Form*, ed. Jay Leyda (New York: Harcourt, Brace & Co., 1949), pp. 45–63.

27. Alfred Stieglitz, "How I Came to Photograph Clouds," *Amateur Photographer & Photography* 56, no. 1819 (1923): 255; reprinted in *Photographers on Photography*, ed. Nathan Lyons (Englewood Cliffs, N.J.: Prentice-Hall, 1966), pp. 111–112.

28. Walt Whitman, *Leaves of Grass: Comprehensive Readers Edition*, ed. Harold W. Blodgett and Scully Bradley (New York: W. W. Norton, 1965). All quotations are from this edition.

29. Tashjian, *Skyscraper Primitive*, p. 281.

30. Quoted ibid., p. 54.

31. Alfred Stieglitz, "How the Steerage Happened," *Twice-A-Year* 8/9 (1942): 105–136; reprinted in Lyons, *Photographers on Photography*, p. 130.

32. Abigail Solomon-Godeau, "The Return of Alfred Stieglitz," *Afterimage* 12, nos. 1–2 (Summer 1984): 22.

33. Paul Strand, "Photography the New God," *Broom* 3, no. 4 (1922): 252–258; reprinted in Lyons, *Photographers on Photography*, p. 130.

34. Ibid., in Lyons, *Photographers on Photography*, p. 141.

35. Ibid., p. 143.

12

The City Viewed
The Films of Leyda, Browning, and Weinberg

WILLIAM URICCHIO

Jay Leyda's *A Bronx Morning* (1931) opens with images of rapidly shifting abstract patterns intercut with street views taken from the window of an elevated train. The patterns, distorted reflections thrown onto various surfaces, move by with such speed that they are difficult to identify. The alternate and more naturalistic shots of passing street views, however, contextualize the abstractions as a particular kind of visual experience. These more familiar images with their views of pedestrians, traffic, and streets include within them the edges of the train window from which the shots were taken, literally re-framing and motivating the abstractions as details of shadow and light cast upon the passing cityscape.

These dual representational strategies—abstractions and rhythms available only to the camera, and more easily recognizable imagery rooted in Albertian perspective—recall, broadly speaking, the categories of avant-garde and nonfiction film as they were discussed in the 1920s and 1930s. Yet, almost coincident with the entry of this terminology into the medium's critical vocabulary, challenges to any easy correlation between signifying practices and categories began to appear. Nowhere was this challenge more systematic than in the wave of city films that culminated in productions such as Walter Ruttmann's *Berlin: The Symphony of a City* (1926), and resonated throughout the production of American counterparts.

In the pages that follow, the city films of Jay Leyda (fig. 12.1), Herman G. Weinberg, and Irving Browning are examined in terms of the two discursive realms within which they were most often positioned, and

Figure 12.1.
Photo of Jay Leyda and Serge Koussevitzky, no date. Courtesy of Museum of Modern Art, Film Stills Library

which they did the most to challenge: that is, the nonfiction film and the avant-garde film.[1] More than any other production category of the period, the city symphony and its variants managed simultaneously to broaden existing notions of the nonfiction film and to re-work the aesthetic agenda of avant-garde practice.

In the case of documentary, the city films of Ruttmann, Dziga Vertov, Leyda, and Browning, among others, introduced an alternative to the two dominant nonfiction strategies of "description" (travelogues, for example) and character-based "interpretation" (as in Nanook of the North, 1922). In the case of the avant-garde, the social spaces and conditions encountered by city filmmakers often seemed to redefine the aesthetic implications of formal devices drawn from movements such as *Neue Sachlichkeit*, Precisionism, and Dada, directing them toward an actively critical and socially committed end. The frequent presence particularly of European city films in the screenings and critical reception of both documentary and avant-garde communities attests as well to the flexible nature of these categories prior to their institutional reification. In this context, the films of Leyda and Browning, and to some extent Weinberg, may be used to interrogate the status of these emerging critical categories and interpretive communities.

The avant-garde city films produced within the United States, with the major exceptions of Paul Strand and Charles Sheeler's *Manhatta* (1921) and Robert Flaherty's *Twenty-Four Dollar Island* (1927), appeared in the wake of such films as Ruttmann's *Berlin*, Jean Vigo's *A Propos de Nice* (1930), and Vertov's *The Man with a Movie Camera* (1929). The films upon which this essay focuses—Leyda's *A Bronx Morning*, Browning's *City of Contrasts* (1931), and Weinberg's *Autumn Fire* (1933)—together with Weinberg's *A City Symphony* (1930) and Lewis Jacobs' *City Block* (1934) and *As I Walk* (1934), for example, seem indebted to the continental "city symphonies" in specific ways. Not only do they construct the city as a dynamic physical and social experience rather than simply as a space to be described and documented, but they also share the use of many distinctive signifying practices with their European predecessors. And their makers more often than not began their productions already well informed of the broader cultural orientations of their continental counterparts. But while in many senses derivative, these films also lay claim to a distinctness rooted in domestic conditions of production, together, of course, with the visions of their creators.

Poorly received upon their initial appearance and all but ignored over the intervening years, American experimental city films of the early 1930s suffered a fate common to many marginalized production areas—that is, the loss of potentially key films together with production documentation.[2] Absent even from the canon of city films, and with minimal claim for influence of any kind on subsequent generations of filmmakers, the films of Leyda, Browning, Weinberg, Jacobs, and the others nevertheless appeared at a crucial moment in the history of both documentary and avant-garde production and reception.

FROM DOCUMENTARY TO AVANT-GARDE

The New York City Writers' Project's organization of article and review citations in the pages of *The Film Index*, while by no means representing a universally accepted typology, nevertheless provides an insight into the period's conceptual framing of the medium.[3] The breakdown of the "factual film" into four subcategories is particularly interesting in light of the crossover status the city film would occupy in the early 1930s. The *Index* draws a revealing distinction between the "descriptive" function of so-called interest films (i.e., newsreel and record films, travel films), and the "interpretive" function of documentaries, finding very different production patterns for films and criticism within each of these categories.[4] Documentary films, according to the *Index*, are "factual films conceived as dramatic interpretations of reality. Related factual films, considered to be less interpretation than description, information, novelty or record, will be found under the several divisions of Interest films, Newsreel and Record films, and Travel films."[5] The bulk of the documentary entries appear between 1929 and 1935, and the category is described as "a genre relatively recent in development." Interest, record, and travel films, by contrast, have the bulk of their entries for the years prior to 1915 "by reason of the diminished attention paid individual interest [travel and record] films following the advent of the feature film."[6]

The *Index*'s definition of documentary as "interpretive" owes a great deal to John Grierson's *Moana*-inspired formulation of the term. The interpretive process, in this case, included strategies generally associated with the classic Hollywood cinema, bound together with a sense of imagistic "realism" consistent with the earlier interest, record, and travel films, characterized by the *Index* as "descriptive." "Descriptive" films tended to foreground their unplayed status and minimize reliance on characters or story, constructions evidently seen as "interpretive" by the editors of the *Index*. From a position of historical hindsight, the "progression" from description to interpretation might be reframed more broadly as a shift in nonfiction representational strategy—a change in interpretive mode—rather than as an assertion of generic difference.[7]

Rooted in the dominant representational practices of the nineteenth century and the Victorian didactic tradition, early nonfiction film, so often retrospectively labeled naive, maintained a remarkably stable set of signifying practices.[8] The first two decades of city films, for example, tended to position the camera as a viewfinder on the world, emphasizing spatial exposition through relatively long takes and minimal deployment of analytic editing techniques, in the process maintaining the urban iconography widely circulated through stereographic photography and postcards by the turn of the century.[9] *Nanook*, by contrast, emblematized the shift to a narrative conception of documentary, one more voyeuristic than exhibitionistic in orientation, to use Tom Gunning's distinction.[10] The construction of an elaborate artifice dependent upon sets, story, and psychologically credible characters, and the effacing of narrative agency, all contributed to a documentary form with far greater similarity to the classical Hollywood cinema than the preceding decades of nonfiction production.

The efforts of Ruttmann, Vertov, Eugene Deslaw, and others with the city film of the late 1920s provided an alternative for nonfiction representational strategies—one that *A Bronx Morning, City of Contrasts*, and *Autumn Fire* would reference. These films drew upon the earlier exhibitionistic mode, this time reformulated by modernist movements such as Cubism, Futurism, and Dada, and *Neue Sachlichkeit*. Often specifically indebted to the deployment of compositional and cutting techniques in films ranging from *Ballet Mécanique* (1925) to *Potemkin* (1925), the city film reworked these techniques in terms of the site-specific tangibility and social construction that the period's urban subject entailed. "Documentaries" within Grierson's sense of interpretation, these films nevertheless broke from the narrative trajectory which *Nanook* had mapped out and which films such as *Rien que les Heures* (1926) followed, profoundly changing both the style of urban depiction and the parameters of nonfiction representation. Non-city films would follow in this vein (for example, Joris Iven's *Phillips-Radio*, 1931, and Ruttmann's *Mannesmann*, 1937), but the widely circulated and reviewed city film served as the primary site for the articulation of this documentary alternative.

A new conceptual orientation appeared not only in the nonfiction film, but in that other category in which city films were often discussed—the avant-garde film. The impact of the city film here is more difficult to chart, since avant-garde or experimental practice is by definition far less systematic and evades easy formal codification. Nevertheless, at least within the particular avant-garde discourses referenced by certain city films, a reworking of the aesthetic agenda seems apparent. City films often contributed an explicitly critical edge to the deployment of avant-garde technique, leading to a far more "politicized" effort than that evident in other experimental, more personally expressive, films.[11]

The point is obviously overdetermined, and it would be a mistake to attribute the politicization of the cinematic avant-garde to the city film.[12] Yet, in their address of concrete living and working conditions, of specific physical, social, and economic environments, these films emblematized the shift from an essentially romantic tradition of self-expression to a socially engaged and often critical aesthetic.

The agents of this approach were usually intimate with the tenets of modernism either as practitioners in other art forms or as critics. The centrality of individuals active in photography, painting, music, and poetry (such as Strand, Sheeler, Lázló Moholy-Nagy, Ruttmann, Leyda, Weinberg, and Browning) in the city's cinematic reformulation attests to the array of aesthetic influences to which this particular film form was subject.[13] Despite divergent aesthetic referents, their city films simultaneously addressed the urban realities before the camera and the film medium itself.

Ute Eskildsen's discussion of *Neue Sachlichkeit* and photography in this period offers a useful insight in this regard.[14] Eskildsen argues that the ideology of objectivity in the photographic medium (always a problem, given its dominant cultural construction as realist) developed in two main directions during the 1920s. In the first, the camera was used as a "mechanical recording device," portraying the pro-filmic object in the form that most accurately resembled its appearance. In the second, the camera was used as a resource for new visionary perspectives, emphasizing the materiality of the medium itself as a means of extending perception.[15]

Films such as *Berlin* embody both of these concerns, extending them to a durational level. *Berlin* analyzes and reconstructs the visual and temporal rhythms of human, animal, and mechanical processes, of the city as an object, organism, and mentality, and the day as its organizing principle. Through compositional and editing strategies, Ruttmann also manages to develop and exploit a dissonance between the screen as transparent access to "reality" and as a formal graphic surface in its own right. The formal concerns so evident in the promotional campaigns for *Berlin* and *The Man with a Movie Camera*—the photomontage constructions of Umbo and Vladimir and Georgi Stenberg—were consistent with the efforts of such Dada-inflected artists as Hanna Hoch and Paul Citroen, suggesting the synthesis of these dual approaches in static terms. Even in the absence of the films themselves, these widely circulated photomontages implicitly addressed the construction of realism, strategies of fragmentation and restructuring, and the potentials for visual rhythms. And the durational extension of these concepts and strategies served as a key stimulus for the American film practice that followed.

AMERICAN EXPERIMENTAL CITY FILMS

Experimental, amateur, independent, avant-garde—the nomenclature may have varied, but the filmmaking constituencies and their stylistic reference points often overlapped. America's avant-garde in this broad sense owed a specific and frequently acknowledged debt to the European modernist tradition. Beyond the major galleries and exhibitions that served both as a showcase of the new and a meeting ground for shared concerns, public critical coverage of movements such as Cubism, Constructivism, and Expressionism was extensive and largely well-informed in the 1920s.[16] This aesthetic discourse crucially shaped the avant-garde that would emerge in American film production.

Manhatta's production provides an early example of European modernism's generalized influence on American city films. One of the first systematic reworkings of urban imagery, *Manhatta* broke from the traditional ordering of the city's image, mapping the contours of a new formal vocabulary. Paul Strand's work with Alfred Stieglitz and his increasing concern with "clear focus" photography and "accidental" abstraction and segmentation merged with Charles Sheeler's discovery of a "new direction," which Sheeler attributed to Francis Picabia, Man Ray, and Marcel Duchamp. *Manhatta*'s violently angled compositions, its planar abstractions of surface and volume, and its imagistic specificity all reflect the synthesis of these two sets of concerns. The film's vision of intersecting spaces and forms, massive shifts in scale and human placement within it, relied upon a break from the street-positioned camera obscura, and at the same time asserted the materiality of surface both of objects *within* the image and of the screen-projected image itself. A vision of the city familiar to the observer on the street was abandoned through this energetic reorientation of perspective. In contrast to earlier city films, where claims for visual dynamism were created through camera movements, *Manhatta* relied upon compositional construction and contradiction.[17]

European modernism, and, more specifically, modernist film practice, deeply influenced the subsequent American avant-garde, although the route was sometimes circuitous. Leyda wrote of *A Bronx Morning*:

> Thanks to my devotion to journals it had echoes of *Rien que les Heures*, *Berlin*, *L'Etoile de Mer*, *Ballet Mecanique* before I ever saw those films, *The Man with the Movie Camera* (the first Soviet film I saw in New York),

and there's even one shot that derives directly from the cover photograph on an issue of *La Revue du Cinema!* Never underestimate the influence on filmmakers of print and photoengraving.[18] (fig. 12.2)

European film practice also influenced Weinberg's production of *Autumn Fire.* "I never saw Steiner's H_2O, but I know Kirsanoff's *Brumes d'Automne,* a sort of "forerunner" of *Autumn Fire,* s.v.p. I don't know where there's any echo of Dreyer in it tho' there is of Ruttmann's *Berlin,* and of Eisenstein's explosive cutting and overtonal montage."[19]

Leyda's experience, like that of Weinberg and even to some extent Sheeler, seems based upon a translation, a re-presentation, of the tenets of European modernism. Affinities of intent and content bind American and European city films together, particularly in terms of earlier nonfiction approaches to the city. But despite frequent reliance on shared techniques, the representational strategies of the American avant-garde reveal a systematic reworking and reformulation of European impulses.

Figure 12.2.
Frame enlargement from *A Bronx Morning* (1931), directed by Jay Leyda. Courtesy of George Eastman House

In the context of films such as Ruttmann's *Berlin*, Vigo's *A Propos de Nice*, and Vertov's *The Man with a Movie Camera*, American productions have often been received as tentative, even naive. Several factors account for this. American avant-garde city films in many cases were the first motion pictures produced by people engaged largely in other activities (in this context, the nomenclature "amateur" seems appropriate). Excepting Sheeler and Strand's *Manhatta* and Flaherty's *Twenty-Four Dollar Island*, the city films under discussion emerged after 1930 — that is, after (to borrow Jacobs' term) the "Golden Age" of Europe's avant-garde, and after a growing politicization of the American experimental scene.[20] Erratic exhibition opportunities and the different social organization and place of artistic movements and support groups in Europe and America all combined to create very distinct modes of production. Contrasting the level of production support enjoyed by Ruttmann (through Fox-Europa) and Vertov (Ukrainian Film and Photography Administration) with Leyda's reliance on photography jobs for *Vanity Fair* and *Arts Weekly* to finance *A Bronx Morning*, or Weinberg's work as a theater manager and film critic to underwrite *A City Symphony*, puts the production process in better perspective.

These distinctions are not intended as an apologia. They simply attest to the very different cultural place and function of the avant-garde in America and its structural distinction even from the European models it so often emulated. Despite a shared stance in terms of urban depiction, despite shared reference points, the two movements expressed themselves in substantially different fashion.

Leyda's *A Bronx Morning*, Browning's *City of Contrasts*, and pieces of Weinberg's *A City Symphony* in *Autumn Fire* all share a common legacy with the seminal and distinctive image base of Strand and Sheeler's *Manhatta*. Leyda, Browning, and Weinberg's films reveal a compositional insistence on sharply defined and intersecting planes of building mass, light, and shadow. Sequences of rapid cutting intensify the extremity of perspective and radical shifts in shot-to-shot relations, extending the graphic exhilaration of space to an emphatically durational level. Neither European urban space nor architectural structures encouraged this photographic approach, although its formal genesis in the work of the Analytic Cubists (most clearly seen in Citroen's *Metropolis* photomontage series) suggests distinctly continental origin.

Yet a common heritage with films like *Berlin* also structurally links Leyda's and Browning's films. An event-oriented, vaguely chronological structure—with clusters of thematized shots grouped around occupations, gestures, locations, time of day, and so on—recalls the overall organization and sequence-editing strategies of the European city film. Leyda's repeated intercutting of revolving barbershop poles and mannequins (fig. 12.3) evokes Ruttmann, as his extended series of intercuts including repeated torso shots of a heavily breathing woman and a coal truck slowly raising its bed recalls Fernand Léger. But despite structural similarities and even possible quotations, a difference in orientation emerges with consideration of the individual films.

A BRONX MORNING

Jay Leyda came to New York from Dayton, Ohio, in 1930 in response to Ralph Steiner's advertisement in the *New Yorker* for an "assistant on experimental films."[21] He came as a published poet with photographic

Figure 12.3.
Frame enlargement from A *Bronx Morning* (1931), directed by Jay Leyda. Courtesy of George Eastman House

experience, familiar with the contemporary American and continental arts scene, at least as represented in journals like *Arts Weekly, Theatre Arts Monthly,* and *Der Querschnitt.*[22] Leyda initially assisted Steiner, and later Julien Levy, in, among other things, providing photographs for *Vanity Fair, Arts Weekly,* and other periodicals. This employment offered far more than the fiscal means to produce *A Bronx Morning.* It thrust Leyda into the center of a community in the process of defining key aspects of modernism in photography, painting, literature, and film.[23] Judging by his poetry, Leyda entered the New York scene firmly positioned within the progressive wing of a traditionally conceived fine arts aesthetic. Within two years, he would embrace a far more politicized notion of the arts, as his activities with the Film and Photo League and departure for the Soviet Union suggest. *A Bronx Morning* stands at the juncture of these two orientations, although shortly after its completion Leyda would dismiss the film as "ideologically, filmically, politically" removed from his beliefs.[24]

Although Steiner and Levy shared a commitment to formal innovation, celebrating the new vision possible through progressive continental and domestic art movements, they differed not only in their respective roles as creator and dealer, but in their appraisals of the ends served by artistic production. Steiner, who enjoyed an international reputation as a photographer, maintained an active interest in film. His filmmaking activities in the period around Leyda's involvement with his studio mapped a shift from formal aesthetic concerns (evident in H_2O, 1929) to social concerns (*Hands*, 1934) that paralleled Leyda's own development. And Steiner's interaction with members of the Film and Photo League, like Leyda's, reinforced his growing sense of film as a weapon in the struggle for social justice.

Levy, by contrast, both depended upon the patronage of an economic elite and held firmly to a transcendent rather than an overtly politicized aesthetic. He organized important retrospectives of American and European photography in his Madison Avenue gallery during 1931 and 1932, presumably with Leyda's involvement.[25] (Among the Americans represented were Strand, Sheeler, Edvard Steichen, Clarence White, Stieglitz, and Steiner; Europeans included Eugene Atget, Moholy-Nagy, Man Ray, Helmar Lerski, and Umbo.) A passionate and well-connected proponent of the avant-garde in photography, painting, and film, Levy worked with Dudley Murphy (Léger's cameraman on *Ballet Mécanique*) in the Cosmopolitan Studios, maintained active involvement with film, and frequently used his gallery for informal screenings of continental and American avant-garde films, including Leyda's *A Bronx Morning*.[26]

Leyda, of course, had his own agenda. He had come to New York with considerable awareness of independent film, at least as presented on the pages of *La Revue du Cinema, Hound & Horn, Close-Up*, and *Theatre Arts Monthly*, and shortly after his arrival contributed to the amateur filmmaking community by publishing technical tips in *Amateur Movie Makers*.[27] While Leyda's specific rationale for producing *A Bronx Morning* remains unclear, he offered at least three motives: learning about film by making one; using the project to attract Guggenheim support and as a springboard for subsequent projects; and using the film to gain admission to Eisenstein's classes.[28] Whatever the reason, his conception of the project, although obviously informed by his sense of the cinematic avant-garde, clearly positioned it as a "travel film." In a letter to Caroline Lejeune of *The Observer* inquiring about the film's dismal British reception, Leyda wrote:

> You have asked for and advocated "films of travel" in your book, that is, films that give one a feeling of the place as well as facts about that place. I find myself in the position of having made a film that I may be mistakenly putting in this class, and having it intensely disliked by the audiences it was meant for. It is a short film, considered by me simple and communicative, about a place that in addition, has hitherto been untouched by a movie camera. It is neither an exotic nor a romantic place. Because of this, and because it is so near to an American audience, I have never attempted a public showing in America.[29]

Although the film had indeed been publicly (but not commercially) screened in New York at Levy's gallery and at the New School for Social Research, Lincoln Kirstein's review suggests at least one reason for the film's poor reception: "The film is a documentary background of a part of New York and the photography is competent. Mr. Leyda has chosen to eliminate human figures and hence his continuous background is merely a background to which there is no foreground."[30] Leyda agreed, faulting the film for its formalism and lack of social engagement.

A Bronx Morning, as mentioned, generally offers multiple points of view of a given subject. The opening shots of abstract patterns created by the reflected light and shadows of a passing train create visual interest through the constant shifting of apparent screen depth. The film shifts between these full-screen abstractions and a secondary perspective that calls attention to the position of the viewer—replicating a "familiar" perspective framed by the window of the train through which all is seen. This approach recalls the prelude of Ruttmann's *Berlin:* abstract, even disorienting, imagery is followed by a perspective that serves to naturalize it (a device echoed somewhat differently in *The Man with a Movie Camera*). Throughout the film, whether exploiting the abstract visual potential offered by high-angle coverage of pedestrians' shadows on the streets or swish-pan coverage of pigeons in flight, the editing process reframes abstraction to reveal its grounding in ordinary experience.

This process, which recontextualizes the abstract within a fabric of easily comprehensible causal motivations, is evident on a compositional level as well. At several key transitions in the film, a slow wipe seems to occur—an effect actually caused by the extension of a building's awning within the shot over the range of the frame, so that the moving awning or its shadow intrudes across the image. This image addresses the dual strategy described earlier, preoccupied with the object while simultaneously foregrounding the mode of presentation in a manner consistent with modernist practice. It compresses the concerns motivating much of the film's editing strategy into a single composition embracing alternate meanings and contexts.

Leyda's use of fragmentation strongly distinguishes him from his European counterparts. Rather than using analytic editing to articulate process or to imbue spaces and objects with special qualities (for instance, the evocative status of *Berlin*'s early-morning street scenes, or the frantic pace of its morning rush-hour sequence), Leyda uses it to draw the viewer's attention to the specificity of the object. At the same time that the film creates this sense of the particular, it maintains a carefully studied compositional balance.

One sequence, for example, involves a series of sunlit apartment building façades, with the camera on a directly perpendicular axis. The intensity of light and shadow, together with the tranquility and stillness of the buildings' carefully etched and balanced surfaces and windows, recalls the compositions of Edward Hopper. The sequence, moving from multiple long-shot façades to closer details of individual units, stands in sharp contrast to *The Man with a Movie Camera* or *Berlin*'s exclusively graphic use of similar compositions. Despite its calculated formal balance, the sequence encourages a sense of tangibility by drawing us ever closer to the experience of a particular space at a specific moment.

One senses a "particularity" or concern for the specificity of objects in Leyda's approach, shared in Browning's *City of Contrasts* and the work of the Precisionists, that the European city films lack, despite broadly shared technique and subjects. This "particularity" recalls Barbara Novak's characterization of the American representational tradition: "Through it all, the *thing* dominated, amounting, in fact, to a preoccupation with *things*, amplified by concerns with light, space, weather, and time that were often additional routes to the character of an environment shaped by things, as well as extensions from the world at large to the thing."[31]

The continual appearance of the signs of American commerce reflects this preoccupation with the particular in another way. The state of the American economy in 1930–1931, apparent in numerous sale announcements and store windows, is more generally evident in the omnipresence of consumer culture and its decline, combining to give the Bronx an economic specificity that Berlin, Montparnasse, and Nice lack. Browning's *City of Contrasts*, far more emphatic in its critical vision of the economy, nevertheless remains rooted in the particular rather than, as critics often noted of European counterparts, the metaphoric. One has the sense that Leyda shares social concerns with Ruttmann and Deslaw, acknowledging economic inequity as part of life's fabric, but his emphasis on carefully structured form and his respect for the specificity of objects and light lack the critical rhetorical edge of Vigo, Vertov, and Browning.

CITY OF CONTRASTS

Reversing the usual career pattern of amateur filmmakers, Irving Browning worked in motion pictures first (with the Vitagraph Company), before turning his attention to still photography.[32] In 1922–1923, he opened the Irving Browning Studios in New York and concentrated on architectural and commercial photography, documenting the construction of the Daily News and Chrysler buildings, as well as life on Fifth Avenue, the Lower East Side, the city's rooftops, and "Hooverville" shanty towns. Many of these images, in terms of both subject and composition, recur in *City of Contrasts*. Interested in photomontage, Browning refined the production process for clients like *Cosmopolitan*, quickly gaining a reputation as a specialist in this area as well. The film is deeply indebted to this interest, and includes photomontage constructions as well as their

durational extension through the editing process.[33] Browning's awareness
of avant-garde European developments, whether in photomontage or
film, remains unknown, although *City of Contrasts* contains images and
sequences reminiscent of continental city films, and Browning maintained active contact with European photographic colleagues. For example, his film contains an extended evening sequence of lights in the
city, closely paralleling the finale to Ruttmann's *Berlin* and the whole of
Deslaw's *La Nuit Electronique* (1930).

Browning's inclusion with such Film and Photo League luminaries as
Ralph Steiner, Margaret Bourke-White, and Bernice Abbott in an
exhibition at the League's first annual Motion Picture Costume Ball in
1934 suggests an alliance with the organization and members of the New
York experimental filmmaking community.[34] And the pointed social
criticism of many of the "contrasts" in his film reinforces the sense of
ideological affiliation with progressive causes.

In this sense, *City of Contrasts* builds upon a different approach to the
city than that apparent in *A Bronx Morning*.[35] Superficially the film is
structured upon chronology, much like its continental counterparts, and
geography, where it departs from the rather generic (or nontouristic)
urban visions of Leyda, Ruttmann, and Vigo. Browning instead covers
New York as a kind of tourist commodity with visits to Chinatown,
Washington Square, 42nd Street, and so on, initially suggesting a
traditional travelogue. Yet the contrasts promised by the film's title work
to undercut any such comparison. The static image under the film's title
depicts a dense cluster of variously angled skyscrapers, foregrounded by
a curved, elevated train track defining the top of the frame. The
composition, with its compressed and jumbled structures, appears to be a
photomontage (recalling the advertising stills for *Berlin* or Citroen's
work), which the film's second shot, clearly a photomontage of people
and places, seems to confirm. The third shot, a return to the first image
but this time in motion, subverts and even contradicts our access to the
space. The "contrasts" promised in the film's title have begun — contrasts
in scale, composition, direction, and even in our perception of the image
as static or in motion. These opening three shots suggest two dominant
strategies that pervade the film: contrast, evident in theme, composition,
and editing, and the exploitation of illusion.

These strategies also form the basis for the film's social criticism and
often cynical commentary. Browning's use of contrast is most apparent in
extended social discrepancy sequences, where, for example, the film cuts

between an upper West Side mansion and an extensive waterfront shanty town, or between elaborately (and often absurdly) costumed doormen and human billboards and the more fortunate citizenry enjoying themselves in elegant restaurants, rooftop gardens, and spas.[36] But the structuring of these scenes suggests a broad critique of the social condition rather than a pointed indictment of particular social formations or economic practices, suggesting a position akin to Vigo's, as Leyda was closer to Ruttmann. Jacobs reports that the film was shot over six or seven years, which may account for the uneven development of the film's social critique.[37]

Extremes of scale, perspective, direction, and motion pervade the film's images, often working in tandem to complicate the spatial cues of particular compositions. Horizontal elevated trains cut the predominantly vertical, static compositions of skyscrapers; massive silhouettes of foreground structures dominate highly detailed building surfaces; deep spaces contrast with flat surfaces; curves offset the rectilinear; and so on. The editing process carries this compositional complexity a step further. Contrasts between architectural mass and fragile human detail, between rooftops and street scenes, and between direction and tone in shot-to-shot relationships, all enhance the dynamic of the city while suggesting Eisenstein's theories of conflict.

This constant play with contradiction enhances the film's other dominant concern—the manipulation of illusion. For example, street vendors, most of whom are engaged in selling novelty items such as magic devices and illusion-producing gadgets, demonstrate their tricks for an audience (recalling Vertov's magician in *The Man with a Movie Camera*). In another sequence, the camera takes a more active role in the construction of an illusion as a shot of what appears to be a yacht bobs up and down, emulating the motion of waves. Only later do we realize that the scene is set on a rooftop sunbathing deck with a nautical theme, and that we have been the audience for a camera trick.

Editing both enhances and shatters these illusions. In the midst of a rooftop novelty sequence (the yacht-sundeck, gardens, and so on), Browning presents a rooftop scene of children playing under sprinklers. Cutting to another shot of what appears at first to be the same space, we see children diving into a pool and splashing about in relatively deep water. However unlikely it is that this, too, is on the roof, we are prepared for it. The next shot reveals that the pool is indeed on the ground, effectively reversing the expectations we have been led to develop. On a simpler level, cutting between the Statue of Liberty and its replica atop the Liberty Storage Building sustains a process of spatial disorientation. Swish pans, used throughout the film to connect sequences and suggest spatial continuity (where it exists as well as where it does not), are exploited throughout the Liberty sequence. Just when we are sure that the pan is disguising a cut and location change, the space is revealed to be intact, and vice versa.

One of the most interesting uses of illusion emerges in an extended sequence on humans as advertisement, a subject very much a part of Browning's photographic career. The film shows men dressed as "British policeman," "Cossack," "farmer," and even top-hatted "gentleman," in close and medium shots, and only later reveals the men as sandwich-board carriers—walking advertisements. Browning holds the close head shots for what seems an uncomfortably long time, creating the impression that several of the men, too, are ill at ease under the camera's scrutiny, an awkwardness easily extended to their encounters with the general public. And, lest the point remain ambiguous, the next sequence provides the sharp contrast of elegant restaurants and rooftop leisure scenes, where we not only see differences in class composition but are kept from intruding by shot distance and brevity. Significantly, the film's only other use of lingering individual closeups occurs with unemployed men advertising their availability and references as they play accordions and drums on the street. The sequence powerfully communicates the commodification of humans, but the recurrent cynicism suggested by Browning's use of camera tricks blunts sustained critical analysis.

A CITY SYMPHONY

Trained as a musician at the Institute of Musical Art of New York, Herman G. Weinberg (fig. 12.4) worked as musical consultant and later publicist for the 5th Avenue Playhouse. In 1929, he became managing director of an important venue for experimental and European film, the Baltimore Little Theatre, which contributed to his work as a critic and subtitler of foreign films, and to his filmmaking activities.

Weinberg, deeply interested in the avant-garde films circulating in the little theater circuit, acknowledged their role in his creative formation. "My films contain fleeting passages here and there that, I think, are original; but, for the most part, they have been influenced by the

Figure 12.4.
Photographic portrait, Herman Weinberg. Courtesy of Museum of Modern Art, Film Stills
Library

memories of passages in far more ambitious achievements."[38] Specifying
Flaherty, Ruttmann, Eisenstein, Kirsanoff, Pudovkin, and Dupont as
influences, Weinberg seems to have been far more traditional in his
appraisal of avant-garde film's aesthetic status as personally expressive
than Leyda, Jacobs, Steiner, and Browning, noting that "a sense of poetry
is almost a *sine qua non* of expressive filmmaking, which is *au fond* a
poetic medium."[39]

Weinberg's inclusion in this essay is based on A *City Symphony*—
sadly, a lost film. Yet some footage remains, recut into *Autumn Fire*,
leaving us with some suggestive bits with which to speculate about his
approach. *Autumn Fire*, a rich and evocative film, merits serious reap-
praisal on its own terms, rather than simply for the depiction of the city
it contains. Its cutting strategies present the city as an externalization of
character and emotion, metaphorically contrasting the city (man) with
nature (woman), the water common to both realms linking them
together. The specific treatment of elements within any one of these
image-sets provides the character's emotional range. Despite this use of
the city as metaphor, there are grounds to consider Weinberg's urban
images as closely related to those in A *City Symphony*.

The urban images in the film reveal a striking compositional dynamism: extreme angles, exploitation of the massive façades and contrasting
deep spaces of walled streets, the "urban heights and canyons" described
by Jacobs in writing about *Manhatta*. Strand and Sheeler's approach to
New York closely parallels Weinberg's compositional concerns, and their
use of Whitman's poetry seems to reverberate with *Autumn Fire*'s
romantic contextualization of the urban image. The film's romanticism
runs deep, extending from Weinberg's conception of experimental film to
his specific purpose in making the film—that is, wooing the actress he
cast in the lead (fig. 12.5).[40]

Weinberg's writings on film, particularly around the time of A *City
Symphony*'s production, permit at least speculation as to his approach. In
Amateur Movie Makers, Weinberg offered advice on the role of composition in film, using examples drawn from Eisenstein, Dreyer, and perhaps
his own work. He argued that judicious composition would result in
"pictorial expressiveness" equivalent to that of the dramatic film, with
composition itself serving as a continuity motif. Contrasting the earlier
"descriptive" with the new evocative mode of documentation, he wrote:

Which gives a greater sense of the height of a skyscraper—a scene
photographed from a block away, which shows the complete building and

Figure 12.5.
Still from *Autumn Fire* (1933), directed by Herman Weinberg, with Erna Bergman. Courtesy of Museum of Modern Art, Film Stills Library

its relation to other buildings, or one made by shooting the building upward from the sidewalk, with the camera tilted to catch its remote peak? . . . It is the camera placement that gives the desired composition . . . to produce a definite, emotional effect.[41]

Such sentiments had been circulating in photographic form at least since Strand's efforts on the eve of *Manhatta*'s production, and they continued to circulate, as *Close Up*'s publication of Francis Bruguière's images of skyscrapers in 1933 attests.[42] Although we cannot be sure if the city sequences that appear in *Autumn Fire* replicate the cutting patterns of *A City Symphony*, Weinberg's use of contrast editing seems to grow from the strong graphics of each shot(fig. 12.6). Shot-to-shot conflict, with rapid intercutting, creates a sense of vertigo, of dynamic tension and rhythm. What little we know of *A City Symphony* comes through Harry Alan Potamkin's scathing review in the pages of *Close Up*, and suggests that these sequences may be intact. "It is a montage-film—if montage means, as it does not, the

Figure 12.6.
Still from *Autumn Fire* (1933), directed by Herman Weinberg. Courtesy of Museum of Modern Art, Film Stills Library

pell-mell piling of fragments.... The entire film is unorganized, no pattern, rhythm, formal intention, is apprehended. And as for photographic work: it is a beginner's.... First films like first poems should be writ and discarded."[43] Perhaps Weinberg selected only the more successful bits for inclusion in *Autumn Fire*, or perhaps Potamkin was excessively harsh, but those urban sequences which remain strike the contemporary eye as visually compelling and highly patterned.

Potamkin's review, prominently positioned and withholding any encouragement whatsoever, may have prompted Weinberg to destroy the film and redirect his subsequent creative effort to an audience of one (although *Autumn Fire* was circulated and included in early experimental film collections). Given his romanticized understanding of experimental filmmaking as highly personal and expressive, his comments on unreceptive audiences, written in 1934, probably give a better indication of his views: "It would never occur to these people to believe that they were incapable of appreciating the author's intent."[44]

Because he also worked on the exhibition side of the experimental movement, Weinberg's views of audience reception, although still shrouded by the veil of artist intentionality, reveal something of the fate of these films. Speaking of the response to "certain exotic films" shown in the Baltimore Little Theatre, Weinberg wrote that the audience did not understand the films, is afraid of anything it does not understand, "and, being afraid, rejects or is bored by it, or shrugs it off in mirthless laughter."[45]

Leyda's A Bronx Morning did not fare much better. One of the few reviews appeared in The Cinema: " 'A Bronx Morning' an alleged impression of life in a suburb of New York was apparently designed on entirely new lines of continuity and composition. For that reason its significance must remain obscure, as indeed must the purpose of its production."[46] Apparently audiences responded rather more passionately. After the film's London premiere at the Film Society, Leyda had scheduled followup bookings at the Tatler Cinema, "a small theatre whose programs are devoted entirely to news and interest pictures." J. M. Harvey, Secretary of the Society, wrote to Leyda, breaking the news gently:

> Unfortunately, for some reason which I cannot explain, the film was so badly received at its first two performances that the management had to cancel the bookings, and substitute something else. . . . I have known it to happen before in cases where an audience has considered a film too 'highbrow' for their taste. The Manager of the theatre himself was most enthusiastic about your film and was extremely distressed at its reception, which was inexplicable to him.[47]

A paucity of substantial reviews makes the fate of Browning's City of Contrasts rather more mysterious. Like Flaherty's Twenty-Four Dollar Island, however, it seems to have been withdrawn after its initial release, reappearing in substantially altered form. Browning's images seem to have survived intact, but a nonstop, wisecracking voiceover narration by Ben Witzler was added, disrupting the argument and visual rhythm of the film.

In her response to Leyda's query regarding A Bronx Morning's negative reception, Caroline Lejeune suggested a reason that may have applied generally to American city films of the 1930s:

I believe that your trouble has been mainly bad luck in coming out last, after a series of very similar films from the continent—English audiences have been so overdone lately with films of 'mean streets' in Berlin, Vienna, Amsterdam, Marseilles and all the rest of it that one more slice of everyday life ... was more than they could bear! I think we are going through a psychological phase at the moment when film audiences are unconsciously demanding, not observation, but construction. They want to be assured that things are not as bad as they seem. ... Two years ago, you could have got away with "A Bronx Morning." Today, I doubt whether you could even get away with "Berlin."[48]

Yet, although quite possibly overshadowed by their European counterparts and playing to audiences weary of the real world, the city films of Leyda, Browning, and perhaps Weinberg and Jacobs nevertheless intervened at an important moment in the trajectories of both documentary and avant-garde. Reworking continental developments through the American vernacular, these films continued the project of invigorating documentary with a new language of rhythm and evocation, while infusing avant-garde practice with a dose of reality and a capacity for social criticism.

NOTES

Thanks to Elena Pinto Simon of New York University's Tisch School of the Arts and the staff of the Tamiment Collection at NYU's Bobst Library for access to the Jay Leyda papers; to Eileen Bowser of New York's Museum of Modern Art and to Wendy Shadwell and the staff at the New York Historical Society for help with the Irving Browning material.

1. I do not mean to suggest any set of essential distinctions between avant-garde and nonfiction, but rather seek to reflect period discourse.

2. Herman Weinberg's *A City Symphony* and Lewis Jacobs' several city films—*City Block* and *As I Walk*, for example—seem not to have physically survived even the 1930s. Several reports state that Weinberg's film was disassembled in order to provide the Manhattan footage for *Autumn Fire*, constituting the grounds for *Autumn Fire*'s inclusion in this discussion. See R. A. Haller, "Early American Avant-Garde Film, *Program Notes: Pittsburgh Film-Makers* (7 December 1979).

3. New York City Writers' Project, *The Film Index: A Bibliography*, vol. 1 (New York: Museum of Modern Art Film Library and H. W. Wilson Co., 1941).

4. This basic distinction is maintained in many general studies of documentaries, which tend to label the nonfiction films produced before Nanook—more than two decades worth of work—as "precursors," "prophets," or "prototypes" for the documentary proper. See, for example, Lewis Jacobs, *The Documentary Tradition: From Nanook to Woodstock* (New York: W. W. Norton, 1971); Eric Barnouw, *Documentary: A History of the Non-Fiction Film* (New York: Oxford University Press, 1974); Richard Meran Barsam, *Non-Fiction Film: A Critical History* (New York: Dutton, 1973). Although the contemporary literature on documentary has drawn upon a much wider range of discourses for its reconsideration and theorization of the form, attention remains largely directed to the films produced after 1922.

5. New York City Writers' Project, *Film Index*, p. 572.

6. Ibid., p. 583.

7. For a closer look at the implications of this categorization, see William Uricchio, "Il patrimonio rappresentativo dei documentari," *Bianco e Nero* 4 (1988): 56–78.

8. Early fiction (played) and nonfiction (unplayed) films fail to share techniques in some curious and significant ways. For example, camera mobility (tilts, pans, tracks) pervades nonfiction city films from 1900 onward, yet remains relatively rare in fiction films until nearly a decade later. Conversely, techniques such as the analysis and fragmentation of time and space through multiple shot angles, distances, and cutting strategies, common by 1912 in narrative cinema, appear far less frequently in nonfiction city films of the same period.

9. Charles Musser has pointed to the important role played by some exhibitors in explaining and even narrativizing these nonfiction subjects, practices that complicate the simple distinction in representational strategies asserted in the *Film Index* (and maintained in this essay for heuristic purposes). See Charles Musser with Carol Nelson, *High-Class Moving Pictures* (Princeton: Princeton University Press, 1991), for an extended presentation of this practice.

10. In his discussion of the cinema of attractions, Gunning points out Louis Lumière and Georges Méliès' shared concern with cinema's "exhibitionistic" values, contrasting this concern with the voyeuristic strategies of the narrative cinema. The primacy of this exhibitionistic character—of direct audience stimulation or "making images seen"—was, Gunning argues, precisely what made film attractive to the avant-garde. See Tom Gunning, "The Cinema of Attractions: Early Film, Its Spectator and the Avant-Garde," *Wide Angle* 8, nos. 3–4 (Fall 1968): 63–70.

11. The "pattern films" that followed in *Berlin*'s wake, such as Ivens' *The Bridge* (1928) and *Rain* (1929), and Steiner's *H₂O* (1929), while formally similar to the city symphonies, tended to remain socially nonspecific, perhaps accounting for their more frequent categorization as avant-garde than as documentary.

12. Among the many complicating factors, ideological orientation is notoriously difficult to define or even locate as a force (producer's intent? period

reception?). The case against any essentialist ideological implications on the level of technique has been convincingly argued by Noel Carroll, *Mystifying Movies: Fads and Fallacies in Contemporary Film Theory* (New York: Columbia University Press, 1988), and even within the period, although artists like Hanna Hoch and John Heartfield saw photomontage as explicitly bound up with the project of ideological critique, many of their peers found the connection anything but evident. These issues aside, many in the period nevertheless associated specific formal strategies with a critical position toward the status quo. By the late 1920s and early 1930s, filmmakers like Eisenstein had demonstrated the critical potentials of certain "nonclassical" signifying practices, while from a very different direction the growing economic and political crisis helped to account for the growing explicitness of social criticism in avant-garde practice.

13. Although never produced, Moholy-Nagy's heavily illustrated sketch for a film, "Dynamic of the Metropolis," appeared in his *Malerei, Fotografie, Film,* volume 8 of the *Bauhausbücher* (Munich: Albert Langen, 1925) and was reissued in 1927. While not a "city film," Moholy-Nagy's project stands as a prominent exemplar of the form.

14. Ute Eskildsen, "Photography and the Neue Sachlichkeit Movement," in *Germany: The New Photography 1927–1933,* ed. David Mellor (London: Arts Council of Great Britain, 1978), pp. 101–112.

15. While factions within *Neue Sachlichkeit* used these two approaches to argue for "objectivity," a related debate took place among film critics and theorists, with the difference that "creationists" like Rudolf Arnheim and Bela Balasz essentially reframed what Eskildsen has presented as a second argument for pointedly antirealist ends; "realists" like Siegfried Kracauer and Erwin Panofsky inclined toward a sense of mechanically reproduced reality.

16. See Susan Platt, *Modernism in the 1920s: Interpretations of Modern Art in New York from Expressionism to Constructivism* (Ann Arbor: UMI Research Press, 1981).

17. Strand and Sheeler's *Manhatta* stands at an important juncture in terms of both urban depiction and the involvement in film of artists primarily associated with other media. For a fuller discussion, see Jan-Christopher Horak, "Modernist Perspectives and Romantic Desire: *Manhatta, Afterimage* 15, no. 4 (November 1987): 8–15, reprinted in an abridged version as Chapter 11 in this volume.

18. Jay Leyda, typewritten notes for FIAF Symposium, Lausanne (1979), Leyda File, Film Department, Museum of Modern Art (MOMA).

19. Letter, H. G. Weinberg to R. A. Haller, 7 August 1979. Cited in Haller, "Early American Avant-Garde Film."

20. *Experimental Cinema's* concern with Soviet developments during its 1930–1934 run and the strong Soviet presence at the Film Arts Guild theater are instructive in this regard, as are the activities of the Film and Photo League.

21. Steiner's work received attention in at least one venue with which Leyda was familiar before coming to New York: *Theatre Arts Monthly.* "Stage Settings in

the Streets of New York: Four Photographs" appeared in February 1927, and "Dramatic Photography: Four Studies" appeared in January 1930.

22. Leyda's early publications include "Half-Soles," *The Whirl* 1 (1930); "It May Have Been the Sweet Evening" and "The River," *Blues: A Magazine of New Rhythms* 8 (Spring 1930). Authors published in this issue of *Blues* included William Carlos Williams and Gertrude Stein. Leyda also had some experience as an art dealer. He recalled that his sale of a sculpture of Henry Ward Beecher to Mrs. Rockefeller permitted him to purchase the camera used in the production of *A Bronx Morning*. "Note sur *A Bronx Morning*," *Travelling* 55 (1979): 85.

23. During his first years in New York, Leyda was on familiar terms with Alfred Stieglitz, Alfred Barr, Lincoln Kirstein, and members of the Film and Photo League, among many others. Leyda retained much of his correspondence from this period. See the Correspondence Files, especially Boxes 1 and 4, Jay Leyda Papers (JLP), Tamiment Collection, Bobst Library, New York University.

24. Jay Leyda to Michael Rowan, *Cinema Quarterly* (Edinburgh), 3 July, 1933. Box 4, JLP. Despite this opinion, Leyda attempted to have the film shown in workers' clubs such as the London Workers' Film Society as late as 1933.

25. The Julien Levy Gallery at 602 Madison Avenue opened on 2 November 1931 with a retrospective of American photography. Exhibits during the first year included "Surrealism: Paintings, Drawings, Photographs," "Modern Photography," "Modern European Photographers," and "Photographs of New York by New York Photographers." Levy is perhaps best known for having saved Atget's work from destruction, but his gallery also became an early center for the U.S. exhibition of Surrealist paintings, drawings, and photographs. See Julien Levy, *Memoir of an Art Gallery* (New York: G. P. Putnam's, 1977).

26. For a detailed example of Levy's film exhibitions, see Lincoln Kirstein, "Experimental Films," *Arts Weekly* 1 (25 March 1932): 52, 62. A columnist characterized Levy's screenings less generously, while giving a glimpse into the range of period filmmaking activities: "Julien Levy returned from Paris in July with some esoteric films, one, I understand, being one of the most tremendous dramas ever done in the films, the others being criticized as being tinged with art snobbism. . . . Lincoln Kirstein and Henwar Rodakiewicz made a 16mm movie of life on Cape Cod. Margaret Bourke-White and Jay Leyda also worked on a film. Leyda did *A Day in the Bronx* with Leo Hurwitz." Walter Gutman, "News and Gossip" [undated, uncited clip, probably 1932], Box 10, JLP. I have not been able to substantiate Leo Hurwitz's collaboration on *A Bronx Morning*. On Levy's photographic interests generally, see David Travis, *Photographs from the Julien Levy Collection, Starting with Atget* (Chicago: Art Institute of Chicago, 1976).

27. Leyda's "Tips on Topicals," *Amateur Movie Makers* 6, no. 1 (January 1931): 13–14, is particularly interesting in light of his film.

28. Leyda clearly had other film projects in mind, as demonstrated by his correspondence with Walter Sidler in 1930 regarding Sidler's translation of a

Leyda scenario, and as outlined in his 1931 Guggenheim application. See Box 4, Box 10, JLP.

29. Leyda to Lejeune, 6 June 1933, Box 4, JLP.

30. Kirstein, "Experimental Films," p. 52.

31. Barbara Novak, *American Painting of the Nineteenth Century* (New York: n.p. 1969), p. 262.

32. Letter, H. V. Browning (Browning's wife) to Wendy Shadwell, 3 November 1981, Browning Collection, Landauer Collection, New York Historical Society (NYHS). See also the Browning Photograph Collection, NYHS, and Wendy Shadwell, "The Browning Collection at the New York Historical Society," *American Society of Picture Professionals* 14 (1983): 1–3. The details of Browning's career remain sketchy. He worked as a motion picture cameraman at least in the 1930s and 1940s, specializing in ringside boxing coverage and newsreels (for Universal Newsreel, among others). In later years, his primary interest was Camera Mart, Inc., where he manufactured and sold specialty photographic equipment.

33. Browning's renown as a photomonteur was such that the film's announcement in *Experimental Cinema* described it as "done entirely in multiple exposures." The film contains only two such shots. "Experimental Cinema in America,"*Experimental Cinema* 5 (1934): 54.

34. Frank Ward, The Film and Photo League invitation letter, 18 April 1934, Browning Collection, NYHS.

35. Although the MOMA's viewing print and original nitrate negative (obtained from the Museum of the City of New York) contain a wisecracking voiceover narration by Ben Witzler, Eileen Bowser reports that the picture negative was full silent aperture, and this, coupled with the film's more appropriate running speed at 18 fps, indicate that *City of Contrasts* was produced as a silent film. On the basis of this analysis, I have dealt with the film as a silent print, and have not taken up the relation of the soundtrack with the images. See also Eileen Bowser, "The Museum of Modern Art Department of Film: Recent Acquisitions" (unpublished notes, 1978), Browning File, Film Department, MOMA.

36. Browning's socially perceptive contrasts—and, indeed, many of his images—were echoed in Francis Bruguière's observations on New York City, published in "Pseudomorphic Film," *Close Up* 10 (March 1933): 19, 22.

37. Lewis Jacobs in *Travelling* 56–57 (Spring 1980): 103.

38. Herman G. Weinberg, "A Statement on Experimental Work in Cinema," *Film Comment* 4, no. 4 (Summer 1968): 23.

39. Ibid., p. 22.

40. Herman Weinberg, "Autumn Fire," *Travelling* 55 (1979): 82–85.

41. Herman G. Weinberg, "Composing Each View," *Amateur Movie Makers* 9, no. 6 (June 1934): 250.

42. "Note on Five Bruguière Photographs," *Close Up* (March 1933): 25. The introduction to these images stated, "*Close Up* has probably not printed before pictures so intrinsically dynamic, so innately motivated and complete." The commentary goes on to position the images with terms like "transcendental," "mystic," "impressionistic," and "romantic."

43. H. A. Potamkin, "Movie: New York Notes," *Close Up* 7 (October 1930): 251–252.

44. H. G. Weinberg, "Audiences, the Dears," *Motion Picture Herald*, 20 October 1934, p. 44.

45. Ibid.

46. *The Cinema*, 13 December 1939, clipping file, Box 10, JLP.

47. Letter, J. M. Harvey, The Film Society, Ltd., to Jay Leyda, 19 May 1933, Box 3, JLP.

48. Letter, Lejeune to Leyda, 14 July 1933, Box 4, JLP.

13

Mary Ellen Bute

LAUREN RABINOVITZ

In 1940 the Museum of Modern Art (MOMA) Film Library presented a one-week show of exemplary abstract films made during the previous twenty years. The leading showcase in the United States for independent, noncommercial cinema, MOMA had already (only four years after beginning its Circulating Film Program) begun to survey the past and to document a rich international, experimental cinema. The 1940 show consisted of Hans Richter's *Rhythmus 21* (1921), Fernand Léger's *Ballet Mécanique* (1924), Man Ray's *Emak Bakia* (1927), Marcel Duchamp's *Anemic Cinema* (1927), Len Lye's *Color Box* (1935), Mary Ellen Bute's and Ted Nemeth's *Parabola* (1937), Mary Ellen Bute's *Escape* (1937), and Len Lye's *Swinging the Lambeth Walk* (1939).[1] Richter, Duchamp, Léger, Man Ray, and Lye—filmmakers working in Europe—have all become familiar names in any standard text of avant-garde cinema, and their films included in this show have become cinema classics. Mary Ellen Bute and her movies, however, are practically unknown today.

Such a fate was not unusual for prewar American experimental filmmakers. They worked in the 1930s and 1940s within a fragile support network and, after World War II, received only sporadic attention from serious film critics when a new generation of filmmakers achieved prominence. The individual filmmaker of the prewar era had to be not only a filmmaker but also a distributor, critic, and educator for an experimental cinema. The reclamation of the individual filmmaker can reveal a great deal about the definition and workings of an experimental cinema in the United States before World War II. Bute's career exemplifies how the artist-filmmaker during this period successfully invented experimental cinema at both the individual and the systemic levels. She achieved an individual aesthetic style, separate and distinct from her European counterparts, and she devised strategies for the distribution, exhibition, and reception of experimental cinema in the United States.

315

Ten of Bute's films, made between 1934 and 1953, belong to the category of cinema known as "abstract films," "motion paintings," or "experimental animation." They place Bute in a painterly-filmic tradition alongside Richter, Viking Eggeling, Oskar Fischinger, Lye, and Norman McLaren. In such films as *Synchromy No. 2* (1935), *Color Rhapsodie* (1948), *Abstronic* (1952), and *Mood Contrasts* (1953), the relationships between sight and sound, visual and aural rhythms, image and music make up the surface subject matter.

Polka Graph (1947) depicts basic design elements—straight and curvilinear lines, geometric and organic shapes, monochromatic hues of primary colors, single planes—as they move across the field of vision and shrink or enlarge to suggest deep space (fig. 13.1). Their rhythmic movements are synchronized to the music of Shostakovich's polka from the *Age of Gold* ballet. The film historian Lewis Jacobs, an assistant on Bute's first film in 1932, compared her films with Oskar Fischinger's: "[They are] less rigid in their patterns and choice of objects, tactile in

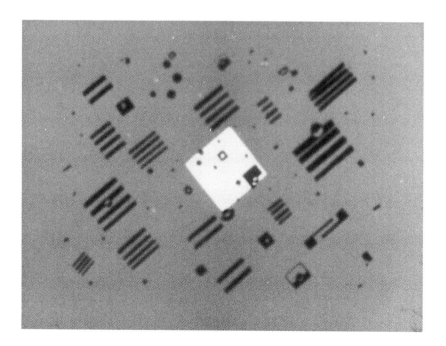

Figure 13.1.
Frame enlargement from *Tarantella* (1940), directed by Mary Ellen Bute. Courtesy of George Eastman House

their forms, more sensuous in their use of light and color rhythms, more concerned with the problems of depth, more concerned with music complementing rather than corresponding to the visuals."[2] These films are about the emotional expressiveness of formal compositional elements. They resonate with a pleasure in visual and aural perception that is rooted in modernist art and its goal of "art for art's sake."

Yet, if Bute's films today seem easily contained within a discrete aesthetic category and tradition of cinema, they were less easily situated within the contemporary avant-garde's rigorous and exclusionary measures for film art. Unlike most experimental filmmakers before and after World War II, Bute did not explicitly claim an anti-Hollywood stance for her aesthetic principles. Indeed, she publicly situated her films not in *resistance* to Hollywood but in conjunction with it, since she marketed her films as short subjects for commercial, theatrical bookings. In the 1940s and 1950s, Bute's films opened for Hollywood features in Radio City Music Hall as well as in theaters across the country. It is, however, precisely this tension between the films' elitist modernist aesthetics and their popular reception as pretty amusements that is worth further exploration.

DRAWING WITH LIGHT

Trained as a painter at the Pennsylvania Academy of Fine Arts in the early 1920s, Bute identified with the dominant intellectual preoccupations of the modernist avant-garde. Like Richter and Eggeling in Europe, Bute tried to express movement and controlled rhythms in time-sequence paintings (fig. 13.2). Like Richter and Eggeling, she subsequently decided that painting itself was too limited a medium to represent time and motion. Throughout the 1920s and early 1930s, she extended painterly concerns to music and light so as to represent the kinetics of modern, fast-paced, highly technologized life. Like many other painters, she understood that such concerns were within the mainstream of contemporary art, the logical outcome of a linear tradition established through Paul Cézanne's abstractions of form and color, Cubism's attempts to produce "surface sensations to the eye," the Italian Futurists, the American Synchronists, and Wassily Kandinsky's paintings of relationships between colors and music, works that Bute herself called "abstract compositions based on an arbitrary chromatic scale of senses."[3]

Figure 13.2.
Mary Ellen Bute at work. Photo by Margery Markley. Courtesy of Yale University, Film
Center

After she graduated from art school and moved to New York City, Bute attempted to transcend the limitations of painting through combining theatrical performance, music, colored lighting, and two-dimensional pieces in stage lighting and design. She attended the Yale School of Drama, and following her graduation in 1925 and a subsequent trip around the world as a drama director for a "floating university," Bute worked with the inventors of the new light organs.[4] She later recalled her significant shift of media to these musical keyboard instruments that could simultaneously produce sound and create moving colors on a screen:

> [I] felt defeated by the medium [of painting]. In an attempt to find a medium other than paint, and to be able to achieve a time element in abstract forms, I began to experiment with optical instruments. The color organ interested me because it seemed like an instrument I could handle the way I do paint but I would be handling light and color.[5]

From the Russian physicist and color organ inventor Leon Theremin, in particular, Bute developed a sophisticated orientation to art as an elaboration of the scientific phenomena of color and light. Theremin taught her how to use light on a static surface and how not to use light haphazardly:

> From the first half hour with Theremin I was installing tiny mirrors, about ⅛th inch in diameter, on minute oscillators in tiny tubes of oil to cut down the friction and make them amenable to control. We would reflect light through prisms on these mirrors to get a range of spectral colors, then move the point of colored light about on the screen. . . . From a vibrating point we got a spiral, the figure 8 "line of beauty" and so on.[6]

Her writing and lectures from this period are specialized discussions of sound and light physics as well as a rich synthesis of the work of color harmonists since the seventeenth century.

Many of Bute's opinions from this period about the limitations of painting were transferred to her later concepts about the limitations of a photographic-based cinema. Even before she became a filmmaker, Bute prepared an implicit critique of the visual image or representation itself as a referent to reality:

In painting, the onlooker is expected to enjoy the clever imitation of nature—to be deceived into thinking the living prototype is before him. Whereas the art of light stimulates our visual sense directly with color, form and rhythm and is thus comparable to the way the aural sense is stimulated by sound in music. In painting, the medium is subordinate to story, symbol or representation.[7]

Bute also took exception to another kind of limitation, the individual medium's targetting of a single sense:

One sense of perception such as sight or hearing is not enough to induce a strong reaction and to put our emotions in balance with the present highly developed intellect. To achieve strong emotional reactions we must charge our perceptive sensual apparatus with greater and more intense exciters. In the field of art these stronger exciters are synchronized art forms."[8]

In other words, Bute called for a multimedia experience (the more media the better) as the only means by which art in a modern world could overpower the conventions of realism that called for intellectual engagement and stimulate, at the level of the physiological, a pure emotional experience.

Although the color organ seemed to meet Bute's requirements for a multifaceted artistic medium, she almost immediately proclaimed it technically inadequate. The projected light forms were only capable of producing either horizontal bands of color or completely diffused color spots, inhibiting the presentation of spatial forms.[9] Moreover, the apparatus was both expensive and undependable, sometimes unable to repeat an effect.[10]

While Bute was working with Theremin, a third person joined the team. A composer interested in applying mathematical concepts to music composition, Joseph Schillinger taught Bute a central means by which she could coordinate musical composition with painting in shared terms of light, form, time, and color:

Visual composition is a counterpart of the sound composition, and once I had learned to do the sound composition, I began to seek for a medium for combining these two and found it in films. I was determined to express this feeling for movement in visual terms, which I had not been able to achieve in painting, and I was determined to paint in film, and that is why I actually started.[11]

Bute's autobiographical account of mastery and discovery resonates with the theme of individual, artistic conquest that is conventional in reflective biographies, but it ignores the ways in which sound cinema in the early 1930s itself involved a renegotiation with increased technologically produced sensations. Such discussion of sound cinema in these terms was culturally available and may even have attracted Bute because the scientific as well as popular discourses of novelty, experimentation, and multiple sensations produced a definition of sound cinema that fitted Bute's qualifications.

ABSOLUTE CINEMA

The outcome of Bute's experimentation with Schillinger was an unfinished short film *Synchromy* (1933), a black and white synchronization of light and sound. According to Bute, *Synchromy* taught her how to plan filmic coordinates from a mathematical formula for musical composition:

> I take the relationship of two or more numbers, for instance 7:2, 3:4, 9:5:4, fraction them around their axis, raise to powers, permutate, divide, multiply, subtract and invert until I have a complete composition of the desired length in numbers. Then I realize this composition in the materials I have started to employ. I use this composition of numbers to determine the length, width and depth of the photographic field and everything in it. This numerical composition determines the length, speed, and duration of a zoom, a travel back with the camera, the curve and angle at which the camera approaches a subject. It determines the shape, size, color and luminosity of the subject; how, when and in what relationship to other elements of the composition it develops and moves. The melody, harmony, rhythm, dynamics, etc. of the sound are elaborated from the same numerical composition, thus setting up an exquisite relationship between the structural and rhythmical interferences of the combined materials.[12]

Bute then applied these concepts to her own "absolute film," a continuation of the collaborative experimentations with Theremin and Schillinger.

Rhythm in Light (1934) was a black and white, five-minute pictorial accompaniment to Edvard Grieg's "Anitra's Dance" from the *Peer Gynt Suite* (fig. 13.3). For the formation of her abstract, graphic compositions, Bute used sheets of crumpled cellophane, an egg-cutter, prisms, toy pyramids, ping pong balls, velvet sparklers, and bracelets. Such materials were both the pictorial objects and translucent windows for the camera, producing effects of rotating cones and floating lights. Bute felt that *Rhythm in Light* abstractly expressed the programmatic music's climax and variations, its moods and psychological moments.[13]

In order to make *Rhythm in Light*, Bute persuaded two friends to co-sign a bank loan so that she could obtain the production funds. Although her friend Melville F. Webber assisted her on the piece, he did not have the technical expertise required to be her cameraman. She located a cameraman during a visit to the New York Film Service Laboratories, where she met the photographer Ted Nemeth. Nemeth, a

Figure 13.3.
Still from *Rhythm in Light* (1934), directed by Mary Ellen Bute. Courtesy of Museum of Modern Art, Film Stills Library

commercial and industrial photographer, taught Bute cinematography and became her production partner until the middle 1950s. (All of Bute's "absolute films" were produced by Ted Nemeth Studios.) Bute and Nemeth married in 1940, had two sons, and eventually separated, although they never divorced.

Bute followed *Rhythm in Light* with *Synchromy No. 2* (1935), a series of representational objects made abstract through camera angles, lighting effects, and lenses. Twelve years later, Jacobs applauded Bute's technique in such films as *Synchromy No. 2*, noting that it differed from Fischinger's reliance on two-dimensional animated drawings and flat lighting on flat surfaces: "The difference in quality ... came largely from a difference in technique."[14] Bute and Nemeth used three-dimensional substances—ping pong balls, paper cutouts, sculptures, cellophane, rhinestone buttons, odds and ends from the five-and-dime store—and achieved "ingenious lighting and camera effects by shooting through long focus lenses, prisms, distorting mirrors, and ice cubes."[15]

Synchromy No. 2 departed from her earlier films in two significant ways: it incorporated vocal music (Richard Wagner's "The Evening Star") and introduced titles that explicitly identified the film as modern art accompaniment to music.[16] Bute felt that this was the important intertextual function of the absolute film, "MUSIC plays an even more salient part in the ABSOLUTE film where it is actually inter-composed with the visual material ... the visual perception of classical and semi-classical music."[17]

Parabola (1937) is Bute's last film in this series, employing stop-motion cinematography, prismatic lenses, and light reflections on objects turned in space. *Parabola* takes as its photographic subject a modern parabolic sculpture by Rutherford Boyd and as its musical subject Darius Milhaud's *Creation of the World*. As the sculpture turns in space, dramatic chiaroscuro effects are produced through highlights and dark shadows cast on a wall. Camera angles, superimpositions, and abstract patterns of light provide the visually expressive corollary to the music.

In 1937, Bute took the absolute film into a second phase. She introduced color, narrative, and dramatic dimensions, and fully animated abstract drawings. *Escape* (1937), also known as *Synchromy No. 4*, began as a "literary idea," a little story with a plot and a musical background (Bach's Toccata from Toccata and Fugue in D Minor) using geometric characters. The "hero" is an orange triangle, who attempts a rhythmic "escape" through a series of backgrounds: a green-blue swirling plane;

black grids that are overlaid, turned, and expanded; grids overlaid and turned on arcs and spirals (fig. 13.4). The movements are almost balletic in their rhythmic and spatial suggestions.

Two years later, Bute produced her fullest work in this vein. *Spook Sport* (1939) is a midnight graveyard ballet of ghosts rising from tombstones, cavorting bats, and dancing skeleton bones set to Camille Saint-Saëns' *Danse Macabre*. Bute collaborated on *Spook Sport* with Norman McLaren, whose animation style and technique pervade the film. Drawing in ink directly on film, McLaren executed simple icons to represent tombstones, bats, bells, and bones. These agitated, nervous, hopping figures suggest McLaren's stylistic sense of visual and rhythmic play, but the fluidity of movement, the dramatic color harmonies, and the rich use of deep space are all more typical of Bute's highly individualized style.

Spook Sport, however, offers greater narrative temporal contours than any other Bute film. It begins with a clock striking midnight, and it ends

Figure 13.4.
Frame enlargement from *Escape* (1937), directed by Mary Ellen Bute. Courtesy of George Eastman House

with the dawning sun and a crowing rooster. In addition, it draws from the conventions of Walt Disney's well-known "Silly Symphony" films, and, indeed, Disney had several years earlier filmed an animated *Danse Macabre* graveyard ballet, *Skeleton Dance* (1928). Unlike any Disney film, however, *Spook Sport* exquisitely balances abstraction and formal experimentation with familiar programmatic music and the representational suggestiveness of popular entertainment genres. It is ironic that Disney's *Fantasia* (1940), released a year later, became the popular standard bearer for this type of animation, since *Spook Sport* beat Disney at his own game. Like Disney's foundations for successful animated art, *Spook Sport* employs a familiar theme and music. But, unlike Disney's work, *Spook Sport* allows the basic formal properties themselves to be foregrounded as the expressive subject matter.

Bute's four films released between 1940 and 1950 represent a third phase of "absolute films" and the most mature of her drawn films. *Tarantella* (1940) is a five-minute color film animated from more than seven thousand drawings to original piano music performed by Edwin Gerchefski. *Polka Graph* (1947) uses the graph pattern of the musical score as a springboard for the visual interpretation.[18] *Color Rhapsodie* (1948) is among Bute's best works, synchronizing rich colored visual forms in motion to the rhythm of Franz Liszt's Hungarian Rhapsody No. 2. In 1976, the experimental cinema critic Jonas Mekas declared, "I like the romantic flair of *Color Rhapsodie*, its visual density."[19]

As in many of her previous films, *Color Rhapsodie*'s music was well-known programmatic fare. Bute depended upon musical selections that were, indeed, already popular staples of classical concert performances and radio programs. Film reviewers acknowledged the success of this strategy: "Familiar acceptability of the music is a good basis for audience and theatre approval."[20] In this way, the unfamiliar synchronization of abstract visual and musical elements became mediated by the familiarity of the musical signature—both melodically and stylistically.

Pastorale (1950) takes the subject of the musical inscription as popular concert performance one step further. The film opens with scenes of the star conductor Leopold Stokowski conducting Johann Sebastian Bach's "Sheep May Safely Graze."[21] But even here Bute disrupts the representational realism of the sequence by overlaying the images with washes of floating liquid primary colors. The images become sharper for a brief moment before the titles: "Leopold Stokowski Conducting 'Pastorale.' " After the credits, the fluid, flowing colors become the cinematic material for the film, and Stokowski as the film's dramatic performer or on-screen bodily "auteur" of the musical soundtrack does not return until the film's closing repeat of the opening shot.

Textual inscriptions that introduced each of these films marked Bute's cinema as educationally edifying. She regularly used credit titles like "A Seeing Sound Film," "Fun With Music," "Let Your 👁 's and 🎵 's Dance This One," as well as paragraphs announcing the film's intention "to present a new type of film-ballet." Such titles presented Bute's cinema from the outset as promoting appreciation for tunes already popularly canonized as acceptable highbrow music.

The fourth and last phase of Bute's "absolute cinema" in 1952 and 1953 is marked by her shift from animation techniques to electronically generated images through the use of an oscilloscope. While Bute was making *Pastorale*, a scientist at Bell Laboratories came to her studio to see her films. Bute told him she "was tired of the laborious animation technique, and that [she] should rather use light to draw with instead of making thousands of drawings."[22] The Bell scientist discussed with her the possible use of an oscilloscope for electronic image generation, and he designed a circuit for her. Bute then had it built by an engineer. The oscilloscope allowed her to pattern composition right on the oscilloscope through the kind of mathematical models she had earlier employed. She was so happy with the results that she adopted the oscilloscope as her "true pencil of light":

> We got the pattern so that we could make it come forward or backward on the screen and move around and come in any side of the screen so that you also have horizontal and vertical control. . . . You can also channel music through the Oscilloscope and work (draw) right on the Oscilloscope with the music on the soundtrack going through the machine, thus coordinating the two. You can also alter and distort the forms taking the fundamental dictation from the music as it goes through the Oscillo-scope.[23]

Bute's appropriation of the oscilloscope, at least ten years before Nam June Paik began working with similar tools, provided the most physically direct method for "drawing" abstract cinema images.

Bute first used the oscilloscope in *Abstronic* (1952), an absolute film structurally and thematically similar to her work of the previous decade. Although the oscilloscope apparatus may have allowed for more exact rhythmic matches to music pitch, it also seems to have limited her visual range to spiraling lines looping and jumping around the foreground. Unlike her earlier films, *Abstronic* depends on the central core imagery of a circular shape or defined space for the actual movement and for supplying field definition (fig. 13.5). This pared-down visual ballet set to folk music by Aaron Copland and Don Gillis may superficially resemble the contemporary canvases of Abstract Expressionist painters. This is probably because contemporary painting always provided Bute with a conventional vocabulary from which to operate, and here she may have had to rely more fully on the aesthetic currency of a nonfilmic medium because of the oscilloscope's visual limitations. Indeed, Bute herself suggests that in the first oscilloscope-based film, she sought music and

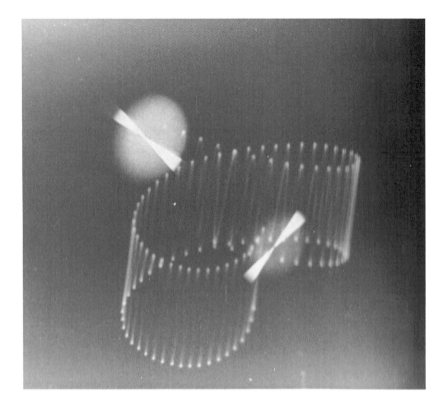

Figure 13.5.
Frame enlargement from *Abstronic* (1952), directed by Mary Ellen Bute. Courtesy of George Eastman House

visual materials that would foreground the technological apparatus: "I wanted something that was clear and definite. . . . I was looking for something that would fit the Scope and its clear-cut patterns."[24]

Bute overcame whatever limitations the technology posed for her personal style in *Mood Contrasts* (1953), her last absolute film and one of her best. *Mood Contrasts* employs oscilloscope-generated images layered over animated backgrounds to music by Nicolai Rimsky-Korsakov and Dmitri Shostakovich. By combining oscilloscope and animation techniques, Bute recaptured the sense of dynamic, deep space so intrinsically a part of her earlier films. After the initial voiceover and credits announcing the edifying nature of this film, *Mood Contrasts* is a series of swirling colors and concentric circles periodically set against a flat checkerboard that gives the illusion of a background plane. In this film, color changes and harmonies of highly saturated monochromes and complementaries offer rich visual excitement.

When international film festivals became prominent after World War II, Bute entered her short "seeing sound" films. *Polka Graph* won a Venice Film Festival award, while *Mood Contrasts* was named "Best Short Film" at the 1958 Brussels International Experimental Film Festival. It is interesting that the postwar community of avant-garde filmmakers, who so heavily publicized their members' awards, ignored and even snubbed Bute's award-winning abstract films. Although her films captured some of the graphic qualities of Abstract Expressionism and were reproduced by a seemingly perfect or balanced combination of scientific, modern technique and psychological expressionism, Bute's critical discourse of cinema contradicted the prevailing ideological goals of the New York avant-garde. Her publicity statements especially opposed the modernist distanciation from mass tastes: "The nice thing about 'seeing sound' is that the people don't take the films seriously, as something pretty advanced, find them amusing. Even gallery types can tolerate the idea of dancing rhomboids and moving prisms and geometric forms because the films don't last very long anyway."[25] Such a statement may acknowledge Bute's aesthetic position within avant-garde art but contextualizes the individual films as well as the filmmaker's social and economic positions inside a commercial, mass entertainment industry. Although such an attitude does not run counter to the political discourse regarding modernist film in Europe or the United States before World War II, it opposes the political platform of "commercial resistance" that prevailed in the United States after the war.[26]

DISTRIBUTING "SEEING SOUND" FILMS AS AMUSING NOVELTIES

Bute learned how to distribute and market her films early in her career. After completing *Rhythm in Light*, she took the film to Leopold Stokowski in the hope that he would be interested in a future collaboration. While she was waiting for Stokowski to arrive at the Philadelphia theater, the projectionist ran the film and suggested that Bute take it to New York's Radio City Music Hall. She took his advice, brought *Rhythm in Light* to a somewhat skeptical Radio City manager, and told him to run it as a short before the feature on a trial basis. When she called back a few days later, the manager agreed to book the film for a run with *Becky Sharp* (1935). Bute attributes this model of success to contemporary industry practices: "I didn't talk about money at all, but what they gave me practically paid for all the costs of the film. You see they were trained by Disney, and Disney always got very good prices. So I've a lot to be grateful to Disney for."[27] In an era when Walt Disney had already struggled successfully to manage his own independent distribution, Bute could capitalize on an increasingly regular industry practice for nonfeature materials. In this way she positioned her short films in commercial movie theaters as toney introductions, "class" or "art" acts that would precede specific Hollywood prestige productions.

Although feature-length films were block-booked at major urban movie theaters, theater managers individually booked shorts, newsreels, and even vaudeville acts. Bute approached these "powerful impresarios" one by one at the big New York City movie palaces.[28] She describes how they helped develop her distribution network: "The people at Radio City [would] give you the names of other theater managers around the country and you'd send your print out, write them a letter and say it was used at Radio City, and it just worked out."[29] In this manner, Bute became the theatrical distributor for her own films.

Once Bute proved that her films could be commercially successful, she continued to distribute them herself. She made more money as an independent distributor than by selling outright or leasing to a Hollywood distributor. For example, MGM offered her $3,000 for *Spook Sport* after it played at Radio City Music Hall, but Bute made $3,000 from a single subsequent booking of the film at the Trans-Lux Theater in New York City.[30] *Synchromy No. 2* premiered at Radio City Music Hall with *Mary of Scotland* (1936). *Tarantella* opened for *Paris Waltz* at New York

City's Paris Theatre, where Bute's original animation art was displayed in the lobby.[31] *Polka Graph* played for twelve weeks in 1952 at the Sutton Theatre, a New York City art house. *Color Rhapsodie* ran for seven weeks at Radio City Music Hall in 1951; immediately afterward it accompanied *Hans Christian Andersen* (1952) at the Criterion Theatre in New York City. *Pastorale* premiered in 1953 at the Paris Theatre with the French film *Seven Deadly Sins* (1951). *Mood Contrasts* accompanied *The Barretts of Wimpole Street* (1957) at Radio City Music Hall.

Often, the films' commercial premieres occurred a few years after their completion. But if the films did not always win immediate commercial success, they enjoyed longevity without regard for timeliness or topicality. Bute attributed their long runs to the films' abstract nature: "It's just like music. You can see it over and over."[32] In 1952, for example, *Polka Graph*, *Color Rhapsodie*, and *Spook Sport* were playing simultaneously at major New York City theaters with popular first-run features.[33] In the same year, Bute collected orders from thirty-nine feature film houses nationwide for extended showings of her films.[34]

The rise of independent art cinema houses in the 1950s, a direct result of the Paramount Decree, appears to have helped Bute's commercial success. Since her films had generally been paired with prestige pictures (adaptations, big-budget "serious" films) in the 1930s or 1940s, they commercially adapted to pairings with foreign films like *Seven Deadly Sins* or *The Man in the White Suit* (1951), which were themselves being promoted as a new class of art cinema. *Rhythm in Light*, although almost thirty years old, accompanied *Last Year at Marienbad* at the Boston art house, the Exeter Theatre.[35]

In addition, Bute's absolute cinema was well suited for exhibition and marketing discourses of technological novelty circulating in the early 1950s. For example, when *Color Rhapsodie* played at the Plaza Theatre in Washington, D.C., the exhibitor advertised the film on the marquee as an "extra" — "An Exciting Technicolor Novelty."[36] Amidst the new promotion campaigns for widescreen, color, and improved sound extravaganzas, Bute's absolute films foregrounded through their subject, credits, and publicity the significance of heightened sound-image cinematic properties.

Although Bute quit making absolute films in 1953, she completed two live-action narrative films: the short *The Boy Who Saw Through* (1956) and the feature-length *Passages from Finnegans Wake* (1965). *Finnegans Wake's* sensitive evocation of James Joyce's book received significant critical attention, and the film won an award at the 1966 Cannes International Film Festival.[37] While Bute worked on a short film adaptation of Walt Whitman's writings and attempted to finance and produce an adaptation of Thornton Wilder's *The Skin of Our Teeth*, she occasionally lectured or taught a new generation of film studies and production students.

In 1976 Robert Russett and Cecile Starr's book *Experimental Animation* focused new attention on Bute.[38] Starr herself took an active interest in reintroducing Bute's films at film festivals and colleges.[39] Bute began to lecture at such places as the Art Institute of Chicago and Cinewomen of Los Angeles.[40] In 1982 the Walker Art Center in Minneapolis ran a Bute retrospective, and in 1983 MOMA featured Bute and her films as part of the museum's "Cineprobe" series. Mary Ellen Bute died of heart failure six months later.

Bute's reception in the early 1980s was part of a reclamation of women filmmakers and animation pioneers who had been marginalized in the history of cinema. The critic Lillian Schiff characterized the audience response at Bute's Cineprobe appearance: "We've just met a real, curious, stubborn, optimistic, courageous, talented person who has been an important part of twentieth century film and video history."[41] The emphasis on the individual personality here is appropriate because, despite widespread rejection of auteurism among film scholars in the 1980s, Bute's individualism is also a function of the nature of the prewar avant-garde.

NOTES

My thanks to David Rodowick, director of the Yale Film Study Center, Yale University, during the time I was completing the research for this article. He not only helped me to locate the Mary Ellen Bute papers, which were stored at a Yale University warehouse; he also drove me to the warehouse, where we climbed over stacks of dirty cartons in order to find the collection. He carried and transported the boxes back to the Yale Film Study Center and then made his office available to me. David also provided me with screening facilities for Bute's films and happily discussed the details of my research with me. I truly could not have completed the research without his enthusiastic support.

1. Herman G. Weinberg, "A Forward Glance at the Abstract Film," *Design* 42, no. 6 (February 1941): 24.

Although William Moritz in Chapter 5 has argued that *Ballet Mécanique* should be designated as a co-authored work by Dudley Murphy and Man Ray and not as Léger's, I have maintained the historical attribution as it was used in 1940, since I am trying to make a point about how certain names, including Léger's, became routinely cited and well-known in film histories for their authorship of these films.

2. Lewis Jacobs, "Experimental Cinema in America, Part 1," *Hollywood Quarterly* 3, no. 2 (Winter 1947–1948): 124.

3. Mary E. Bute, "Light*Form*Movement*Sound," *Design* 42, no. 8 (April 1941): 25.

4. Mary Ellen Bute amplified the circumstances: "The director told me a Columbia University professor already had the job I wanted. I didn't 'hear' him. My father got me a secretary and I began working on drama pages for the *Ryndam*. Every few days I mailed some pages to the director, including plans for a collapsible stage set based on lead pipes. Six weeks before the sailing date, the man originally hired, cancelled, and I got the job." Mary Ellen Bute, as quoted by Lillian Schiff in "The Education of Mary Ellen Bute," *Film Library Quarterly* 17, nos. 2–4 (1984): 54.

5. Mary Ellen Bute, "Abstract Films," unpublished typescript, n.d., p. 1, Mary Ellen Bute papers, Yale Film Studies Center, Yale University.

6. Mary Ellen Bute, "Film Music: New Film Music for New Films," untitled magazine 12, no. 4 (1952): n.p., Bute papers.

7. Mary Ellen Bute, "Light as an Art Material and Its Possible Synchronization with Sound," lecture before the New York Musicological Society, 30 January 1932, New York City, unpublished typescript, p. 1, Bute papers.

8. Mary Ellen Bute, "Composition in Color and Sound," unpublished lecture typescript, n.d., p. 1, Bute papers.

9. Bute, "Light as an Art Material," p. 7.

10. Bute, "Abstract Films," p. 1.

11. Ibid., p. 3.

12. Bute, "Film Music."

13. Untitled press release, 13–19 June 1935, pp. 2–3, Bute papers.

14. Jacobs, "Experimental Cinema in America," p. 124.

15. Ibid.

16. The film begins with the title: "The following is designed by a modern artist" and identifies the film as a "seeing sound" production.

17. Bute, "Film Music."

18. Ibid.

19. Jonas Mekas, "Movie Journal," *Soho Weekly News*, 23 September 1976, as quoted in publicity release, n.d., Bute papers.

20. Cecile Starr, "Animation: Abstract & Concrete," *Saturday Review* 35 (13 December 1952): 48.

21. Ted Nemeth filmed the live-action sequence, and he was assisted by the experimental filmmaker Hillary Harris.

22. Bute, "Abstract Films," pp. 4–5.

23. Ibid., pp. 5–6.

24. Ibid., p. 10.

25. Virginia Irwin, "She Sets Music to 'Seeing Sound' Movies," *St. Louis Post-Dispatch*, n.d., Bute papers.

26. The notion of "commercial resistance" is a complex one and not a monolithic description of the economic, critical context for all experimental films in the postwar era. But the ideological stance of "commercial resistance" permeated the experimental filmmakers' community in the 1950s and was a significant structural issue. By the time such films as *Scorpio Rising* (1963) and Andy Warhol's films of a few years later enjoyed popular success as midnighters in commercial theaters, the issues of commercial and popular culture opposition themselves became discursive subjects. For further discussion, see David E. James, *Allegories of Cinema: American Film in the Sixties* (Princeton: Princeton University Press, 1989), and Lauren Rabinovitz, *Points of Resistance: Women, Power and Politics in the New York Avant-Garde Cinema, 1943–1971* (Urbana and Chicago: University of Illinois Press, 1991).

27. "Mary Ellen Bute," *American Film Institute Newsletter* (n.d.): 41, Bute papers.

28. Mary Ellen Bute, "Professor Howard Beckermann lecture," handwritten manuscript, n.d., p. 109, Mary Ellen Bute papers.

29. "Mary Ellen Bute," *American Film Institute Newsletter*, p. 41.

30. Ibid.

31. Untitled press release, Bute papers.

32. "Mary Ellen Bute," *American Film Institute Newsletter*, p. 41.

33. "The Early Films of Mary Ellen Bute," publicity release, n.d., Bute papers.

34. Howard Thompson, "Random News on Pictures and People," *New York Times*, 13 April 1952, Bute papers.

35. "Early Films of Mary Ellen Bute."

36. "Exclusive Distribution Ted Nemeth Studios," publicity release, n.d., Bute papers.

37. For selected film reviews of *Passages from Finnegans Wake*, see Margaret Tarratt, "Passages from James Joyce's Finnegans Wake," *Films and Filming* 16, no. 5 (February 1970): 4, 42; Albert Johnson, "The Dynamic Gesture: New American Independents," *Film Quarterly* 19, no. 2 (Winter 1965–66): 8–11; Stanley Kaufmann, *Figures of Light* (New York: Harper & Row, 1971), pp. 26–28; Dwight MacDonald, *Dwight MacDonald on Movies* (Englewood Cliffs, N.J.: Prentice-Hall, 1969), pp. 461–462; Vincent Canby, "Passages from James Joyce's Finnegans Wake," *New York Times*, 10 October 1967.

38. *Experimental Animation: An Illustrated Anthology,* ed. Robert Russett and Cecile Starr (New York: Van Nostrand Reinhold, 1976), pp. 102–105.

39. Schiff, "Education of Mary Ellen Bute," p. 60.

40. An article assembled from Bute's remarks at the Art Institute of Chicago on 7 May 1976 is: "Mary Ellen Bute: Reaching for Kinetic Art," *Field of Vision* 13 (Spring 1985), n.p.

41. Schiff, "Education of Mary Ellen Bute," p. 60.

14

Machines That Give Birth to Images

Douglass Crockwell

TOM GUNNING

> But, wander as you will, free animation is very exciting.
> —Douglass Crockwell

A DOUBLE LIFE

When P. Adams Sitney chose to begin his history of the American avant-garde with the work of Maya Deren, he was responding to more than the unique crystalization of form, theme, and influences that make up *Meshes in the Afternoon* (1943).[1] Deren's decision to understand herself primarily as a filmmaker, to create, at enormous financial and emotional cost to herself, a series of works that truly could be considered a corpus, provided the essential model for the emergence of the American avant-garde. Beyond the extraordinary achievement of her filmmaking, her definition of herself as a film artist (a definition that united rather than contradicted her many other interests in ritual, dance, and the metaphysics of time) mounted a challenge to both the Hollywood mode of production and the lifestyle and attitude toward one's work that it implied. For the American avant-garde filmmakers who followed in her wake, this model of a film artist provided as essential an inspiration as her films did. Stan Brakhage's reorientation of Deren's trance-based aesthetic to a direct exploration of his own life was founded on Deren's allegiance to an artisanal mode of production that provided the freedom to create films from a personal aesthetic and sense of exploration. Filmmaking not only defined Brakhage's lifestyle; it also subsumed it, as the most intimate details of marriage and child bearing were fused with

335

the artist's avocation. And this fusing of profession and lifestyle constitutes one of the avant-garde's defining acts; from the works of Jordan Belsen to those of Ken Jacobs or Ernie Gehr.

Turning to the first generation of American avant-garde filmmakers, we encounter a very different situation. Few of the many experimental filmmakers before Deren produced a full and developed corpus of works in the way Deren, Brakhage, and Kenneth Anger have. Instead we have fugitive films, either scattered over a long period of time and separated by large gaps, or concentrated in a limited (often youthful) stage in their creator's life. These works are frequently tangential to the filmmakers' other pursuits—in other art forms, professions, or nonexperimental films.[2] Further, rather than defining a lifestyle, the films made by the first generation of American experimental filmmakers frequently stand apart from their maker's principal profession and way of life. They often seem to arise from a much more disjunctive impulse, one not totally foreign to the idea of a hobby, an oasis of private obsession and personal discipline precisely defined against the demands of a more conventional public life.

Perhaps no early American experimental filmmaker exemplifies this better than Douglass Crockwell. His film work consists of a small number of animated films, only two of which seem actually to exist: *Glens Falls Sequence* and *The Long Bodies*.[3] And far from building a life around filmmaking and related activities, Crockwell's films stand in stark contrast to his successful career as a commercial artist, creating covers for the *Saturday Evening Post* and images of typical American life for a variety of advertisers (fig. 14.1). In no sense, however, do I believe that Crockwell's apparently seamless integration into a typical American life trivializes the role filmmaking played for him. Rather, like the greatest American poets of his generation, William Carlos Williams and Wallace Stevens, Crockwell was able to oscillate between an experimental mode of modernist art making and a fully engaged professional or commercial career. It was, of course, the dean of all American experimentalists, the composer and insurance executive Charles Ives, who noted that innovative ideas seem to be more readily accepted in business than in official American culture and academia. As avant-garde filmmakers have moved increasingly into teaching careers, the fissures of artistic and professional life may have simply become less noticeable but no less biting. In fact, one might wonder whether the split managed by artists like Crockwell is more salutary to art making than an academic career.

Figure 14.1.
Artwork for the *Saturday Evening Post*, by Douglass Crockwell (no date). Courtesy of George Eastman House

Crockwell seems to have enjoyed the double quality his filmmaking gave his life. On the one hand, he was always quick to emphasize that as a commercial artist he was hardly a bohemian. His official résumé described him as "a steady, hard-working, prosperous family man who contributes much to his civic surrounding,"[4] and in his hometown of Glens Falls, New York (from which his best-known film derives its title), he served as chairperson for the City Planning Commission and president of the Chamber of Commerce, and was involved in the local Boy Scouts, Rotary Club, and YMCA. This public aspect of his life seems to harmonize perfectly with much of his commercial art, which included not only *Saturday Evening Post* covers but other commissions that portrayed American life at its most average.[5] The earliest *Saturday Evening Post* cover by Crockwell that I have located (for the issue of 26 January 1935) conforms to the Norman Rockwell pattern of narrativized images of bourgeois life, showing an adolescent brother pursuing a younger sister who is making off with his love letter, her eyes fixed on the page as she runs.[6] Crockwell apparently integrated portraits of family and neighbors into his work, picturing his real life environment in the typical and idealized images that Americans expected as they were coaxed to consume.

But Crockwell was also well aware that his role as experimental artist left a private side to his public image. While Crockwell the creator of Scenes of American Home Life was well known to his neighbors, a feature for the local paper informed them: "Only among his friends, locally and among a small number of advanced artists, critics, museum directors and interested individuals in other places, is it known that his real creative interest is in the field of animated motion pictures."[7] For Crockwell the contrast between the two types of imagery he produced— the well-paid, familiar, and static versus the unprofitable, esoteric, and moving—seemed less a cause for despair at a fragmented existence than the recognition of an essential fold in his life, even a traditionally conceived one—between the public and the private, between the practical and the libidinal, between profession and avocation (as he listed filmmaking on his résumé). He does not seem to have regarded himself as the tragic victim of a split between his own personal taste and that of publishers and mass audiences, or as a cynical artist who managed to use his skill to supply what sold while keeping the real stuff for his own (and a small elite's) delectation (fig. 14.2).

Figure 14.2.
Portrait of Douglass Crockwell at work, ca. 1947. Courtesy of George Eastman House

In trying to describe the way in which Crockwell seems to have negotiated his identity as American artist, I think the key lies in a certain reversal of modes. His commercial work was created for mass distribution, of course, but it was produced with the traditional hand-directed tools of the artist. His experimental work, destined for a much smaller audience, was the product of machines, not simply the camera that photographed them, but the variety of machines that Crockwell designed (and patented) to create the imagery he filmed. Crockwell's films are the product of personally designed and operated machines, and I believe this was the source of his fascination with animation and specifically nonrepresentational animation. For Crockwell, then, the traditional tools of the artist—brushes, paints, and easels—could supply a broad-based need for familiar mass-produced imagery. An intricate and personally designed machine, however, produced images direct from the creator's fantasies and desires, a hobby of libidinal investment that would also interest a small network of similar obsessed aficionados. Inventing a machine that creates unusual and even esoteric imagery defines Crockwell's unique situation in the history of filmmaking. And I believe that Crockwell's machines were created (as were their products, his films) in imitation of, and homage to, a machine that saw the height of its exploration during Crockwell's early childhood: the Mutoscope.

THE MUTOSCOPE AND THE FLOW OF IMAGES

> Ah, yes. Mutoscope pictures in Capel street:
> for men only. Peeping Tom. Willy's hat and
> what the girls did with it. Do they snapshot
> those girls or is it all a fake?
> —James Joyce, *Ulysses*

The Mutoscope was more than a nostalgic memory for Crockwell. Throughout his adult life he was devoted to preserving the machine on a number of levels: physically, by collecting and restoring the apparatuses as they were being junked by amusement entrepreneurs; historically, by producing not only pioneering research on their history but also an exhibit at the Museum of Modern Art in 1967; and aesthetically, by producing animated wheels for Mutoscope exhibition, becoming certainly one of the last (if not the last) Mutoscope artists (and in some senses the first). In fact, Crockwell's last works as a creator of animated images exist not on film, but on wheels of cards designed for Mutoscope.[8]

The Mutoscope was patented in 1893 by a group of businessmen and engineers working in upstate New York, including Henry Marvin, Hermann Casler, and one of the most fascinating figures in early American cinema, William Kennedy Laurie Dickson.[9] Dickson had been the leading inventor of the first moving picture machine, Thomas Edison's Kinetoscope (fig. 14.3). However, for a variety of motives (ranging from simple profit to a degree of pique over the lack of credit he was given on Edison's invention), he also aided the endeavors of Edison's rivals, usually somewhat surreptitiously, contributing both his expertise and his intimate knowledge of the specifications of Edison's patents. The

Figure 14.3.
Edison Kinetoscope parlor, ca. 1900. Courtesy of George Eastman House

Mutoscope was, like the Kinetoscope, a peep show device that showed moving pictures to a single viewer. While the projected motion pictures that eventually dominated the moving image industry were inspired by the projection of magic lantern slides to a large audience, the peep show devices that were cinema's first film apparatuses seemed to derive from such single-viewer devices as the stereoscope, the three-dimensional viewer designed for parlor use in the Victorian era. Although the basic technology that produced the images—that is, the camera—was identical for both projected and peepshow viewing, their spectorial reception is quite different, a difference that was acknowledged both in the types of film made for each apparatus and in their ultimate commercial fates.

The Mutoscope not only circumvented Edison's patents in a number of ingenious ways, but also improved on the Kinetoscope in a manner that ensured that the new invention would eclipse its peep show predecessor. While the Kinetoscope consisted of spools of motion picture film that moved automatically between a light source and a viewing lens, the Mutoscope consisted of a reel of circularly mounted still photographs that flipped past a viewing lens (creating the illusion of motion in the manner of a flip book) when propelled by a crank operated by the viewer. The advantages of the machine lay in its simplicity. The wheel of photographs was actually more resilient than Edison's spool of film, which was subject to warping, snapping, and scratching. The viewer's control of the crank could also be seen as an improvement. The viewer could make the wheels of cards spin fast or slow, and could even make a single photograph pause for longer contemplation. In the "Girlie" reels that were always important to the Mutoscope (whose voyeuristic nature seemed embodied in its single-viewer peep show nature), the ability to suspend motion could pose a definite advantage.

But if the Mutoscope triumphed in the peep show marketplace of the penny arcade, the peep show mode of exhibiting motion pictures was soon to be marginalized by the triumph of theatrically projected films. The Mutoscope, however, was not quite an invention without a future. Rather, the peep show became increasingly marginalized, as its association with furtive erotic viewing institutionalized both its voyeur nature and its exile from respectable entertainments. While the public nature of screen projections and the expansive program they allowed could be associated with educational lectures and adapted to fully developed narratives, the Mutoscope remained limited to brief doses of scopic pleasure, an attraction associated with either eroticism or pure curiosity, lacking clearly defined social benefits. The American Mutoscope and Biograph Company ceased producing Mutoscopes after 1909, undoubtedly because of its entry into the Motion Picture Patents Company, the film trust that sought to control the motion picture industry and whose motto "Moral, Educational and Cleanly Amusing" disavowed cinema's origins in the scopic curiosity of the penny arcade. The Mutoscope business was sold to the International Mutoscope Reel Company, which understood (and accepted) the penny-ante, side-show nature of the attraction, and targeted amusement parks and fairgrounds. As if underscoring their small-time, parasitic relation to theatrical films, the new Mutoscope company produced some anodyne reels, two minutes of silent film with well-known stars (Charles Chaplin, Tom Mix, Mabel Normand) , cut from the longer features produced by the industry mainstream. But "the glory of the International Mutoscope Company must rest on its 'Girlies', dance and strip-tease subjects," to quote Crockwell,[10] home-produced short erotic scenes of women disrobing or dancing in skimpy costumes. Mutoscopes now were among the less featured attractions of amusement arcades, and in the 1940s and 1950s Crockwell began collecting them as they were being cast off from a dying branch of show business.[11]

What fascinated Crockwell about the Mutoscope? While the ultimate answer to this question may be as complex and contradictory as the illustrator's passion for nonobjective film making, Crockwell has provided an answer that throws light on his filmmaking as well. In a draft of program notes for the MOMA exhibit that he put together in 1966, Crockwell defines the essence of Mutoscope art:

> Visually the motion picture is sequential art. . . . Motion is but one of the incidental byproducts. In essence the Mutoscope reel presents one image after another, after another, after another— —. Timing of the interval has no basic importance. The raw material of this art is the topological arrangement in time of a given set of images.[12]

Crockwell provides a radical definition of the origins of film art, against the grain of the traditional interpretation of the essence of film as the reproduction of motion (and one, it might be added, that Crockwell shares with the Austrian experimental filmmaker Peter Kubelka).[13] And one can see how the viewer-controlled aspects of the Mutoscope in its original form might have aided Crockwell in his anti-Edison redefinition of the essence of cinema. Rather than providing the most powerful simulacrum of reality by conquering the reproduction of motion, motion pictures become a sort of serial art based on the temporal permutations of images, the intervals between which could be immensely varied.

Animation, in spite of its name, is the form of cinema that most naturally questions the primacy of the illusion of motion. Animation does not record motion, because it does not actually record anything. The freedom of drawn animation springs from the fact that it short-circuits the indexical relation to a previous reality that photography entails. The animator can create his or her images strictly from fancy, and the possibility of the illusion of motion comes only from a disciplined imitation of the slight variations between the film frames that motion picture photography produces. The repetitive and painstaking labor necessary for such drawings caused the industrialization of animation studios that soon overtook the commercial branches of cartoon making, with rows of drawers and inkers producing the images that would animate a character or section of a landscape.[14] In the early 1930s Crockwell was attracted to cartoon animation as a way to fuse his commercial art skills and his fascination with temporal images. But the assembly-line nature of the animation studio and its need for nonexperimental themes seemed to deny the synthesis he desired.[15] Instead, his work was split between his illustrations of traditional popular images and his experimental films.

But the split allowed him to explore his fascination with sequential art without subordinating it to the conventions of recognizable motion or story. By circumventing the conventions of commercial animation, Crockwell was in some sense returning to both the primal sequential fascination of the Mutoscope and the roots of animated films, particularly the style and methods of production used by the greatest of all early animators, Emil Cohl. Like Crockwell, this early French filmmaker was a commercial artist, a caricaturist who supplied covers for political and satirical magazines of the turn of the century. However, the sorts of publications that Cohl worked for and the culture of his time and place did not force a split between his experimental interests and his commercial life. As Don Crafton has shown in his definitive biography,[16] Cohl's allegiance with the proto-Dadaist "Incoherents" was fully integrated with his commercial life. Likewise, as Cohl moved into filmmaking in 1907, cinema still sought out the sort of unnarrativized magical or absurd attractions that characterized the trick films of its first decade. Cohl's first animated films were untrammeled by narrative or character logic, or, one could add, much logic at all.

Cohl's first fully animated film, *Fantasmagorie* (1908), shares more than a title with Crockwell's work. Although it is basically figurative (its stark black and white contrast sharply with Crockwell's interest in color harmonies), the essence of sequential animation for Cohl is less the illusion of motion than a constant whimsical transformation that undermines any consistency of space, object, or identity. Although Cohl was also a master of gags, and his films (and comic strips) often include comic scenarios worthy of Buster Keaton, it is this ceaseless flow of transformation that gives his animation its wonderfully incoherent flavor. Films like Cohl's and, before him, the trick films of stop motion that prepared the way for animation, show that early cinema's fascination with motion was as much a product of wonder at instantaneous change as it was of scientific satisfaction in the capturing of realistic movement.[17] Likewise, in the classic Mutoscope reels that Crockwell collected (and especially in the reel of Mutoscopes that he photographed from his collection for MOMA,[18] the initial fascination of motion owes as much to its uncanny nature as its familiarity. The cards could be flipped at speeds that broke motion down into separate still images, and the rather slow speed at which Crockwell filmed the reels for MOMA allows one to sense the push/pull between moving *gestalt* and separate still fragments (fig. 14.4).

This sense of an unstoppable flow of imagery is the dominant impression of Crockwell's surviving work. The dates given for *Glens Falls Sequence* and *The Long Bodies* are 1946 and 1947, respectively,[19] dates that come a fair time after the earliest abstract experiments of Oskar Fischinger and Hans Richter or the Americans Mary Ellen Bute and Dwinell Grant. It is clear, however, that the films known under these titles are actually anthologies of works made over the previous decade, beginning, Crockwell indicates, in 1934.[20] Correspondence between

Figure 14.4.
Installation photo from Crockwell mutoscope exhibition, Museum of Modern Art (1967), with mutoscopes constructed by Douglass Crockwell. Courtesy of George Eastman House

Crockwell and MOMA dating from May 1937 already speaks of his "abstract color film" containing a "Tanguy landscape," most likely a reference to material that ended up in *Glens Falls Sequence*.[21] And a letter to Iris Barry of MOMA from April 1938 speaks of a film that includes a "Calvary" sequence, undoubtedly the "Crucifixion" sequence from the same film.[22] In August 1937 Crockwell filed documents with a patent attorney for a device that allowed one to create animated films by painting on the reverse side of a piece of glass. The papers clearly show images that appear in *Glens Falls Sequence*.[23] Clearly much of the material for the surviving films came from early works that were cannibalized in the late 1940s, guaranteeing Crockwell a pioneering date in American abstract animation.

My purpose in detailing the anthology nature of Crockwell's finest films, however, is less to establish historical priority than to make a point about the films' structure. Both *Glens Falls Sequence* and *The Long Bodies* are made up of discontinuous suites of films, whose only continuity comes from the endless transformations that run through them. This was apparently just as true of the earlier lost films, since his 1938 letter to Barry speaks of the discontinuity in his work and indicates that the short sequences originally had separate titles. In fact, both surviving films include a variety of methods of animation.[24] Although the painting-on-glass method dominates *Glens Falls* and the sliced-wax process gives *The Long Bodies* both its name and its dominant method, each film includes sections of stop-motion and cutout animation, and other processes (such as the molding of clay over a pane of glass in *Glens Falls*).

Crockwell's films often give the impression, then, of an avant-garde vaudeville show where pace and variety are everything. In this regard they contrast sharply with the tendencies in abstract animation that precede him (and in a sense link him more closely to a later filmmaker like Robert Breer). The dominant metaphor for abstract animation had been a merging of abstract painting with music. From Viking Eggeling through Fischinger, the European tradition frequently defined such films as visualization of (often preexisting) music. This tradition has a clear impact on the pioneers of American abstract animation, particularly Bute. For Crockwell, however, it involved a basic misunderstanding of the sources of fascination of the moving image, exemplified by the flipping images of the Mutoscope. As he stated in his discussion of "Free Animation" in *Film Culture*: "Music I have neglected, for the need has not been apparent. . . . Unfortunately others have allowed the music to dominate, even to keying every motion to a musical beat. I believe the beauties of abstract animation in their own right."[25]

The issue here involves more than the presence of sound or the technique of synchronization. If we take Fischinger's work as perhaps the most extreme example, the music not only dominates, but determines the sorts of transformations possible. Movement of abstract shapes is keyed primary to tempo and rhythm, and shape and size seem to correspond to timber, volume, and pitch. Further, Fischinger's films employ a series of variations on a rather limited number of forms, as if the shapes on the screen represent the regularities of a tonal scale. In other words, the abstraction used in animated films before Crockwell usually makes use of a limited vocabulary of shapes and permutations that seem to imitate the regularities of Western music. The abstraction therefore (and this applies also to films not synchronized with music) tends to be geometrical and constructivist. The film's total form is orchestrated, with recurring shapes and motifs supplying a sense of unity. The lack of representation in these films seems compensated for by a clearly indicated sense of total shape and structure.[26]

This is why Crockwell's films recall more immediately the flow of transforming imagery found in Cohl's cartoons than the work of his immediate predecessors in abstract animation. There is no dominant recurring abstract vocabulary of shapes in Crockwell's films. His forms are plastic and pliable, stretching and shrinking, biomorphic rather than geometric. Further, they seem to respond to an endless line of caprice rather than a predetermined plan and orchestration. Like Cohl's transforming lines, they are the product of a free association seeming to unfold before our eyes, rather than a predetermined series. This explains why Crockwell's reference point in speaking of his films was most frequently surrealism. Not only did he compare the opening image of *Glens Falls Sequence* to a Tanguy landscape, but his animation technique corresponds to surrealist ideas of the creative process in a way the methods of earlier animators could not (fig. 14.5). The painting-on-glass technique of most selections of *Glens Falls Sequence* necessitated a fairly rapid work process (so that the paint would remain liquid enough to be manipulated) and entailed a large number of aleatory effects. The way paint moves over the surface (or, in the "crucifixion" sequence, some sort of plasticene or clay) has expressive effects the maker can neither fully predict nor control. Rather, the maker has the opportunity to respond to

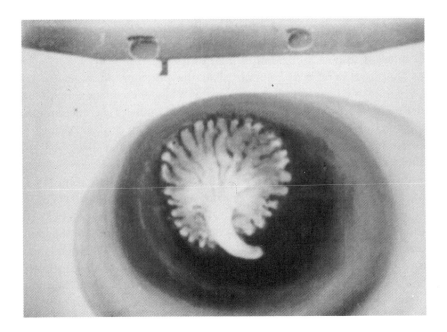

Figure 14.5.
Frame enlargement from *Glens Falls Sequence* (1946), directed by Douglass Crockwell.
Courtesy of George Eastman House

and interact with the shapes as they appear. In this way the films convey a strong sense of action painting, since the process takes place as it is recorded, rather than fulfilling a entirely predetermined scheme. Further, the flow of images follows an entirely different logic than that of the orchestrated animations that precede Crockwell. In his letter to Barry, Crockwell actually described his method as "automatic," with "each movement and form suggesting the character of the following movement form."[27] The logic partly evolves as the film is being made, giving the films their extraordinary sense of free association.

This free-flowing process of association endows Crockwell's biomorphic shapes with a protean energy lacking any concept of identity or consistency, driven by primary process without regard to secondary revisions. And if I am right that this dream analogy constitutes part of the drive behind these films, it might also explain the recurrent appearance of the somewhat surprisingly representational and symbolic elements. Crockwell's statements on his films and his working notes on sequential art refer to the importance of symbolism and "totems."[28] Although this last term seemed to have a significance for Crockwell which I cannot fully define, it is clear that part of the fascination with transformation in his filmmaking lies in the shifting, dreamlike associations that become attached to his imagery as it unfolds. A manuscript page of Crockwell's notes entitled "Suggestions for animation," quoted by Andrew Eskind, lists topics Crockwell wished to explore, including, "Inducing associations between abstract forms and colors and ideas and emotions," followed immediately by "Psychopathic effects" and "Hypnotic effects." Clearly Crockwell did not intend here the sort of transparent representations of meanings and moods found in commercial art.

A dreamlike process of association shapes the succession of forms in his films. Out of a matrix of moving material, an image will arise with a recognizable shape, or an identifiable action. Crockwell plays with these recognitions, delighting in both creating and dissolving them, blending one recognizable form into another unexpected one. As in Freud's most radical image of the dream process (before secondary revision has intervened to create stories and consistencies out of radically juxtaposed elements), Crockwell's images breed a series of associations rather than ever truly creating a narrative.

At points these mergings of symbolic totems take on an exhilarating obscenity, as the circular shapes in both *Glens Falls Sequence* and *The Long Bodies* sprout squirming tentacles and appendages, dripping out liquids and generally behaving like the ceaselessly procreating and swelling organs of an invertebrate sexuality (fig. 14.6). At other points the forms recall more specific icons in transformation, with the opening of *Glens Falls Sequence* providing the most dizzying of alterations. The initial shape appears first as a pink, heartlike object which become compressed and forced into a sphere. A fleshy tube emerges from the sphere until the whole form becomes serpentlike, then forms an eye with lid and pupil from which a teardrop falls. A description of this sort, however, not only fails to account for all the transformations taking place, but threatens to congeal these shifting images into familiar forms. The experience of this brief sequence is actually one of furtive recognition, as no sooner does the material take definable shape than it is on its way to becoming something else. And while everybody may not find the same references I do, I think that part of Crockwell's method is to summon up Rorschach-like associations, like the fragments of a dream that never coheres.

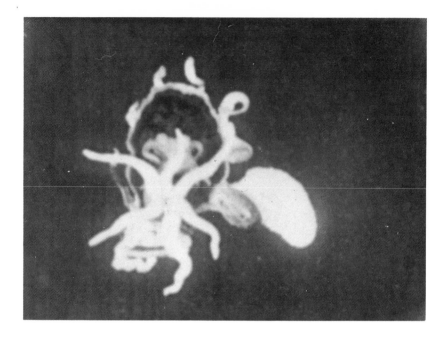

Figure 14.6.
Frame enlargement from *Glens Falls Sequence* (1946), directed by Douglass Crockwell.
Courtesy of George Eastman House

When Crockwell films were shown in the San Francisco "Art in Cinema" program in April 1947 they were described (and Crockwell may be the source of the description) as "experiments in surrealist poetry."[29] Certainly the automatic writing of André Breton or Paul Eluard is as useful a reference for these films as imagery from surrealist painters (and marks again Crockwell's difference from most preceding abstract animators). The flow of imagery in *Glens Falls Sequence* takes on the power of surrealist metaphors as one totem becomes another. In the sequence of the film that takes my breath away, a form recalling the curve of an eyelid appears within an area that has functioned as a sort of stage for previous cavorting objects. From this eyelid curve a white flat material is lowered, looking like a movie screen. Figures are drawn on this surface. The screen becomes a darkened square and shapes appear in front of it and spurt a red liquid that dyes them crimson. Then the screen is raised, revealing behind it the blackened shadow of the red form.

Soon after this Crockwell presents his most symbolic and narrative image. As swirls of matter (plasticene pressed over glass, I believe) seem to divide the screen into a ground and a horizon, a cross appears. Crockwell seems to fix the flow of imagery here by summoning up such a culturally loaded image. However, as a figure appears on the cross, its body begins to be transformed. It sways and stretches, expressing less the agony of the crucifixion than a rhythmic bopping to unheard music. Its arms become stretched to chewing gum–like strands and its belly swells to obesity. Briefly an image of a traditional Christ appears, and then the icon itself is swept away by another squall of heaving matter. If Crockwell here flirts with allegory, his purpose seems essentially playful. As with the other recognizable imagery, it is the dreamlike transformation that counts, rather than any static signification.

DESIRING MACHINES

Desire is not in the subject, but in the machine in desire—with the residual subject off to the side, alongside the machine, around the entire periphery, a parasite of machines, an accessory of vertebromachinate desire.
—Gilles Deleuze and Felix Guattari, *Anti-Oedipus*

This ability to create a flow of imagery whose sense would be a process of association and transformation rather than an orchestration of abstract geometry or the representations of cartoon characters was a product of Crockwell's unique animation machines. Crockwell designed two basic processes for creating animation, both of which were patented. The first is the painting on the reverse side of a sheet of glass that is used in many sections of *Glens Falls Sequence*. His second method, which dominates *The Long Bodies*, consisted of slicing long pieces (hence the title) of prepared wax. Crockwell would prepare the wax block carefully, combining a variety of shapes in different colors, surrounded, or interacting with, other shapes and colors. The actual apparatus consisted of a mount that would hold the prepared-wax blocks while a slicer took off a sixty-fourth of an inch. This cross-section, with its particular configuration of shapes and colors, would then be photographed. The precision screws of the device would then move the wax an increment further, it would be sliced again, and the new configuration would be photographed. The resulting series of cross-sections would produce patterns of transformation and apparent growth and movement of forms, which the filmmaker could partially determine by the preparation of the wax, but which would also display a margin of aleatory effects.[30]

Crockwell seems to have been as fascinated by the process itself as by its results, and he frequently commented on its temporal implications. The relation between the wax block and the slicer provided a rich image of the configuration of time and motion: "This solid block contains within itself the past, present and future of an animated sequence suspended in time. When the solid is sliced consecutive cross sections are revealed and photographed, and the sequence joins the flow of time."[31] For Crockwell *Long Bodies* imaged "the four dimensional trail left by an object as it moves and exists in time and space."[32] The machine, then, both freezes and liberates time, figuring all its possibilities in the wax body before slicing. The film itself creates a temporal series by recording the machine as it slices into this congealed time, creating momentary cross-sections. But the film presents these slices as a continuous flow, creating a temporal process that mediates between the frozen simultaneity of the block and the successive units of the slicer. Through his machines Crockwell regulates and creates a sense of time totally liberated from the normal time produced by the illusion of motion. This is a sequential art in which the intervals between slices are eclipsed and a time of synthesis intervenes.

If we see Crockwell as in some sense a hobbyist, it also makes sense to see his films less as final artistic works, the end products of an aesthetic process, than as by-products of a tinkering obsession and pleasure. It would seem that the devices that made them possible were as important to Crockwell as the films, and the same fascination is evident in his collection of Mutoscope wheels. One senses again that the driving purpose behind these works was as much to bring Crockwell into a close relation to the machine of his desires as to produce an artwork. Soon after *Glens Falls Sequence* came to its final form, Crockwell approached the International Mutoscope Reel Company to see if a section could be transferred to a Mutoscope wheel.[33] Crockwell persuaded the company's executives to cooperate, and a peep show machine with Crockwell's movie was installed in the offices of MOMA.[34]

It was probably soon after this that Crockwell began to make card wheels directly intended for Mutoscopes. Most of the wheels preserved at the George Eastman House are titled "Color Wheels" and consist of a series of cards of single colors that create a sense of alternating and blending colors when flipped (*Color Wheels* 1, 2, 3, 4, 5). Others combine disparate material, such as *Duopusses*, which includes letters playing an anagramic game with the title and sequences photographed from *Glens Falls Sequence,* and *Animation #1,* which includes color photos of animation (possibly made by the sliced-wax process) and images from an old Mutoscope "Girlie" reel of a skimpily clad dancer in a top hat. The same "Girlie" material reappears in what I find to be the most fascinating of Crockwell's Mutoscope wheels (which would date from the early to mid-1960s). Entitled *Playboy and Dancer Reel,* it consists of images of the top-hatted dancer interspersed with fragments from the pages of *Playboy* magazine. These fragments alternate printed matter with images from *Playboy* ads and cartoons in black and white and color. Luxury goods such as tobacco pipes and liquor, gourmet foods, radios and cars, and items of men's apparel (especially socks and underwear) interweave with fragments of women's bodies and the recurring Mutoscope dancer. This seems to be the one time Crockwell brought together his fascination with fragmented moving images with imagery from the advertising industry he worked in. The fragmentation here triumphs over the lure of consumer goods, while the titillation of the flesh seems merged with the flipping motion of the cards. As works of animation, these wheels also share a noticeable quality of Crockwell's films: unlike orchestrated animated films, they come to no climax, have no grand finale. They simply stop. Or, as these wheels indicate, they can simply begin again, in an endlessly repeatable circuit of imagery.

In all of his animated work, but perhaps most clearly in this late Mutoscope reel, Crockwell evokes one of the enduring paradoxes of modern culture—the extraordinary exchange of connotations that take place between machines and sexuality, as seeming ontological opposites recurringly figure each other. The repetitive rhythms of sexual actions can invoke the workings of machines, while machines from at least as far back as Henry Adams' dynamo have provided images for sexual energy. The Mutoscope seems to have invited an erotic interpretation as much from the rapid rhythm of its manual crank as from its voyeuristic visuality. Linda Williams' pioneering work on film pornography, *Hard Core,* describes a film included in the Kinsey Institute collection of stag films.[35] *A Country Stud Horse,* although not designed for Mutoscope viewing, shows a Mutoscope in operation as a man peers into the viewer and turns the crank. The film next reveals the pornographic film the man is presumably watching and then cuts back to the man as he begins to masturbate (with, as Williams felicitously puts it, "one hand cranking the machine, another cranking himself").[36] The film continues as a flesh and blood woman woos the man away from his scopic, manual, and mechanical pleasure. As Williams indicates in a recent essay discussing this stag film, the apparatus of the Mutoscope plays an important role here, not only as a *faute de mieux*, but as a form of technological foreplay. As such it foregrounds the free-flowing displacement that circulates between machine and body, transforming both through sexual energy. The Mutoscope in this instance cranks out sex as well as moving imagery. And in this free flow of libido, who is to say which is the primary apparatus, and which the substitute? As Williams puts it, "This body moves, and is moved by, the machine."[37]

And this is what Crockwell understood so well about the variety of motion picture apparatuses, which Thomas Edison once called machines that make images dance: that they are what Deleuze and Guattari call "desiring machines," machines that both produce a flow of material and slice into it ("like a ham slicing machine").[38] It is desire that causes the flow, as well as the breaks in the flow, and what the machine produces is desire. If the poststructuralist implications of this are intentionally elusive, with Crockwell it serves as a nearly literal description, almost a definition, of what he termed sequential art. Not only the wax-slicing machine, but also Crockwell's Ur-Machine, the Mutoscope of his childhood, produces a flow of material and transforms this flow by slicing it into suspended moments of time. But as Crockwell indicates, it rejoins the flow of time in its animation. For Crockwell that motion is rarely (if ever) a representation. It is rather a new production, a production that embodies the free flow of association and transformation, the very image of desire. The sexual imagery of the "Girlie" Mutoscopes, or of Crockwell's antediluvian lifeforms, provides no clearer images of desire than the untrammeled motion of the machine itself does, set free from representation and released into the paths of libidinal cathexis.

As a collector and historian, Crockwell was as fascinated by the Mutoscope machines as by their wheels of turning imagery: "Looking back I remember the 'image' of the Mutoscope as a machine and a rather tawdry machine at that. It was a fascinating image, however, and I believe the public felt the same."[39]

Crockwell not only created what may be the last Mutoscope reels; he also designed his own version of the machine itself. On display at MOMA in 1967, his machine was simplified and streamlined, a clear plastic box enclosing the reel of cards in such a way that the mechanism itself was clearly visible.[40] For Crockwell understood that in this exhibit the viewer's interest, like his own, would be as much in the process as in the moving image product. In this regard he was again returning to some of the primal fascination of the cinema, which focused as much on the machines as on the motion pictures they displayed. At the turn of the century, motion pictures were initially exhibited as demonstrations of the apparatus that photographed and projected them, rather than simply images on the screen. For the first years of projected motion pictures, it was the apparatuses—the Cinematograph, the Vitascope, the Biograph, the Phantoscope, or the Eidoloscope—that were advertised as the attraction, while the films themselves went untitled. Quite rapidly, however, the subject matter of the film or the name of the production company took pride of place, and the apparatuses were tucked away, remaining essential equipment, but in the hands of technicians, far from the public's view. Except, of course, for the amusement arcade Mutoscope, which still stood there, subject to viewer manipulation and object of some residual fascination, in the dustier corners of Coney Island or Santa Monica Pier.

I believe that Crockwell made films because they put him in contact with the machine of his desires, a desire imaged by the flow of transformation and its possibility of suspension. He made the type of film he did because it allowed a direct and intense connection to these desiring machines. Most of his machines are gone (although some were donated to the George Eastman House), but the films remain. Properly viewed, they are not simply fragments of an early phase of American avant-garde cinema. They are desiring machines themselves, which connect viewers to their own production of the desire for moving, transforming images. Just as, I feel, they once transformed the double sensibility of Douglass Crockwell, commercial artist and experimental filmmaker. His machines released him from his own production of commercial images (in which desires had to be carefully channeled toward an illusory satisfaction through a circuit of consumption), transforming the image of desire—allowing it to divest itself of its familiar iconography and, like a Mutoscope Girlie, dance around naked. At least for a little while.

NOTES

1. P. Adams Sitney, *Visionary Film: The American Avant-Garde 1943–1978*, 2d ed. (Oxford: Oxford University Press, 1979), pp. 3–46.

2. In this sense, the career of the co-author of *Meshes in the Afternoon*, Alexander Hammid (a.k.a. Hackenschmied), relates more strongly to the histories of the early filmmakers: youthful experimental films in Czechoslovakia and the collaboration with Deren, alternated with professional work as a cinematographer and director of documentaries.

3. A third title, *Fantasmagorie*, sometimes appears in filmographies. However, the footage bearing this title at the George Eastman House (GEH) consists of footage that also appears in the two other films, albeit in a different order. *Glens Falls Sequence* and *The Long Bodies* are preserved in 16mm copies by both George Eastman House in Rochester and the Museum of Modern Art (MOMA) in New York City. MOMA also distributes both films. The colors in the prints vary in hue between the archives, and the MOMA and GEH prints of *The Long Bodies* are reversed left to right.

4. Résumé in file of Douglass Crockwell material at GEH. I would like to thank Dr. Jan-Christopher Horak for making this material available to me, and in fact, for suggesting that I write on Crockwell and introducing me to his work.

5. A series of paintings done for the U.S. Brewers Foundation, for instance, was designed to show the role of beer drinking in typical family gatherings. Titles include: *Meeting Her Parents, A Television Party, Gathered Around the Piano,* and *An Evening of Bowling.*

6. Andrew H. Eskind gives 1933 as the date for the first Crockwell *Saturday Evening Post* cover. He also lists General Motors, General Electric, Metro-Goldwyn-Mayer, Coca-Cola, Camel Cigarettes, the Army, and the Marine Corps as Crockwell clients. See Andrew H. Eskind, " 'She banked in her stocking' or 'Robbed of her all': Mutoscopes Old and New," *Image* 19, no. 1 (March 1976): 1–6.

7. Clipping of article by Joseph J. Dodd, *Glens Falls Post Star*, Crockwell file, George Eastman House (GEH), Rochester, N.Y.

8. These wheels are preserved at GEH in Rochester, along with a substantial collection of early Mutoscope wheels, donated to the museum by Crockwell.

9. Besides Crockwell's own pioneering article for *Image*, scholarly studies of the Mutoscope include Gordon Hendricks' encyclopedic *Beginnings of the Biograph: The Story of the Invention of the Mutoscope and the Biograph and Their Supplying Camera* (Reprint. New York: Arno Press, 1972), and Charles Musser's recent history, *The Emergence of Cinema: The American Screen to 1907* (New York: Scribners, 1990).

10. Douglass Crockwell, *Mutoscopes*, a text written by Crockwell and distributed in connection with the exhibit of Mutoscopes and machines that he set up at MOMA in 1967. I have worked, however, from a draft of this text entitled "Peep Show: The Past and Future Mutoscope, a World-Wide Folk Art From Since 1895. Created and Almost Totally Produced in New York State is now in Resurgence," preserved in the Crockwell file, GEH, which includes

passages not found in the published version. Large sections of both the MOMA text and the unpublished text at GEH are reprinted in Eskind, " 'She banked in her stocking.' " It might be noted that the "Girlie" Mutoscopes were an element of production from the beginning. A Mutoscope fragment among some papers left by the company head, Henry Marvin, includes images of a nude dancer. The much tamer reel *What the Girls Did with Willie's Hat*, mentioned by Joyce in *Ulysses*, was an actual mutoscope and was among a number of early Girlie Mutoscope reels banned from Coney Island in 1897 after a raid staged by the Reverend Frederick Bruce Russell. See Musser, *Emergence of Cinema*, p. 187.

11. The Crockwell file, GEH, includes letters from Crockwell's negotiations with an amusement arcade owner in Coney Island to buy his Mutoscopes.

12. Douglass Crockwell, "Peep Show," GEH file.

13. See Peter Kubelka, "The Theory of the Metrical Film," in *The Avant-Garde Film: A Reader of Theory and Criticism*, ed. P. Adams Sitney (New York: New York University Press, 1978), p. 140.

14. For a full account of the origin and development of the cartoon industry, including its full industrialization, see Don Crafton, *Before Mickey: The Animated Film 1898–1928* (Cambridge, Mass.: MIT Press, 1982). See also Mark Langer, "Institutional Power and the Fleischer Studios: *The Standard Production Reference*," *Cinema Journal* 30, no. 2 (Winter 1991): 3–22.

15. Douglass Crockwell, "A Background to Free Animation," *Film Culture* 32 (Spring 1964): 30–31.

16. Donald Crafton, *Emil Cohl, Caricature and Film* (Princeton: Princeton University Press, 1990). Did Crockwell know Cohl's films? I have found no mention of them, but MOMA has a Cohl reel in its collection, and Crafton has told me that Theodore Huff had a print of *Fantasmagorie* that he showed in his film clubs in the New York area during the 1930s and 1940s, so Crockwell may have been aware of his predecessor. However, nothing in Crockwell's work indicates strongly that he saw Cohl's films. The connections between the two filmmakers are more primary than direct influence, though the influence may be there.

17. For a consideration of the relation between the trick film and the illusion of motion in early cinema, see Tom Gunning, " 'Primitive Cinema'—A Frame-Up? or The Trick's on Us," *Cinema Journal* 28, no. 2 (Winter 1989): 3–12, and "An Aesthetic of Astonishment: Early Film and the [In]credulous Spectator," *Art & Text* 34 (Spring 1989): 31–45.

18. Crockwell's selection of reels from his own collection is distributed by MOMA in 16mm under the title *The Classic American Mutoscope*. It includes *The Tramp and the Muscular Cook, Reginald's First High Hat* (misidentified as *A Wringing Good Joke*), *The Horsethief, A Affair of Honor, How the Old Maid Got a Husband* (incorrectly identified as *Old Maid and the Burglar*), *A Fight for a Bride, The Convict's Bride* (incorrectly identified as *Jail Break*), *Waltzing*

Walker, and *Robbed of Her All.* Although intended primarily as a record of the original reels, a few effects managed by Crockwell, such as the freeze frames, a shot of a Mutoscope viewer, and the rather slow speed of shooting (which I discuss here) actually make this the last Crockwell film work.

19. See, for instance, *Circulating Film Catalogue* (New York: Museum of Modern Art, 1984), pp. 175–176.

20. Douglass Crockwell, "A Background to Free Animation," Crockwell file, GEH.

21. Letter, Douglass Crockwell to John Abbott, 27 May 1937, MOMA correspondence file. I thank Eileen Bowser for drawing my attention to this material and for reading it to me over the phone.

22. Letter, Douglass Crockwell to Iris Barry, 27 April 1938, MOMA. Thanks again to Eileen Bowser.

23. Patent application in Crockwell file, GEH.

24. The letter to Barry (27 April 1938) even indicates that the early films included sequences of "realistic photography"—presumably nonanimated shots—which Crockwell cautioned were not to be taken seriously.

25. Crockwell, "Background to Free Animation," p. 30.

26. This characterization applies, of course, only to Fischinger's best-known work. As William Moritz points out in his monograph-length article, "The Films of Oskar Fischinger," *Film Culture* 58–60 (1974): 37–188, Fischinger's early films and a number of works scattered throughout his career were conceived without musical accompaniment. However, even Moritz acknowledges the tendency I discuss here: "The one limitation that music did impose on Fischinger is in the area of circumscribing the potential for all but certain styles and movements. The hard edged tones, evenly-spaced harmonies, recurrent melodic phrases, and regular/simple-peasant dance rhythms of much of 19th century European classical music seem to call for a certain limited kind of geometrical figure and choreographical movement." Moritz, "Fischinger," p. 80.

27. Letter, Crockwell to Iris Barry, 27 April 1938, Crockwell file, MOMA.

28. Notes accompanying the draft of the Mutoscope article preserved at GEH mention such topics as "Art as an organisational system of totems," and "The future of the 'non-useful' value totem in the natural organisation of mankind." Likewise, program notes for his films preserved at GEH state that through abstract animation, "there are many latent totemic values of great importance to be discovered." These comments show that he had elaborated this concept personally, although its full implications remain enigmatic. Donald Crafton suggested to me that totems may parallel Jungian archetypes, a theory with some currency in the American avant-garde in the 1940s. I would like to thank Crafton for reading a draft of this article and his comments.

29. Program notes for "Art in Cinema" showing of *The Long Bodies* in San Francisco, April 1947, preserved in Crockwell file, GEH.

30. The patent drawings (Patent no. 2.444.729, issued 6 July 1948, filed 16 March 1944) for this machine are preserved in the Crockwell file, GEH. This process is particularly well illustrated by photographs showing both the various stages of wax preparation and Crockwell operating the slicer in *Experimental Animation: An Illustrated Anthology*, ed. Robert Russett and Cecil Starr (New York: Van Nostrand Reinhold, 1976), pp. 109–110. The book also includes a description of the process by Crockwell's assistant, William Smith. (Crockwell also held patents for a number of other devices related to motion picture photography, including a panoramic camera capable of what he termed "sweep photography.")

Fischinger created and used a similar wax-slicing machine in Weimar, Germany, beginning in 1921, and he made a number of films with this process, as did other, later animators. See Moritz, "Fischinger," pp. 43–45, 83–85. Crockwell may have known of Fischinger's apparatus and experiments, or he may have arrived at the process independently, since Fischinger does not seem to have brought the apparatus with him to the United States or to have made films by this process there. Although Crockwell's and Fischinger's films are very different stylistically, the apparatuses they used had many parallels. Besides the wax-slicing machines, Fischinger also devised an apparatus for creating animated films by painting on glass (ibid., pp. 70–71), and around 1945 he also created a small number of Mutoscope reels (ibid., p. 159). Moritz notes "the astounding coincidence" between the two filmmakers' work (p. 172), but I have found no evidence that they ever met. Fischinger's extensive career, in both number of films and decades of productive work, his critical and commercial recognition, his off and on relationship with established commercial film studios in Germany and in the United States, and his European background all contrast with Crockwell's more limited and "private" career. Fischinger also managed a sort of synthesis between abstract animation and commercial career (two realms that Crockwell kept separate), since many of his films served as advertisements for commercial products. Moritz states that "Crockwell's films lack the finesse and style evident in the work of Fischinger" (ibid., p. 173). Precisely (and thank goodness).

31. Crockwell, program notes, in Crockwell file, GEH.

32. Crockwell, "Background to Free Animation," (p. 31.

33. Eskind indicates that Crockwell had already had the International Mutoscope Reel Company manufacture a black and white reel from one of his animated films in 1939, apparently paying for the work. See Eskind, " 'She banked in her stocking,' " p. 6.

34. Interestingly, this Mutoscope was coin-operated, and Crockwell indicates that it eventually broke down from too many coins in its coin box. It would seem that the commercial side of the Mutoscope, the deposit of the coin, was part of Crockwell's essential fascination with the device. He was, after all, a commercial artist.

35. Linda Williams, *Hard Core: Power, Pleasure and the "Frenzy of the Visible"* (Berkeley: University of California Press, 1989), pp. 78–80.

36. Linda Williams, "Corporealized Observers: Visual Pornographies and the 'Carnal Densities of Vision,' " in *Fugitive Images From Photography to Video*, ed. Patrice Petro (Bloomington: Indiana University Press, 1995), p. 19.

37. Ibid., p. 10.

38. Gilles Deleuze and Felix Guattari, *Anti-Oedipus: Capitalism and Schizophrenia* (Minneapolis: University of Minnesota Press, 1983). The concept of desiring machines is used throughout this work, but see pp. 36–41 for a key presentation.

39. Crockwell, draft of *Image* article, Crockwell file, GEH.

40. Crockwell's machine could also be viewed by more than one person at a time, since the peep show viewer masking device was removed. Unlike the version in the MOMA offices, this display machine did not take coins.

FILMMAKERS OF THE FIRST AMERICAN
AVANTE-GARDE

BIBLIOGRAPHY

INDEX

FILMMAKERS OF THE FIRST
AMERICAN AVANT-GARDE

Sara Katheryn Arledge
(Born 28 September 1911, Mojave, Calif.)
Artist
Films: *Introspection* (1941); *What Is a Man?* (1958); *Tender Images* (1978); *Interior Garden* (1978); *Interior Garden II* (1978); *Iridum Sinus* (*Cave of the Rainbows*) (1980); *What Do Two Rights Make?* (1982).

Roger Barlow
(3 March 1912, Minneapolis–9 May 1990, Charlotte, Va.)
Cameraman/director
Films: *New Architecture* (1934); *Danger on the Streets* (1936); *Educated Feet* (1936); *Federal Theatre Project* (1936); *CCC at La Purissima* (1937); *CCC at Mono* (1937); *Even As You and I* (1937, with Hay, Robbins); *Give Us This Day* (1938); *The City* (1939); *Man and Medicine* (1939); *Sarah Lawrence* (1940); *Valley Town* (1940); *One Tenth of a Nation* (1940); *Wings of Youth* (1940); *Letter from Camp* (1940); *Home Front* (1940); *A Place to Live* (1941); *Autobiography of a Jeep* (1943); *To Your Health* (1950); *Round Trip* (1952); *Confidential File* (1955, TV); *Oedipus Rex* (1956); *An Affair of the Skin* (1963); *The Royal Hunt of the Sun* (1969); *The Plastic Dome of Norma Jean* (1970).

Josef Berne
(1904, Kiev–19 December 1964, Los Angeles)
Film director/producer
Films: *Destiny* (ca. 1932); *Dawn to Dawn* (1934); *Mirele Efros* (1939); *Seven Beers with the Wrong Man* (1941); *Nightmare of a Goon* (1942); *From the Indies*

to the Andes (in His Undies) (1942); *Hong Kong Blues* (1942); *You Made Me Love You* (1942); *The Good Newsreel* (1942); *Heavenly Music* (1943); *New Orleans Blues* (1944); *Sweet Swing* (1944); *Hilda Was a Darn Good Cook* (1944); *They Live in Fear* (1944); *Down Missouri Way* (1946); *Catskill Honeymoon* (1950).

Thomas Bouchard

(1896–5 March 1984, Brewster, Mass.)
Photographer
Films: *Underground Printer* (1934, with Jacobs); *The Shakers* (1938); *Queen of the Gypsy Dancers* (?); *The Golden Fleece* (?); *Fernand Leger in America—His New Realism* (1942); *Jean Helion: One Artist at Work* (1946); *The Birth of Painting* (1950); *Joan Miro Makes a Color Print* (1948); *Around and About Miro* (1959).

Irving Browning

(15 May 1895, New York–1961, New York)
Photographer
Films: *House of Secrets* (1929); *Unmasked* (1930); *City of Contrasts* (1931); *The New Legion* (1934, with Manon Miller); *Edward Steichen—Master of the Camera* (1936); *Getting Your Money's Worth* (1937, camera); *United States Military Academy, West Point* (1940, camera); *Women in Photography* (1941); *Babies by Banister* (?).

Francis Joseph Bruguière

(16 October 1879, San Francisco–8 May 1945, London).
Photographer
Films: *Danse Macabre* (1922, with Murphy, A. Bolm); *The Way* (1923, unfinished); *Theory* (1925?); *Light Rhythms* (1931, with Oswell Blakeston).

Jules V. D. Bucher

(?)
Cameraman
Films: *The Child Psychology Series* (1930–1931): *A Study in Infant Behavior, The Growth of Infant Behavior: Early Stages, The Growth of Infant Behavior: Later Stages, Posture and Locomotion, From Creeping to Walking, A Baby's Day at Twelve Weeks, A Thirty-Six Week Behavior Day, A Behavior Day at Forty-eight Weeks, Behavior Patterns at One Year, Learning and Growth, Early Social Behavior, Life Begins; Child of Mother India* (1933); *The Lord Helps Those* (1934); *The New World* (1934); *A Study of Negro Artists* (1935); Julian Bryan Travelogues (1935–1938); *The Negro and YMCA* (1938); *The City* (1939, camera); *New Worlds* (1940); *Men and Dust* (1940); *America's Making* (1940); *High Plain* (1943, camera); *Good Neighbor Family* (1943); *The Window Cleaner* (1945).

Rudy Burckhardt
(Born 1914, Basel)
Photographer
Films: *145 West 21* (1936); *Seeing the World—Part One: A Visit to New York* (1937); *Haiti* (1938); *The Pursuit of Happiness* (1940); *The Uncle's Return* (1940); *Montgomery, Alabama* (1941); *Trinidad* (1943); *How Wide Is Sixth Avenue?* (1945); *Up and Down the Waterfront* (1946); *The Climate of New York* (1948); *Mounting Tension* (1950); *See Naples . . . And the Island of Ishia* (1951); *Under the Brooklyn Bridge* (1953); *The Automotive Story* (1954); *The Aviary* (1954, with Cornell); *Nymphlight* (1955–1957); *A Fable for Fountains* (1955– 1957); *Verona* (1955); *What Mozart Saw on Mulberry Street* (1956); *Eastside Summer* (1959); *Millions in Business As Usual* (1961); *Shoot the Moon* (1962); *Lurk* (1964); *Daisy* (1966); *Square Times* (1967); *The Apple* (1967); *Money* (1968); *Paradise Arms* (1968); *Tarzam* (1969); *Summer* (1970); *Inside Dope* (1971); *Made in Maine* (1972); *Doldrums* (1972); *Avenues of Communication* (1973); *Caterpillar* (1973); *Slipperella* (1973); *City Pasture* (1974); *Default Averted* (1975); *Saroche* (1975); *The Bottle of the Bulge* (1975); *Dwellings* (1975); *Sodom and Gomorrah, New York 10036* (1976); *Good Evening Everybody* (1977); *Six Days* (1978); *Alex Katz Painting* (1978); *Mobile Homes* (1979); *Neil Welliver Painting in Maine* (1980); *Sonatina and Fugue* (1980); *Rads on Wheels; Cerveza Bud* (1981); *Yvonne Jacquette Painting "Autumn Expansion"* (1981); *Bach's Last Keyboard Fugue* (1981); *All Major Credit Cards* (1982); *Indelible, Inedible* (1983); *Untitled* (1984); *Around the World in Thirty Years* (1984); *The Nude Pond* (1985); *Central Park in the Dark* (1985); *Dancers, Buildings and People in the Street* (1986); *In Bed* (1986); *Zipper* (1987).

Paul Burnford
(Born 19 July 1914, London)
Director
Films: *Symphony of Nature* (1933); *Moods of Nature* (1935); *Rooftops of London* (1936); *Statue Parade* (1936); *To-day We Live* (1937, camera); *Free to Roam* (1938); *Zoo Babies* (1938); *The Zoo and You* (1938); *Birth of the Year* (1938); *Time in the Sun* (1939, editor); *Speed of the Plow* (1939, camera); *Storm Warning* (1940); *Kid in Upper Four* (1943); *Patrolling the Ether* (1944); *Nostradamus IV* (1944); *Return from Nowhere* (1944); *Storm* (1944); *Brothers in Blood* (1944); *Fall Guy* (1945); *It Looks Like Rain* (1945); *Little White Lies* (1945); *Strange Destiny* (1945); *Adventures of Rusty* (1945); *Seven Little Ducks* (1946); *Girls' Basketball for Beginners* (1946); *What Is a City?* (1947); *Insect Zoo* (1947); *Firehouse Dog* (1955); *Discovering Dark and Light* (1965); *Paper in Art* (1967); *Our Immigrant Heritage* (1968); *Fiber in Art* (1968); *Rhythm and Movement in Art* (1969); *Art, People, Feelings* (1971); *Frame by Frame* (1973).

Mary Ellen Bute
(25 November 1906, Houston, Tex.–17 October 1983, New York)
Artist
Films: *Synchromy* (1933, unfinished, with Schillinger, Jacobs); *Rhythm in Light* (1934, with Webber, Nemeth); *Synchromy No. 2* (1935); *Dada* (1936); *Parabola* (1937, with Nemeth); *Escape—Toccata and Fugue* (1937, with Nemeth); *Spook Sport* (1939, with Norman McLaren); *Tarantella* (1940, with Nemeth); *Polka Graph* (1947); *Color Rhapsodie* (1948); *Imagination* (1948); *New Sensations in Sound* (1949); *Pastorale* (1950); *Abstronic* (1952); *Mood Contrasts* (1953); *The Boy Who Saw Through* (1956, producer); *Passages From Finnegans Wake* (1965).

Joseph Cornell
(24 December 1903, Nyack, N.Y.–29 December 1972, Flushing, N.Y.)
Artist
Films: *Rose Hobart* (1936); *Cotillion* (1937–1970, edited by Larry Jordan); *The Children's Party* (1937–1970, edited by L. Jordan); *The Midnight Party* (1937–1970, edited by Larry Jordan); *Aviary* (1954, with Burkhardt); *Joanne, Union Sq.* (1954, with Burkhardt); *A Legend for Fountains* (1954, with Burkhardt); *Gnir Rednow* (1955, with Stan Brakhage); *Centuries of June* (1955, with Stan Brakhage); *Nymphlight* (1957, with R. Burkhardt); *Angel* (1957, with Burkhardt); *Seraphina's Garden* (1958, with Burkhardt); *Flushing Meadows* (1965, with Larry Jordan).

Stanley Cortez (Stanislaus Krantz)
(Born 4 November 1908, New York)
Photographer/cameraman
Films: *Sherzo* (1932, with Vorkapich); *Four Days Wonder* (1936); *Armoured Car* (1937); *The Wildcatter* (1937); *Danger on the Air* (1938); *Exposed* (1938); *Lady in the Morgue* (1938); *The Last Express* (1938); *For Love of Money* (1939); *The Forgotten Woman* (1939); *Hawaiian Nights* (1939); *Laugh It Off* (1939); *Risky Business* (1939); *They Asked for It* (1939); *Alias the Deacon* (1940); *The Leather Pushers* (1940); *Love, Honor, and Oh Baby* (1940); *Margie* (1940); *Meet the Wildcat* (1940); *The Badlands of Dakota* (1941); *The Black Cat* (1941); *A Dangerous Game* (1941); *Moonlight in Hawaii* (1941); *San Antonio Rose* (1941); *Sealed Lips* (1941); *Bombay Clipper* (1942); *Eagle Squadron* (1942); *The Magnificent Ambersons* (1942); *The Powers Girl* (1942); *Flesh and Fantasy* (1943); *Since You Went Away* (1944); *Smash Up* (1947); *Secret Beyond the Door* (1948); *Smart Woman* (1948); *The Man on the Eiffel Tower* (1949); *The Admiral Was a Lady* (1950); *The Whipped* (1950); *The Basketball Fix* (1951); *Fort Defiance* (1951); *Abbott and Costello Meet Captain Kidd* (1952); *Models, Inc.* (1952); *Stronghold* (1952, Mexico); *The Diamond Queen* (1953); *Shark River* (1953); *Dragon's Gold* (1954); *Riders to the Stars* (1954); *Black Tuesday* (1955);

The Night of the Hunter (1955); *The Man from Del Rio* (1956); *The Three Faces of Eve* (1957); *Top Secret Affair* (1957); *The Angry Red Planet* (1959); *Thunder in the Sun* (1959); *Vice Raid* (1959); *Dinosaurus* (1960); *Back Street* (1961); *Shock Corridor* (1963); *The Candidate* (1964); *The Naked Kiss* (1964); *Nightmare in the Sun* (1964); *They Saved Hitler's Brain* (1964); *Young Dillinger* (1965); *Ghost in the Invisible Bikini* (1966); *The Navy Vs. the Night Monsters* (1966); *Blue* (1968); *The Bridge at Remagen* (1969); *Another Man, Another Chance* (1970).

Douglass Crockwell
(29 April 1904, Columbus, Ohio–30 November 1968, Glens Falls, N.Y.)
Magazine illustrator
Films: *Fantasmagoria I* (1938); *Fantasmagoria II* (1939); *Fantasmagoria III* (1940); *The Chase* (1942); *Glens Falls Sequence* (1946); *The Long Bodies* (1947). Mutoscope reels: *Red* (1949); *A Long Body* (1950); *Random Glow* (ca. 1950s); *Stripes* (ca. 1950s); *Ode to David* (ca. 1950s); *Around the Valley* (ca. 1950s).

Floyd Crosby
(12 December 1899, New York–30 September 1985, Ojai, Calif.)
Cameraman
Films: *Tabu* (1930); *Nesting of the Sea Turtle* (1933); *Pueblo* (unfinished); *The River* (1936); *Fight for Life* (1940); *Power and the Land* (1940); *Look to Lockheed for Leadership* (1940); *It Is for Us the Living* (1940); *Youth Gets a Break* (1940); *The Land* (1942); *My Father's House* (1947); *The Brave Bulls* (1951); *High Noon* (1952); *Man Crazy* (1953); *Man in the Darkness* (1953); *Mystery Lake* (1953); *The Steel Lady* (1953); *The Fast and Furious* (1954); *The Monster from the Ocean Floor* (1954); *Apache Woman* (1955); *Five Guns West* (1955); *Hell's Horizon* (1955); *The Naked Street* (1955); *Shack Out on 101* (1955); *Attack of the Crab Monsters* (1957); *Carnival Rock* (1957); *Hell Canyon Outlaws* (1957); *Naked Paradise* (1957); *Reform School Girl* (1957); *Ride Out for Revenge* (1957); *Rock All Night* (1957); *Teenage Doll* (1957); *The Cry Baby Killer* (1958); *Hot Rod Gang* (1958); *Machine Gun Kelly* (1958); *The Old Man and the Sea* (1958); *She-Gods of Shark Reef* (1958); *Suicide Battalion* (1958); *Teenage Cavemen* (1958); *War of the Satellites* (1958); *Wolf Larsen* (1958); *Crime and Punishment* (1959); *I, Mobster* (1959); *The Miracle of the Hills* (1959); *The Rookie* (1959); *The Wonderful Country* (1959); *Freckles* (1960); *The High-Powered Rifle* (1960); *House of Usher* (1960); *Twelve Hours to Kill* (1960); *Talk Tall* (1960); *Cold Wind in August* (1961); *The Explosive Generation* (1961); *The Gambler Wore a Gun* (1961); *Little Shepherd of Kingdom Come* (1961); *The Pit and the Pendulum* (1961); *The Purple Hills* (1961); *Seven Women from Hell* (1961); *The Two Little Bears* (1961); *The Firebrand* (1962); *Hand of Death* (1962); *The Premature Burial* (1962); *Tales of Terror* (1962); *Terror at Black Falls* (1962); *Woman Hunt* (1962); *X—The Man with X-Ray Eyes* (1963); *Black Zoo* (1963); *The Haunted Palace*

(1963); *The Raven* (1963); *The Yellow Canary* (1963); *The Young Racers* (1963); *Bikini Beach* (1964); *The Comedy of Terrors* (1964); *Pajama Party* (1964); *Raiders from Beneath the Sea* (1964); *Beach Blanket Bingo* (1965); *How to Stuff a Wild Bikini* (1965); *Indian Paint* (1965); *Sallah* (1965, Israel); *Sergeant Deadhead* (1965); *Fireball 590* (1966); *The Arousers* (1973).

Boris Deutsch
(4 June 1895, Krasnogorka, Russia–16 January 1978, Los Angeles)
Artist
Films: *Lullaby* (1925).

Emlen Etting
(24 August 1905, Merion, Pa.–20 July 1993, Philadelphia)
Artist
Films: *Oramunde* (1933); *Poem 8* (1933); *Laureate* (1940); *Encounters* (1941); *Make Love, Not War* (1969); *Face Values* (1969).

Paul Fejos
(24 January 1897, Budapest–23 April 1963, New York)
Anthropologist
Films: *The Last Moment* (1928); *Lonesome* (1929); *Broadway* (1929); *The Last Performance* (1929); *Captain of the Guard* (1930, uncredited); *Menschen Hinter Gittern* (1931, German version of *Big House*), *Fantomas* (1931); *Marie* (1932); *Itel a Balaton* (1932); *Sonnenstrahl* (1933); *Frühlingsstimmen* (1933); *Flugten Fra Millionerne* (1934); *Fange Nr. 1* (1935); *Det Gyldne Smil* (1935); *Horizons Noir* (1935–1936); 1937-38: *The Tribe Lives On, The Age of Bamboo at Mentawei, The Chief's Son Is Dead, The Dragon of Komodo, The Village near the Pleasant Fountain, Tambora, To Sail Is Necessary; A Handful of Rice* (1938); *Yagua* (1941).

Ben Finney
(?)
Films: *Ob-seen* (1926).

Robert Flaherty
(16 February 1884, Iron Mountain, Mich.–23 July 1951, Brattleboro, Vt.)
Filmmaker
Films: *Nanook of the North* (1922); *The Pottery Maker* (1925); *Moana* (1926); *Twenty-four Dollar Island* (1927); *White Shadows of the South Seas* (1928); *Tabu* (1931); *Industrial Britain* (1933); *Man of Aran* (1934); *Elephant Boy* (1937); *The Land* (1942); *Louisiana Story* (1948).

Robert Florey
(14 September 1900, Paris–16 May 1979, Los Angeles)
Director
Films: *The Mad Doctor* (1926, unfinished); *That Model from Paris* (1927); *One Hour of Love* (1927); *The Romantic Age* (1927); *Face Value* (1927); *The Life and Death of 9413—A Hollywood Extra* (1928, with Vorkapich); *The Love of Zero* (1928); *Johann the Coffin Maker* (1928); *Alice Boulden* (1928); *Eddie Cantor* (1928); *Night Club* (1929); *Back in Your Own Back Yard* (1929); *Borah Minnevitch and His Harmonica Rascals* (1929); *Lillian Roth and Her Band* (1929); *Lillian Roth and Her Piano Boys* (1929); *Songs and Dances of Lillian Roth* (1929); *Songs of Alice Boulden* (1929); *Tito Schipa* (1929); *Elinor Glynn* (1929); *The Pusher-in-the-Face* (1929); *Bonjour, New York!* (1929); *Skyscraper Symphony* (1929); *Trees of England* (1929); *The Hole in the Wall* (1929); *Glorifying the American Girl* (1929); *The Cocoanuts* (1929); *The Battle of Paris* (1929); *La Route Est Belle* (1930); *L'Amour Chante/Komm' zu Mir zum Rendezvous/El Professor de Mi Señora* (Germany) (1930); *Le Blanc et le Noir* (1930); *Murders in the Rue Morgue* (1932); *The Man Called Back* (1932); *Those We Love* (1932); *Girl Missing* (1933); *Ex-Lady* (1933); *The House on 56th Street* (1933); *Bedside* (1934); *Smarty* (1934); *Registered Nurse* (1934); *I Sell Anything* (1934); *I Am a Thief* (1935); *The Woman in Red* (1935); *The Florentine Dagger* (1935); *Don't Bet on Blondes* (1935); *Going Highbrow* (1935); *The Pay-off* (1935); *Ship Cafe* (1935); *The Preview Murder Mystery* (1936); *Till We Meet Again* (1936); *Hollywood Boulevard* (1936); *Outcast* (1937); *King of Gamblers* (1937); *Mountain Music* (1937); *This Way Please* (1937); *Daughter of Shanghai* (1937); *Dangerous to Know* (1938); *King of Alcatraz*(1938); *Disbarred* (1939); *Hotel Imperial* (1939); *The Magnificent Fraud* (1939); *Death of a Champion* (1939); *Parole Fixer* (1940); *Women Without Names* (1940); *The Face Behind the Mask* (1941); *Meet Boston Blackie* (1941); *Two in a Taxi* (1941); *Dangerously They Live* (1942); *Lady Gangster* (1942); *The Desert Song* (1943); *Man from Frisco* (1944); *Roger Touhy—Gangster* (1944); *God Is My Co-Pilot* (1945); *Danger Signal* (1945); *Monsieur Verdoux* (1946); *The Beast with Five Fingers* (1946); *Tarzan and the Mermaids* (1948); *Rogues' Regiment* (1948); *Outpost in Morocco* (1949); *The Crooked Way* (1949); *The Vicious Years* (1950); *Johnny One-Eye* (1950); *Four Star Playhouse: The Last Voyage* (1953, TV).

John A. Flory
(28 July 1910, Cleveland–7 October 1987, Cleveland)
Industrial filmmaker
Films: *Panther Woman of the Needle Trades, or The Lovely Life of Little Lisa* (with Steiner, 1931); *This Is America* (production assistant, 1933); *Mr. Motorboat's Last Stand* (1933, with Huff); *The Harbor* (1935); *Liberty for the Housewife*

(1936); *Want to Go Fishing?* (1937); *The City* (1938); *Song of a City* (1941); *Airlift to Berlin* (1949).

Roman Freulich
(1 March 1898, Czenstockowa, Poland–2 March 1974, Hollywood)
Photographer
Films: *Prisoner* (1934), *Roan Stallion* (1934, unfinished); *Broken Earth* (1936); *Stevedore* (1937-1938, unfinished).

Jo Gerson (Josef Morris Gerson)
(Born 1907, Philadelphia)
Art instructor
Films: *Transition* (1927, with Hirshman, Jacobs); *Mobile Composition No. 1* (1928, with Hirshman, Jacobs); *The Story of a Nobody* (1930, with Hirshman).

Dwinell Grant
(Born 11 August 1912, Springfield, Ohio)
Artist
Films: *Composition 1 (Themis)* (1940); *Composition 2 (Comtrathemis)* (1941); *Abstract Experiments* (1941–1942); *Composition 3 (Spelean Dance)* (1942); *Color Sequence* (1943); *Three Themes in Variation* (1945); *Composition 4 (Stereoscopic #1)* (1945); *Composition 5 (Fugue)* (1949); *Pepsi-Cola Commercial* (1960); *Composition 6* (1975).

Harry Hay
(Born 7 April 1912, Worthing/Sussex, England)
Trade union and gay rights activist
Films: *Even As You and I* (1937, with Barlow, Robbins); *Suicide* (unfinished, 1938).

(James) Jerome Hill
(1905, St. Paul, Minn.–21 November 1972, New York)
Artist
Films: *Tom Jones* (1927, with Bill Hinkel); *The Magic Umbrella* (1927); *Fortune Teller* (1932); *Death in the Forenoon, Or Who's Afraid of Ernest Hemingway?* (1933/1965); *Snow Flight* (1938); *Seeing Eye* (1940); *Grandma Moses* (1950); *Salzberg Seminar* (1950); *Cassis* (1950); *Albert Schweitzer* (1957); *The Sand Castle* (1961); *Open the Door and See All the People* (1964); *Bach* (1965); *The Artist's Friend* (1966); *The Canaries* (1968); *Merry Christmas* (1969); *Film Portrait* (1970).

Hy Hirsch
(1911, Chicago–1960, Paris)
Photographer
Films: *Even As You and I* (1937, actor); *Horror Dream* (1947); *Clinic of Strumble* (1947); *Divertissement Rococo* (1952); *Come Closer* (1953); *Change of Key* (1950s); *Chasse des Touches* (ca. 1950s); *Djinn/Recherche* (1950s); *Scratch Pad* (1950s); *Decollages Recolles* (1950s); *Gyromorphosis* (1958); *Autumn Spectrum* (1958); *Double Jam* (1958); *Eneri* (1958); *Defense d'Afficher* (1959); *Le Couleur de la Forme* (1960).

Louis Hirshman (Hershell Louis)
(21 August 1905, Russia–26 July 1986, Philadelphia)
Artist
Films: *Transition* (1927, with Jacobs, Gerson); *Mobile Composition* (1928, with Jacobs, Gerson); *The Story of a Nobody* (1930, with Gerson).

John Ivan Hoffman
(1904, Hungary–6 January 1980, Altedena, Calif.)
Special effects cameraman
Films: *One Night of Love* (1934); *Between Two Women* (1937); *Navy Blue and Gold* (1937); *Man-Proof* (1938); *Moods of the Sea* (1942, with Vorkapich); *Crimson Canary* (1945); *Strange Confession* (1945); *Prelude to Spring* (1946); *The Fabulous Suzanne* (1946); *The Wreck of the Hesperus* (1948); *The Lone Wolf and His Lady* (1949); *I Killed Geronimo* (1950); *Five* (1951); *Storm Over Tibet* (1952); *Bwana Devil* (1953); *The Nun and the Sergeant* (1962); *War Hunt* (1962).

Theodore Huff (Edmund Newell Huff)
(December 1905, Englewood, N.J.–15 March 1953, Farmingdale, N.Y.)
Film historian
Films: *Hearts of the West* (1931); *Little Geezer* (1932); *Mr. Motorboat's Last Stand* (1933, with Flory); *Ghost Town: The Story of Fort Lee* (1935, with Mark Borgatte); *The Uncomfortable Man* (1948, with Kent Munson); *The Stone Children* (1948, with Kent Munson).

Lewis Jacobs
(Born 22 April 1906, Philadelphia)
Filmmaker/historian
Films: *Transition* (1927, unfinished, with Gerson, Hirshman); *Mobile Composition No. 1* (1928, with Gerson, Hirshman); *Western Pennsylvania and Kentucky Miners' Strike* (1931, with Joseph Hudyma, Tom Brandon); *Scottsboro Trial* (1932 with T. Brandon); *Commercial Medley* (1933); *The Scottsboro Boys* (1933,

with Leo Hurwitz, Leo Seltzer); *Footnote to Fact* (1934); *Synchromy* (unfinished, with Bute, Schillinger); *Underground Printer* (1934, with Bouchard); *Hopi* (1935); *From Tree Trunk to Head* (1939); *To My Unborn Son* (1943, script); *Return from Nowhere* (1944, script); *Sunday Beach* (1947–1948); *Birth of a Building* (1950); *Lincoln Speaks at Gettysburg* (1950); *A Sculpture Speaks* (1952); *Buma: African Sculpture Speaks* (1952); *Matthew Brady: Photographer of an Era* (1953); *The Raven* (1954); *Ode to a Grecian Urn* (1954); *The Book of Job* (1945); *Case History* (1956, released 1964 as *Another Time . . .*); *The World That Nature Forgot* (1956); *Old Art, New Magic* (1957); *The Stylists* (1957); *Fibers and Civilization* (1959); *Ages of Time* (1960); *Face of the World* (1960); *The Rise of Greek Art* (1960); *Gothic Art* (1960); *Another Time: Another Place* (1964).

Merle Johnson
(?)
Artist
Films: *Knee Deep in Love* (1926).

Elia Kazan (Elia Kazanjoglou)
(Born 7 September 1909, Istanbul)
Director
Films: *Pie in the Sky* (1934, with Steiner, Lerner, M. D. Thatcher); *People of the Cumberland* (1938); *It's Up to You* (1941); *A Tree Grows in Brooklyn* (1945); *The Sea of Grass* (1947); *Boomerang* (1947); *Gentleman's Agreement* (1947); *Pinky* (1949); *Panic in the Streets* (1950); *A Streetcar Named Desire* (1951); *Viva Zapata!* (1952); *Man on a Tightrope* (1953); *On the Waterfront* (1954); *East of Eden* (1955); *Baby Doll* (1956); *A Face in the Crowd* (1957); *Wild River* (1960); *Splendour in the Grass* (1961); *America America* (1963); *The Arrangement* (1969); *The Visitors* (1972); *The Last Tycoon* (1976).

Charles Klein (Karl Friedrich Klein)
(28 January 1898, Namedy, Germany–20 December 1962, Cologne)
Film director
Films: *The Tell-Tale Heart* (1928); *Blindfold* (1928); *The Lion and the Mouse* (1928); *Pleasure Crazed* (1929); *The Sin Sister* (1929); *Wenn am Sonntag die Dorfmusik spielt* (1933); *Zigeunerblut* (1934); *Urlaub auf Ehrenwort* (1937); *Der Vierte kommt nicht* (1939); *Die Frau ohne Vergangenheit* (1939); *Ihr Privatsekretär* (1940); *Urlaub auf Ehrenwort* (1955).

Francis Lee
(Born 1913, New York)
Artist
Films: *1941* (1941); *Le Bijou* (1946); *Idyll* (1948); *The Black Fox* (1962, animation sequence); *Film-Makers' Showcase* (1963); *Craftsmen in Concert*

(1969); *Cooking in the 70's* (1970); *Images* (1970); *Soundroundus* (1973); *A Scream Away from Happiness* (1973); *Synthesis* (1975); *Sumi-E* (1975); *Illuminations #1* (1976, video); *Illuminations #2* (1976, video).

Irving Lerner

(7 March 1909, New York–25 December 1976, Hollywood)
Documentary filmmaker
Films: *Hunger 1932* (1933, with Leo Seltzer, Leo Hurwitz, Sam Brody); *Pie in the Sky* (1934, with Kazan, Steiner, M. D. Thatcher); *The World of Today: Sunnyside* (1936); *The World of Today: Black Legion* (1936); *China Strikes Back* (1937, with Leyda); *One Third of a Nation* (1938); *Valley Town* (1940); *The Children Must Learn* (1940); *A Place to Live* (1941); *Tall Tales* (1941); *The Land* (1942); *The Autobiography of a Jeep* (1943); *Good Neighbor Family* (1943); *Toscanini: The Hymn of Nations* (1944); *For Better Tomorrow* (1945); *Library of Congress* (1945); *Till the Ends of the Earth* (1945); *Human Growth* (1945); *To Hear Your Banjo Play* (1946); *Muscle Beach* (1948); *Oedipus* (1953); *Man Crazy* (1953); *Edge of Fury* (1958); *Murder by Contract* (1958); *City of Fear* (1959); *Studs Lonigan* (1960); *Cry of Battle* (1963); *Custer of the West* (1968); *The Royal Hunt of the Sun* (1969); *Executive Action* (1973); *Steppenwolf* (1974); *The River Niger* (1976); *New York, New York* (1977).

Jay Leyda

(12 February 1910, Detroit–15 February 1988, New York)
Film historian/archivist
Films: *A Bronx Morning* (1931); *China Strikes Back* (1937, with Lerner); *People of the Cumberland* (1938, with Sidney Meyers); *Youth Gets a Break* (1940); *Mission to Moscow* (1943).

Charles MacArthur

(5 May 1895, Scranton, Pa.–21 April 1956, New York)
Scriptwriter
Films: *Ob-Seen* (1926, with Finney); *The Girl Said No* (1930); *Paid* (1930); *Way for the Sailor* (1930); *The Front Page* (1931); *The New Adventures of Get-Rich-Quick Wallingford* (1931); *The Sin of Madelon Claudet* (1931); *The Unholy Garden* (1931); *Rasputin and the Empress* (1932); *Crime Without Passion* (1934); *Twentieth Century* (1934); *Barbary Coast* (1935); *The Scoundrel* (1935); *Once Upon a Blue Moon* (1936); *Soak the Rich* (1936); *Gone with the Wind* (1939); *Gunga Din* (1939); *Wuthuring Heights* (1939); *His Girl Friday* (1940); *I Take This Woman* (1940); *The Senator Was Indiscreet* (1947); *Lulu Belle* (1948); *Perfect Strangers* (1950); *Jumbo* (1962); *The Front Page* (1974).

M. G. MacPherson (Artkino)
(?)
Director
Films: *War Under the Sea* (1929, with Michelson); *The Trap* (1930, with Michelson); *The Power of Suggestion* (1930, with Michelson); *Oil—A Symphony in Motion* (1933, with Michelson).

Mylon Meriam
(Born 1900, Brooklyn, N.Y.)
Artist
Films: Untitled abstract films (1941).

Jean D. Michelson (Artkino)
(?)
Editor
Films: *War Under the Sea* (1929, with MacPherson); *The Trap* (1930, with MacPherson); *The Power of Suggestion* (1930, with MacPherson); *Oil—A Symphony in Motion* (1933, with MacPherson); *Sweden—Land of the Vikings* (1934).

Dudley Murphy
(10 July 1897, Winchester, Mass.—22 February 1968, Los Angeles)
Film director
Films: *The Soul of the Cypress* (1920); *Aphrodite* (1920); *Anywhere out of the World* (1920); *The Way of Love* (1921); *The Romance of the White Chrysanthemum* (1921); *Danse Macabre* (1922, with Adolph Bolm, F. Bruguière); *High Speed Lee* (1923); *O Sole Mio* (1923); *Ballet Mècanique* (1924, with Fernand Léger); *Alex the Great* (1928); *Stocks and Blonds* (1928); *The Traveller* (1929); *The Burglar* (1924); *St. Louis Blues* (1929); *Jazz Heaven* (1929); *Black and Tan* (1929); *Frankie and Johnny* (1930); *Dracula* (1931, script); *Confessions of a Co-ed* (1931); *Twenty-four Hours* (1931); *A Lesson in Golf* (1932); *The Sport Parade* (1932); *The Emperor Jones* (1933); *The Night Is Young* (1935); *Don't Gamble with Love* (1936); *One Third of a Nation* (1938); *Main Street Lawyer* (1939); *Abercrombie Had a Zombie* (1941); *Alabamy Bound* (1941); *Easy Street* (1941); *I Don't Want to Set the World on Fire* (1941); *Jazzy Joe* (1941); *Carrying the Torch for Jim* (1941); *Lazybones* (1941); *Merry-go-round* (1942); *Mountain Dew* (1942); *Yes, Indeed* (1942); *Yolanda* (1942, Mexico); *Alma del Bronce* (1944).

C. O. Nelson
(Born Chicago)
Labor organizer
Films: *Hunger: The National Hunger March to Washington* (1932); *Halsted Street* (1934).

Theodore J. Nemeth
(1911, Cambridge, Mass.–December 1986, New York)
Industrial filmmaker
Films: *Rhythm in Light* (1934, with Bute); *Synchromy No. 2* (1935, with Bute); *Parabola* (1937, with Bute); *Escape—Toccata and Fugue* (1937, with Bute); *Tarantella* (1940, with Bute); *Pastorale* (1950, with Bute); *The Boy Who Saw Through* (1956, with Bute, G. Stoney); *The Time Piece* (1966); *Fable Safe* (1971).

Warren A. Newcombe
(Born 28 April 1894, Waltham, Mass.)
Artist/special-effects technician/studio executive
Films: *The Enchanted City* (1922); *The Sea of Dreams* (1923); *Dr. Jekyll and Mr. Hyde* (1941); *The Feminine Touch* (1941); *Smilin' Through* (1941); *Tarzan's Secret Treasure* (1941); *They Met in Bombay* (1941); *I Married an Angel* (1942); *Keeper of the Flame* (1942); *Mrs. Miniver* (1942); *Reunion in France* (1942); *Rio Rita* (1942); *Tarzan's New York Adventure* (1942); *Tennessee Johnson* (1942); *Tortilla Flat* (1942); *A Yank at Eton* (1942); *Bataan* (1943); *A Guy Named Joe* (1943); *Lassie, Come Home* (1943); *Madame Curie* (1943); *Presenting Lily Mars* (1943); *Whistling in Brooklyn* (1943); *Dragon Seed* (1944); *Gaslight* (1944); *Kismet* (1944); *Mrs. Parkington* (1944); *National Velvet* (1944); *Thirty Seconds Over Tokyo* (1944); *The White Cliffs of Dover* (1944); *Adventure* (1945); *Her Highness and the Bellboy* (1945); *Son of Lassie* (1945); *The Valley of Decision* (1945); *What Next, Corporal Hargrave?* (1945); *Yolanda and the Thief* (1945); *The Harvey Girls* (1946); *Holiday in Mexico* (1946); *The Hoodlum Saint* (1946); *The Sailor Takes a Wife* (1946); *Till the Clouds Roll By* (1946); *The Yearling* (1946); *The Beginning or the End* (1947); *Cass Timberlane* (1947); *Green Dolphin Street* (1947); *High Barbaree* (1947); *The High Wall* (1947); *The Hucksters* (1949); *The Sea of Grass* (1947); *Song of Love* (1947); *B. F.'s Daughter* (1948); *A Date with Judy* (1948); *Easter Parade* (1948); *Homecoming* (1948); *Julia Misbehaves* (1948); *A Southern Yankee* (1948); *The Three Musketeers* (1948); *The Bribe* (1949); *The Great Sinner* (1949); *Little Women* (1949); *On the Town* (1949); *The Stratton Story* (1949); *Take Me Out to the Ball Game* (1949); *Crisis* (1950); *Kim* (1950); *Pagan Love Song* (1950); *To Please a Lady* (1950); *Two Weeks with Love,* (1950); *Watch the Bride* (1950); *An American in Paris* (1951); *The People Against O'Hara* (1951); *Royal Wedding* (1951); *Show Boat* (1951); *The Strip* (1951); *Texas Carnival* (1951); *The Bad and the Beautiful* (1952); *The Merry Widow* (1952); *Pat and Mike* (1952); *Plymouth Adventure* (1952); *The Prisoner of Zenda* (1952); *Scaramouche* (1952); *Singin' in the Rain* (1952); *Above and Beyond* (1953); *The Actress* (1953); *All the Brothers Were Valiant* (1953); *Dream Wide* (1953); *Escape from Port Bravo* (1953); *Julius Caesar* (1953); *Kiss Me Kate* (1953); *Latin Lovers* (1953); *Lili* (1953); *Sombrero* (1953); *Deep in My Heart* (1954); *The Long, Long Trailer* (1954); *Rhapsody*

(1954); *Rose Marie* (1954); *Diane* (1955); *Green Fire* (1955); *I'll Cry Tomorrow* (1955); *It's Always Fair Weather* (1955); *Love Me or Leave Me* (1955); *The Prodigal* (1955); *Trial* (1955); *Meet Me in Las Vegas* (1956); *The Opposite Sex* (1956); *Raintree County* (1957); *The Wings of Eagles* (1957).

Claire Parker

(Boston–October 1981, Paris)
Animator
Films (all with Alexej Alexeieff): *Une Nuit sur le Mont Chauve* (1934); *La Belle aux Bois Dormant* (1935); *Lingner-Werke* (1935); *Opta-Empfang* (1935); *L'Orchestre Automatique* (1935); *Parade des Champeaux* (1936); *Le Trône de France* (1936); *Franck Aroma* (1937); *L'Eau d'Evian* (1937); *Huilor* (1937); *Nestor Martin* (1937); *Le Crème Simon* (1937); *Les Vêtements Sigrand* (1937); *Étoile Nouvelle* (1937); *Jaffa* (1938); *Balatum* (1938); *Les Fonderies Martin* (1938); *Cigarettes Bastos* (1939); *Les Gaines Roussell* (1939); *Ceupa* (1939); *Le Gaz* (1939); *En Passant* (1943); *Fumées* (1952); *Masques* (1953); *Nocturne* (1954); *Pure Beaute* (1954); *Rimes* (1954); *Seve de la Terre* (1955); *Le Buisson Ardent* (1955); *Bain d'X* (1956); *Osram* (1956); *Quatre Temps* (1956); *Cent pour Cent* (1957); *Cocinor* (1957); *Constance* (1958); *Anonyme* (1958); *Divertissement* (1960); *The Trial* (titles, 1962); *Le Nez* (1963); *L'Eau* (1965); *Tableau D'Exposition* (1972); *Three Moods* (1980).

Man Ray (Emmanuel Radenski)

(27 August 1890, Philadelphia–18 November 1976, Paris)
Artist
Films: *Le Retour à la Raison* (1923); *Entr'acte* (1924, with René Clair); *Emak Bakia* (1926); *Anemic Cinema* (1927, with Marcel Duchamp); *L'Étoile de Mer* (1928); *Les Mystères du Château de Dés* (1929); *Essai de Simulation de Délire Cinematographique* (1935, unfinished); *Dreams That Money Can Buy* (1947, with Hans Richter).

Lynn Riggs

(August 1899, Claremore, Okla.–30 June 1954, New York)
Playwright
Films: *A Day in Sante Fe* (1931); *Stingaree* (1934); *The Garden of Allah* (1936); *The Plainsman* (1937); *Destination Unknown* (1942); *Madame Spy* (1942); *Sherlock Holmes and the Voice of Terror* (1942); *Sherlock Holmes in Washington* (1943); *Oklahoma* (1955).

LeRoy Robbins

(14 June 1904, St. Louis–24 January 1987, San Diego)
Photographer/soundman

Films: Advertising films (1930–1931); *Imperial Valley* (1932, unfinished); *Dawn to Dawn* (1933); *Even As You and I* (1937, with Barlow, Hay); *Suicide* (unfinished, 1935–1937); *The Staff of Life* (1938); *The City* (1939, cameraman); *Symphony in Stone* (1939); *School for Dogs* (1940); *Pipeline* (1942); *Freedom to Learn* (1945); *Letter from Stalingrad* (1945); *Southern California Gas* (1945); *Survival in the Aleutians* (1948). Sound only: *Confidential File* (1955, TV); *Stake out on Dope Street* (1958); *The Untouchables* (1961); *Out of the Tiger's Mouth* (1962); *An Affair of the Skin* (1963); *America, America* (1963); *The Shepherd of the Hills* (1964); *The Young Sinner* (1965); *Born Losers* (1967); *Hell's Angels on Wheels* (1967); *Psych-Out* (1968); *The Savage Seven* (1968); *Easy Rider* (1969); *The Plastic Dome of Norma Jean* (1970); *The Last Movie* (1975).

Henwar Rodakiewicz
(19 September 1902, Vienna–12 February 1976, New York)
Films: *The Barge* (1930); *Portrait of a Young Man* (1931), *Faces of New England* (1931); *Pueblo* (1933, unfinished, with Stern); *The Wave* (1934); *The City* (1939); *It Is for Us the Living* (1940); *Mr. Trull Finds Out* (1940, with Joseph Krumgold); *One Tenth of Our Nation* (1940); *The Capital Story* (1945); *East by North* (1947); *International Ice Patrol* (1947); *Land of Enchantment* (1948); *People to People* (1949); *Jose Martinez—American* (1950); *To Your Health* (1950); *Birth of a Building* (1950); *Henry Lends a Hand* (1952); *Home at the Wheel* (1953); *Roots to Happiness* (1953); *The Search: Speech Clinic in Iowa* (1954); *The Search: Waco Toronado—Texas* (1954); *Point of View* (1955); *The Search: Report on Mental Illness—Tulane* (1954); *To All Who Believe in Youth* (1954); *Puerto Rico: The Peaceful Revolution* (1954).

Joseph Schillinger
(1895–23 March 1943, New York)
Composer
Films: *Synchromy* (1933, unfinished, with Bute, Jacobs).

Leon Shamroy
(16 July 1901, New York–7 July 1974, Hollywood)
Cameraman
Films: *Tongues of Scandal* (1927); *Pirates of the Sky* (1927); *The Mystery Trunk* (1927); *Catch-As-Catch-Can* (1927); *Hidden Aces* (1927); *The Land of the Lawless* (1927); *The Last Moment* (1928); *The Tell-Tale Heart* (1928, with Charles Klein); *Out with the Tide* (1929); *Alma de Gaucho* (1930); *Women Men Marry* (1932); *Stowaway, A Strange Adventure* (1932); *Jennie Gerhardt* (1932); *Her Bodyguard* (1932); *Three-Cornered Room* (1933); *Good Dame* (1934); *Thirty Day Princess* (1934); *Kiss and Make-Up* (1934); *Ready for Love* (1934); *Behold, My Wife* (1934); *Private Worlds* (1935); *She Married the Boss* (1935); *Accent on

Youth (1935); *She Couldn't Take It* (1935); *Mary Burns, Fugitive* (1935); *Soak the Rich* (1936); *Fatal Lady* (1936); *Spendthrift* (1936); *Wedding Present* (1936); *You Only Live Once* (1937); *Her Husband Lied* (1937); *The Great Gambini* (1937); *She Asked for It* (1937); *Blossoms on Broadway* (1937); *The Young in Heart* (1938); *Made for Each Other* (1939); *The Story of Alexander Graham Bell* (1939); *The Adventures of Sherlock Holmes* (1939); *Little Old New York* (1940); *I Was an Adventuress* (1940); *Lillian Russell* (1940); *Four Sons* (1940); *Down Argentine Way* (1940); *Tin Pan Alley* (1940); *That Night in Rio* (1941); *The Great American Broadcast* (1941); *Moon Over Miami* (1941); *A Yank in the R.A.F.* (1941); *Confirm or Deny* (1941); *Roxie Hart* (1942); *Ten Gentlemen From West Point* (1942); *The Black Swan* (1942); *Crash Dive* (1943); *Stormy Weather* (1943); *Buffalo Bill* (1944); *Greenwich Village* (1944); *Wilson* (1944); *A Tree Grows in Brooklyn* (1945); *Where Do We Go from Here?* (1945); *State Fair* (1945); *The Shocking Miss Pilgrim* (1945); *Leave Her to Heaven* (1946); *Forever Amber* (1947); *Daisy Kenyon* (1947); *That Lady in Ermine* (1948); *Prince of Foxes* (1949); *Twelve O'Clock High* (1949); *Cheaper by the Dozen* (1950); *Two Flags West* (1950); *On the Riviera* (1951); *David and Bethsheba* (1951); *With a Song in My Heart* (1952); *Wait till the Sun Shines* (1952); *Down Among the Sheltering Palms* (1952); *The Snows of Kilimanjaro* (1952); *Tonight We Sing* (1953); *Call Me Madam* (1953); *The Girl Next Door* (1953); *White Witch Doctor* (1953); *The Robe* (1953); *King of the Khyber Rifles* (1953); *The Egyptian* (1954); *There's No Business Like Show Business* (1954); *Daddy Long Legs* (1955); *Love Is a Many-Splendored Thing* (1955); *Good Morning, Miss Dove* (1955); *The King and I* (1956); *The Best Things in Life Are Free* (1956); *The Girl Can't Help It* (1956); *The Desk Set* (1957); *His Other Woman* (1957); *South Pacific* (1958); *The Bravados* (1958); *Rally 'Round the Flag, Boys!* (1958); *Porgy and Bess* (1959); *The Blue Angel* (1959); *Beloved Infidel* (1959); *Wake Me When It's Over* (1960); *North to Alaska* (1960); *Snow White and the 3 Stooges* (1961); *Tender Is the Night* (1962); *Cleopatra* (1963); *What a Way to Go!* (1964); *John Goldfarb* (1964); *The Agony and the Ecstasy* (1965); *Do Not Disturb* (1965); *The Glass Bottom Boat* (1965); *Caprice* (1965); *Planet of the Apes* (1968); *The Secret Life of an American Wife* (1968); *Skidoo* (1968); *Justine* (1969).

Charles Sheeler

(16 July 1883, Philadelphia–7 May 1965, New York)
Photographer/painter
Films: Untitled Shamberg film (ca. 1914); *Katherine Baird Shaffer* (ca. 1919); *Manhatta* (1921).

Mike Siebert

(1898–December 1948, Los Angeles)
Actor/assistant director
Films: *Breakwater* (1931); *Olvera Street* (1935).

Stella Simon (nee Furchtgott)
(8 February 1878, Charleston, S.C.–15 March 1973, San Francisco)
Photographer
Films: *Hände/Hands* (1928).

Harry Smith
(1923, Portland, Oreg.–1991, New York)
Painter
Films: *No. 1* (1939); *No. 2* (1940–1942); *No. 3* (1942–1947); *No. 4* (1950); *No. 5* (1950); *No. 6* (1951); *No. 7* (1951); *No. 8* (1954); *No. 9* (1954); *No. 10* (1956); *No. 11/Mirror Abstractions* (1956); *No. 12/Heaven and Earth Magic* (1958); *No. 13/Oz Kaleidoscope* (1962); *No. 14/Late Superimpositions* (1965); *No. 15* (1966); *No. 16/Tin Woodsman's Dream* (1967); *Mahagonny* (1972–1980).

Ralph Steiner
(8 February 1899, Cleveland–13 July 1986, Thetford, Vt.)
Photographer
Films: *City Film* (1927); H_2O (1929); *Silo* (1929); *People Playing Croquet* (1929); *Mechanical Principles* (1930); *Surf and Seaweed* (1930); *Panther Woman of the Needle Trades, or The Lovely Life of Little Lisa* (1931); *May Day in New York* (1931, with Lerner); *Dance Film* (1931); *Granite/The Quarry* (1932); *Harbor Scenes* (1932); *Mechanical Principles* (1933); *G-3* (1933); *Cafe Universal* (1934); *Pie in the Sky* (1934, with Kazan, Lerner, M. D. Thatcher); *Hands* (1934); *The World Today: Sunnyside* (1935); *The World of Today: Black Legion* (1935); *The Plow That Broke the Plains* (1936); *People of Cumberland* (1938); *The City* (1939); *Sara Lawrence* (1940); *New Hampshire Heritage* (1940); *Youth Gets a Break* (1941); *Troop Train* (1942); *Earth and Fire* (1950); *Seaweed, a Seduction* (1960); *Of Earth and Fire* (1968); *One Man's Island* (1969); *Glory, Glory* (1970); *A Look at Laundry* (1971); *Beyond Niagara* (1973); *Look Park* (1974); *Hooray for Light!* (1975); *Slowdown* (1975).

Seymour Stern
(22 February 1908, New York–22 January 1978, New York)
Film critic/historian
Films: *Imperial Valley* (1932); *Pueblo* (1933, unfinished); *Land of the Sun* (1933); *Dawn to Dawn* (1934); *The Good Job* (1942).

Paul Strand
(16 October 1890, New York–31 March 1976, Orgeval, France)
Photographer
Films: *Manhatta* (1921); *Crackerjack* (1925); *Betty Behave* (1927); *Where the Pavement Begins* (1928); *Redes/The Wave* (1934); *The Plow That Broke the Plains*

(1936); *Heart of Spain* (1937); *People of Cumberland* (1938); *Native Land* (1942, with Leo Hurwitz); *It's Up to You* (1943); *Tomorrow We Fly* (1944).

Leslie P. Thatcher
(Born Toronto, Canada)
Films: *Mighty Niagara* (1933); *Another Day* (1934).

Molly Day Thatcher Kazan
(16 December 1906, East Orange, N.J.–13 December 1963, New York)
Playwright
Films: *Pie in the Sky* (1934, with Kazan, Lerner, Steiner).

William C. Vance
(1915, Chicago–8 December 1961, New York)
Advertising executive
Films: *Dr. Jekyll and Mr. Hyde* (1932); *Hearts of the Age* (1934).

Willard Van Dyke
(5 December 1906–23 January 1986, Jackson, Tenn.)
Photographer
Films: *Hands* (1934); *Self-Help Cooperatives in California* (1935); *The World Today: Sunnyside* (1935); *The River* (1937); *The City* (1939); *Valley Town* (1940); *Sara Lawrence* (1940); *New Hampshire's Heritage* (1940); *A Year's Work* (1940); *Tall Tales* (1941); *The Bridge* (1942); *International House* (1942); *Evander Childs High School* (1942); *Oswego Story* (1943); *Chicago* (1943), *Cowboy* (1943); *Steeltown* (1944); *Conference at Yellow Springs* (1945); *Northwest USA* (1945); *San Francisco— 1945* (1945); *To Hear Your Banjo Play* (1945); *Journey Into Medicine* (1947); *The Photographer* (1948); *Mount Vernon in Virginia* (1949); *High Adventure with Lowell Thomas* (1958); *Land of White Alice* (1959); *Skyscraper* (1959); *Ireland, the Tear and the Smile* (1960); *Harvest* (1962); *So That Men Are Free* (1962); *Frontier of News* (1964); *Rice* (1964); *Frontline Camera 1935–1956* (1965); *Corbit-Sharp House* (1965); *Shape of Films to Come* (1968).

Charles Vidor
(27 July 1900, Budapest–4 June 1959, Vienna)
Film director
Films:*The Bridge* (1929); *The Mask of Fu Manchu* (1932); *Sensation Hunters* (1933); *Double Door* (1934); *Strangers All* (1935); *The Arizonian* (1935); *His Family Tree* (1935); *Muss 'em Up* (1936); *A Doctor's Diary* (1937); *The Great Gambini* (1937); *She's No Lady* (1937); *Romance of the Redwoods* (1939); *Blind Alley* (1939); *Those High Grey Walls* (1939); *My Son, My Son!* (1940); *The Lady*

in Question (1940); *Ladies in Retirement* (1941); *New York Town* (1941); *The Tuttles of Tahiti* (1942); *The Desperadoes* (1943); *Cover Girl* (1944); *Together Again* (1944); *A Song to Remember* (1945); *Over 21* (1945); *Gilda* (1946); *The Loves of Carmen* (1948); *It's a Big Country* (1952); *Hans Christian Andersen* (1952); *Thunder in the East* (1953); *Rhapsody* (1954); *Love Me or Leave Me* (1955); *The Swan* (1956); *The Joker Is Wild* (1957); *A Farewell to Arms* (1958); *Song Without End* (1960).

Slavko Vorkapich
(17 March 1892, Yugoslavia–20 October 1976, Mijas, Spain)
Special-effects technician
Films: *Prisoner of Zenda* (1922); *Scaramouche* (1923); *The Life and Death of 9413—A Hollywood Extra* (1928); *Dancing Lady* (1933); *Past of Mary Holmes* (1933); *Manhattan Melodrama* (1934); *Crime Without Passion* (1934); *Millions of Us* (1935, direction); *David Copperfield* (1935); *The Good Earth* (1937); *The Last Gangster* (1937); *They Gave Him a Gun* (1937); *Broadway Melody of 1938* (1938); *Test Pilot* (1938); *The Crowd Roars* (1938); *Yellow Jack* (1938); *Marie Antoinette* (1938); *Boy's Town* (1938); *Girl of the Golden West* (1938); *Sweethearts* (1938); *Idiot's Delight* (1939); *San Francisco* (1939); *Mr. Smith Goes to Washington* (1939); *Air Waves* (1939); *The Howards of Virginia* (1940); *Moods of the Sea* (1942, with Hoffman); *Mail Call* (1944); *Fingal's Cave* (1946); *Forest Murmurs* (1947); *Hanka* (1955); *The Mask* (1961, Canada).

James Sibley Watson, Jr.
(10 August 1894, Rochester, N.Y.–31 March 1982, Rochester)
Doctor
Films: *The Dinner Party* (1925, unfinished); *The Fall of the House of Usher* (1928, with Webber); *Tomatoes Another Day/It Never Happened/What May Happen* (1930); *The Eyes of Science* (1931); *Rochester Newsreel* (1931, with Webber); *Rochester Newsreel* (1933, with Webber); *Lot in Sodom* (1933, with Webber); *Highlights and Shadows* (1937); *Experiments in X-ray motion pictures* (1940s).

Melville Webber
(8 October 1989, Boston–1 October 1947, Canandaigua, N.Y.)
Poet
Films: *The Fall of the House of Usher* (1928, with Watson); *Rochester Newsreel* (1931, with Watson); *Lot in Sodom* (1933, with Watson); *Rhythms in Light* (1936, with Bute).

Herman Weinberg
(1908, New York–7 November 1983, New York)
Film critic
Films: *City Symphony* (1930); *Autumn Fire* (1933); *Rhapsody* (1934, unfinished); *The Artist* (1950).

James Whitney
(Born 1922, Altadena, Calif.)
Artist
Films: *Variations* (1939–1943); *Five Abstract Film Exercises* (1944); *House of Cards* (1947, assistant); *Yantra* (1950–1955); *Lapis* (1963–1966); *Dwi Ja* (1976); *Wu Ming* (1970–1977); *Hsiang Sheng* (1977).

John Whitney
(Born 1917 Altadena, Calif.)
Artist
Films: *Variations* (1939–1943); *Five Abstract Film Exercises* (1943–1944); *Journal* (1947); *Mozart Rondo* (1947–1949); *Hot House* (1949); *Celery Stalks at Midnight* (1951); *Lion Hunt* (1955); *Blues Pattern* (1956); *Performing Painter* (1956); *Celery Stalks at Midnight 2* (1957); *Catalog* (1962); *Permutations* (1967); *Experiments in Motion Graphics* (1968); *Cria* (1969); *Binary Bit Patterns* (1969); *Osaka 1-2-3* (1970); *Matrix I* (1971); *Matrix II* (1971); *Arabesque* (1975).

Christopher Baugham Young
(1908, Jenkintown, Pa.–1 December 1975, Hartford, Conn.)
Films: *Object Lesson* (1941); *Subject Lesson* (1955); *Nature Is My Mistress* (after 1955); *Search for Paradise* (after 1955).

BIBLIOGRAPHY

Abbott, Jere
1931   "Film and Music." *Creative Art* 8, no. 4 (April): 283.

Agel, Henri
1965   *Robert Flaherty*. Paris: Cinéma d'Aujourd'hui/Editions Seghers.

Alexander, William
1981   *Film on the Left: American Documentary from 1931 to 1942*. Princeton: Princeton University Press.

1991   "Paul Strand as Filmmaker, 1933–1942." In Stange (1991): 148–160.

Allen, Richard
1983   "*The Life and Death of 9413—A Hollywood Extra (1928)*." *Framework*, no. 21 (Summer): 12–14.

Anonymous
1927   "Cranking Your Own." *National Board of Review Magazine* 2, no. 6 (June): 3.

Anonymous
1927   "More Anent the Little Theatre." *National Board of Review Magazine* 2, no. 11 (November): 5, 7.

Anonymous
1928   "Four Screen Theatre Being Built Here (Interview with Frederick Kiesler)." *New York Times*, 9 December, sec. II.

Anonymous
1928   "*The Life and Death of 9413—A Hollywood Extra (1928)*." *Close Up* 2 (April): 55–57.

Anonymous
1928   "Suicide of Hollyw'd Extra." *Variety*, 20 June, n.p.

Anonymous
1929   "Some Amateur Movies." *New Republic* 58 (6 March): 71–72.

Anonymous
1929   "H_2O (1929)," *National Board of Review Magazine* 4, no. 10 (December): 12.

Anonymous
1933   "The Face of New England (Rodakiewicz)." *Experimental Cinema* 1, no. 5: 35.

Anonymous
1934   "Experimental Cinema in America." *Experimental Cinema* 1, no. 5:54–55.

Anonymous
1936   "*Underground Printer.*" *Film Art* 3, no. 9 (Autumn): 28.

Anonymous
1936   "Expanding Cinema's Synchromy 2." *Literary Digest* 122, no. 6 (8 August): 20–21.

Anonymous
1936   "Color, Sound, Light Dance with Harmonious Steps in 'Synchromy,' Art Form Created by Texas Girl." *New York World-Telegram*, 20 July.

Anthology Film Archives
1977   "A Tribute to Anthology Film Archives' *Avantgarde Film Preservation Program:* An Evening Dedicated to Frederick Kiesler." Program brochure. Museum of Modern Art, 19 October 1977; American Film Institute, 10 November 1977. pp. 22–45.

Arledge, Sara Kathryn
1981   "Brief Statements." *Cinemanews* 1, no. 6: 3–4.

Barrett, Gerald R., and Erskine, Thomas L.
1973   *From Fiction to Film: Ambrose Bierce's "An Occurrence at Owl Creek Bridge."* Encino: Dickenson Publishing Co.

Barrett, Wilton A.
1929   "*The Fall of the House of Usher.*" *National Board of Review Magazine* 4, no. 1 (January): 5–6.

Basquin, Kit
1991   "Mary Ellen Bute's Film Adaptation of *Finnegans Wake.*" *James Joyce's "Finnegans Wake": A Casebook,* ed. John Harty III. New York/London: Garland.

Batten, Mary
1962   "Notes on Rudy Burckhardt: Motion Seen." *Vision (Film Comment)* 1, no. 1 (Spring): 15–16.

1962   "Actuality and Abstraction (Interview with M. E. Bute)." *Vision (Film Comment)* 1, no. 2 (Summer): 55–59.

Beyerle, Mo
1988   "Ästhetische Erfahrung und urbane Idylle: Jay Leydas *A Bronx Morning* (1931)." *Amerikastudien/American Studies* 37: 75–84.

Blakeston, Oswell
1929   "*Hands* (1928)." *Close Up* 5, no. 2 (August): 137–138.
1937   "A Note on the Camera and Philosophy (*The Way*)." *Film Art* 4, no. 10 (Spring): 24.

Blakeston, Oswell, and MacPherson, Kenneth
1932   "We Present a Manifesto!" *Close Up* 9, no. 2 (June): 92–105.

Bond, Kirk
1934   *"Lot in Sodom."* *Film Art* 1, no. 4 (Summer): 69.

Brahkage, Stan
1991   *Film at Wit's End: Eight Avant-Garde Filmmakers.* New York: McPherson & Company.

Brandon, Tom
1979   "Survival List: Films of the Great Depression: The Early Thirties." *Film Library Quarterly* 12, nos. 2–3: 34–40.

Braun, B. Vivian
1934   *"Dawn to Dawn."* *Film Art* 2, no. 5 (Winter): 35.

Browning, Irving
1944   "Francis Doublier, Cameraman Fifty Years Ago." *American Cinematographer* (October).

Buache, Freddy
1979   "Le cinéma independent et d'avant-garde à la fin du muet: Le Congrès de La Sarraz (1929)." *Travelling* (special issue), no. 55 (Summer): 17–20.
1980   "Le cinéma independent et d'avant-garde a la fin du muet: Notes sur quelques films independent ou d'avant-garde." *Travelling*, nos. 56–57 (Spring).

Burckhardt, Rudy
1992   "How I Think I Made Some of My Films." In James (1992): 97–99.

Bute, Mary Ellen
1941   "Light*Form*Movement*Sound." *Design* 42, no. 8 (April): 25.
1954   "Abstronics." *Films in Review* 5 (June–July): 263–266.
1985   "A Conversation with Mary Ellen Bute at the Art Institute of Chicago (1976)." Presented at the Art Institute of Chicago.

Caditz, Judith Freulich
1991   "Roman Freulich: Hollywood's Golden Age Portraitist." *The Rangefinder* (July): 46–47, 57.

Calder-Marshall, Arthur
1970   *The Innocent Eye: The Life of Robert Flaherty.* London: Penguin Books.

Camper, Fred
1976   "Cornell: Joseph Cornell Films." *Soho Weekly News*, 11 March, p. 27.

Char
1934   *"Dawn to Dawn* (1934)." *Variety*, 9 January. Reprinted in *Variety Film Reviews*, vol. 4. New York and London: Garland Publishing 1983.

Corliss, Richard
1973   "Robert Flaherty: The Man in the Iron Myth." *Film Comment* 9, no. 6 (November–December): 38–42.

Crockwell, Douglass
1964   "A Background to Free Animation," *Film Culture* 32 (Spring): 30–31.

Curtis, David
1971   *Experimental Cinema*. New York: Universe Publishing Co.

Dal Co, F.
1974   "Cinema citta' avanguardia 1919–1939." *Bianco e Nero* 35 (September–December): 294–320.

Dwoskin, Stephen
1975   *Film Is . . .: The International Free Cinema*. Woodstock, N.Y.: Overlook Press.

Enyeart, James L.
1977   *Bruguière: His Photographs and His Life*. New York: Knopf.

Eskildsen, Ute, and Horak, Jan-Christopher
1979   *Film und Foto der zwanziger Jahre*. Stuttgart: Verlag Gerd Hatje.

Fejos, Paul
1929   "Illusion on the Screen." *National Board of Review Magazine* 4, no. 6 (June): 3–4.

Ferguson, Otis
1934   "Genesis, 19:8" (*Lot in Sodom*, 1933). *New Republic* 78 (21 March): 160–161.

Fischer, Lucy
1987   "The Films of James Sibley Watson, Jr., and Melville Webber: A Reconsideration." *Millennium Film Journal* 19: 40–49.

Flaherty, Frances Hubbard
1937   *Elephant Dance*. New York: Scribners Sons.

Flaherty, Robert
1934   "Filming Reel People." *Amateur Movie Makers* 9, no. 12 (December). Reprinted in *The Documentary Tradition: From Nanook to Woodstock*, ed. Lewis Jacobs. New York: W. W. Norton, 1971.

Flint, Ralph
1931   "Boris Deutsch," *Creative Art* 8 (June): 430–432.

Foster, Richard, and Stauffacher, Frank
1947   "The Avant Garde." *Cinema* 1, no. 3 (August): 12–13.

Gale, Arthur
1928   "Amateur Clubs: Unchartered Seas." *Amateur Movie Makers* 3, no. 2 (February): 100–101.

Gallen, Ira H.
1979   "Notes on a Film Historian: Seymour Stern." Manuscript, Museum of Modern Art, New York.

Gartenberg, Jon
1985   "Reframing Experimental Cinema." In *Black Maria Film Festival* (brochure), n.p.

Geller, Evelyn
1973   "Paul Strand as Documentary Filmmaker." *Film Library Quarterly* 6, no. 2 (Spring): 28–30.

Glassgold, C. Adolph
1929   "The Films: Amateur or Professional?" *The Arts* 15, no. 1 (January): 56–59.
1929   "H_2O (1929)," *The Arts* 15, no. 3 (March): 204–205.

Gould, Symon
1926   "The Little Theatre Movement in the Cinema." *National Board of Review Magazine* 1, no. 5 (September–October): 4–5.

Gray, Hugh
1950   "Robert Flaherty and the Naturalist Documentary." *Hollywood Quarterly* 5, no. 1 (Fall): 41–48.

Grierson, John
1951   "Flaherty as Innovator." *Sight and Sound* 21, no. 2 (October–December): 64–68.

Gunning, Tom
1986   "The Cinema of Attractions: Early Cinema, Its Spectators and the Avant-Garde." *Wide Angle* 8, nos. 3–4: 63–70.

Hacker, Leonard
1934   "*Lot in Sodom* (1933)." *Film Art* (London) 1, no. 3 (Spring): 23.

Haller, Robert
1980   "*Autumn Fire* (1933)." *Field of Vision* (Spring): n.p.

Hamilton, James Shelley
1934   "*Lot in Sodom* (1933)." *National Board of Review Magazine* 9, no. 2 (February): 14–15.

Hammer, Barbara
1981   "Sara Kathryn Arledge." *Cinemanews* 1, no. 6: 3–4.

Hammond, Richard
1931   "Pioneers of Movie Music." *Modern Music* 8 (March): 35–38.

Hein, Birgit
1971   *Film im Underground.* Frankfurt/Main: Ullstein Buch.

Hein, Birgit, and Herzogenrath, Wulf
1977   *Film als Film: 1910 bis Heute.* Cologne: Kölnischen Kunstverein.
1980   *Film as Film.* London: Arts Council of Britain.

Herring, Robert
1929   "Art in the Cinema: The Work of Robert Florey." *Creative Art* 4 (1 May): 360–361.

Highams, Charles
1970   *Hollywood Cameramen.* Bloomington/London: Indiana University Press.

Hill, Jerome
1964   "Some Notes on Painting and Film-making." *Film Culture* 32 (Spring): 31–32.

Hoberman, James
1980   "Explorations: The Strange Films of Joseph Cornell." *American Film* 5, no. 1 (January–February): 18–19.

Horak, Jan-Christopher
1979   "Film and Foto: Towards a Language of Silent Film." *Afterimage* 7, no. 5 (December): 8–11.
1980   "Discovering Pure Cinema: Avant-Garde Film in the 1920s." *Afterimage* 8, nos. 1–2 (Summer): 4–7.
1987   "Modernist Perspectives and Romantic Desire: *Manhatta*." *Afterimage* 15, no. 4 (November): 9–15.
1991   "Manhatta." In Stange (1991): 55–71.
1992   "L'avanguardia cinematographica americana 1921–1945." In *Il grande occhio della notte: cinema d'avanguardia americano 1920–1990,* ed. Paolo Bertetto. Torino: Museo Nationale del Cinema. Pp. 61–79.
1993   "The Avant-Garde Film." In *Grand Design: Hollywood as a Modern Business Enterprise, 1930–1939,* ed. Tino Balio. New York: Scribners. Pp. 387–404.

Huff, Theodore
1932   "The Mirror of Burlesque." *Amateur Movie Makers* 7, no. 10 (October): 429, 448.
1933   "Spoken Titles." *Amateur Movie Makers* 8, no. 11 (November): 456, 470–472.

Hutchins, John
1929   "L'Enfant Terrible: The Little Cinema Movement." *Theatre Arts Monthly* 13, no. 9 (September): 694–697.

Jacobs, Lewis
1930   "The New Cinema." *Experimental Cinema* 1, no. 1:13–14.
1932   "*Highway 66*: Montage Notes for a Documentary Film." *Experimental Cinema,* 1, no. 4: 40–41.
1947   "Experimental Cinema in America (Part 1)." *Hollywood Quarterly* 3, no. 2 (Winter): 111–124. Reprinted as "Avant-Garde Production in America"

in *Experiment in the Film*, ed. Roger Manvell. London: Grey Walls Press, 1949; New York: Arno Press, 1970). Pp. 113–152. Also reprinted in Jacobs (1968): 543–582.

1958   "Free Cinema I." *Film Culture*, no. 17: 9–10.

1959   "Morning for the Experimental Film." *Film Culture*, no. 19: 8.

1968   *The Rise of the American Film*. 2d ed. New York: Teachers College Press.

1979   "Intervention de Lewis Jacobs," *Travelling* 56 (Fall); 27.

Jacoby, Irving
1976   "Henwar Rodakiewicz, 1903–1976." *Sightlines* (Spring): 4.

James, David E. (ed.)
1992   *To Free the Cinema: Jonas Mekas and The New York Underground*. Princeton: Princeton University Press.

Joseph, Robert
1938   "The Unimportance of Budget . . . *The Wave*." *Hollywood Spectator* 13 (25 June): 11.

Josephson, Matthew
1931   "Modern Music for the Films." *New Republic* 66 (1 April): 183.

Kiesler, Frederick
1928   "100 Per Cent Cinema." *Close Up* 3, no. 2 (August): 39–40.

1929   "Building a Cinema Theatre." *New York Evening Post* (February). Reprinted in Anthology Film Archives (1977): 34–35.

Kirstein, Lincoln
1932   "Experimental Films." *Arts Weekly* 1, no. 3 (25 March): 52, 62.

Klaue, Wolfgang, and Leyda, Jay (eds.)
1964   *Robert Flaherty*. East Berlin: Henschelverlag.

Kleinhans, Chuck
1975   "Reading and Thinking About the Avant-Garde." *Jump Cut*, no. 9 (March–April): 21–25.

Kuttner, Alfred B.
1926   "The Little Motion Picture Theatre." *National Board of Review Magazine* 1, no. 2 (May–June): 3.

Lawder, Standish D.
1967   *Structuralism and Movement in Experimental Film and Modern Art, 1896–1925*. Ph.D. diss., Yale University.

1975   *The Cubist Cinema*. New York: New York University Press.

Le Grice, Malcolm
1977   *Abstract Film and Beyond*. Cambridge, Mass.: MIT Press.

Lehman, Peter
1984   "The Avant-Garde: Power, Change, and the Power to Change." In *Cinema Histories, Cinema Practices*, ed. Patricia Mellencamp and Philip Rosen. Los Angeles: American Film Institute. Pp. 120–131.

1985   For Whom Does the Light Shine? Thoughts on the Avant-Garde. *Wide Angle* 7, nos. 1–2: 68–73.

Leyda, Jay
1931   "Tips on Topicals." *Amateur Movie Makers* 6, no. 1 (January): 13–14, 39.
1945   "Exploration of New Film Techniques." *Arts & Architecture* 62 (December): 38–39.

Lichtenstein, Manfred; Meier, Gerd; and Lippert, Klaus
1981   *American Social Documentary.* East Berlin: Staatliches Filmarchiv der DDR.

Lopate, Phillip
1987   "Rudy Burkhardt: Man with a Movie Camera." *Museum of Modern Art Program Notes* (6–24 February).

McBride, Joseph
1972   *Welles.* New York: Viking Press.

MacCann, Richard Dyer
1947   "Hollywood Letter: Nonfiction Man in Fiction Film." Newsclipping, Paul Burnford file, Museum of Modern Art, New York.

MacDonald, Scott
1987   "Amos Vogel and Cinema 16." *Wide Angle* 9, no. 3: 38–51.
1993   Avant-Garde Film: Motion Studies. Cambridge: Cambridge University Press.

McKay, H. C.
1938   "Abstract Films: Mechanism of Perception, Association of Ideas, Abstract Motion." *American Photographer* 32 (November): 817–820.

MacPherson, Kenneth
1928   "As Is." *Close Up* 2, no. 6 (June): 5.

Martin, Marcel
1966   "Flaherty." *Anthologie du Cinéma* 1: 121–172.

Markopoulos, Gregory
1962   "The Films of Mary Ellen Bute: Beyond Audio Visual Space," *Vision (Film Comment)* 1, no. 2 (Summer): 52–54.

Mekas, Jonas
1955   "The Experimental Film in America." *Film Culture* 1, no. 3 (May–June): 15–18.
1972   "Francis Lee's First Films." *Village Voice*, 17 February. Reprinted in Russett (1976): 115.
1972   *Movie Journal: The Rise of a New American Cinema 1959–1971.* New York: Collier Books.
1972   "Movie Journal (Jerome Hill)." *Village Voice*, 7 December.
1973   "An Interview with Jerome Hill." *Film Culture*, nos. 56–57 (Winter): 3–16.

Merriam, Mylon
1936   A Film Technique for Artists. London: the author.

Mitry, Jean
1974   Le cinéma expérimental. Paris: Edition Seghers.

Moritz, William
1996   "Visual Music and Film-As-An-Art in California Before 1950." In On the
        Edge of America: California Modernist Art, 1900–1950, eds. Paul Karl-
        strom and Ann Karlstrom. Berkeley: University of California Press.

Moore, James W.
1933   "Lot in Sodom." Amateur Movie Makers 8, no. 9 (September): 372.

Moore, Marianne
1933   "Lot in Sodom" (1933)." Close Up 10, no. 3 (September): 318–319.

Needham, Wilbur
1928   "The Future of the American Cinema." Close Up 2, no. 6 (June): 45–50.

Parker, Robert Allerton
1921   "The Art of the Camera: An Experimental Movie." Arts and Decoration
        15, no. 6 (October): 369, 414.

Penley, Constance, and Bergstrom, Janet
1978   "The Avant-Garde: Histories and Theories." Screen 19, no. 3 (Autumn):
        113–127. Reprinted in Movies and Methods, vol. 2, ed. Bill Nichols.
        Berkeley: University of California Press. Pp. 288–299.

Perkins, Elizabeth
1928   "The Civic Cinema: A Unique Movie Move Planned for Manhattan."
        Amateur Movie Makers 3, no. 4 (April): 254.

Petric, Vlada
n.d.   "Legacy of a Great Teacher: Slavko Vorkapich (1894–1976)." Manuscript.
        Museum of Modern Art, New York.

Pike, Robert Marvin
1960   "A Critical Study of the West Coast Experimental Film Movement."
        M.A. thesis, University of California at Los Angeles.

Polan, Dana
1985   The Political Language of Film and the Avant-Garde. Ann Arbor: UMI
        Research Press.

Potamkin, Harry Alan
1929   "Francis Bruguière." Transition (Paris), no. 18 (November): 81–82.
1930   "A City Symphony (1929)." Close Up 5 (October): 251–252.
1933   "Spectator's Groups in America." Close Up 10, no. 1 (March): 78–79.

Renan, Sheldon
1967   An Introduction to the American Underground Film. New York: Dutton.

Richter, Hans
1929   Filmgegner von heute, Filmfreunde von morgen. Halle/Saale: Verlag
        Wilhelm Knapp. Reprint ed., Zurich: Verlag Hans Rohr, 1968.

1947   "A History of the Avant-Garde." In Stauffacher (1947).

1976   *Der Kampf um den Film*. Munich: Carl Hanser Verlag.

1986   *Struggle for Film: Towards a Socially Responsible Cinema*, trans. Ben Brewster. New York: St. Martin's Press.

Rodakiewicz, Henwar

1929   "Something More Than a Scenic." *Amateur Movie Makers* 7, no. 6 (June): 249, 262.

1970   "Treatment of Sound in *The City*." In *The Movies as Medium*, ed. Lewis Jacobs. New York: Farrar, Straus & Giroux.

Rotha, Paul

1930   *The Film Till Now*. London: n.p. Reprint ed., London: Spring Books, 1967.

Ruoff, Jeffrey

1991   "Home Movies of the Avant-Garde: Jonas Mekas and the New York Art World." *Cinema Journal* 30, no. 3 (Spring): 6–28.

Russett, Robert, and Starr, Cecile

1976   *Experimental Animation: An Illustrated Anthology*. New York: Van Nostrand Reinhold. Reprint ed., New York: Da Capo Press, 1988.

Sargent, Epes W.

1929   "The Lesson of Poverty Row." *Amateur Movie Makers* 4, no. 1 (January): 26.

Scheugl, Hans, and Schmidt, Ernst, Jr.

1974   *Eine Subgeschichte des Films: Lexikon des Avantgarde-, Experimental-und Underground films*. Frankfurt/Main: Edition Suhrkamp.

Schillinger, Joseph

1934   "Excerpts from a Theory of Synchronization." *Experimental Cinema* 1, no. 5: 28–31.

Seldes, Gilbert

1929   "Some Amateur Movies." *New Republic* 528 (6 March): 71–72.

Simon, Elena Pinto, and Stirk, David

1987   *Jay Leyda: A Chronology*. New York: Tisch School of the Arts.

Singer, Marilyn

1976   *A History of the American Avant-Garde*. New York: American Federation of the Arts.

Sitney, P. Adams

1962   "A View of Burkhardt." *Film Comment* 1, no. 1 (Spring): 13–15.

1970   *Film Culture Reader*. New York: Praeger.

1975   *The Essential Cinema: Essays on the Films in the Collections of Anthology Film Archives*. New York: New York University Press.

1978   *The Avant-Garde Film: A Reader of Theory and Criticism*. New York: New York University Press.

1979   *Visionary Film: The American Avant-Garde 1943–1978.* 2d ed. New York: Oxford University Press.

1982   "The Cinematic Gaze of Joseph Cornell." In *Joseph Cornell.* New York: Museum of Modern Art.

1983   *"Rose Hobart."* In "13. Internationales Forum des Jungen Films," program notes, Berlin Film Festival (19 Feb.–1 March).

Spearing, O.

1922   "A Valuable Service." *Exceptional Photoplays* 2 (March).

Stange, Maren

1991   *Paul Strand: His Life and Work.* New York: Aperture.

Starr, Cecile

1972   *Discovering the Movies.* New York: Van Nostrand Reinhold.

1980   "Programming Early Avant-Garde Films." *Sightlines* 13, no. 2 (Winter): 19–21.

Stauffacher, Frank

1947   *Art in Cinema.* San Francisco: San Francisco Museum of Modern Art. Reprint ed., New York: Arno, 1970.

Stearns, Myron M.

1922   "The Art of Suggested Motion." *Arts and Decoration* 12, no. 3 (July): 191, 221.

Steiner, Ralph

1934   "Revolutionary Movie Production." *New Theatre* (September): 22–23.

Stern, Seymour

1931   "Principles of the New World-Cinema, Part II: The Film as Microcosmos." *Experimental Cinema* 1, no. 3: 29–34.

1931   "A Working-Class Cinema for America?" *The Left* 1, no. 1 (Spring): 69–73.

1933   "Eisenstein and Upton Sinclair." *Film Art* 1, no. 2 (Winter): 68.

Strand, Paul

1950   "Realism: A Personal View." *Sight and Sound* 18 (January): 23–26.

1950   "International Congress of Cinema, Perugia." *Photo Notes* (Spring): 8–11, 18.

Tafuri, Manfredo

1979   *Projet et utopie: de l'avant-garde à la metropole.* Paris: Éditions Dunod.

Taves, Brian

1987   *Robert Florey: The French Expressionist.* Metuchen, N.J.: Scarecrow Press.

Tazelaar, Marguerite

1928   "The Story of the First Little Film Theatre." *Amateur Movie Makers* 3, no. 7 (July): 441.

1929   "Amateurs Point the Way." *Amateur Movie Makers* 6, no. 6 (September): 599–600.

1936   *"The Plow That Broke the Plains—*Grand Central Palace." *New York Herald Tribune,* 26 May.

Testa, Bart
1992   *Back and Forth: Early Cinema and the Avant-Garde.* Toronto: Art Gallery of Ontario.

Thomas, Kevin
1976   "The American Avant-Garde." *Los Angeles Times,* 20 March.

Toeplitz, Jerzy
1969   "Underground Cinema: Americki Podzemni Film." *Filmska Kultura* (Zagreb), nos. 66–67: 83–102.

Troy, William
1934   *"Lot in Sodom* (1933)." *The Nation* 138 (17 January): 82–84.

Tyler, Parker
1949   "Experimental Film: Layman's Guide to Its Understanding and Enjoyment." *Theatre Arts Monthly* 33 (July): 46–48.
1958   "A Preface to the Problems of the Experimental Film." *Film Culture* no. 17 (February): 5–8.
1969   *Underground Film: A Critical History.* New York: Grove Press
       1970 *Der Film im Untergrund.* Frankfurt/Main: März Verlag.

Van Dongen, Helen
1965   "Robert Flaherty (1884–1951)." *Film Quarterly* 18, no. 4 (Summer): 3–14.

Van Dyke, Willard
1973   "Documentaries of the Thirties." *University Film Association Journal* 25, no. 3 (Fall): 45–46.

Verdone, Mario
1977   *Le avanguardie storiche del cinema.* Turin: Societa Editrice Internationale.

Vogel, Amos
1974   *Film as a Subversive Art.* New York: Random House.

Vorkapich, Slavko
1930   "Cinematics: Some Principles Underlying Effective Cinematography." *Cinematographic Annual* 1: 29–33.
1938   "Montage: A Look Into the Future With Slavko Vorkapich." *Cinema Progress* 2, no. 5 (December–January): 18–22, 34.
1959   "Toward a True Cinema." *Film Culture,* no. 19 (March): 10–17. Reprinted in *Introduction to the Art of the Movies,* ed. Lewis Jacobs. New York: Noonday Publications, 1960. Pp. 288–296. Also reprinted in *A Montage of Theories,* ed. Richard Dyer MacCann. New York: Dutton, 1966. Pp. 171–179.

Waldman, Diane
1967   *Joseph Cornell.* New York: Solomon Guggenheim Foundation.

Webber, Melville
1930   "Simplified Settings." *Amateur Movie Makers* 5, no. 3 (March): 146–147, 179.

Weinberg, Herman
1929   "A Paradox of the Photoplay: A Professional Turns Amateur." *Amateur Movie Makers* 4, no. 1 (January): 866–867, 879–881.
1933   "*Lot in Sodom* (1933)." *Close Up* 10, no. 3 (September): 266–268.
1934   "American Notes." *Film Art* 1, no. 4 (Summer): 96–97.
1934   "*The Prisoner.*" *Film Art* 2, no. 5 (Winter): 39.
1936   "Herman Weinberg Interviews Roman Freulich." *Film Art* 3, no. 8 (Summer): 41.
1941   "A Forward Glance at the Abstract Film." *Design* 42, no. 6 (February): 24.
1946   *Film Index Series, no. 6 — Robert Flaherty*. London: British Film Institute.
1951   "30 Years of Experimental Film." *Films in Review* 2, no. 10 (December): 22–27.
1970   *Saint Cinema: Writings on Film, 1929–1970*. New York: Drama Book Specialists. Reprint eds., New York: Dover, 1973; New York: Frederick Ungar, 1980.
1982   *A Manhattan Odyssey: A Memoir*. New York: Anthology Film Archives.

Weiss, Peter
1963   "Avantgarde Film." *Akzente* 10:297–319.

Winton, Roy W.
1927   "For the Love of It." *National Board of Review Magazine* 2, no. 7 (July): 4.

Wolfe, Charles
1993   "The Poetics and Politics of Nonfiction: Documentary Film." In *Grand Design: Hollywood as a Modern Business Enterprise, 1930–1939*, ed. Tino Balio. New York: Scribner's. Pp. 351–386.

Zimmermann, Patricia
1986   "The Amateur, the Avant-Garde, and Ideologies of Art." *Journal of Film and Video* 38, nos. 3–4 (Summer–Fall): 63–85.

Zuckerman, Art
1965   "Focus on Willard Van Dyke." *Popular Photography* 56, (April): 118–119, 127–129.

Zuker, Joel
1978   *Ralph Steiner: Filmmaker and Still Photographer*. New York: Arno.

INDEX

Abstract Expressionism, 42, 327, 328
Abstronic (1952), 316, 326, 327, 366
Adams, Ansel, 243
Amateur Cinema League (ACL), 17, 18, 25, 26, 28, 51, 56, 139, 143, 146, 148, 153, 182, 184, 187, 190, 200
amateur film, 18, 19, 30, 137–53, 180, 245, 264, 298
Amateur Movie Makers, 28, 56, 57, 58, 59, 63, 137–39, 141, 143, 144, 146, 148, 185, 186, 190, 298, 305
American Cinematographer, 142
Anemic Cinema (1927), 315
Anger, Kenneth, 4, 178, 336
animation, 39–42, 124, 125, 129, 211, 315–31, 335–55
Another Day (1934), 26, 380
Anthology Film Archives, 4, 6, 62, 65, 128
A Propos De Nice (1930), 289, 295
A Quoi Revent les Jeunes Films (1924), 120, 229
Arledge, Sara, 14, 29, 44, 45, 63, 125, 363
Arnheim, Rudolf, 28
Art Deco, 70, 75, 77
"Art in Cinema" series, 4, 5, 12, 27, 55, 62, 63, 65, 66, 195, 200, 350

Artkino, 19, 36, 61, 374
Art Nouveau, 30, 70, 77
As I Walk (1934), 28, 33, 289, 372
Autumn Fire (1931), 33, 59, 144, 289, 291, 294, 295, 305–8, 382
avantgarde film, American, 3, 6, 7, 15, 27, 28, 30, 81, 113, 119, 144, 152, 160, 175, 176, 180, 226, 234, 249, 270, 295, 308, 309, 315, 336
avantgarde film, European, 3, 6, 17, 24, 29, 30, 35, 40, 42, 50, 52, 67, 68, 84, 86, 118, 146, 160, 163, 176, 249, 275, 295, 315, 346

Baillie, Bruce, 226, 230
Ballet Mécanique (1924), 119, 120, 122, 126–30, 133, 135, 215, 291, 293, 315, 332
Barlow, Roger, 14, 17, 18, 26, 29, 52, 65, 363
Beggar On Horseback (1925), 84–86, 93
Belson, Jordan, 4, 336
Berlin, die Sinfonie einer Großstadt (1927), 35, 151, 238, 245, 261, 275, 277, 287, 289, 292–95, 299, 301
Berne, Josef, 14, 28, 49, 50, 363, 364
Beyond Niagara (1973), 225, 229, 379
Big Parade, The (1925), 67

Birth of a Nation, The (1915), 196, 198
Black and Tan (1929), 122, 132, 133, 136, 374
Blakeston, Oswell, 12, 28, 40, 63, 259
Blitzstein, Marc, 43, 62, 226, 233, 245, 255, 264
Blood of a Poet (1930), 51, 166, 178, 192
Blue Bird, The (1918), 71–73, 91
Blum, Viktor Albrecht, 43
Bolm, Adolph, 43, 123, 125
Bordwell, David, 68, 69, 91, 249
Bouchard, Thomas, 14, 44, 364
Bovington, John, 43, 63
Brakhage, Stan, 4, 30, 176, 335
Brandon, Tom, 25, 64
Bridge, The / The Spy (1929), 18, 24, 49, 64, 380
Broadway (1929), 87
Broken Earth (1936), 18, 50, 370
Bronx Morning, A (1931), 25, 32, 59, 247, 287, 291, 293–301, 308, 373
Broughton, James, 30
Browning, Irving, 14, 33, 287–89, 292, 295, 300–303, 305, 308, 364
Bruguière, Francis, 14, 40, 61, 118, 133, 306, 314, 364
Bucher, Jules V. D., 364
Burckhardt, Rudy, 14, 29, 34, 35, 60, 365
Burnford, Paul, 14, 365
Bute, Mary Ellen, 14, 28, 40, 42, 62, 315–34, 345, 366

Cafe Universal (1934), 28, 219, 229, 379
Cameo Theatre, 20, 27, 56
Camille (1922), 75, 76, 92
Canyon Cinema, 4, 12
Cavalcanti, Alberto, 35, 151, 152, 233
Chaplin, Charles, 67, 89, 93, 98, 110, 114, 128, 129, 146, 180, 182, 189, 195–96, 199, 219, 342
China Strikes Back (1937), 253, 373
Chomette, Henri, 120, 126, 134, 229
Cinema Club of Rochester, 19
Cinema Crafters of Philadelphia, 16, 19, 48, 249
Cinema 16, 4, 12, 55, 66, 200

City, The (1939), 34, 224–25, 240, 242, 244, 245, 250, 251, 363, 364, 377, 379, 380
City Block (1934), 289
city films, 17, 31–35, 150, 238, 245, 247, 259, 275, 287–309
City of Contrasts (1931), 33, 289, 291, 295, 300–303, 308, 364
City Symphony (1930), 33, 59, 60, 277, 289, 295, 303–6, 382
Clair, René, 17, 52, 120, 376
classical Hollywood style, 6, 50, 68, 69, 163, 250
Close Up, 5, 27, 56, 63, 64, 263, 306
Cocteau, Jean, 166, 171, 178, 192
Cohl, Emil, 5, 344, 347, 357
Collins, Russell, 219
Color Rhapsodie (1948), 316, 325, 330, 366
Composition I (Themis) (1940), 42, 370
Composition 2 (Contrathemis) (1941), 42, 370
Composition 3 (1942), 42, 370
Composition 4 (1945), 42, 370
Constructivism, 3, 149, 160, 164, 237, 293
Copeland, Aaron, 224, 226, 229, 233, 245, 246, 264, 327
Cornell, Joseph, 6, 14, 25, 29, 53, 55, 366
Cortez, Stanley, 14, 366, 367
Craig, Edward Gordon, 70
Crisis (1938), 253
Crockwell, Douglass, 14, 42, 62, 335–55, 367
Crosby, Floyd, 367, 368
Crowd, The (1928), 80, 81
Cubism, 30, 71, 157, 160, 170, 234, 291, 293, 317
cummings, e. e., 158, 166–72, 176
Cyrano de Bergerac (1923), 24

Dadaism, 3, 119, 126, 129, 234, 288, 291, 292, 344
Dahme, F. A. A., 124
dance, 43–45, 123–25
Danse Macabre (1922), 43, 123–25, 128, 133, 324, 374

Das Cabinet des Dr. Caligari (1919), 21, 45, 46, 48, 84, 95, 103, 110, 130, 160, 162, 163, 166, 272

Dawn To Dawn (1934), 49, 50, 363, 377, 379

Day in Santa Fe, A (1931), 25, 376

de Beaumont, Comte Etienne, 120, 126

Deren, Maya, 4, 6, 7, 12, 45, 55, 125, 192, 335

Deslaw, Eugene, 291, 300, 301

Deutsch, Boris, 14, 30, 45, 50, 63, 368

Dial, The, 157–60, 170, 175, 176–78, 237

Die Leuchte Asiens (1926), 24, 117

Disney, Walt, 325, 329

documentary, 30, 33, 140, 146, 151, 192, 224, 234–58, 288–90

Duchamp, Marcel, 119, 293, 315

early cinema, 5, 6, 12, 68, 197, 310, 340–43

Eastman Kodak Co., 18, 137, 156

Eccentric Films, 19

Eggeling, Viking, 120, 229, 242, 316, 317, 346

Eisenstein, Sergei, 52, 146, 147, 164, 165, 193, 208, 215, 244, 276, 298, 305, 310

Emak Bakia (1926), 62, 120, 121, 133, 315, 376

Enchanted City, The (1922), 39–40, 50, 375

Emperor Jones (1933), 131, 133, 374

Emschwiller, Ed, 30

Entr'acte (1924), 52, 120

Epstein, Jean, 47, 162, 178

Escape (1937), 315, 323, 324, 366, 375

Etting, Emlen, 14, 53, 54, 55, 66, 125, 368

Even as You and I (1937), 26, 52, 65, 363, 370, 371, 377

Exceptional Photoplays, 20, 27

Experimental Cinema, 27, 28, 240, 241, 244, 249, 263

Eyes of Science, The (1930), 156, 381

Face Value (1927), 105, 106–8, 369

Fall of the House of Usher, The (1928), 6, 23, 25, 26, 46, 67, 150, 151, 156–58, 160–68, 171, 381

Fejos, Paul, 18, 24, 49, 50, 67, 80, 87–90, 144, 145, 368

Fifth Avenue Playhouse, 21, 27, 114, 117, 178, 303

Film Art, 27, 65, 163, 166, 175

Filmarte Theatre (Los Angeles), 24, 49, 57, 117

Film Art Guild (New York), 20, 23, 27, 108, 146, 271

Filmfront, 238, 249

Filmmakers' Cinémathèque, 4, 12

Finney, Ben, 118, 368

Fischinger, Oskar, 4, 7, 40, 90, 211, 229, 316, 345–47, 358, 359

Flaherty, Robert, 14, 30, 32, 59, 67, 146, 236, 255, 256, 289, 295, 305, 308, 368

Florey, Robert, 14, 17, 24, 27, 30, 37, 50, 58, 67, 94–117, 144, 150, 285, 369

Flory, John, 14, 26, 46, 51, 180, 188–92, 200, 204, 369, 370

Footnote to Fact (1934), 34, 372

Fortune Teller, The (1932), 53, 66, 370

Frank, Robert, 219

Freud, Sigmund, 40

Freulich, Roman, 14, 18, 24, 49, 50, 64, 65, 370

Friberg, Conrad, 247

Frontier Films, 242, 244, 253

Futurism, 3, 71, 85, 129, 157, 160, 234, 291, 317

Gale, Arthur, 19, 25, 56, 57

Garrison Films, 25

George Eastman House, 56, 57, 63, 64, 66, 90, 132, 134, 145, 148, 151, 152, 169, 173, 177, 194, 200, 202, 203, 251, 352, 355–57

German Expressionism, 30, 49, 70, 77, 85, 110, 113, 130, 144, 156, 160, 161, 234, 293

Gerson, Jo, 14, 19, 24, 29, 48, 64, 370

Ghost Town: The Story of Fort Lee
(1935), 191, 371
Glassgold, C. Adolph, 18, 56
Gleason, Marion, 56, 57
Glens Falls Sequence (1946), 42, 62,
336, 345–53, 367
Glory, Glory (1971), 225, 227, 229, 379
Gold Rush, The (1925) 89, 146
Gottheim, Larry, 226, 227, 230, 233
Gould, Symon, 20, 23, 25, 27, 58, 117
Grant, Dwinell, 14, 42, 62, 345, 370
Greed (1923), 49, 80, 81, 84
Grierson, John, 235, 290, 291
Griffith, David Wark, 74, 80, 181, 195,
199, 248
Group f.64, 243, 244, 262
Group Theater, The, 28, 219, 221

H_2O (1929), 25, 26, 36, 50, 150,
205–13, 223, 225, 226, 228, 229,
233, 242, 246, 294, 297, 310, 379
Hacker, Leonard, 149, 150, 154, 172,
179, 245, 263
Halsted Street (1934), 247, 374
Hammid (Hackenschmied), Alexander,
4, 356
Hands (1928, Simon), 23, 29, 43, 379
Hands (1934, Steiner), 222–23, 229,
253, 297, 379
Hay, Harry, 14, 26, 52, 65, 370
Heart of Spain, The (1937), 252, 380
Hearts of the Age (1934), 51, 52, 380
Hearts of the West (1931), 51, 184–87,
371
Highlights and Shadows (1937), 156,
381
Hill, Jerome, 14, 53, 54, 55, 66, 119,
370
Hine, Lewis, 247
Hirsch, Hy, 65, 371
Hirshman, Louis, 14, 19, 24, 29, 48, 58,
64, 371
Hoffman, John, 14, 37, 38, 371
Hollywood, 15, 28, 37, 50, 53, 67–93,
94, 97, 108, 130, 137, 139, 141, 144,
146, 181, 194, 236, 248, 317

Hollywood Film Guild, 20
Hooray For Light! (1975), 225, 227–29,
379
Huff, Theodore, 14, 26, 28, 51, 65,
180–202, 371
Hurwitz, Leo, 205, 206, 219, 229, 242,
245, 248, 249, 312, 372

Idyll (1948), 41–42, 62, 372
In Pursuit of Clouds (1985), 207, 229
Intolerance (1916), 74, 197
Introspection (1941), 44, 63, 363
It Never Happened (a.k.a. *Tomatoes
Another Day*) (1930), 46, 47, 156,
168, 169, 381
Ivens, Joris, 17, 246, 248, 264, 291, 310

Jacobs, Lewis, 7, 13, 14, 15, 19, 27, 28,
33, 34, 44, 48, 59, 60, 63, 64, 67, 90,
93, 196, 244, 249, 253, 262, 267, 289,
295, 305, 316, 371, 372
Johann the Coffin Maker (1928), 46,
108–10, 113, 114, 117, 369
Johnson, Merle, 19, 372
Julien Levy Gallery, 25, 297, 298, 312

Kazan, Elia, 14, 51, 190, 219, 372
Kiesler, Frederick, 19, 23, 56, 57, 135
Kinetoscope, 341
Kirsanoff, Dmitri, 294, 305
Klein, Charles, 14, 25, 30, 48, 63, 64,
67, 285, 372
Kloven (1927), 24
Knee Deep in Love (1926), 19, 372
Knight, Arthur, 7, 62
Koolish, Elman, 219–21, 256
Koyaanisqatsi (1983), 225
Kubelka, Peter, 4, 343
Kuchar, George and Mike, 4

Land, The (1942), 255, 367, 368, 373
Last Laugh, The (1925), 146, 163, 167
Last Moment, The (1928), 18, 49, 67,
68, 87–89, 93, 144, 145, 368, 377
Last Warning, The (1929), 87, 368
Laureate (1940), 53, 54, 368

Le Bijou (1945), 42, 62, 372
Lee, Francis, 14, 29, 40, 61, 372, 373
Léger, Fernand 62, 119, 127, 133, 215, 237, 260, 297, 315, 332
Le Retour à la Raison (1923), 119, 376
Lerner, Irving, 17, 51, 190, 219, 242, 373
L' Etoile de Mer (1927), 133, 293, 376
Leyda, Jay, 5, 6, 12, 14, 25, 28, 32, 58, 59, 203, 242, 247, 287–89, 292, 293, 295–300, 305, 308, 373
Liberty, 26, 52
Life and Death of 9413—A Hollywood Extra, The (1928), 18, 24, 27, 37, 46, 51, 56, 94–100, 103, 110, 113, 114, 116, 117, 144, 150, 271, 369, 381
Light Rhythms (1931), 40, 118, 364
Little Geezer (1932), 51, 187–88, 371
Little Review, The, 237,
Little Theaters, 20–25, 28, 49, 57, 59, 148, 303, 308
Long Bodies, The (1947), 336, 345, 346, 349, 351, 352, 367
Look at Laundry, A (1971), 225, 226, 229, 379
Look Park (1974), 225, 226, 229, 379
London Film Society, 120, 269, 308
Lorentz, Pare, 90, 242, 245, 249, 254
Lot in Sodom (1933), 25, 29, 47, 58, 59, 64, 156–58, 163, 165, 166, 168, 172, 175, 177, 381
Love of Zero, The (1928), 18, 24, 46, 50, 94, 100–105, 113, 114, 116, 285, 369
Lullaby (1925), 45, 46, 63, 368
Lye, Len, 229, 315, 316

MacArthur, Charles, 373
McLaren, Norman, 316, 324
MacPherson, Kenneth, 12, 27, 58
MacPherson, M. G., 14, 19, 61, 374
Mad Doctor, The (1926), 95, 369
Madame Cubist (1916), 70, 71, 91
Maddow, Ben, 255
Man of Aran (1934), 256, 368
Man With a Movie Camera, The (1929), 35, 146, 151, 215, 238, 260, 275, 289, 292, 293, 295, 299, 302

Manhatta (1920), 25, 27, 31, 32, 50, 119, 205, 224, 241, 245, 267–84, 289, 293, 295, 305, 306, 378, 379
March of Time, The, 256
Marievsky, Joseph, 100, 103
Markopoulos, Gregory, 4, 203
Maxim, Hiram Percy, 19
Mechanical Principles (1933), 36, 213–16, 223, 225, 229, 233, 242, 379
Mekas, Jonas, 4, 13, 15, 55, 59, 325
Méliès, Georges, 5, 12, 94
Men and Dust (1940), 252, 255, 364
Menzies, William Cameron, 46, 77, 94, 100, 108, 114
Meriam, Mylon, 374
Meshes in the Afternoon (1943), 335
Michelson, Jean D., 14, 19, 61, 374
Millions of Us (1935), 37, 254, 381
Mindlin, Michael, 21
Mr. Motorboat's Last Stand (1933), 26, 51, 180, 188–92, 203, 369, 371
Moana (1926), 32, 146, 256, 290, 368
Mobile Composition No. 1 (1928), 48, 370, 371
modernism, 70, 71, 156–57, 159, 166, 176, 234, 242, 267, 271, 283, 291, 293, 294, 317, 328, 336
Moholy-Nagy, László, 40, 237, 242, 263, 275, 291, 297, 311
Mol, Jan, 17, 35
montage, 74, 75, 98, 126, 151, 164, 190, 209, 248, 276, 291, 302, 306
Mood Contrasts (1953), 316, 328, 330, 366
Moods of the Sea (1942), 37, 38, 61, 117, 371, 381
Moore, Grace, 118, 119, 133
Moore, Marianne, 158, 166, 238
Mumford, Lewis, 240, 256, 261
Munson, Kent, 180, 182, 192–95, 371
Murders in the Rue Morgue (1931), 110, 369
Murnau, Friedrich Wilhelm, 80, 146, 149, 163
Murphy, Dudley, 14, 30, 43, 62, 119–36, 215, 297, 374

Muse, Clarence, 50
Museum of Modern Art, The (MOMA),
  6, 29, 51, 55, 59, 60–62, 128, 178,
  182, 197–98, 200–202, 206, 211,
  232, 258, 304, 313, 315, 331, 343,
  345, 346, 352, 354
music, 38, 43, 53, 54, 62, 121–23, 126,
  224, 226, 229, 233, 245, 246, 255,
  264, 322, 325, 327, 329
Mutoscope, 340–46, 352–55, 367
Mystèries du Chateau de Dés (1929),
  133, 376

Nanook of the North (1922), 32, 146,
  256, 288, 290, 291, 368
National Archives, Washington, D.C.,
  182, 196, 197
National Board of Review, 20, 23, 26,
  27, 28, 56, 57, 137
Native Land (1942), 242, 251, 252, 255,
  256, 380
Nazimova, 75–77, 117
Nelson, C. O., 374
Nemeth, Theodore, 14, 40, 315, 322,
  323, 375
Neue Sachlichkeit, 3, 237, 261, 288,
  291, 292, 311
New Deal, The, 17, 222, 234, 242, 249,
  254, 265
New Hampshire Heritage (1940), 224,
  229, 379, 380
New York, 31, 32, 33, 56, 99, 113, 122,
  180, 193, 213, 237, 267, 268, 271,
  277, 279, 295–303
New York University, 182, 198–99
Newcombe, Warren, 14, 30, 39, 42, 61,
  375, 376
1941 (1941), 40–42, 62, 372
Nykino, 242–44, 255

Object Lesson (1941), 54, 55, 66, 382
Oil — A Symphony in Motion (1933),
  19, 36, 56, 374
Old Swimmin Hole, The (1921), 68, 69,
  77–80, 88, 92
145 West 21 (1936), 34, 365

One Man's Island (1969), 225, 226, 229,
  379
Oramunde (1933), 53, 125, 368

painting, 31, 39–42, 45, 48, 53, 54, 157,
  210, 215, 237, 238, 274, 292, 297,
  317, 320
Painleve, Jean, 36
Panther Woman of the Needle Trades, or
  The Lovely Life of Little Lisa (1931),
  51, 65, 188, 217, 229, 230, 369, 379
Parabola (1937), 315, 323, 366, 375
Parker, Claire, 376
Passages From Finnegans Wake (1965),
  330, 366
Pastorale (1950), 325, 326, 330, 366
People of Cumberland (1937), 223, 229,
  253, 255, 256, 372, 373, 379, 380
Peterson, Sidney, 4
Phillips-Radio (1931), 291
photography, 118, 135, 209, 224, 230,
  234, 236, 237, 243, 244, 245, 262,
  268, 273, 275, 280, 292, 297, 300
Photoplay, 26, 181
Photo-Secession, 239
Pie in the Sky (1934), 28, 51, 190,
  219–22, 229, 230, 255, 256, 372,
  373, 379, 380
Platt, David, 244, 249, 263
Plow That Broke the Plains, The (1936),
  223, 229, 242, 243, 245, 252, 379
Poem 8 (1933), 53, 54, 66, 368
Polka Graph (1947), 316, 325, 328, 330,
  366
Portrait of a Young Man (1931), 25, 36,
  37, 48, 242, 245, 377
Potamkin, Harry A., 27, 58, 60, 64, 144,
  149, 150–52, 248, 260, 264, 306, 307
Potemkin (1925), 52, 146, 164, 215, 291
Pound, Ezra, 126, 127, 129, 130,
  170–74, 176, 179, 278
Power and the Land (1940), 246, 255,
  367
Precisionism, 238, 288
Prelude to Spring (1946), 38, 61, 371
Print Generation (1966), 227

Prisoner, The (1934), 18, 24, 49, 65, 370
production budgets, 18, 89, 95, 96, 100,
    114, 115, 122, 123, 126, 150, 185,
    186, 269, 329
Prunella (1918), 71, 73, 74, 91
Pursuit of Happiness, The (1940), 35,
    365

Rainer, Yvonne, 4, 222, 232, 258
Rambova, Natacha, 75–77
Ray, Charles, 68, 77–80
Ray, Man, 4, 62, 118–20, 126, 127,
    133, 134, 293, 297, 315, 376
Redes / The Wave (1934), 65, 242, 244,
    377, 379
Rhythm in Light (1934), 322, 323, 329,
    330, 366, 375, 381
Richter, Hans, 4, 6, 17, 30, 42, 52, 56,
    59, 118, 163, 199, 229, 242, 315, 317,
    345
Rien que les Heures (1925), 35, 151,
    152, 291, 293
Riggs, Lynn, 14, 25, 376
River, The (1937), 90, 244, 246, 255,
    256, 367, 380
Robbins, LeRoy, 14, 17, 26, 29, 52, 65,
    376, 377
Robeson, Paul, 131, 255
Rodakiewicz, Henwar, 14, 17, 25, 28,
    34, 36, 37, 60, 61, 242, 245, 312, 377
*Romance of the White Chrysanthemum,
The* (1922), 123, 374
Romantic Age, The (1927), 105, 106, 369
Rose Hobart (1936), 6, 25, 53, 366
Rotha, Paul, 235, 258
Ruttmann, Walter, 17, 35, 120, 125,
    151, 230, 238, 242, 245, 287–89,
    291, 294, 295, 299, 301

Salome (1923), 76, 77, 117
Saturday Evening Post, 42, 336–38
Salvation Hunters, The (1924), 18,
    80–84, 89, 93, 115
Schillinger, Joseph, 14, 28, 321, 377
Seaweed, a Seduction (1960), 225, 229,
    230, 379

Seeing the World—Part I (1937), 35,
    365
Shamberg, Morton, 238, 269
Shamroy, Leon, 377, 378
Sheeler, Charles, 25, 30, 50, 119, 205,
    232, 238, 241, 263, 267–84, 289,
    292, 293, 295, 297, 305, 378
Siebert, Mike, 14, 378
Sight and Sound, 182
Simon, Stella, 14, 29, 43, 62, 379
Sitney, P. Adams, 4, 6, 12, 31, 59, 156,
    176, 179, 232, 335
Skyscraper Symphony (1929), 46, 63,
    110–13, 117, 369
Slowdown (1975), 225, 379
Smith, Harry, 4, 379
Soul of the Cypress, The (1921),
    121–23, 125, 134, 374
sound films, 99, 105, 130, 131, 146,
    168, 224, 226, 228, 245, 253
Soviet cinema, 146, 149, 160, 163, 203,
    208, 218, 223, 238, 248, 249, 259,
    311
Spanish Earth, The (1936), 252–55
Spook Sport (1937), 324, 325, 329, 330,
    366
St. Louis Blues (1929), 131, 133, 374
Stark Love (1927), 80, 84
Stauffacher, Frank, 5, 12, 27, 58, 60,
    62–66, 195
Steiner, Ralph, 14, 17, 25, 28, 29, 34,
    36, 50, 51, 60, 144, 150, 188,
    205–28, 240, 242, 245, 246, 256,
    262, 294, 296, 301, 305, 379
Stern, Seymour, 14, 27, 64, 263, 379
Stieglitz, Alfred, 25, 118, 239, 240, 245,
    268, 270, 272, 273, 276, 280, 281,
    293, 297
Stokowski, Leopold, 325, 326, 329
Stone Children, The (1947) 194–95, 371
Story of a Nobody, The (1930) 24, 29,
    48, 370, 371
Strand, Paul, 14, 17, 25, 29, 31, 50, 65,
    67, 119, 205, 238, 239, 241, 245, 261,
    263, 267–84, 289, 291–93, 295, 297,
    305, 379, 380

Sunrise (1927) 80, 84, 146
Surf and Seaweed (1930), 36, 212, 213, 215, 223, 225, 229, 230, 233, 242, 379
Surrealism, 3, 52, 118, 160, 234, 350
Sweden—Land of the Vikings (1934), 24
Synchromy (1933), 28, 321, 366, 372, 377
Synchromy No. 2 (1935), 316, 323, 329, 366, 375

Tarantella (1940), 316, 325, 329, 366, 375
Tell-Tale Heart, The (1928), 25, 47, 48, 63, 285, 372, 377
Ten Days That Shook the World (1927), 147
Thatcher, Leslie P., 14, 26, 380
Thatcher, Molly Day, 51, 190, 219, 380
Thayer, Scofield, 159, 160
Theatre Arts Monthly, 24, 63, 297, 298
Theremin, Leon, 319, 320
Thomson, Virgil, 246
Tomatoes Another Day. SEE *It Never Happened*
Tourneur, Maurice, 71, 73, 74, 91
Turin, Victor, 146, 238
Turksib (1929), 146, 147, 149, 260
Twenty-Four Dollar Island (1926), 32, 259, 289, 295, 308, 368
Two Days (1928), 23
Tyler, Parker, 202

Uncomfortable Man, The (1948), 51, 180, 192–93, 195, 203, 371
Underground Printer (1934), 44, 63, 364, 372
University of Southern California (USC), 182, 194, 198

Valley Town (1940), 255, 363, 373, 380
Vance, William, 14, 51, 380
Van Dyke, Willard, 17, 29, 34, 224, 225, 230, 240, 242, 243, 251, 380

Vanity Fair, 274, 295, 297
Vertov, Dziga, 35, 146, 151, 215, 238, 275, 288, 289, 291, 295, 300, 302
Vidor, Charles, 14, 18, 24, 49, 50, 64, 380, 381
Vigo, Jean, 289, 295, 300, 301
Vogel, Amos, 58, 66
von Sternberg, Joseph, 18, 80–84, 115
von Stroheim, Erich, 80, 84
Vorkapich, Slavko, 14, 17, 37, 46, 61, 94, 95–98, 114, 116, 254, 263, 381

Watson, Jr., Dr. James Sibley, 6, 14, 19, 25, 46, 47, 50, 51, 63, 67, 144, 150, 151, 156–79, 381
Webber, Melville, 6, 14, 25, 51, 67, 144, 156–79, 322, 381
Weinberg, Herman, 6, 14, 15, 17, 27, 28, 33, 56, 57, 59, 60, 65, 108, 117, 144, 150, 155, 277, 287, 289, 292, 293, 295, 303–9, 381, 382
Welles, Orson, 14, 51
Weston, Edward, 65, 244
White Gold (1927), 80, 81, 84
Whitman, Walt, 269, 277–80, 305, 331
Whitney Brothers, 4, 6, 135, 382
Williams, William Carlos, 238, 278, 336
Winton, Roy, 17, 137, 139, 153
Workers Film and Photo League, 25, 33, 150, 218, 220, 230, 242, 244, 248–50, 266, 297, 301, 312
Works Progress Administration (WPA), 222, 253
World Today, The (1937), 255, 373, 379, 380

Yellow Girl, The (1915), 71, 72
Young, Christopher Baughman, 14, 54, 55, 66, 382
Youth Gets a Break (1941), 224, 367, 379, 380

Zayas, Marius de, 25, 268
Zinnemann, Fred, 65, 242